Higher Grade Physics

STUART G. BURNS BSC(HONS), DIP ED

Paisley Camphill High School

D1494219

The English Universities Press

To John Burns

ISBN O 340 16738 6

First printed 1974

Copyright © S. G. Burns

The English Universities Press Ltd.,
St Paul's House, Warwick Lane, London EC4P 4AH

Printed and bound in Great Britain by
Hazell, Watson and Viney Ltd, Aylesbury

Contents

Author's Preface

In preparing for the S.C.E. examination in Physics at 'Higher' Grade, it is insufficient to study only those topics included in the third cycle of the Examination Board's 'Syllabuses and Notes'. Much of the present examination is concerned with material required for the 'Ordinary' Grade examination—this material being examined at a greater level of difficulty in the 'Higher'.

With this in mind, I have written 'Higher Grade Physics'. I have included all third cycle topics along with those second cycle topics taught only once for the 'Ordinary' and 'Higher' Grade examinations. These second cycle topics have been written at the 'Higher' level of difficulty. I hope therefore that the textbook will provide the pupil with the complete material for his course.

I have included mathematical ideas throughout the textbook and have tried to arrange these so that the more able pupil will be able to consult them as additional material, while the less able pupil may by-pass them without jeopardizing his examination prospects. I have included these mathematical discussions because I think that part of physics is to derive satisfaction from seeing nature obey mathematical relationships. Mathematical discussions will also benefit those who are intending studying physics at the post-Higher level since much of this physics tends to be mathematically based.

If the textbook is adopted at 'Ordinary' Grade, teachers should guide pupils to the relevant material, and guard against the pupil reading too far into the 'Higher' Grade material for the 'Ordinary' Grade examination. For those pupils using the textbook in preparation for the 'Higher' Grade examination, a programme of ('Ordinary') revision home reading should be prepared by the teacher, so that the pupil may upgrade the standard of 'Ordinary' Grade topics while studying fresh topics for the 'Higher' Grade Examination. (In very few schools will time permit the complete coverage of the book in the classroom and in the fifth year).

Problems have been included at the end of each chapter. It must be realised that these problems are intended to supplement the 'Higher' Grade problems which are reprinted each year from the S.C.E. examination. My problems must not be taken as a substitute for the S.C.E. problems.

I should like to thank Mr. John Douglas for taking some of the photographs, and my wife Liz for typing the manuscript. I should also like to thank Mr. Roger Stone for his editorial guidance at all stages of preparation of the manuscript; Mr. Raymond Dunphy for providing answers to the problems; and Mr. Iain MacInnes for introducing me to E.U.P. I wish all who use the book success. If it helps clarify physics by serving as a useful teaching aid, then the time spent preparing it will have been time well spent.

Stuart G. Burns
Paisley Camphill High School

Chapter 1

Vectors

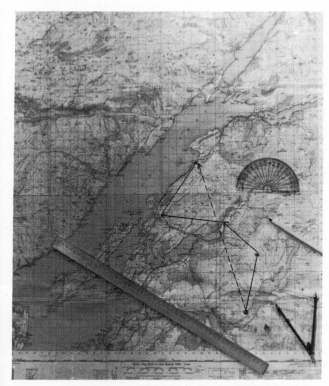

Fig.1.0 The combination of arrows represents the addition of displacement vectors. (Reproduced from the Ordnance Survey Map with the sanction of the Controller of H.M. Stationery Office, Crown Copyright reserved.)

If we were asked to divide the quantities we use in physics into two disjoint sets, that is two sets whose intersection is empty, we could perhaps do so in a few different ways. A most useful division, however, would be that whereby those quantities described by size alone were separated from others requiring direction and size for their complete description. On achieving such a separation we would label the first set 'the set of scalar quantities' and the second set, 'the set of vector quantities' respectively.

A scalar quantity is one which is completely described by a number, whereas a vector quantity is one which requires a direction in addition to a number for its complete description. The mass of a body, defined as the amount of matter contained in the body, is a scalar quantity, and so too is the number of people in Scotland. Both quantities are undirected. On the other hand, displacement, defined as the distance gone in a particular direction, is a vector quantity since it describes the direction, as well as the size of a movement between two points. Such a quantity is obviously necessary in mechanics since we have to watch which way a body is travelling as well as the distance which it travels. So too, velocity, defined as

the rate of displacement, is a vector quantity, since it describes the direction in which a body is travelling as well as its speed.

Considering the four quantities,

$$3 \text{ m} \qquad 5 \text{ m s}^{-1} \qquad 3 \text{ m North} \qquad 5 \text{ m s}^{-1} \text{ West}$$

we see that the first two are scalar quantities and the last two are vector quantities. The physical quantities represented by the four are in order; distance, speed, displacement, and velocity.

The third quantity, the displacement 3 metres North is of considerable interest. Consider two points P and Q such that Q is 3 metres North of P. If a person moves from P to Q, we say his displacement is 3 metres North. By this, we mean that the person has effectively moved a distance of 3 metres in the direction North. This is not to say however that the total distance which the person has actually travelled in going from P to Q is 3 metres. It is quite possible that he could follow the path indicated in Fig. 1.1, the length of which is certainly greater than 3 metres. The distance travelled along this path from P to Q might be about 8 metres, but the displacement from P to Q is 3 metres North.

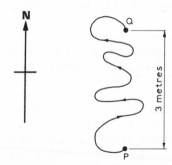

Fig.1.1 The displacement from *P* to *Q* is 3 metres North. The distance travelled between *P* and *Q* might be about 8 metres however.

Having distinguished between scalar quantities and vector quantities, and realising that such a distinction will have to be borne in mind since it does exist, we now consider the rules for dealing with vector quantities. In physics we perform many mathematical operations on physical quantities such as addition, subtraction, multiplication, division, and differentiation. We are already familiar with such operations on scalar quantities, but since the set of scalar quantities is a subset of the set of all physical quantities, we must turn our attention to such operations on vector quantities. An operation on two scalar quantities is obviously going to be a different process from the equivalent operation on two vector quantities since the scalar operation involves only the treatment of two numbers, whereas the equivalent vector operation must involve the treatment of two combinations of direction and number.

For the purpose of this course we shall confine our attention to the operations of addition and subtraction of vector quantities.

1.1 The Addition of Vector Quantities

Our first consideration as far as vector addition is concerned is that we must only attempt to add vector quantities of a like nature. We would never attempt to add two scalar quantities of an unlike nature such as mass and distance, and so it would be somewhat ridiculous to attempt to add two vector quantities of an unlike nature. We shall thus be concerned with the addition of such quantities as displacement and displacement, or velocity and velocity.

Our second consideration is that while the addition of two or more scalar quantities is purely and simply a matter of arithmetical addition of the numbers representing the quantities, the addition of two or more vector quantities cannot be achieved quite so simply, since the process of arithmetical addition takes no account of the directions inherent in the vector quantities. How then are we to add or combine vector quantities?

Since a vector quantity is an entity which has size and a definite direction in space, we can represent it very conveniently by a straight line with an arrow head—the length of the line representing the size of the vector quantity according to a suitably chosen scale, and the direction of the line, as indicated by the sense of the arrow head, representing the direction of the vector quantity. A vector quantity can thus be represented as in Fig. 1.2. For the symbolic representation of a vector quantity it is common practice to use a single small letter underlined. For example: $\underline{u}$. Some textbooks however use a boldface type to indicate a vector quantity which would thus appear **u**. Other common representations of the vector quantity are $\vec{u}$, $\bar{u}$, u. For our purposes we shall employ the first representation $\underset{\sim}{u}$ and we shall also employ the symbol u to denote the size of the vector quantity $\underline{u}$.

Fig.1.2 Since the arrow has direction and size, it incorporates in itself the features of the vector quantity it represents.

Using this directed line or arrow representation of vector quantities, we can attempt to add vector quantities by combining or adding their representative arrows graphically, so that the problem of vector addition becomes geometrical in nature. Let us first attempt to add two displacements by this approach.

If we make a displacement of 6 metres North from point A to point B, followed by a displacement of 8 metres East from point B to point C, the result is the same as if we had made a single displacement from point A to point C. Relating this exercise to a scale drawing as in Fig. 1.3, in which we represent our displacements by arrows, we find by direct

measurement and reference to the scale, that the resultant displacement from point A to point C is 10 metres, 53° East of North. This result can be verified by calculation if desired, using the fact that the triangle ABC is right angled.

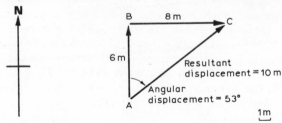

Fig.1.3 Addition of the displacements 6 m North and 8 m East.

The addition or combination of displacements is thus achieved by choosing a suitable scale and drawing the displacements according to this scale, nose to tail, each in its correct direction. The resultant displacement, that is the sum of displacements, is found by direct measurement and reference to the chosen scale.

If we denote the displacement AB by $\underline{u}$, the displacement BC by $\underline{v}$, and the displacement AC by $\underline{w}$, then we can write

$$\underline{u} + \underline{v} = \underline{w}$$

This is an equation relating vector quantities, and its full meaning is: 'a displacement of 6 metres North, followed by a displacement of 8 metres East is equivalent to a displacement of 10 metres 53° East of North'. The equation is different from an equation relating scalar quantities in so far as it is relating directions as well as sizes. The equation most certainly does *not* mean that $u + v = w$. The symbols $+$ and $=$ in the vector equation have quite different meanings from the symbols $+$ and $=$ in the scalar equation purely because of the totally different attributes of vector and scalar quantities themselves.

A correct scalar equation for the combination of the two displacements is

$$u^2 + v^2 = w^2$$

We have thus achieved addition of vector quantities by *drawing representative arrows of the quantities nose to tail, (each in its correct direction) and taking the size and direction of the resultant arrow as the total or sum of the vector quantities being added.* Since we have done this only for displacements (perhaps the simplest vector quantities of all) it may be wise to examine the procedure for another type of vector quantity, say velocity, so that we may feel justified in adopting the geometrical method in all problems of vector addition.

Consider a ship moving through the water with a velocity of 12 km h^{-1} North being driven off course by a current whose velocity is 5 km h^{-1} East. Let us attempt to calculate the resultant velocity of the ship as observed by a stationary observer on land.

If the water surface was perfectly still, then the ship would make a displacement of 12 km North each hour. However since the whole water surface is moving East, and therefore carrying the ship with it, at a speed of 5 km h⁻¹, the ship also makes a displacement of 5 km East each hour. In one hour the ship therefore has a resultant displacement of 13 km 23° East of North as measured from the displacement diagram in Fig. 1.4, so that the actual velocity of the ship as noted by the stationary observer is 13 km h⁻¹ 23° East of North. This follows from the definition of velocity which states that velocity is the rate of displacement.

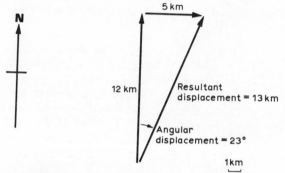

Fig.1.4   Addition of the displacements 12 km North and 5 km East.

We note with satisfaction that had the scale been chosen as ⅓ cm to 1 km h⁻¹ in Fig. 1.4, then we would have achieved exactly the same result namely that the resultant or actual velocity of the ship is 13 km h⁻¹ 23° East of North, thereby proving that velocities can be added or combined in exactly the same way as displacements, that is, by the geometrical method.

In fact all vector quantities can be added or combined using this geometrical method.

Although we have employed this method to add only two vector quantities in each example, it is perhaps fairly obvious that it can be extended to add any number of vector quantities in a given problem.

The last point to be made as far as the addition of vector quantities is concerned is that the order in which the quantities are added is of no importance. That is to say the operation of vector addition is commutative as is the operation of scalar addition.

In scalar addition for example: $3 + 4 = 4 + 3 \ (= 7)$, so that the result is the same regardless of the order in which we add the quantities.

So too for vector quantities $\underline{a}$ and $\underline{b}$ of a like nature we can say that

$$\underline{a} + \underline{b} = \underline{b} + \underline{a}$$

The order in which the quantities are added or combined

has no effect on the result.

We can prove this commutative property of the addition of vector quantities by considering the quantities shown in Fig. 1.5. We see that the resultant vector $\underline{a} + \underline{b}$ obtained when the quantities are added in the order $\underline{a}$, $\underline{b}$ is exactly the same vector as $\underline{b} + \underline{a}$, the resultant vector obtained when the quantities are combined in the order $\underline{b}$, $\underline{a}$.

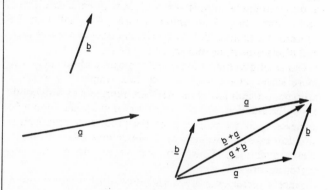

Fig.1.5   The resultant quantity $\underline{a} + \underline{b}$ is the same vector as the resultant quantity $\underline{b} + \underline{a}$.

In our first example we added our displacements in the order 6 metres North, 8 metres East. Check that this gives exactly the same result as when the displacements are added in the order 8 metres East, 6 metres North. Check too that the order in which the velocities were added in the second example has no effect on the result.

In adding two vector quantities we have been finding convenience in replacing the two quantities being added by a vector quantity equivalent to their sum. Frequently in mechanics, however, we find it convenient to take one vector quantity and express it as two or more vector quantities. That is, we sometimes find it convenient to replace a given vector quantity by a set of components. This process, the reverse of addition, is known as the *resolution of a vector quantity*. The components of a vector quantity when considered together are equivalent to the vector quantity itself, and when considered separately, each may be of use in reducing the overall complexity of a given problem.

Let us consider a vector quantity $\underline{a}$ inclined to each of a pair of rectangular co-ordinate axes labelled X and Y. Let the angle which $\underline{a}$ makes with the positive X direction be θ. If it becomes necessary in a problem to discuss the vector quantity with respect to the X axis and subsequently to discuss it quite independently with respect to the Y axis, it is most convenient to resolve the quantity into two components, one in the X direction and the other in the Y direction.

Referring to Fig. 1.6, we have labelled the projections of $\underline{a}$, OA on the X axis, and OB on the Y axis.

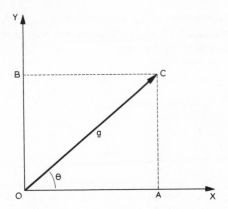

Fig.1.6 Projections of the vector quantity $\underline{a}$ on to the X and Y axes.

By definition,

$$\frac{OA}{a} = \cos\theta$$

and $$\frac{OB}{a} = \sin\theta \quad \text{since} \quad OB = AC$$

Hence, $\quad OA = a\cos\theta \quad$ and $\quad OB = a\sin\theta$

If we now consider a vector $\underline{a}_X$ whose direction is that of the positive X direction and whose length is OA, and another vector $\underline{a}_Y$ whose direction is that of the positive Y direction and whose length is OB, then we can say that

$$\underline{a} = \underline{a}_X + \underline{a}_Y \quad \text{where} \quad a_X = a\cos\theta$$
$$a_Y = a\sin\theta$$

This relationship is represented graphically in Fig. 1.7.

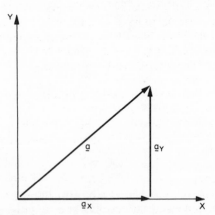

Fig.1.7 $\quad \underline{a} = \underline{a}_x + \underline{a}_y.$

The quantities $a\cos\theta$ and $a\sin\theta$ are known as the X and Y components of the vector quantity $\underline{a}$. Their consideration becomes necessary in problems where motion has to be related to two independent co-ordinate axes along neither of which the original vector quantity is directed.

Having resolved a vector quantity into its components, we can use these components to describe the quantity completely. Before resolution our vector quantity was described by the quantities a and θ. After resolution, it is described by the quantities a_X and a_Y. The relationships involving the complete description of the vector quantity before and after resolution are

$$a = \sqrt{a_X{}^2 + a_Y{}^2}$$

and $$\tan\theta = \frac{a_Y}{a_X}$$

Two vector quantities can be added by reference to their components alone. Addition by this approach is known as the analytical method of addition and differs from the geometrical method in so far as it is algebraic whereas the geometrical method is graphical.

Consider two vector quantities $\underline{a}$ and $\underline{b}$ which lie in the XY plane, each of which is inclined to both the X and Y axes in direction. Let the sum of these quantities be the quantity $\underline{c}$. That is, $\underline{a} + \underline{b} = \underline{c}$.

Relating this equation to a vector diagram as in Fig. 1.8, we can see that as far as the X and Y components of the three vector quantities are concerned,

$$c_X = a_X + b_X \quad \text{and} \quad c_Y = a_Y + b_Y$$

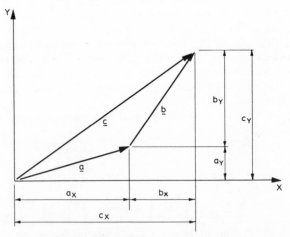

Fig.1.8 Illustrating the analytical approach to the addition of vector quantities.

This tells us that the component of the sum of two vector quantities in a given direction is equivalent to the sum of the components of the quantities being added, in that direction.

If the vector quantities $\underline{a}$ and $\underline{b}$ are completely defined, then their components $(a_X\ a_Y)$ and $(b_X\ b_Y)$ can be calculated. From this calculation, the components of the sum of the quantities can be found, and so finally, the size and direction of the sum can be calculated.

This method, although more demanding than the geometrical method, is more powerful in so far as the addition of vector quantities can be achieved in the absence of satisfactory instruments for drawing and measurement.

For the purpose of our course, it will be sufficient for us to refer to the geometrical method in problems involving the addition of vector quantities. Our consideration of the analytical method however is perhaps a more interesting exercise and one which will be of much use in our study of vector quantities at a more advanced level.

1.2 The Subtraction of Vector Quantities

When we realise that the operation of subtraction of any two quantities is really the addition of one quantity and the negative of the other quantity, then the problem of subtraction of two vector quantities reduces to an extension of that of the addition of two vector quantities. This being the case, the foregoing discussion on the addition of vector quantities is directly applicable to the problem of subtraction.

If we are required to subtract the vector quantity $\underline{b}$ from the vector quantity $\underline{a}$, we can say that since the subtraction of the quantities $\underline{a}$ and $\underline{b}$ is really the addition of the quantities a and $(-b)$ then

$$\underline{a} - \underline{b} = \underline{a} + (-\underline{b})$$

The most sensible interpretation of the quantity $(-\underline{b})$ is that $(-\underline{b})$ is a vector quantity whose size is b but whose direction is opposite to that of $\underline{b}$.

As an example of vector subtraction, consider a body whose velocity at one instant is 6 m s^{-1} North and at a later instant is 8 m s^{-1} West. Suppose that we wish to find the change in velocity of the body.

Let us denote the velocity of 6 m s^{-1} North by $\underline{u}$ and the velocity of 8 m s^{-1} West by $\underline{v}$.

The change in velocity is found from the expression:

$$\text{change in velocity} = \text{final velocity} - \text{initial velocity}$$

$$= \underline{v} - \underline{u}$$

$$= \underline{v} + (-\underline{u})$$

The change in velocity can thus be found from the addition of the vector quantities $\underline{v}$ and $(-\underline{u})$. This addition is performed in Fig. 1.9.

By direct measurement on the scale drawing in Fig. 1.9 and reference to the chosen scale, we find that the change in velocity of the body is 10 m s^{-1} 38° South of West.

This result may seem very strange considering that the change in the speed of the body is 2 m s^{-1}.

The result, however strange, emphasises the fact that velocity, a vector quantity, is a much more complicated concern than speed, a scalar quantity. 'Complication' arises from the interaction of both number and direction in the vector quantity. It is hoped that a result of this kind, no matter how strange at present, will become extremely meaningful in the next few chapters when we consider velocity vector quantities in a broader context.

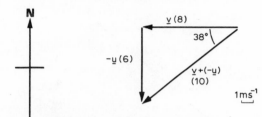

Fig.1.9 The subtraction of 8 m s^{-1} West and 6 m s^{-1} North is treated as the addition of 8 m s^{-1} West and 6 m s^{-1} *South*.

Problems

1. Add the displacements
   (a) 2 cm East and 3 cm Northwest
   (b) 8 km South and 4 km East.

2. A man in a maze walks 6 metres East, 4 metres North, 5 metres East, 8 metres South, 8 metres West, 2 metres North, 7 metres East, 4 metres North, 3 metres West, 2 metres South, 7 metres West.
   How far has he walked, and what is his resultant displacement from the starting point?

3. Prove geometrically by consideration of any three vector quantities $\underline{a}$, $\underline{b}$, $\underline{c}$ of a like nature, that vector addition is associative. That is, prove that

   $$\underline{a} + (\underline{b} + \underline{c}) = (\underline{a} + \underline{b}) + \underline{c}$$

4. An aircraft pilot wishes to fly North at a speed of 800 km h^{-1}. What speed and course must he select in order to achieve this if a wind is blowing from West to East at a speed of 80 km h^{-1}?

5. An aircraft has a cruising air speed of 900 km h^{-1}. The pilot wishes to travel to an airfield distant 2400 km due South of his home base. There is a wind blowing from West to East at a speed of 80 km h^{-1}.
   (a) What course should the pilot select if he decides to fly at cruising air speed?
   (b) How long will the trip last assuming cruising air speed is maintained throughout?

6. Using the analytical method of addition, add the displacements $\underline{a}$ and $\underline{b}$ whose components are given by

   $$a_X = 3 \text{ metres} \qquad b_X = 2 \text{ metres}$$
   $$a_Y = 4 \text{ metres} \qquad b_Y = 2 \text{ metres}$$

7. Using the analytical method of addition, add the displacements 4 metres 30° North of East, and 8 metres 60° North of East. (Take the direction East as the positive X axis and the direction North as the positive Y axis.)

8. A particle is describing a circle at a steady speed of 5 m s^{-1}. Find the change in its velocity over one sixth of the circumference of the circle.

Chapter 2

Motion in a Straight Line

Fig.2.0   The motion of this aircraft along the runway is an accelerated motion. This chapter is concerned with such motion. (By kind permission of IPC Transport Press Ltd.)

If we were asked to select two physical quantities which could be employed to describe the motion of a body, then with reference to the contents of the last chapter, we might well choose the quantities displacement and velocity. The displacement of the body would be a description of its change of position, while the velocity of the body would describe its rate of displacement.

We now discuss the quantity velocity more fully than in the last chapter, with a view to providing material which will be of use to us in our development of the present chapter.

2.1 The Meaning of Velocity

Suppose we are told that a car made a displacement of 1000 metres North in 250 seconds. From this information, and the knowledge that velocity is defined as rate of displacement, we might be tempted to conclude that the velocity of the car during this interval was 4 metres (North) per second. Such a conclusion would be inaccurate however in as much as it implies that the velocity of the car was constant at 4 metres (North) per second throughout the 250 seconds. If we are told further that the car was travelling Northwards along a straight North–South road throughout the 250 seconds, (so that its direction was constant), then such a conclusion would imply that the speed of the car was constant at 4 metres per second.

The correct conclusion to be drawn from the information given is that the *average* velocity of the car during the 250 second interval was 4 metres (North) per second, and given the additional information that the road was North–South and straight, then the *average* speed during the interval was 4 metres per second. We must introduce the term 'average'

since we are given no information as to the motion of the car at any particular time during the 250 second interval. The motion during this interval could have been steady or erratic but we cannot tell since we are given only a net displacement, and the total time taken for this displacement.

To elaborate on the statement that the motion 'could have been steady or erratic', let us suppose that the displacement of 1000 metres North was made through part of a busy town as illustrated in Fig. 2.1.

In the day-time situation it is most unlikely that the speed of the car would remain constant at 4 m s^{-1}. The car might for example be slowed down at point A by traffic lights, but might make good progress between points B and C. Then again, it might be stopped altogether by say pedestrians crossing at D. In the night-time situation it is quite possible that the car could travel the 1000 metres at a steady speed of 4 m s^{-1}, unhindered by any other road users or controls.

The important point is that the net displacement of the car and the time taken for this displacement enable us to calculate only an *average* velocity for its complete journey. We cannot calculate or estimate the velocity of the car at some instant of the journey—for example, the velocity of the car at the instant when it passes point P in Fig. 2.1.

When using the term 'velocity', we therefore have to use it carefully by deciding whether we mean *average* velocity—the velocity which is calculated for a journey between two points, or *instantaneous* velocity—the velocity which is measured at some instant in a given journey. An instantaneous velocity is found by calculating an average velocity over a very short interval of time (including the instant)—so short that the velocity has not time to change during it.

6

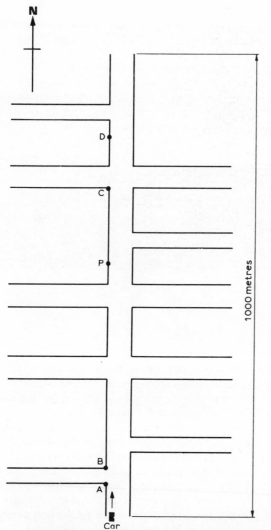

Fig.2.1 The total distance travelled (1000 m) and the total time taken (250 s) enable us to calculate an average speed for the journey, but not the instantaneous speed at any particular time.

In our example, we could hardly call 250 seconds a short interval of time, since the velocity of the car could change continually throughout. In fact *one* second cannot be treated as a short interval of time when we are trying to measure an instantaneous velocity, since the velocity of any object can change quite considerably in one second (or even in a hundredth of one second).

To measure the instantaneous velocity of an object we must find its displacement Δs which occurs in the shortest time interval imaginable, Δt say, and thereby calculate this instantaneous velocity as

$$\text{instantaneous velocity} = \lim_{\Delta t \to 0} \frac{\Delta s}{\Delta t}$$

That is, the instantaneous velocity is the limiting value of an average velocity calculated over the extremely short time interval Δt which is so small as to be approaching zero.

To summarise the discussion this far, we quote four important formulae:

(1) Average velocity $= \dfrac{\text{total displacement}}{\text{total time taken}} = \dfrac{s}{t}$

(2) Instantaneous velocity $= \lim_{\Delta t \to 0} \dfrac{\Delta s}{\Delta t}$

(3) Average speed $= \dfrac{\text{total distance}}{\text{total time taken}} = \dfrac{s}{t}$

(4) Instantaneous speed $= \lim_{\Delta t \to 0} \dfrac{\Delta s}{\Delta t}$

(It is customary to denote these quantities by the following symbols):

average velocity—$\bar{v}$ average speed—$\bar{v}$

instantaneous velocity—v instantaneous speed—v

In our example, the car was travelling in a straight line so that its direction was constant. Its velocity and speed were thus numerically equal.

Since we are considering motion in a straight line in this chapter we are concerned with motion in an unchanging direction. It is thus sufficient for us to refer to the speed of a body rather than its velocity since the two are numerically equal. Similarly we can refer to the distance travelled by a body rather than the displacement which it makes. In short, it is sufficient for use to consider scalar quantities rather than vector quantities for motion in a straight line since the problem of changing direction does not arise.

Although motion in a straight line has a constant direction, it can have either of two senses for a given direction. If we draw a horizontal line, we can do so in the sense left to right or in the sense right to left, and the direction of the line will be the same in each case (horizontal). To account for the problem of sense when it arises we shall adopt one sense of a direction as positive and the opposite sense as negative. All quantities related to the positive sense we shall describe by positive numbers, and all quantities related to the negative sense we shall describe by negative numbers.

The consideration of sense will become important later in this chapter in our study of the motion of a body under gravity, since the sense of motion in the vertical direction can be upwards or downwards.

2.2 The Definition and Meaning of Acceleration

In our example in the last section we discussed the possibilities of a car having an 'erratic motion' by which we meant a velocity which was non-uniform.

When the velocity of a body is changing the body is said to be accelerating and the acceleration of the body is defined as the rate at which its velocity changes. Since velocity is a vector quantity it is only completely described by size and direction. If either or both of these change, then velocity changes. A body can thus accelerate by:

1 changing its speed while maintaining a constant direction,

or 2 changing its direction while maintaining a constant speed,

or 3 changing its speed and direction simultaneously.

The first of these possibilities will concern us for the remainder of this chapter. The second possibility we shall consider briefly in the next chapter although its discussion is not specifically required for the purposes of the course. The third possibility we shall also consider in the next chapter.

We now consider the acceleration of a body moving in a straight line.

Consider a car starting from rest and accelerating along a straight road. Suppose that its instantaneous speed is recorded by someone looking at the speedometer at the end of each second after the motion begins. Let us suppose further that these instantaneous speeds have the values shown in the following table:

time after motion begins (t)	0	1	2	3	4	5	6	7	8	s
speed after a time t (v)	0	2	4	6	8	10	12	14	16	m s^{-1}

Since the speed of the car is increasing by 2 metres per second *every* second, we can say that the car is accelerating uniformly. Further, this uniform acceleration has the value 2 metres per second every second—usually written as 2 metres/second², 2 m/s² or 2 m s^{-2}.

In this case, the statement 'the acceleration of the car is 2 m s^{-2}' means that the speed of the car is increasing by 2 metres per second every second.

If we draw a graph of the results in the table, then this would appear as in Fig. 2.2. An important result to be noted from this graph is that

the speed-time graph of a body which is being accelerated uniformly in a straight line, is a straight line inclined to each axis.

Result 1

The gradient of this graph (m) would be defined in the normal way, thus

$$m = \frac{v_2 - v_1}{t_2 - t_1}$$

where ($t_1 v_1$) and ($t_2 v_2$) are two points on the graph such that $t_2 > t_1$ and $v_2 > v_1$. If we denote the term ($v_2 - v_1$) by Δv, and the term ($t_2 - t_1$) by Δt, then:

$$m = \frac{\Delta v}{\Delta t}$$

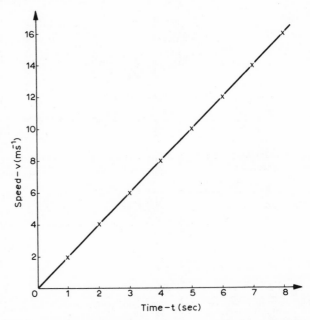

Fig.2.2 The speed-time graph of a body being accelerated uniformly at 2 m s^{-2}.

If we choose two points P_1 and P_2 on the graph as shown in Fig. 2.3, then the gradient of the graph can be calculated as follows:

$$m = \frac{\Delta v}{\Delta t}$$

$$= \frac{v_2 - v_1}{t_2 - t_1}$$

$$= \frac{12 - 6}{6 - 3}$$

$$= \frac{6}{3}$$

$$= 2$$

We note that the gradient of the graph is *numerically equal*

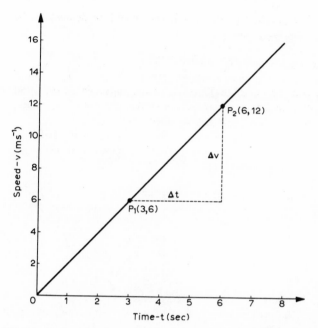

Fig.2.3 Determination of the gradient of the speed-time graph.

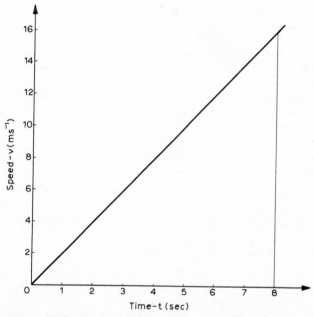

Fig.2.4 The area under the graph between 0 and 8 s is the area of the triangle shown.

to the acceleration of the car.

(The units of the gradient can be derived from a consideration of the dimensions of Δv and Δt as follows:

$$m = \frac{\Delta v}{\Delta t}$$

hence

$$[m] = \frac{[\Delta v]}{[\Delta t]} \quad \text{(where } [m] \text{ means 'the dimensions of } m\text{')}$$

$$= \frac{LT^{-1}}{T}$$

$$= LT^{-2}$$

Since the unit of L is the metre and the unit of T is the second, the units of the gradient are m s^{-2}.)

We are thus provided with a second important result:

the gradient of a speed-time graph is a measure of the acceleration present in the motion which the graph represents.

Result 2

(Had the graph been non-linear, that is, had the car speed not been increasing uniformly with time, so that the acceleration was non-uniform, then the instantaneous acceleration could be calculated at any time as the gradient of the graph at the point representing that time. We shall discuss instantaneous acceleration at the end of this chapter.)

We recall from the first section of this chapter that

$$\text{average speed} = \frac{\text{total distance gone}}{\text{total time taken}}$$

hence, total distance gone = (average speed) × (total time taken). As far as the motion of the car is concerned, the average speed over the 8 second period is calculated as

$$\bar{v} = \frac{\text{(initial speed)} + \text{(final speed)}}{2}$$

$$= \frac{0 + 16}{2} = 8 \text{ m s}^{-1}$$

hence total distance gone $= 8 \times 8$ metres

$$= 64 \text{ metres}$$

If we calculate the area under the speed-time graph between 0 and 8 seconds, this area is the area of the triangle in Fig. 2.4.

Since the area of a triangle $= \frac{1}{2}$(base × altitude),

then area under the speed-
time graph between 0
and 8 seconds $= \frac{1}{2} \times 8 \times 16$

$$= 64$$

The area under the graph is thus *numerically equal* to the distance travelled by the car.

(The units of the area can be derived from a consideration of the dimensions of 'base' and 'altitude' as follows:

$$\text{area} = \frac{1}{2}(\text{base} \times \text{altitude})$$

9

hence,   [area] = [base] × [altitude]

$$= T \times LT^{-1}$$

$$= L$$

The area under a speed-time graph is therefore measured in *metres*.)

We are now provided with a third important result:

the distance travelled by a body in a given time interval can be calculated as equal to the area under its speed-time graph for that interval.

Result 3

In deriving 'Result 2' we found the car to have an average speed of 8 m s^{-1} where the average was calculated between 0 and 8 seconds. With reference to Fig. 2.2, we see that the car had an instantaneous speed of 8 m s^{-1} after 4 seconds.

We are now provided with a fourth important result:

when a body is being accelerated uniformly, its instantaneous speed becomes equal to its average speed half way through the time interval over which the average speed was calculated.

Result 4

The four results which we have obtained are essential for our study of uniformly accelerated motion in a straight line and we now adopt them as propositions for use in our later discussions. This we may do since the results are mathematically consistent with the definition of acceleration. We have shown that the results apply in a particular situation and so we may therefore derive a certain confidence regarding their more general usage.

2.3 An Experiment to Measure Acceleration

We now consider an experimental approach to measuring the acceleration of a body which is accelerating uniformly in a straight line.

The body concerned is a dynamics trolley which is allowed to run (from rest) down a plane. The plane is inclined at a sufficiently steep angle to the bench to ensure that the trolley will run freely and accelerate.

To record the motion of the trolley, we attach a paper tape to it and feed this tape through a ticker-tape timer which is illustrated in Fig. 2.5.

The apparatus is arranged as illustrated in Fig. 2.6.

Let us suppose that the paper tape representing the motion appears as in Fig. 2.7(a).

Since the arm of the timer vibrates 50 times each second,* one complete vibration must take $\frac{1}{50}$th of a second. That is, the time between the arm stamping one dot and the next

* The frequency of the a.c. input is 50 Hertz (50 cycles per second).

dot on the tape is $\frac{1}{50}$th second. The interval between any two consecutive dots on the tape (called a *dot-interval*) is therefore worth $\frac{1}{50}$th second in time.

Since measuring the length of one dot-interval would be less accurate than measuring the length of five dot-intervals, we shall mark off the experimental tape in a series of five dot-intervals as shown in Fig. 2.7(b). Each 'five dot-interval' (AB, BC, etc.) will then be worth $\frac{1}{10}$th second in time.

Measuring the length of each 'five dot-interval', that is, the distance travelled by the trolley during each $\frac{1}{10}$th second, we find the following:

interval	AB	BC	CD	DE
duration (s)	$\frac{1}{10}$	$\frac{1}{10}$	$\frac{1}{10}$	$\frac{1}{10}$
length (cm)	1	3	5	7

Knowing the distance travelled each $\frac{1}{10}$th second, we can calculate the *average* speed of the trolley during each $\frac{1}{10}$th second by using the formula

$$\text{average speed} = \frac{\text{total distance gone}}{\text{total time taken}}$$

The average speed of the trolley over the first $\frac{1}{10}$th second of its motion is thus 1 cm/$\frac{1}{10}$ s or 10 cm s^{-1}.

The average speed of the trolley over each $\frac{1}{10}$th second of its motion is given in the following table:

interval	AB	BC	CD	DE
average speed (cm s^{-1})	10	30	50	70

Let us now assume that the acceleration of the trolley is uniform over such a short time interval as $\frac{1}{10}$th second. We can then employ 'Result 4' in considering each successive tenth of a second of the motion.

It follows that the trolley had an instantaneous speed of 10 cm s^{-1} half way through the first $\frac{1}{10}$th second of its motion—that is, after $\frac{1}{20}$th second. The trolley had an instantaneous speed of 30 cm s^{-1} half way through the second $\frac{1}{10}$th second of its motion—that is, after $\frac{3}{20}$th second. Its instantaneous speed was 50 cm s^{-1} after $\frac{5}{20}$th second, and 70 cm s^{-1} after $\frac{7}{20}$th second.

The graph of trolley speed against time thus appears as in Fig. 2.8. We see that this graph is a straight line inclined to both axes and so by using 'Result 1' we may say that the overall motion of the trolley has been that of uniform acceleration—as intended. We would expect the acceleration to be uniform since the trolley was acted on by a constant

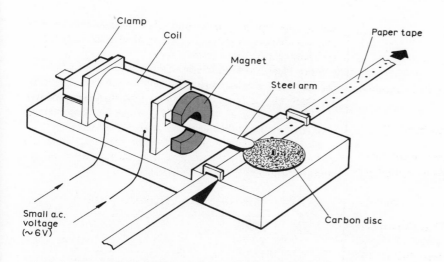

Fig.2.5   The ticker-tape timer. The a.c. voltage supplied to
the coil sets up an alternating axial magnetic field
which magnetises the steel arm in one direction
and then in the other. The free end of the arm is thus
set vibrating between the poles of the fixed magnet.

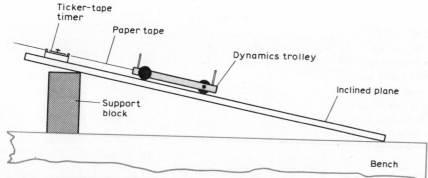

Fig.2.6   The experimental arrangement for determining the
acceleration of a dynamics trolley on an inclined
plane.

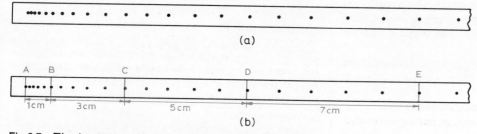

Fig.2.7   The beginning of the paper tape representing the
motion of the dynamics trolley on the inclined plane:
(a) originally, (b) divided into a series of five dot-
intervals.

component of the Earth's gravitational pull as it moved down the plane.

From this graph we can calculate the acceleration of the trolley, using 'Result 2', as follows:

$$\text{acceleration} = \text{graph gradient} = \frac{\Delta v}{\Delta t}$$

Choosing Δt as the interval between 0 and $\frac{4}{10}$th second, the corresponding change in speed Δv is 80 cm s^{-1}.

Hence
$$\text{acceleration} = \frac{80 \ (\text{cm s}^{-1})}{\frac{4}{10} \ (\text{s})}$$
$$= 200 \ \text{cm s}^{-2}$$
$$= 2 \ \text{m s}^{-2}$$

The acceleration of the trolley is thus 2 m s^{-2}.

(As a check on the validity of 'Result 3', we can calculate the distance travelled by the trolley in the first $\frac{4}{10}$th second of its motion as the area under the speed-time graph between times 0 and $\frac{4}{10}$th second, and compare this with the length of tape stamped during the same period.)

With reference to the graph in Fig. 2.8:

area under the graph between times 0 and $\frac{4}{10}$th second

$$= \frac{1}{2} \times \frac{4}{10} \times 80$$
$$= 16 \ \text{cm}.$$

Now the actual distance gone in the first $\frac{4}{10}$th second is just the length of the experimental tape interval AE

The length of the interval AE = 1 cm + 3 cm + 5 cm + 7 cm
$$= 16 \ \text{cm} - (\text{as required})$$

2.4 The Equations of Uniformly Accelerated Motion in a Straight Line

Although uniformly accelerated motion in a straight line occurs more as an exception than a rule in nature, its study is an essential starting point for the study of more complicated accelerated motions. We now treat this 'exceptional' motion in more general terms, and in so doing we shall derive three equations to describe it completely.

Let us consider the motion of a body as represented by the speed-time graph in Fig. 2.9.

This graph tells us that when the body was first observed its speed was u (m s^{-1}) and that after t seconds, it had reached a speed of v (m s^{-1}). That is, the body was being accelerated. Since the graph is of a straight line nature, we can say from 'Result 1' that the acceleration was uniform. Let us suppose that the value of the uniform acceleration was a (m s^{-2}), and that the total distance travelled by the body during the t seconds was s metres.

We now attempt to relate the five quantities u, v, t, a, and s.

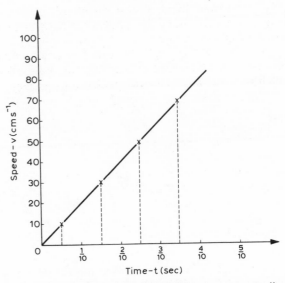

Fig. 2.8 The speed-time graph for the dynamics trolley on the inclined plane. This has been drawn from consideration of the average speed of the trolley each $\frac{1}{10}$th second of its motion.

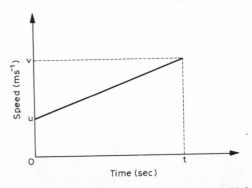

Fig. 2.9 The speed-time graph of a body whose initial speed was u, and which was uniformly accelerated for a time t, until its speed was v.

Since acceleration = gradient of graph = $\frac{\Delta v}{\Delta t}$, then choosing Δt as the interval between 0 and t seconds, the corresponding change in speed Δv is $(v - u)$, hence

$$a = \frac{v - u}{t}$$

$$\Leftrightarrow \qquad at = v - u$$

$$\Leftrightarrow at + u = v$$

or
$$\boxed{v = u + at} \quad \ldots \ldots (2.1)$$

We know from 'Result 3', that the distance travelled by a body in a certain time can be calculated as the area under its speed-time graph for that time.

The area under the graph can be thought of as a rectangle of sides u, t, surmounted by a triangle of altitude $(v - u)$ and base t. The area under the graph is thus given by

$$\text{area} = ut + \tfrac{1}{2}t(v - u)$$

hence distance gone,

$$s = ut + \tfrac{1}{2}t(v - u)$$

But $(v - u) = at$, since $v = u + at$, hence $s = ut + \tfrac{1}{2}tat$

$$\Leftrightarrow \boxed{s = ut + \tfrac{1}{2}at^2} \ldots\ldots\ldots\ldots(2.2)$$

Equation 2.1 states that

$$v = u + at$$

hence

$$t = \frac{v - u}{a}$$

Substituting this value for t into Equation 2.2 we have

$$s = u\left(\frac{v - u}{a}\right) + \tfrac{1}{2}a\left(\frac{v - u}{a}\right)^2$$

$$= \frac{u(v - u)}{a} + \frac{a}{2}\left(\frac{v^2 - 2uv + u^2}{a^2}\right)$$

$$= \frac{u(v - u)}{a} + \frac{v^2 - 2uv + u^2}{2a}$$

hence

$$2as = 2uv - 2u^2 + v^2 - 2uv + u^2$$

$$\Leftrightarrow 2as = v^2 - u^2$$

$$\Leftrightarrow \boxed{v^2 = u^2 + 2as} \ldots\ldots\ldots\ldots\ldots\ldots (2.3)$$

We have thus derived three equations connecting the five important variable quantities encountered in the study of uniformly accelerated motion in a straight line.

In using these equations, as in using any equations, we must pay particular attention to the consistency of units. Equation 1 for example would lack validity if we were to quote each of u and v in m s^{-1} and t in min. To maintain consistency among the units it is perhaps good practice to quote u and v in m s^{-1}, s in m, a in m s^{-2}, and t in s — at all times. This may necessitate some preliminary conversions in some problems— as would be the case if say speeds were originally quoted in km h^{-1}—but this is a small price to pay for correctness.

We consider a problem which can be solved quite easily by the application of these equations of motion.

Problem 1 A motor cycle accelerates uniformly in top gear from 14 m s^{-1} to 30 m s^{-1} in 16 seconds. Find the value of its acceleration, and the distance travelled during these 16 seconds.

Here $u = 14$, $v = 30$, $t = 16$.

Using the equation $\quad v = u + at$

we have $\qquad\qquad 30 = 14 + 16a$

hence $\qquad\qquad\quad 16 = 16a$

hence $\qquad\qquad\quad a = 1 \text{ m s}^{-2}$

The acceleration of the motor cycle is thus 1 m s^{-2}.

Using the equation $\quad s = ut + \tfrac{1}{2}at^2$

we have $\qquad\qquad s = (14 \times 16) + (\tfrac{1}{2} \times 1 \times (16)^2)$

$$= 224 + (\tfrac{1}{2} \times 256)$$

$$= 224 + 128$$

$$= 352 \text{ m}$$

The motor cycle thus travels 352 metres during acceleration.

2.5 Vertical Motion under Gravity

Perhaps the most frequent example of uniformly accelerated motion in a straight line in our everyday experience is that of an object falling towards the surface of the Earth. The acceleration of a freely falling body is called the acceleration due to gravity and is denoted by the symbol g. Its size is approximately 9.8 m s^{-2} and it is directed downwards towards the centre of the Earth.

The presence of this acceleration means that any object which is dropped near the surface of the Earth will have its speed increased by approximately 9.8 m s^{-1} every second until it strikes the Earth's surface. On the other hand, an object projected vertically upwards from the Earth's surface will have its speed reduced by approximately 9.8 m s^{-1} every second since the gravitational acceleration is directed downwards. After reaching its highest point however the object will have its speed increased by approximately 9.8 m s^{-1} every second as it proceeds downwards.

The topic of vertical motion under gravity will thus have to be considered in an upward sense or in a downward sense, depending on the motion of the body concerned. To avoid having to quote the terms 'vertically upwards' and 'vertically downwards' in our every problem, we shall label the downwards sense positive, (since it is the sense in which the gravitational acceleration acts) and upwards sense negative. Having done this, we shall then describe speeds in the downwards sense by positive numbers, speeds in the upwards sense by negative numbers, and the ever-present acceleration due to gravity by a positive number.

In doing this we are preparing to equip our equations of uniformly accelerated motion in a straight line (derived to relate scalar quantities) to accommodate the vectorial property of sense. Consequently the variable s in the equations, instead of referring to a distance gone, will refer to a linear *displacement* with respect to a chosen origin. If in a particular problem, s is calculated to have a negative sign, we shall decide that it represents a net displacement above the chosen origin, whereas if it is calculated to have a positive sign, we shall decide that it represents a net displacement below the chosen origin: (The chosen origin is usually the starting point of the motion.)

The solution of a problem should demonstrate the use of this sign convention.

Problem 2 A stone is projected vertically upwards from the top of a deep mine shaft with a speed of 20 m s^{-1}. Taking g as 10 m s^{-2}, find

    a) the height to which the stone will rise

    b) its position after 1, 3, and 5 seconds

a) Here $u = -20$, $v = 0$ (since the stone is at rest at its highest point)

$$a = 10,$$

Using the equation $v^2 = u^2 + 2as$

we have $0 = (-20)^2 + (2 \times 10s)$

$$= 400 + 20s$$

hence $20s = -400$

hence $s = -20$ m

The stone thus rises *20 metres above* the top of the shaft ('above' as indicated by the minus sign).

b) Here $u = -20$, $a = 10$, $t = 1, 3, 5$.

Using the equation $s = ut + \frac{1}{2}at^2$

we have $s = (-20 \times 1) + (\frac{1}{2} \times 10 \times 1^2)$

                    (for $t = 1$)

$$= -20 + 5$$

$$= -15 \text{ m}$$

After one second, the stone is *15 metres above* the top of the shaft.

Again using $s = ut + \frac{1}{2}at^2$

we have $s = (-20 \times 3) + (\frac{1}{2} \times 10 \times 3^2)$ (for $t = 3$)

$$= -60 + 45$$

$$= -15 \text{ m}$$

After 3 seconds the stone is again *15 metres above* the top of the shaft.

Again using $s = ut + \frac{1}{2}at^2$

we have $s = (-20 \times 5) + (\frac{1}{2} \times 10 \times 5^2)$ (for $t = 5$)

$$= -100 + 125$$

$$= 25 \text{ m}$$

After 5 seconds the stone is *25 metres below* the top of the shaft. That is, it has fallen back into the shaft after 5 seconds.

These results are represented diagramatically in Fig. 2.10.

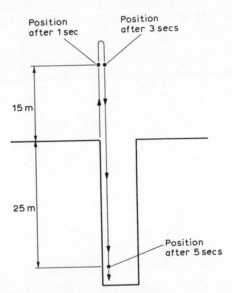

Fig.2.10 The results of Problem 2 (text).

2.6 Limitations of the Equations of Motion

However interesting and potentially valuable the three equations of motion may seem, they are but the starting point for a more general and complete study of accelerated motion. The equations function as tools for the treatment of motion in a straight line in which the acceleration is constant. Such motion however is the exception rather than the rule in our everyday lives and in nature.

We have already solved problems about cars accelerating *uniformly* along straight roads, and objects accelerating *uniformly* under gravity. In actual practice however we would observe a car accelerating *uniformly* along a straight road only occasionally. (Not because cars are incapable of being accelerated uniformly but because of the way in which they are usually driven.) Again if we decided to test the validity of the equations of motion for a body falling freely under gravity, we might begin to doubt their value. If we calculated the time of fall of an object dropped from a very high tower (using the equations), and compared this with the time as actually measured with a stopwatch, we would most likely find the results to be in disagreement no matter how often we carried out the measurement. The reasons for the disagreement would be:

1   The object would tend to reach a terminal or ultimate speed beyond which it would suffer no acceleration at all (Fig. 2.11). This terminal speed is reached because air

Fig.2.11 During free fall, the sky-diver reaches a terminal or ultimate speed. As he leaves the aircraft however, he is accelerating at approximately 10 m s⁻². (By kind permission of The British Army Freefall Parachute Team—'The Red Devils'.)

resistance builds up as the object speeds up so that the object cannot be regarded as falling freely. Were we able to conduct the same experiment on the moon, would we be any more fortunate in finding agreement between our calculations and experimental results?

2 The acceleration due to gravity is not constant. Its value changes (slightly) as we move away from the surface of the earth.

2.7 Motion in a Straight Line and the Use of Calculus

When a body moves along a straight line we can describe its motion by means of an equation which gives the position of the body as a function of the time which has elapsed from the start of the motion. For example in the case of a body

falling freely under gravity from a rest position, the equation which describes its position or distance fallen in terms of the elapsed time is

$$s = \tfrac{1}{2}gt^2 \quad \text{where } g \text{ is the acceleration due to gravity}$$

In the general case, the equation of motion of a body is

$$s = f(t) \quad \text{where } f(t) \text{ denotes 'a function of time'}$$

Let us try to derive expressions for the speed and acceleration of a body at some time t, taking the equation of motion of the body as

$$s = f(t)$$

If the body has travelled a distance s in a time t, and then travels a further distance Δs in a subsequent time Δt

$$\text{then since} \qquad s = f(t)$$
$$\text{we can say} \quad s + \Delta s = f(t + \Delta t)$$

Hence the distance travelled Δs in the time Δt is given by:

$$\Delta s = f(t + \Delta t) - f(t)$$

The *average* speed of the body, $\bar{v}$, during the interval Δt is calculated as $\dfrac{\Delta s}{\Delta t}$, so that

$$\bar{v} = \frac{f(t + \Delta t) - f(t)}{(t + \Delta t) - t}$$

$$= \frac{f(t + \Delta t) - f(t)}{\Delta t}$$

To obtain the *instantaneous speed* of the body, v, at time t, we must compute the average speed over the shortest interval of time imaginable. The instantaneous speed of the body at time t must therefore be the limiting value of the average speed $\bar{v}$ as Δt approaches zero. That is

$$v = \lim_{\Delta t \to 0} \bar{v}$$

$$= \lim_{\Delta t \to 0} \frac{\Delta s}{\Delta t}$$

$$= \lim_{\Delta t \to 0} \frac{f(t + \Delta t) - f(t)}{\Delta t}$$

This equation is by definition the derivative of s with respect to t.
That is

$$v = \frac{\mathrm{d}s}{\mathrm{d}t} = f'(t) \quad [= g(t) \text{ say}]$$

Let us suppose that the instantaneous speed of the body is v at time t but at time $t + \Delta t$ the instantaneous speed has increased to $v + \Delta v$.

If the relationship between v and t is $v = g(t)$, then
$$v + \Delta v = g(t + \Delta t).$$
Hence the change in speed Δv occurring in the time Δt is given by
$$\Delta v = g(t + \Delta t) - g(t)$$
The *average* acceleration of the body during the time Δt, $\bar{a}$ say, is $\dfrac{\Delta v}{\Delta t}$ so that

$$\bar{a} = \frac{g(t + \Delta t) - g(t)}{(t + \Delta t) - t}$$
$$= \frac{g(t + \Delta t) - g(t)}{\Delta t}$$

To obtain the *instantaneous acceleration* of the body, a say, at time t, we must compute the average acceleration over the shortest time interval imaginable. The instantaneous acceleration of the body must therefore be the limiting value of the average acceleration as Δt approaches zero. That is

$$a = \lim_{\Delta t \to 0} \bar{a}$$
$$= \lim_{\Delta t \to 0} \frac{\Delta v}{\Delta t}$$
$$= \lim_{\Delta t \to 0} \frac{g(t + \Delta t) - g(t)}{\Delta t}$$

This equation is by definition the derivative of v with respect to t. That is

$$a = \frac{dv}{dt} = f''(t)$$

Thus given the distance travelled by a body, s say, as a function of time, for example $s = f(t)$, we can calculate the instantaneous speed of the body (v) and the instantaneous acceleration of the body (a), according to the equations

$$v = f'(t)$$
$$a = f''(t)$$

This set of results is particularly useful and the only feasible approach when the motion of a body is characterised by a *non-uniform* acceleration.

By way of example, let us solve one problem where the motion of a body is of this nature.

Problem 3 The distance, s (metres), travelled by a body t (seconds) after the motion has begun is defined by the equation:
$$s = 2t^3 + 5t - 3$$

Find expressions for the instantaneous speed and instantaneous acceleration of the body at time t. What are the values of these quantities one second after the motion has begun?

In this case $s (= f(t)) = 2t^3 + 5t - 3$

hence $v (= f'(t)) = 6t^2 + 5$—instantaneous speed

and $a (= f''(t)) = 12t$—instantaneous acceleration

After 1 second, $v = 11$ and $a = 12$

Hence after one second the instantaneous speed of the body is 11 m s^{-1} and its instantaneous acceleration is 12 m s^{-2}.

Problems
(Where necessary take g as 10 m s^{-2}.)

1 A car moves 40 metres North, then 16 metres West and finally 40 metres South. If the journey lasts 12 seconds, calculate the average speed of the car and also its average velocity.

2 The table shows the distance of a car from its starting point at various times after its motion begins.

Time after start (t)	0	1	2	3	4	5	seconds
Distance (s) from starting point	0	1	4	9	16	25	metres

Draw a speed-time graph of the motion of the car (by consideration of its average speed over each second) and use this to estimate its instantaneous speed after 4 seconds.

3 Figure 2.12 shows part of a paper tape which was attached to a trolley being accelerated from rest. The ticker-timer used in the investigation had a frequency of vibration of 50 Hertz (50 vibrations per second). The tape has been divided into a series of ten dot-intervals.

Using the information on the tape, draw a speed-time graph for the trolley's motion. From the graph estimate the acceleration of the trolley and also the time which had elapsed between the start of the motion and the stamping of the first dot on the portion of tape shown.

4 A motor car starts from rest and accelerates uniformly at 2 m s^{-2}. How long will it take to reach a speed of
a) 20 m s^{-1} b) 108 km h^{-1}?

5 An aircraft 'lifts off' at a ground speed of 180 km h^{-1}. If it accelerates uniformly from rest and reaches this speed after 50 seconds, what length of runway does it require for take-off?

6 A car is travelling at 13 m s^{-1} in a restricted zone. On entering the de-restricted zone, the driver increases the car's speed to 26 m s^{-1} in 10 seconds.
a) What was the acceleration of the car during the 10 second interval (assuming it to be uniform)?
b) How far did the car travel during acceleration?

7 A folded collapsible life raft is dropped from a hovering helicopter. It strikes the sea 3 seconds after release. Find its speed on impact and the height of the helicopter at the

moment the raft was released. Are there any factors in this problem which might cause errors in the calculation?

8 The graph in Fig. 2.13 represents the motion of a parachutist after bailing out of an aeroplane.

i) How long did he fall before opening his parachute?

ii) What was his deceleration after opening it?

iii) From what height did he bail out?

iv) In what respects is the portion of the graph between 0 and 5 seconds inaccurate?

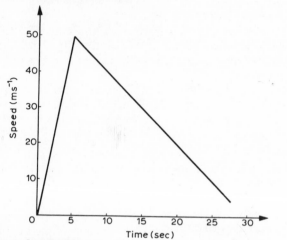

Fig.2.13 See Problem 8.

9 A sandbag is allowed to fall from a balloon when the balloon is 80 metres above ground and ascending vertically at a steady speed. If the sandbag reaches the ground after 5 seconds, find the speed of the balloon.

10 The distance travelled by a body (s metres), t seconds after its motion has begun is given by the equation:

$$s = At^3 - Bt$$

What are the units of A and B? If the numerical values of A and B are 3 and 1 respectively, find the speed of the body and also the distance which it has gone after 2 seconds. Find an expression for the acceleration of the body.

11 The equation $s = ut + \frac{1}{2}at^2$ is derived for *uniformly* accelerated motion. Show, by considering

$$s = f(t), \quad v = f'(t), \quad \text{and} \quad a = f''(t)$$

that (1) $v = u + at$

(2) the acceleration is constant.

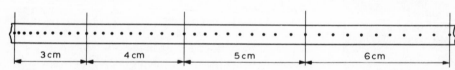

Fig.2.12 See Problem 3.

Chapter 3

Force and Acceleration

Fig.3.0 A portrait of Sir Isaac Newton. We shall be concerned with Newton's first two laws of motion in this chapter. (By kind permission of The Science Museum, London. Neg. no. 1080.)

In the last chapter, our attention was focussed mainly on the topic of acceleration. We discussed its meaning, its measurement, and its calculation. We now concentrate on the most fundamental issue of all—the *cause* of acceleration. For this purpose we introduce and discuss two laws of motion first enunciated by Isaac Newton in his 'Philosophioe Naturalis Principia Mathematica' of 1687. (In this work, Newton actually enunciated three laws of motion, but as far as we are concerned, the third law will find application in our next chapter.) For many years after 1687 it was believed that the laws of motion were infallible in their description of dynamical systems. In more recent years however, it has been shown that this is not quite the case, and in fact the laws are somewhat inaccurate for the description of extreme macroscopic and microscopic systems. Nevertheless the laws find widespread application by engineers and physicists in less extreme situations where any errors due to limitations in the laws are quite insignificant in comparison to errors of experimental observation. The impact of the laws of motion on physical science is perhaps well described by Professor Feynman who tells us that

'The discovery of the laws of dynamics, or the laws of motion was a dramatic moment in the history of science. Before Newton's time, the motion of things like the planets were a mystery, but after Newton there was complete understanding. . . . The motions of pendulums, oscillators with springs and weights in them, and so on, could all be analysed completely after Newton's laws were enunciated.'

Let us then look at the formulations of the first two laws of motion before discussing their explanation of the cause of acceleration.

Newton's First Law of Motion
The first law may be formulated as follows:

Every body remains at rest or moves at a constant speed in a straight line unless it is acted upon by a net (i.e. unbalanced) external force.

(This law is sometimes referred to as the 'Principle of Inertia.')

Newton's Second Law of Motion
This law may be formulated as

The net (i.e. unbalanced) external force acting on a body provides the body with an acceleration which is directly proportional to, and in the same direction as, the net force.

The idea of 'force' as employed in these two laws is perhaps a difficult one to analyse. It is generally agreed that the definition of the word 'force' is embodied in the second law although this is perhaps seemingly unsatisfactory. As far as we are concerned in our everyday lives, a force is something we apply to a body to push it, pull it, topple, turn, or twist it. The idea of force is an intuitive one so that the understanding and description of the basic nature of force is somewhat intangible. It is hoped that our discussions in this chapter will consolidate whatever intuitive ideas we have on the term 'force' so that we may employ it with more than sufficient understanding for the purposes of our course.

Let us then discuss the implications of the two laws of motion.

The first law provides us with a perfect account of non-accelerated motion. We are well acquainted with the fact that a stationary object will remain stationary until it is acted upon by a net external force. We are perhaps not so well acquainted with the fact that an object, once started, will continue to move in a straight line at steady speed provided no external force acts on it. This statement may seem contrary to our experience. After all, to move a heavy crate across a level floor at steady speed, we must apply a constant force to the crate. This would seem to suggest that a constant force is necessary to maintain a steady speed. The important point to be borne in mind however is that the force applied at the crate is not a net force. When the crate is moving at steady speed, this applied force is equal and opposite to the force of friction between the crate and the floor, so that the net force on the crate is zero. Its steady speed is thus accounted for by the first law.

It is highly unlikely that we should ever observe an object upon which there are *no* forces acting and which would move consequently at a constant speed in a straight line. In most of the problems we shall meet, constant speed in a straight line is achieved by an object which is acted upon by a balanced set of forces. That is, an object on which the *net* force is zero.

Near constant speed can be achieved in the laboratory using the linear air track shown in Fig. 3.1. The air track provides a cushion of air for the track vehicle which may therefore move effectively without frictional resistance. Which two forces still act on the vehicle?

Fig.3.1   The linear air track and its accessories. (By kind permission of M.L.I. Ltd.)

Since the first law describes the motion of an object which is acted upon by a balanced set of forces, it is quite essential that the second law should describe the motion of an object which is acted upon by some net force. This is in fact the case. The second law tells us that when a net force F_{net} acts on an object, then the object is accelerated by an amount a in the direction of F_{net} such that

$$a \propto F_{net}$$

Consequently we may write

$$\frac{F_{net}}{a} = \text{some constant (for a given object)}$$

This constant may be regarded as the measure of the *inertia* or *mass* of the given object because if the ratio F_{net}/a is

large, we conclude that a large net force is necessary to produce a particular acceleration, and this conclusion is quite consistent with our knowledge that a large net force is usually required to accelerate a massive body. If we call the constant 'mass' and denote it by the symbol m then

$$\frac{F_{net}}{a} = m$$

$$\Leftrightarrow \boxed{F_{net} = ma} \quad \dots \dots \dots \dots \dots (3.1)$$

With reference to this equation, we can see that the first law of motion is a specific instance of the second law. That is, if F_{net} is zero, then the acceleration of the object of mass m must be zero. That is, the object must either be stationary or moving at a constant speed in a straight line.

Since we have arrived at equation (3.1) purely by discussion of the second law of motion, it may be advisable at this stage to attempt to verify it by experimental investigation. This we now do.

3.1 Experimental Approach to Newton's Second Law of Motion

Theory   The equation (3.1) predicts that the acceleration 'a' produced in an object of mass 'm' by a net force 'F_{net}' is given by $a = \dfrac{F_{net}}{m}$. That is, acceleration is a function of 'F_{net}' and 'm'. We must therefore investigate the relationship between 'a' and 'F_{net}' for some constant 'm', and then the relationship between 'a' and 'm' for some constant 'F_{net}'.

Part 1   In this part of the investigation, we apply different net forces to a constant mass (one dynamics trolley), and note the resultant acceleration in each case. To arrive at a measure of applied net force, the following procedure is adopted:

The trolley is placed on a running board and the board is gradually inclined to the bench until the angle is reached where in order to keep the trolley in a state of rest, one elastic thread (attached at one end to the lower pillar of the trolley) has to be maintained stretched over the full length of the trolley as in Fig. 3.2. When the thread is then removed and the board maintained at the same angle, *one* unit of net force is said to be acting on the trolley.

Similarly if two identical elastic threads (each attached at one end to the lower pillar of the trolley) have to be stretched over the length of the trolley to keep it at rest when the running board is inclined to the bench at some steeper angle, then *two* units of net force are said to be acting on the trolley when the threads are removed. (The values of three and four units of net force are derived in a similar way.)

The acceleration of the trolley, provided by the application of some net force, is found from the analysis of a ticker tape attached to the trolley and threaded through a ticker tape timer. The analysis of the tape and subsequent calculation of acceleration is performed as in the last chapter.

Fig.3.2   When the thread is removed, one unit of net force will act on the trolley.

When the trolley is subjected to one, two, three, and four units of net force in turn, and the tape for each run analysed to find the acceleration produced by the application of the particular net force, the results obtained are likely to be similar to those shown in the following table:

Net force on trolley — F_{net} (Units)	acceleration produced — a (m s^{-2})	$\dfrac{a}{F_{net}}$
1	0·25	0·25
2	0·48	0·24
3	0·78	0·26
4	0·96	0·24

From this table we can see that the ratio of acceleration to net force is approximately constant.

That is, $\dfrac{a}{F_{net}}$ = a constant, or a = a constant $\times F_{net}$

That is $\boxed{a \propto F_{net}}$ . . . . Result 1

Part 2 In this part of the investigation, we apply a constant net force to different masses in turn. These different masses are one, two, three, and four dynamics trolleys stacked as required. We apply a net force of two units (defined as in Part 1) to each of the four masses in turn, and find the resulting acceleration produced in each case.

In this part of the experiment, it is necessary to reduce the angle of inclination of the running board for each new mass employed. This is because as more mass is added to the original mass (at a certain angle of inclination), the component

of weight acting parallel to and down the plane, is increased. In order that two units of net force should act on the increased mass therefore, the angle of inclination of the running board must be reduced.

The motion of each mass is recorded as before on a paper tape attached to the mass and threaded through a ticker tape timer. Each tape is analysed as before, and the accelerations calculated.

When the different masses are in turn subjected to two units of net force, and the resulting acceleration calculated for each, the results obtained are likely to be similar to those shown in the following table:

mass — m (no. of trolleys stacked)	acceleration produced — a (m s^{-2})	$m \times a$
1	0·25	0·25
2	0·13	0·26
3	0·09	0·27
4	0·06	0·24

From this table we can see that the product of mass and acceleration is approximately constant.

That is, $m \times a$ = a constant, or a = a constant $\times \dfrac{1}{m}$

That is, $\boxed{a \propto \dfrac{1}{m}}$ . . . . Result 2

Result 1 states that $a \propto F_{net}$ for a constant m, while Result 2 states that $a \propto \dfrac{1}{m}$ for a constant F_{net}. If we wish to consider the cases of different net forces being applied to different masses so that neither m nor F_{net} is constant, then we must combine the two results and write

$$a \propto \frac{F_{net}}{m}$$

or, $$\frac{F_{net}}{m} \propto a$$

$$\Leftrightarrow \frac{F_{net}}{m} = ka \quad \text{where } k \text{ is some constant}$$

$$\Leftrightarrow F_{net} = kma$$

If we now define a force of *1 Newton* as that net force which acting on a mass of *1 kilogram* provides it with an acceleration of *1 metre second*$^{-2}$, then by substituting the values $F_{net} = 1$, $m = 1$, and $a = 1$ into the last equation, we have

$$1 = k \times 1 \times 1$$

$$\Leftrightarrow k = 1$$

Provided we measure net force in Newtons, mass in kilograms, and acceleration in metres second^{-2}, then the constant k will always have the value unity. This being the case, we can rewrite the last equation in the form

$$\boxed{F_{\text{net}} = ma}$$

and this agrees with equation 3.1 which was deduced from the second law of motion.

3.2 Mass and Weight

If an object is released near the surface of the Earth, then the net force acting on it is the force of gravitational attraction between the object and the Earth. This force is called the *weight* of the object. The acceleration produced in the object by the presence of this net force has the approximate value of 10 m s^{-2} and is directed vertically downwards regardless of the nature of the object concerned. This acceleration we have previously referred to as g.

Since $F_{\text{net}} = ma$, then for an object near the surface of the Earth, $F_{\text{net}} = mg$

or $\boxed{W = mg}$ where W is the weight of the object.

We note from this equation and from the foregoing discussion that weight and mass are completely different quantities. The weight of an object is the force of gravity acting on it, and as such is a vector quantity. Mass on the other hand is a scalar quantity. Weight, an expression of force, is measured in Newtons, while mass is measured in kilograms.

3.3 Motion in a Plane

The second law of motion tells us that the acceleration produced in an object by the application of a net external force is in the same direction as that in which the force acts. Until now we have been considering only instances where the net external force is applied in the same direction, as that in which the object is moving. The effect of such an application, as we have seen, is to increase the speed of the object while it continues to move along its original direction of travel.

We now come to consider the more general case of a net external force being applied to an object in a direction different from that of the object's motion. As a particularly interesting instance of this more general case, we consider the possibility of the net external force being applied at right angles to the original direction of motion of the object. Obviously the effect of such an application will be somewhat different from the effects we have discussed up to now. For one thing the body will be continually deflected from its original line of travel for as long as it is within the locality of the force.

According to the laws of motion, the body will acquire a steadily increasing speed along the direction of application of the force, while its speed along its original direction of travel should remain constant since the net external force in this direction is zero.

As an example, let us consider the motion of a beam of electrons within a cathode ray tube, as illustrated in Fig. 3.3. The path of the electrons is curved only for as long as the electrons are in the region of the net force. On leaving this region, the electrons travel in a straight line at steady speed since then no net force acts on them. The actual curvature of the path between the deflecting plates is the result of the electrons acquiring a steadily increasing speed in the direction of the applied force in addition to their original speed which must remain unchanged in size. On leaving the region of the deflecting plates, the electrons move with a constant velocity which is different in size and direction from their original constant velocity.

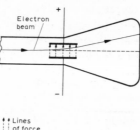

Fig.3.3 The electron path is curved only in the region of the plates.

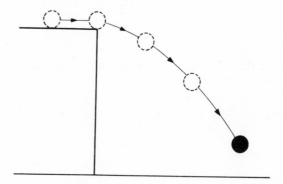

Fig.3.4 The motion of a ball projected from a bench top.

As a second example, let us consider the motion of a body which is projected horizontally near the surface of the Earth. We shall consider the case of a ball being rolled from the top of a bench illustrated in Fig. 3.4. While the ball is in contact with the bench, its weight is being balanced by an upward reaction from the bench. On leaving the bench, however, the weight of the body is no longer supported, and so becomes a net external force acting at right angles to the direction of the ball's motion (neglecting the effects of air buoyancy). According to the two laws of motion, the subsequent motion of the ball is in fact a combination of two independent motions—one of steady speed in the horizontal direction (since no net force acts horizontally), the other of uniform acceleration in the vertical direction (since a net force—the weight of the body—acts vertically). It is reasonable to assume that since the net force acting on the ball is its weight, then the uniform acceleration in the vertical direction will be 'g'.

With reference to Fig. 3.5 we can attempt to explain the shape of the path followed by the ball after it leaves the bench. At point P, the weight of the ball $\underline{W}$ acting at right angles to the line of travel of the ball, deflects it by providing it with a gradually increasing speed in the vertical direction. At the point Q however, the weight of the ball $\underline{W}$ no longer acts at right angles to its direction of travel. Let us resolve the weight $\underline{W}$ into components $\underline{W_1}$ and $\underline{W_2}$ such that $\underline{W_1}$ is directed along the tangent to the path at Q, and $\underline{W_2}$ is directed at right angles to the tangent to the path at Q. It follows that $\underline{W} = \underline{W_1} + \underline{W_2}$, $W_1 = W \cos \theta$, and $W_2 = W \sin \theta$ (where θ is the angle between $\underline{W}$ and the tangent to the path at Q). Since the component $\underline{W_2}$ is now at right angles to the path at Q, then it alone is responsible for further deflection of the ball at Q. Since $W_2 < W$, it is obvious that the amount of bending at Q must be smaller than that occurring at P. (The component $\underline{W_1}$ acting along the direction of travel of the ball at Q is available to increase the speed of the ball in this same direction.) This type of analysis helps to explain why the bending of a horizontally projected body is at a maximum at the start of the projection.

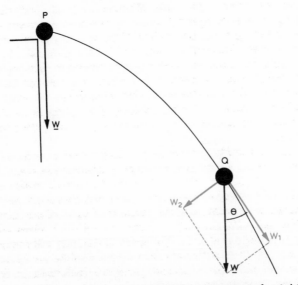

Fig.3.5   As the motion progresses, the component of weight perpendicular to the path is steadily reduced.

Let us now solve a problem on projectile motion to illustrate the mathematical application of the two laws of motion in such a situation.

Problem 1 A steel ball rolls along the inside of a horizontal pipe and reaches the open end of the pipe with a speed of 2 m s^{-1}. If the pipe is supported at a height of 5 m above ground, find the time of flight of the ball between leaving the pipe and striking the ground. Find also the horizontal distance travelled. (Take the acceleration due to gravity as 10 m s^{-2}.)

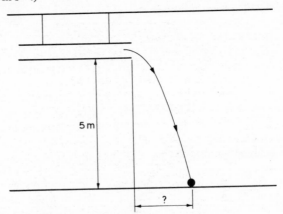

Fig.3.6   See Problem 1 (text).

The situation is illustrated in Fig. 3.6. Since we have decided that the motion of such a body is in fact a combination of two independent motions, we consider each separately.
Vertical motion: a motion of constant acceleration. We shall analyse it using the equations of motion.

Here $u = 0$, $a = 10$, $s = 5$ (all quantities here are to be taken as measured in the vertical direction—'u' is the initial speed in the vertical direction etc).

Using the equation $\quad s = ut + \tfrac{1}{2}at^2$

we have $\qquad 5 = (0 \times t) + (\tfrac{1}{2} \times 10 \times t^2)$

$\qquad\qquad\qquad = 5t^2$

hence $\qquad\qquad t^2 = 1$

$\Leftrightarrow \qquad\qquad t = 1$

The time of flight is thus one second.
Horizontal motion: a motion of constant speed. We shall analyse it using the equation "distance gone = (speed) × (time taken)".
Here speed $= 2 \text{ m s}^{-1}$ time of flight $= 1$ s.
Hence distance gone $= 2$ m
The horizontal distance travelled by the steel ball is thus two metres.

If in a problem we are asked to find the value of a quantity relating to the horizontal motion (say, distance travelled horizontally), then this can only be found from consideration of the horizontal motion. Similarly the value of a quantity relating to the vertical motion (say, distance gone vertically) can only be found from consideration of the vertical motion. Because the two motions are independent, we must always try never to confuse them. The time of flight of the projectile is the only quantity common to both motions, being the same for each.

Our discussion on projectiles has been concerned with horizontal projection. The same principles apply however when the body concerned is projected at some angle to the horizontal—Fig. 3.7 and Fig. 3.8 for example.

Fig.3.7   A 'Bloodhound' missile ready for launching. (Crown Copyright: Ministry of Defence.)

Fig.3.8   The launching of a 'Tiger Cat' missile. (Crown Copyright: Ministry of Defence.)

[In the case of an inclined projection, the initial velocity of the projectile must be resolved into horizontal and vertical components before the separate consideration of horizontal and vertical motions can begin. In considering these motions separately, we bear in mind that the horizontal motion is determined by the constant horizontal component of velocity, while the vertical motion is determined by the continually changing vertical component of velocity. The reader may care to check these facts with reference to the strobe photograph of the inclined projection in Fig. 3.9.]

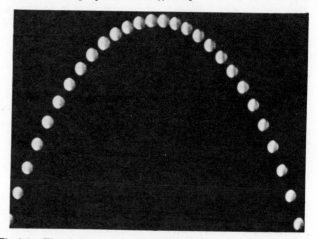

Fig.3.9   The laboratory investigation of an inclined trajectory.

Finally in this chapter, we consider the possibility of constraining a body to move in a circular path. We have already considered the path of a body projected horizontally near the surface of the Earth. We noted for such a body that its path could be explained by the fact that some net force was acting at right angles to its line of travel at any given point on its path. This net force was provided at a given point by a component of the weight of the body, selected at right angles to the direction of travel at that point. It is perhaps fairly obvious that this 'perpendicular' component of weight, which accounts for further bending of the path, assumes a smaller and smaller value as the body progresses along the path.

Let us consider the motion of a body which is continually acted upon by a net external force of constant size which is always directed at right angles to the direction of motion of the body. If the net force acts in this way, then it will never have a component along the direction of travel of the body. This being the case, no acceleration will result along the direction of travel and so the speed of the body will remain constant. The direction of motion however will be continually changing since the net force acts purely in a deflecting capacity. Having already specified that the size of the net force should remain constant, we may conclude that the body will have its direction of motion changed by equal amounts in equal intervals of time. That is, the body will describe a *circular* path. It follows that the net force responsible for this motion will be directed at all times towards the centre of the circle. The net force is therefore 'centre-seeking' or 'centripetal'.

This discussion is quite consistent with the experience of rotating a stone on a string at steady speed and in a horizontal circle above one's head. The presence of the constant tension in the string is quite evident and the necessity for it (if the circular motion is to be preserved) becomes apparent if and when the string is released—the stone then flies off at a tangent to the circle it was describing. Similarly in the 'throwing the hammer' event.

By considering a body which is actually describing a circular path at steady speed, we can substantiate the findings of this last discussion. This we now do.

When a body is moving in a circular path at steady speed, its velocity is continually changing, since the direction of motion is continually changing. Let us consider the velocities of a body at two points of its circular path A and B as shown in Fig. 3.10. When we represent the vector velocities by arrows, the arrows are of the same length but point in different directions. Since the velocity of the body is continually changing, the body is by definition accelerating, and the direction of the acceleration of the body at any point on the path will coincide with the direction of the *change* in velocity of the body in the immediate locality of the point. To determine the direction of the change in velocity of the body, let us consider the points A and B to be separated by only a very short length of arc so that the angle AOB in Fig. 3.10 is extremely small.

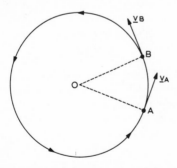

Fig.3.10 The velocity of a body at two points on a circular orbit.

Vectorially, the change in velocity Δv between points A and B is given by

$$\Delta v = v_B - v_A$$
$$= v_B + (-v_A)$$

This operation is performed in Fig. 3.11 in relation to the portion of the circular path concerned. Referring to Fig. 3.11,

we see that the change in velocity Δv can be interpreted as pointing towards the centre of the circle. This becomes more obvious as A and B are chosen closer and closer together thereby making v_B and v_A more and more parallel, so that Δv tends to act at right angles to each.

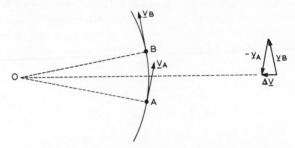

Fig.3.11 Finding the change in velocity between *A* and *B*.

Since the change in velocity of the body is directed towards the centre of the circle, the acceleration must be directed towards the centre, and so the net force acting on the body at any point (the cause of its acceleration) must be directed towards the centre. This is quite consistent with our previous discussion.

Problems
(Where necessary take g as 10 m s^{-2})

1   A dynamics trolley of mass 5 kg is pulled with a horizontal force of 17 N along a flat horizontal table. The forces of friction and air resistance amount to 2 N. Determine the acceleration of the trolley.

2   A packing case of mass 80 kg is dragged along flat level ground by a horizontal force of 250 N. The case is observed to accelerate by $\frac{1}{4}$ m s^{-2}. What is the value of the net resistive force acting on it?

3   The acceleration due to gravity at the surface of the moon is one sixth of that at the surface of the Earth. Estimate the weight of an 80 kg man on the moon and on the Earth.

4   A body of mass 2 kg moves down a frictionless plane. The plane is inclined at 30° to the horizontal. Find the component of the weight of the body acting parallel to the plane and hence determine the acceleration of the body down the plane.

5   A ramp 24 m long has one end raised 12 m above the other end. A 2 kg mass at the top is allowed to move down the plane starting from rest. Frictional forces amount to 5 N. Calculate the net force acting on the body and hence find its acceleration. How long will the body take to travel the length of the ramp?

6   A body is projected horizontally from the top of a cliff at a speed of 15 m s^{-1}. It is observed to reach the sea at a point 45 m from the foot of the cliff (assumed vertical). Determine the time of flight of the body, and calculate the

height of the cliff.

7 A rifle pointing horizontally at the centre of a target fires a bullet at a speed of 200 m s^{-1} which strikes the target 5 cm below the centre. How far is the rifle from the target?

8 A shell is fired with a muzzle velocity of 200 m s^{-1} at an angle of elevation of 30° to the horizontal. By consideration of the vertical and horizontal components of this velocity find (1) the time taken to reach the highest point of the path; (2) the height of this point above the ground; (3) the total time of flight; (4) the horizontal range of the shell.

9 What is the source of the centripetal force present in each of the following circular motions: (1) a satellite orbiting the Earth; (2) a stone describing a horizontal circle at the end of a string; (3) the electron orbiting the proton in a hydrogen atom.

10 Figure 3.12 illustrates an electron orbiting the proton in a hydrogen atom. Calculate the electron speed given that its period of revolution about the proton is $4 \cdot 5 \times 10^{-17}$ s.

By means of a vector diagram find the change in velocity of the electron between points A and B.

From the definition of acceleration $\left(a = \dfrac{\Delta v}{\Delta t} \right)$, calculate the size of the acceleration of the electron. (Use your last result.)

If the electronic mass is 9×10^{-31} kg, what is the size of the net force acting on the electron? Comment on its action.

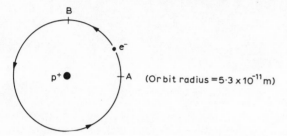

Fig.3.12 See Problem 10.

Chapter 4

Interaction

Fig.4.0   The collision of two vehicles is a process of interaction. Such a process may be analysed in terms of
the principle of conservation of linear momentum
which we shall consider in this chapter. (Picture by
courtesy of The Scottish Daily Record.)

In the last chapter our discussions were based on Newton's first two laws of motion. Having noted that the second law incorporates the first law and also relates the acceleration of a body to the net force acting on it, we may feel that this law is sufficient in itself for the solution of any given problem in mechanics. In actual fact however, very few real problems can be solved exactly by the application of this law in their analyses. For example if we consider the motion of the planets within the solar system, then in using the second law for analysis we are restricted to the consideration of only the interaction of the sun and a given planet. That is, we must neglect the forces of gravitational attraction between different planets so that a simple formula to describe the motion of any two bodies going round the sun cannot be derived. This is not to say that such a three body problem cannot be solved. Indeed such a problem can be solved by 'numerical methods'—an approach used widely when the powers of analysis fall short.

There are also problems in mechanics which can be solved neither by the use of the second law for analysis, nor by the approach known as 'numerical methods'. Such problems are regarded as complicated problems and would include two vehicles colliding, the motion of gas molecules, and the motion of stars in a cluster. These problems are complicated in so far as we cannot study their exact details, and in such a situation we find it necessary to employ a general principle. A most useful general principle for any complicated mechanics problem is 'the principle of conservation of momentum'—a principle which is found to be a direct consequence of

Newton's third law of motion.

Let us then investigate Newton's third law for both the completeness of the laws of motion, and also as a basis for the principle of conservation of momentum. After doing this and discussing the principle, we shall attempt to solve two complicated mechanics problems. We shall consider the problem of bodies colliding in this chapter, and the problem concerning the motion of gas molecules in a later chapter.

4.1 Newton's Third Law of Motion
In Newton's words:

To every action there is always opposed an equal reaction: or, the mutual actions of two bodies upon each other are always equal and directed to contrary parts.

This law is in fact telling us that an isolated object can neither exert a force nor experience a force. Forces are derived by the process of interaction of two bodies, and this interaction may involve actual contact of the bodies or may be of a non-contact nature (as would be the case with two bodies which hold similar electrical charges).

It is perhaps unfortunate that Newton chose the terms 'action' and 'reaction' to describe the forces resulting from interaction. These terms seem to suggest that when two bodies interact, one of the forces appears first (the action) and this causes the second (the reaction). We should in fact think of the forces as being produced simultaneously and not as cause and effect.

Suppose that a body A interacts with a body B—say by

colliding with it. Then a force is exerted on B by A, and simultaneously a force is exerted on A by B. Furthermore these forces are equal in size but opposite in direction. It is important to emphasise the point that the forces act on *different* bodies. (If they were to act on the same body then accelerated motion would be impossible since the net force on any given body would always be zero.)

If we denote the force exerted on A due to B by F_{AB}, and the force exerted on B due to A by F_{BA} then vectorially we may write (according to the third law)

$$\underline{F}_{AB} = -\underline{F}_{BA}$$

If A has mass m_A and B has mass m_B, then we may write

$$m_A \underline{a}_A = -m_B \underline{a}_B$$

(where $\underline{a}_A$ is the acceleration produced in A and $\underline{a}_B$ is the acceleration produced in B, both as a result of the interaction).

If the velocity of A is changed from $\underline{u}_A$ to $\underline{v}_A$ and the velocity of B is changed from $\underline{u}_B$ to $\underline{v}_B$—both as a result of the interaction—then we may write the last equation in the form

$$m_A \left(\frac{\underline{v}_A - \underline{u}_A}{\Delta t} \right) = -m_B \left(\frac{\underline{v}_B - \underline{u}_B}{\Delta t} \right)$$

where Δt is the duration of the interaction (this follows from the definition of acceleration).

$$\begin{aligned} \text{Hence} \quad & m_A(\underline{v}_A - \underline{u}_A) = -m_B(\underline{v}_B - \underline{u}_B) \\ \Leftrightarrow \quad & m_A \underline{v}_A - m_A \underline{u}_A = -m_B \underline{v}_B + m_B \underline{u}_B \\ \Leftrightarrow \quad & \boxed{m_A \underline{v}_A + m_B \underline{v}_B = m_A \underline{u}_A + m_B \underline{u}_B} \end{aligned}$$

Since $\underline{v}_A$ and $\underline{v}_B$ are the velocities of the bodies after the interaction, and $\underline{u}_A$ and $\underline{u}_B$ are the velocities before, then the left hand side of this last equation is a measure of the state of the bodies after interacting, while the right hand side is a measure of their states before. We note also that the sum of terms 'mass × velocity' is the same before and after the interaction—in this case a collision. The term 'mass × velocity' when calculated for a given body is called the *momentum* of the body. Momentum is a vector quantity.

We conclude from our discussion this far, that when two bodies interact—say by colliding—then the sum of their momenta is the same before and after the interaction. That is, the total momentum of the system remains constant.

This result is known as the principle of conservation of momentum. It finds application in all mechanics problems concerned with collision phenomena.

It is important to note that the only forces acting on the bodies considered in the discussion were those due to their mutual interaction. Neither of the bodies was acted upon by any *external* force. Had any net external force been acting

on the system (i.e. the two bodies considered) then the total momentum of the system would have been changed. The total momentum of a system cannot be altered by internal forces arising within the system. This holds true regardless of the nature of the bodies interacting, and of the nature of the interaction. The bodies might be lumps of clay or balls made of steel; the interaction might be a head on collision, an electrostatic repulsion, or a gravitational attraction. The only limitation which we put on the conservation of momentum principle is that it is applied in the context of a *closed* system. That is, to a system in which the bodies considered are not acted upon by forces exerted by bodies outside the system.

Having defined 'momentum', it is now possible to re-phrase Newton's second law of motion in the form:

The rate of change of a body's momentum is a measure of the net force acting on the body.

That is, if a change of momentum Δp is produced in a body by a net force $\underline{F}_{net}$ in a time Δt, then according to this formulation

$$\underline{F}_{net} = \frac{\Delta \underline{p}}{\Delta t}$$

In general the momentum of a body p is calculated as:

$$\underline{p} = m \times \underline{v} \quad \text{(where } \underline{v} \text{ is the velocity of the body)}$$

hence

$$\Delta \underline{p} = \Delta(m \times \underline{v})$$

and assuming the mass of the body to be constant

$$\Delta \underline{p} = m \times \Delta \underline{v}$$

(where $\Delta \underline{v}$ is the change in velocity of the body resulting from the application of the force $\underline{F}_{net}$).

$$\text{Hence} \quad \underline{F}_{net} = \frac{m \times \Delta \underline{v}}{\Delta t}$$

By definition however, $\frac{\Delta \underline{v}}{\Delta t} = \underline{a}$ (the acceleration of the body)

$$\Leftrightarrow \underline{F}_{net} = m \times \underline{a} \quad \text{as previously}$$

(The equation written in vector form tells us that the acceleration produced in the body by the application of $\underline{F}_{net}$ is in the same direction as that of $\underline{F}_{net}$.)

Let us consider the expression $\underline{F}_{net} = \frac{m \times \Delta \underline{v}}{\Delta t}$

We may re-write this as $\underline{F}_{net} \times \Delta t = m \times \Delta \underline{v}$

The quantity ($\underline{F}_{net} \times \Delta t$) is called the *impulse* of the force $\underline{F}_{net}$. We see that it is equal in size and direction to the change in momentum of the body concerned.

In considering the instances of large forces acting for short time intervals, it is usually the case that we do not know the exact values of these forces. For example if we consider the case of a golf club head coming into contact with a golf ball, then the force F_{net} exerted by the club head on the ball would most likely vary with time in such a way that it could not be determined. The size of the force might vary with time according to the theoretical curve shown in Fig. 4.1.

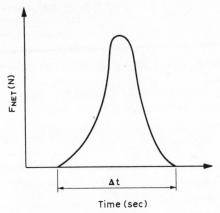

Fig.4.1 The possible nature of the net force exerted by a golf club head on a golf ball.

However indeterminate the force of contact might be, the 'size' of the interaction could be specified by calculating the impulse of the force as equal to the change in momentum of the ball. If after calculating this change we were further instructed as to the duration of contact of the blow, we could then calculate some value for F_{net}. Since it is misleading to think of F_{net} as a constant force in such a situation we would have to decide that the calculated value was representative of the average force exerted on the ball by the club head. In such a problem it is therefore more advisable to express our equation relating impulse and change in momentum in the form

$$(\bar{F}_{net} \times \Delta t) = (m \times \Delta v)$$

where $\bar{F}_{net}$ denotes an average value of the applied force. A steady force of size $\bar{F}_{net}$ applied to the body for a time Δt would provide it with the same change in momentum as the force F_{net} whose size is continually changing over the Δt seconds. This is represented by the equal areas under the graphs shown in Fig. 4.2.

(It is sometimes very convenient to calculate the change in momentum of a body as equal to the area under the graph of net force acting against time.)

So far in this chapter, we have been building up a comprehensive picture of the interaction of two bodies which we hope to refer to in the analyses of some collision phenomena. Before applying the findings as they stand at present, let us consider the role of 'energy' in the interaction of two bodies. Our discussions of energy in this chapter will be with reference to 'mechanical' energy. In the later chapters of the book we will be concerned with energy in the form of heat, in the form of electricity, and in its most potent form of all—within the nucleus of an atom.

By listing the various forms in which energy can exist, we may derive a certain intuitive idea as to what energy really is. For a first consideration, energy is present when work can be done (the term 'work' including such tasks as lifting an object, boiling water, propelling a nuclear submarine, driving an electric current, and so on). In trying to define energy further, we run into much the same difficulty as we encountered in trying to define the term 'force' in the last chapter.

4.2 Mechanical Energy

When a body moves under the application of a force, then work is being done, and energy is being transformed. The amount of energy transformed will depend on the size of the applied force and also on the distance through which it

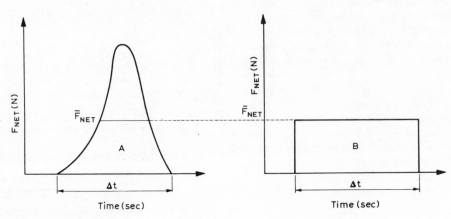

Fig.4.2 The area under each graph is the same.

moves the body. If a force whose size is F moves a body through a distance s in the direction of the force, then the work done is defined as W, where

$$W = F \times s$$

If F is measured in Newtons, and s in metres, then W is measured in Newton metres (Nm) or joules (J). Since the energy expended in this situation has given rise to useful work it is reasonable to equate the energy expended to the work done so that energy too is measured in joules.

If two men do the same amount of work but in different times, we say that one man is more *powerful* than the other. *Power* is defined as the *rate* at which work is done. That is, if a force of size F Newtons moves a body through a distance s metres along its own direction in a time of t seconds, we say that the power of the agency responsible is P, where

$$P = \frac{F \times s}{t} \quad *$$

Since power describes the rate of working it will be measured in joules per second and in most situations it is usual to refer to 1 J s^{-1} as 1 watt (W).

Note that P can be written as $P = F \times \dfrac{s}{t}$ so that we may write $P = F \times \bar{v}$*, where $\bar{v}$ is the average speed of the body moving under the influence of the applied force. When the body is travelling at a *steady* speed v (m s^{-1}) then P may be written as

$$P = F \times v$$

Suppose now that a body of mass m resting on a frictionless surface is subjected to a constant force of size F Newtons over a distance of s metres in the direction of this force. Since this force is unbalanced, it will produce a uniform acceleration $\underline{a}$ in the body such that

$$a = \frac{F}{m}$$

If the speed of the body after travelling the s metres is v, then we can say

$$v^2 = 2as$$

Hence

$$\frac{v^2}{2s} = \frac{F}{m}$$

$$\Leftrightarrow \frac{mv^2}{2s} = F$$

* In this expression P is a measure of the average power of the agency.

$$\Leftrightarrow F \times s = \tfrac{1}{2}mv^2$$

Now the quantity $(F \times s)$ is a measure of the work which has been done in moving the body through the s metres and consequently of the energy which has been expended in doing so. It is reasonable to expect that this amount of energy has been transferred to the body because to stop the body (now moving with speed v) would require the application of a force equal to F, but in opposition to the motion, acting over a distance of s metres.

> The energy of a body of mass m travelling at speed v is thus $\tfrac{1}{2} mv^2$. It is measured in joules when m is measured in kilograms and v in metres per second.

Such energy is called *kinetic energy* and is possessed by all moving bodies. Any stationary body has zero kinetic energy.

If we consider a car of mass 1000 kg travelling at a speed of 30 m s^{-1} then its kinetic energy (k.e.) is calculated according to the formula: k.e. $= \tfrac{1}{2} mv^2$.

Hence
$$\text{k.e.} = \tfrac{1}{2} \times 1000 \times 900$$
$$= 450\,000 \text{ joules}$$

In coming to rest, the car obviously gives up this amount of energy and we may therefore be tempted to think that the energy has been lost or destroyed. The 450 000 joules of kinetic energy has certainly been lost but it has *not* been destroyed. In fact it has been transformed into other forms of energy—into heat energy and possibly sound energy within the braking system of the car during the deceleration.

This simple example illustrates an instance of another conservation principle. The principle considered here is the principle of conservation of energy which states that

the total energy in any closed system is constant although this energy may be transformed from one form to another.

This principle is telling us that the total energy of the universe is constant. For our purposes however it is often convenient and quite permissible to consider the laboratory as a closed system.

Let us consider two examples of energy conservation before proceeding with our discussion of mechanical energy:

1. A petrol driven vehicle

Chemical energy → Heat energy + sound energy + kinetic energy

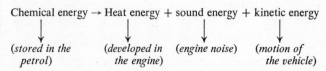

| (stored in the petrol) | (developed in the engine) | (engine noise) | (motion of the vehicle) |

2. A television set

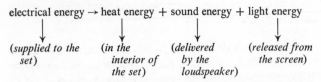

electrical energy → heat energy + sound energy + light energy

(supplied to the set)	*(in the interior of the set)*	*(delivered by the loudspeaker)*	*(released from the screen)*

If we measure the amount of energy being supplied to a system—a piece of apparatus in the laboratory say—then it is only by careful investigation and measurement of the obvious and inconspicuous ways in which energy can leave the apparatus and the laboratory that we may in fact verify that energy is rigorously conserved. The system considered here—the piece of apparatus in the laboratory—must be regarded as a subsystem of some larger system in which total energy remains constant: for example, the Universe.

In our consideration of kinetic energy we found that by doing mechanical work on a body energy of motion was imparted to it. It is also possible to do mechanical work on a body and thereby to store energy within it. We now discuss this possibility.

Consider firstly the case of a body being raised vertically near the surface of the Earth as illustrated in Fig. 4.3. In this case energy is being expended in raising the body against the Earth's gravitational pull. If the body has mass m kg, then the force of gravity acting on it is $(m \times g)$ Newtons and so to raise the body at steady speed we must apply an equal and opposite force. If we apply this force over a vertical distance of h metres, then the work done and hence the energy expended is $(m \times g \times h)$ joules. Since energy cannot be destroyed, this amount of energy is stored with the body as *potential energy*.

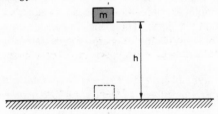

Fig.4.3   A body raised vertically near the surface of the earth.

> The energy of a body of mass m raised through a height h near the surface of the Earth is mgh. It is measured in joules when m is measured in kilograms, g in metres second^{-2} and h in metres.

When the body at the height h is released, its potential energy is gradually converted to kinetic energy so that if the body reaches a speed of $v(\text{m s}^{-1})$ just before contact with the ground we may write (since energy is conserved):

$$\tfrac{1}{2}mv^2 = mgh$$

or

$$v^2 = 2gh$$

which agrees with the third equation of uniformly accelerated motion in a straight line for the case of a body allowed to fall from a height h.

Secondly let us consider the case of a missile being launched from a catapult as illustrated in Fig. 4.4. To stretch the elastic of the catapult requires a steadily increasing force—from zero Newtons when the elastic is unstretched to say F Newtons when the elastic has been stretched over a horizontal distance of s metres. To calculate the work involved in the stretching of the elastic, it is thus reasonable to consider the average value of the stretching force employed. If we denote this by $\bar{F}$, then $\bar{F} = \dfrac{F}{2}$, and so the work done in stretching the elastic is given by W where

$$W = \frac{Fs}{2}$$

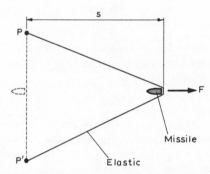

Fig.4.4   The launching of a missile from a catapult.

This work is a measure of the energy expended in the actual stretching of the elastic and since energy cannot be destroyed, this energy must be stored as *potential energy* within the elastic.

If a missile of mass m is now placed at the bend in the elastic, and the elastic is then released, complete energy transfer will take place between the elastic and the missile, provided that no energy is transformed into sound as a result of say the elastic 'twanging'. That is, the potential energy stored in the elastic will appear as kinetic energy of the missile. Further, if the missile has reached a speed v on crossing the line PP', then we may say

$$\tfrac{1}{2}mv^2 = \frac{Fs}{2}$$

It is often convenient to solve problems in mechanics by consideration of the interconversions of potential and kinetic energy—particularly in the case of bodies moving under the influence of gravity.

Our main interest in energy in this chapter is that concerning kinetic energy however. We have discussed both potential energy and kinetic energy for the completeness of mechanical energy, but we find the consideration of kinetic energy to be particularly useful as regards certain collision processes.

We conclude this chapter with analyses of some collision processes, and towards that end we first classify the various processes.

Basically we have to decide whether a given collision occurs in one dimension or in two dimensions—that is, along a straight line or in a plane. Having decided upon the number of dimensions involved for a given process, it is then usual to decide whether or not kinetic energy is conserved. If kinetic energy is conserved, the collision is referred to as 'elastic', while if kinetic energy is not conserved, the collision is referred to as 'inelastic'.

In the collision processes we are about to discuss, we shall have no information regarding the forces of interaction. We know however that the principle of conservation of momentum must apply in any given collision, and further, that if the collision is 'elastic', then the principle of conservation of kinetic energy must apply.* Although lacking the details of a given collision process, we hope to be able to predict the outcome of the process by the application of these principles.

4.3 Collisions in One Dimension

We consider firstly the case of a one-dimensional collision which is almost perfectly elastic.

Imagine two smooth ivory spheres of masses m_1 and m_2 moving along the same straight line with velocities $\underline{u}_1$ and $\underline{u}_2$ respectively. Suppose that the spheres collide and that after colliding their velocities are $\underline{v}_1$ and $\underline{v}_2$ respectively.

Since momentum is conserved during the collision, we may write

$$m_1\underline{u}_1 + m_2\underline{u}_2 = m_1\underline{v}_1 + m_2\underline{v}_2$$

Since kinetic energy is also conserved during the collision we may write

$$\tfrac{1}{2}m_1u_1{}^2 + \tfrac{1}{2}m_2u_2{}^2 = \tfrac{1}{2}m_1v_1{}^2 + \tfrac{1}{2}m_2v_2{}^2$$

(the vector notation has been dropped in this last equation because 'energy' is a scalar quantity, kinetic energy being derived as the scalar product of the vector velocity with itself.)

Since the motion is along the same straight line, we can omit the vector notation from the first equation, but in doing so we must pay attention to the sense of each body's motion. When a body travels in the sense of the positive X direction, it is usual to denote its velocity by a positive number, while if it travels in the opposite sense, it is usual to denote its velocity by a negative number.

If we know the initial velocity of each body, then the two equations provide us with a simultaneous solution of the final

* This principle is experimentally sound and was first proposed by Christiaan Huygens (1629–1695) in a slightly modified form.

velocities.

Let us consider a typical problem concerned with an elastic collision in one dimension:

Problem 1 Two like magnetic pucks, A (of mass 1 kg) and B (of mass 0·5 kg), travelling on a frictionless surface collide 'head on' as shown in Fig. 4.5. The successive positions of each puck before the collision are shown at intervals of $\frac{1}{10}$th second. Find the velocities of the pucks after colliding, assuming their collision to be perfectly elastic.

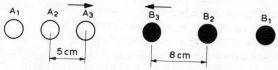

Fig.4.5   See Problem 1 (text).

Let the velocities of A and B be $\underline{v}_A$ and $\underline{v}_B$ respectively after the collision.

Velocity of A before colliding = 5 cm/0·1 s = 50 cm s⁻¹
                                                            = 0·5 m s⁻¹
Velocity of B before colliding = −8 cm/0·1 s = −80 cm s⁻¹
                                                            = −0·8 m s⁻¹

Since momentum is conserved during the collision, total momentum before collision = total momentum after collision.

$$\Leftrightarrow m\underline{u}_A + m_B\underline{u}_B = m_A\underline{v}_A + m_B\underline{v}_B$$

$$\Leftrightarrow (1 \times 0\cdot5) + (0\cdot5 \times (-0\cdot8)) = (1 \times v_A) + (0\cdot5 \times v_B)$$

$$\Leftrightarrow v_A + (0\cdot5 \times v_B) = 0\cdot5 - 0\cdot4$$

$$\Leftrightarrow \boxed{2v_A + v_B = 0\cdot2} \quad\ldots\ldots\ldots\ldots\ldots\ldots\ldots (1)$$

Since the collision is elastic, kinetic energy is conserved. That is, total kinetic energy before = total kinetic energy after

$$\Leftrightarrow \tfrac{1}{2}m_A u_A{}^2 + \tfrac{1}{2}m_B u_B{}^2 = \tfrac{1}{2}m_A v_A{}^2 + \tfrac{1}{2}m_B v_B{}^2$$

$$\Leftrightarrow (\tfrac{1}{2} \times 1 \times (0\cdot5)^2) + (\tfrac{1}{2} \times 0\cdot5 \times (-0\cdot8)^2)$$
$$= (\tfrac{1}{2} \times 1 \times v_A{}^2) + (\tfrac{1}{2} \times 0\cdot5 \times v_B{}^2)$$

$$\Leftrightarrow v_A{}^2 + (0\cdot5 \times v_B{}^2) = 0\cdot25 + 0\cdot32$$

$$\Leftrightarrow \boxed{2v_A{}^2 + v_B{}^2 = 1.14} \quad\ldots\ldots\ldots\ldots\ldots\ldots (2)$$

Solving the equations (1) and (2) simultaneously we find the solution sets to be

$$v_A = \{0\cdot5, -0\cdot37\}$$

and

$$v_B = \{-0\cdot8, 0\cdot94\}$$

If we choose the solutions $v_A = 0\cdot5$ and $v_B = -0\cdot8$, then we are implying that the bodies pass through each other each having no effect on the other. This picture is rather meaningless and is not at all consistent with our idea of an 'elastic' collision.

We therefore choose the solutions $v_A = -0.37$ and $v_B = 0.94$ and interpret these as meaning that puck A rebounds with a speed of 0.37 m s^{-1} and puck B rebounds with a speed of 0.94 m s^{-1}.

Secondly, we consider the case of a one dimensional collision which is *perfectly inelastic*. That is, a collision in which the two bodies colliding stick together after the collision. For example, when two beads of mercury collide, they coalesce, and move on as one bead. In such a collision, kinetic energy is not found to be conserved, and for a prediction of the outcome of the collision, we must rely on the application of the principle of conservation of momentum. Let us solve a problem concerned with such a collision process.

Problem 2 A bead of mercury A, of mass 0.04 kg, travelling at a speed of 0.05 m s^{-1} collides with a stationary bead B of mass 0.06 kg, and the two move on as one. What is their common speed immediately after colliding?

Since momentum is conserved during the collision, total momentum before collision = total momentum after collision.

$$\Leftrightarrow m_A \underline{u}_A + m_B \underline{u}_B = m_A \underline{v}_A + m_B \underline{v}_B$$

Since the beads coalesce, $\underline{v}_A = \underline{v}_B = \underline{v}$ say. Omitting the vector notation and denoting all velocities by positive numbers (since all motion here is in one sense of the particular line of travel) we have

$$m_A u_A + m_B u_B = (m_A + m_B)v$$

$$\Leftrightarrow v = \frac{m_A u_A + m_B u_B}{(m_A + m_B)}$$

$$= \frac{(0.04 \times 0.05) + (0.06 \times 0)}{0.04 + 0.06}$$

$$= \frac{0.0020}{0.10}$$

$$= 0.02$$

The common speed of the beads immediately after the collision is thus 0.02 m s^{-1} along the original direction and sense of travel of A.

4.4 Collisions in Two Dimensions

In the case of two-dimensional collisions, we find that for particularly complicated processes a graphical solution (made possible by the vectorial nature of momentum) is often desirable. This is not to say that an analytical solution is impossible. Rather, an analytical solution may be such as to demand considerable time, patience, and concentration, while an equally correct, and sufficiently accurate, graphical solution might be achieved more quickly and more easily.

The fact that momentum is conserved in two dimensions may be verified in the laboratory by setting up apparatus such as that in Fig. 4.6 or Fig. 4.7. In Fig. 4.6, a frictionless horizontal plane is created by sprinkling tiny polystyrene beads on a clean glass tray. The collision of two like magnetic pucks moving on this surface may then be recorded and analysed by strobe photography. In Fig. 4.7 an air table (a two dimensional extension of the linear air track) provides a frictionless surface on which a collision between two like magnetic pucks may be effected. Such a collision is recorded again by strobe photography—the camera being placed vertically above the table, as in Fig. 4.6.

Fig.4.6   Apparatus used in investigating a collision in two dimensions. Can you label the items *C, S, B, T,* and *P*? (By kind permission of Philip Harris Ltd.)

Fig.4.7   The air table. (By kind permission of M.L.I. Ltd.)

In this our last discussion of the chapter, we shall solve a problem concerning a collision in two dimensions. We shall solve the problem both analytically and graphically, discussing the theory for solution by each method at the outset of each.

Problem 3 A billiard ball A of mass m travelling at a speed of 3 m s^{-1} strikes an identical ball B (at rest) a glancing blow. After the collision, A is moving in a direction which makes an angle of $60°$ with its original direction, and at a speed of 1.5 m s^{-1}. What is the speed and direction of B following the collision?

The situation is represented in Fig. 4.8.

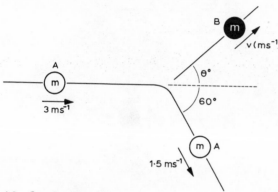

Fig.4.8   See Problem 3 (text).

Since we are not told that the collision is elastic, we must rely on the application of the principle of conservation of momentum for solution. We now consider the two possible solutions.

1. The Analytical Solution

Let the speed of B be v (m s^{-1}) after the collision, and let its direction of travel make an angle θ with the original line of travel of A.

Denoting initial and final velocities by $\underline{u}$ and $\underline{v}$ respectively then since momentum is conserved during the collision we may write

$$m_A\underline{u}_A + m_B\underline{u}_B = m_A\underline{v}_A + m_B\underline{v}_B \quad \text{in the usual notation}$$

In this problem B is initially at rest so that $\underline{u}_B = 0$ and

$$m_A\underline{u}_A = m_A\underline{v}_A + m_B\underline{v}_B$$

If we now resolve each velocity into two perpendicular components along X and Y axes chosen in relation to the collision as illustrated in Fig. 4.9, then we may write

$$m_A(\underline{u}_{AX} + \underline{u}_{AY}) = m_A(\underline{v}_{AX} + \underline{v}_{AY}) + m_B(\underline{v}_{BX} + \underline{v}_{BY})$$

(where $\underline{v}_{AX}$ denotes the X-component of A's velocity after the collision etc.).

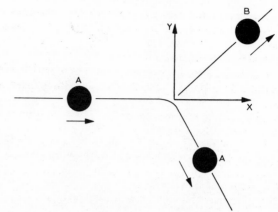

Fig.4.9   The analytical solution of Problem 3 (text).

Equating vector quantities in the X direction we may write

$$m_A\underline{u}_{AX} = m_A\underline{v}_{AX} + m_B\underline{v}_{BX}$$

and equating vector quantities in the Y direction

$$m_A\underline{u}_{AY} = m_A\underline{v}_{AY} + m_B\underline{v}_{BY}$$

We see therefore that in a two dimensional collision process, momentum is conserved along each of two directions at right angles.

In considering quantities related to these directions we may drop the vector notation and revert to the use of numbers, provided that when two quantities are found to be in opposite senses, we describe one by a positive number and the other by a negative number. The positive sense of each axis (already defined) is usually taken as the positive sense of motion, and in our discussion we shall adopt this convention.

Now

$$m_A u_{AX} = m_A v_{AX} + m_B v_{BX}$$

and

$$m_A u_{AY} = m_A v_{AY} + m_B v_{BY}$$

Here $m_A = m_B = m$, and $u_{AY} = 0$ since ball A is travelling in the X direction originally, hence

$$m u_{AX} = m v_{AX} + m v_{BX}$$

and

$$0 = m v_{AY} + m v_{BY}$$

$\Leftrightarrow$

$$u_{AX} = v_{AX} + v_{BX}$$

and

$$0 = v_{AY} + v_{BY}$$

$\Leftrightarrow$

$$3 = 1.5 \cos 60 + v \cos \theta$$

and

$$0 = -1.5 \sin 60 + v \sin \theta$$

$\Leftrightarrow$

$$v \cos \theta = 3 - 1.5 \cos 60$$

and

$$v \sin \theta = 1.5 \sin 60$$

$\Leftrightarrow$

$$v \sin \theta = 1.299$$

and

$$v \cos \theta = 2.250$$

$$\Leftrightarrow \qquad \tan \theta = \frac{1\cdot299}{2\cdot250}$$

$$= 0\cdot577$$

$$\Leftrightarrow \qquad \theta = 30°$$

Since $\qquad v \cos \theta = 2\cdot25,$

$$v = \frac{2\cdot25}{\cos 30°} = 2\cdot6 \text{ m s}^{-1}$$

Ball B thus moves off at $2\cdot6$ m s^{-1} and in a line making an angle of $30°$ with the original line of travel of ball A.

2. The Graphical Solution

Early in the analytical solution we wrote the expression

$$m_A \underline{u}_A = m_A \underline{v}_A + m_B \underline{v}_B$$

so that $\qquad m_B \underline{v}_B = m_A \underline{u}_A - m_A \underline{v}_A$

and $\qquad \underline{v}_B = \dfrac{m_A \underline{u}_A - m_A \underline{v}_A}{m_B}$

Since $\qquad m_A = m_B = m.$

then $\qquad \underline{v}_B = \underline{u}_A - \underline{v}_A$

$\Leftrightarrow \qquad \underline{v}_B = \underline{u}_A + (-\underline{v}_A)$

This last equation can easily be solved by a graphical approach which is as follows:

Choose a scale of 1 cm to 1 m s^{-1}, then the solution for $\underline{v}_B$ is contained in the vector diagram of Fig. 4.10.

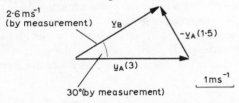

Fig.4.10 The graphical solution of Problem 3 (text).

By measurement we find that ball B is moving at $2\cdot6$ m s^{-1} in a direction making an angle of $30°$ with the original direction of travel of ball A (as previously).

Problems

(Where necessary take g as 10 m s^{-2})

1 A car of mass 1200 kg tows a trailer of mass 500 kg along a level road. The car engine provides a driving force of 1000 N, and the car experiences a resistance of 100 N. The trailer runs freely with negligible resistance. Find the acceleration of the car and trailer, and also the force exerted on the trailer by the car.

2 A ball of mass 0·15 kg travelling horizontally at 25 m s^{-1} strikes a wall at right angles and rebounds at a speed of 15 m s^{-1}. What impulse has been exerted on the ball?

3 A golf ball is struck by a golf club and moves off at a speed of 45 m s^{-1}. If the mass of the ball is 25 gm, and contact with the club head lasts for 0·008 s, find the impulse imparted to the ball and the average force exerted by the club on the ball.

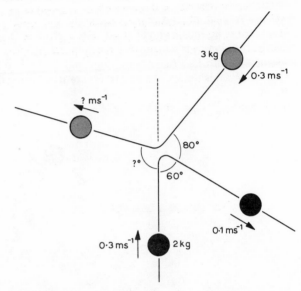

Fig.4.11 See Problem 11.

4 A boy of mass 40 kg climbs a vertical rope of length 5 m in a time of 8 s. What is the power of the boy during the climb, assuming that he climbs at a constant speed?

5 A mass of 1 kg is suspended from a beam by a light cord of length 1 metre. The mass is pulled aside until the cord makes an angle of 30° with the vertical. How much potential energy is stored in the mass? If the mass is released, what will be its speed as it passes through the lowest point of its swing?

6 A railway truck of mass 1000 kg travelling at 4 m s^{-1} strikes a stationary truck of mass 1500 kg. If the trucks couple and move off together, what will be their common speed?

7 A trolley of mass 200 kg is moving at 2 m s^{-1}. A man of mass 100 kg runs straight towards it, meeting it head on, at a speed of 2 m s^{-1}. If the man jumps on the trolley on meeting it, what will be the speed and sense of the motion immediately afterwards?

8 A bullet of mass 5 gm travelling horizontally at a speed of 200 m s^{-1} strikes a block of wood and embeds itself therein. The block of wood has mass 0·5 kg, and is suspended from a ceiling by a light cord of length 1 metre. Find the speed of the block and bullet following the collision and hence estimate the vertical height through which the block will be displaced.

9 A car of mass 1000 kg travelling North at 20 m s^{-1} collides

at a crossroads with a truck of mass 4000 kg travelling East at 8 m s^{-1}. If the vechicles interlock on colliding, what will be the size and direction of the velocity of the wreckage just after the collision?

10 A proton travelling at a speed of 5×10^5 m s^{-1} strikes a stationary α particle, and moves off in a direction at 45° to its original direction at a speed of 2×10^5 m s^{-1}. What is the speed and direction of the α particle following the collision? (The proton mass is $\frac{1}{4}$ of the mass of the α particle.)

11 A metal puck of mass 2 kg travelling at a speed of 0·3 m s^{-1} collides with a puck of mass 3 kg travelling at a speed of 0·3 m s^{-1}. After the collision, the first puck has a speed of 0·1 m s^{-1}. The directions of the motions are shown in Fig. 4.11. What is the speed and direction of the second puck just after the collision?

Chapter 5

Temperature, Heat, and Energy

Fig.5.0 This photograph shows two calorimeters used by Joule in his investigations of the equivalence between mechanical energy and heat. (Kelvin Museum, University of Glasgow.)

In Chapter 4 we met the idea of energy, and observed that its consideration could be particularly useful in the analyses of certain collision processes. We decided that although the idea of energy was somewhat abstract, it had a certain unifying capacity for linking all branches of physics in so far as it could be changed from one form into another without ever being destroyed. Although we were mainly concerned with energy in the form of bulk movement in the last chapter, we suggested that energy could be identified within the atomic nucleus, in the form of electricity, and in the form of heat. We now turn to consider the idea that energy is the content of heat or alternatively, that heat is a form of energy.

5.1 The Caloric Theory

Until the beginning of the nineteenth century heat was regarded as a material substance called *caloric* which was fluid-like, and present in every body. When a body was subjected to heating by say a flame, it was believed that the caloric content of the body was increased. When a 'hot' body was placed in contact with a 'cold' body, the 'hot' body, rich in caloric, lost some caloric to the 'cold' body until some equilibrium was reached between the bodies. That is, until the two bodies reached what we would call the same 'temperature'. The first person to realise that heat was not in fact a material substance was Benjamin Thompson (1753–1814), an American who became Count Rumford of Bavaria (Fig. 5.1). He came to this realisation while supervising cannon boring for the Bavarian government. In the process of boring, the bore of the cannon was supplied with water to prevent overheating of the metal, and this water had to be replenished continually as it boiled away during the boring process. In terms of caloric theory, the water was being boiled because it was receiving caloric continuously—the caloric being derived from the boring process because the process subdivided the metal and hence reduced its capacity for retaining caloric. Benjamin Thompson noticed however that the water continued to boil *even when the boring tool became so blunt that it was no longer cutting or subdividing the metal.* He concluded that heat was being generated purely by motion, and thus gave rise to the idea that mechanical work employed in the boring process was alone responsible for the production of heat.

Fig.5.1 (By kind permission of The Science Museum, London. Neg. no. 4148.)

Thompson seemed to view the process as a disappearance of mechanical energy and a creation of heat, instead of viewing it more correctly as a transformation of energy from one form into another, so that total energy was conserved. It is worth noting however that the whole idea of energy conservation was not properly instituted until the late nineteenth century, so that Thompson's interpretation was perhaps quite excusable in the light of current thought at the time.

Thompson's conclusion on the equivalence between heat and mechanical work was verified experimentally by James Prescott Joule in the mid-nineteenth century. Joule succeeded in showing that when a given quantity of mechanical energy was converted to heat in different ways, the same amount of heat was generated in each case, thus establishing the equiva-

lence of heat and mechanical work as two forms of energy. Joule's conclusion was extended to a satisfactory end by Hermann von Helmholtz who suggested the idea that not only heat and mechanical energy were equivalent, but in fact *all* forms of energy were equivalent. The disappearance of a certain amount of energy in one form was always accompanied by the appearance of an equal amount in some other form (or forms).

5.2 Heat as Unseen Energy

Accepting the discussion so far, it may seem strange that heat being a form of energy is not directly 'visible' as such. For example, if we were to look at a block of cold copper beside a block of warm copper of the same dimensions, we would have no visual information as to which was the warmer. With no visable clues, we may begin to wonder as to the actual form in which the excess energy present in the warmer block existed. We can go some way towards such an understanding of the nature of heat energy by considering the following model.

Imagine two balls of equal mass m, moving inside a stationary box of mass M_b. If the balls are moving in opposite senses along the same direction each at speed v, then the total momentum of the system is zero, and this would be the conclusion of an outside observer who cannot see into the box—assuming it to be opaque. The kinetic energy of the system, although not zero, would appear to be so to the observer however. If the box is now moved relative to the observer at speed V, with the balls inside still moving as before, then the apparent kinetic energy of the system $\frac{1}{2}MV^2$ is but part of the total kinetic energy: $(M = M_b + 2m)$. The amount of energy $\frac{1}{2}MV^2$ takes no account of the energy of *internal motions*.

This simple illustration shows that energy can be confined to forms which make no contribution to the kinetic energy of bulk movement.

If a bullet is fired into a lump of plasticene, then after the collision the kinetic energy of bulk motion is considerably less than the original kinetic energy of the bullet. Some of the original kinetic energy has disappeared from view and has been used to set the plasticene molecules into more agitated motion than before. Such motion is of course invisible to an external observer, but the observer may be able to detect a heating of the plasticene following the collision.

It is thus possible to think of heat energy as energy contained in internal motions of a given body. This suggestion although unproven as such, is sufficiently accurate for our present purposes.

5.3 The Meaning of Temperature

Several times in this chapter we have employed the terms 'hot' and 'cold'. These terms are the names given to certain body sensations which cannot be described in other words.

The scientific name for hotness is temperature, which is defined as the *degree* of hotness of a body, or the *degree* to which the heating of a body has taken place. In describing the degree to which heating has taken place, temperature does *not* describe the amount of heat contained in a body. By way of example let us consider a swimming pool which is full of warm water, and a thimble which is full of boiling water. We would say that although the water in the thimble was at a higher temperature, the water in the pool contained more heat.

In molecular terms, the temperature of a body is interpreted as a representative average of the kinetic energies of the molecules of the body. As such, it gives no information as to the total energy contained in the body, but information as to the general degree of molecular excitation.

Strictly we cannot measure temperature in the true sense of the word, but we can assess differences of temperature. When the temperature of a body is changed, we note that the sizes of most of its physical properties change accordingly. The variation of any one of these properties can thus be chosen to represent the change in temperature which has been responsible. An instrument which is used to 'measure' temperature is called a thermometer, and we now discuss the common mercury-in-glass thermometer before employing it as a means of temperature estimation in an experimental investigation later in the chapter. We shall discuss two other types of thermometer at the end of this chapter.

In the mercury-in-glass thermometer which is illustrated in Fig. 5.2, the volume of the mercury is chosen as the fundamental temperature dependent property. This property is chosen because its size remains constant when temperature is constant, and also because it is single-valued in so far as it never has the same value at two or more temperatures which are different. Although we might not expect the volume of a liquid to have the same value at different temperatures, an examination of Fig. 5.3 will convince us that we cannot exclude the possibility. Mercury is also chosen as a suitable thermometric liquid because it is easily seen, and does not wet the sides of the glass tube containing it, so that no liquid is left adhering to the tube walls when the temperature is falling.

The Celsius or Centigrade scale of temperature has been established for mercury-in-glass thermometers by the selection of *two fixed points*—two temperatures which are accepted as fixed and easily reproducible. These temperatures are recorded as the mercury volume at the temperature of melting ice (the 'ice' point), and the mercury volume at the temperature of steam rising from pure boiling water (the 'steam' point). The interval between these points is then divided into one hundred equal intervals or degrees, and the ice point is thereafter referred to as zero degrees Centigrade (written 0 °C) while the steam point is referred to as one hundred degrees Centigrade (written 100 °C). The Centigrade scale

of temperature has been marked on the thermometer shown in Fig. 5.4.

By employing the mercury-in-glass thermometer as an instrument which can indicate the degree to which the heating of a body has taken place, we can now conduct an experimental investigation in an attempt to show for ourselves that heat is indeed a form of energy.

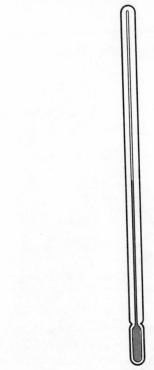

Fig.5.2　The mercury in glass thermometer (uncalibrated).

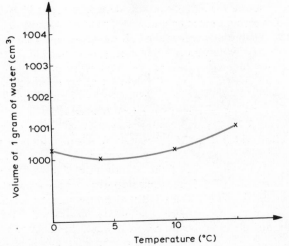

Fig.5.3　The volume of water is not 'single-valued' at low temperatures.

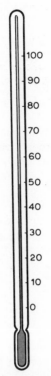

Fig.5.4 The mercury in glass thermometer calibrated according to the Centigrade scale of temperature.

5.4 Experiment

In this investigation we wish to show that heat can be accepted as a definite form of energy. If we can show that the same quantity of heat is developed in a body on separate occasions when equal quantities of energy in different forms are supplied to it, then we will have accomplished our goal. As an indication of the amount of heat developed in the body, we shall measure the temperature rise produced in the body by each amount of energy in turn. If the same temperature rise is produced by each amount of energy, then we shall say that the same amount of heat has been developed in the body by each of the two forms of energy. Consequently the heat developed is equivalent to each of two different forms of energy, and so must itself be a form of energy.

The body under investigation is a small copper drum which is illustrated in Fig. 5.5. The well, which runs some depth into the drum, can accommodate a mercury-in-glass thermometer. In the first part of the investigation, the drum is set up as shown in Fig. 5.6. Mechanical work is done against the force of friction between the drum and the cord by rotating the drum at a steady speed such that the elastic band remains slack and the 10 kg mass is maintained at a fixed height above the floor. The net force exerted on the drum by the cord is that due to the loading. This is equal to 100 N. Hence the value of the applied force at the drum—required to rotate it

at steady speed—must also have the value of 100 N. (The value of the applied force at the handle is considerably less than 100 N however.)

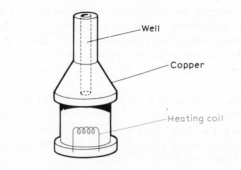

Fig.5.5 The small copper drum.

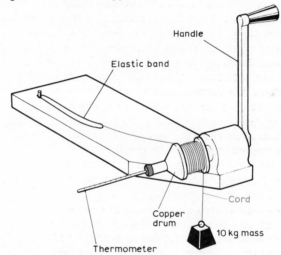

Fig.5.6 Transforming mechanical energy.

The circumference of the drum is 0·1 m and so when the handle is turned say 100 times, the work done against friction is given as $100 \times (0·1 \times 100)$ Nm. The work done or the mechanical energy supplied is thus 1000 joules.

In carrying out this part of the investigation we note the initial temperature of the drum, turn the handle 100 times, and note the highest temperature reached by the drum. The rise in temperature as a result of 1000 J of mechanical energy supplied can thus be found. This is usually found to be about 7·4 °C.

In the second part of the investigation, use is made of the small heating coil which is built into the drum. This heater is known to draw an electric current of 0·71 amp when the heater is connected to a supply of 12 volts. The heater can be used to supply energy to the drum from an electrical circuit, and in particular, 1000 J of energy.

Electrical energy E (measured in joules) is calculated from the formula

$$E = V \times I \times t$$

where V represents voltage (in volts), I represents current (in amperes), and t represents time (in seconds).

If we wish to transfer 1000 J of energy, we must know the time for which the current of 0·71 amp should be drawn from the 12 volt supply. Substituting into the last formula, we find that the time required (t) is given as

$$t = \frac{1000}{12 \times 0·71}$$
$$= 117\,s$$

In carrying out this part of the investigation, we note the initial temperature of the drum, switch on the 12 volt supply for 117 seconds, and note the highest temperature reached by the drum after switching off. The rise in temperature as a result of 1000 J of energy transferred can thus be found. This usually turns out to be about 7·4 °C!

(Why should the cord be wrapped round the arm in this part of the experiment as it was in the first part?)

Since the same body shows the same temperature rise in each part of the investigation, we may conclude that the same amount of heat has been developed by each of 1000 J of mechanical energy, and 1000 J of electrical energy in turn. This amount of heat is thus equivalent to 1000 J of mechanical energy, and also to 1000 J of electrical energy. In fact it is equivalent to 1000 J of energy in any form. Heat therefore seems to be a form of energy.

5.5 Electrical Thermometers

We conclude this chapter by considering two thermometers which are quite different from the common mercury-in-glass thermometer. The main reason for doing this is that the temperature range of the mercury in glass thermometer is limited. Mercury freezes at a temperature of −39 °C and boils at a temperature of 357 °C and so the recording of temperatures beyond these limits would be quite impossible without the use of some other type of thermometer.

Earlier in the chapter we noted that the 'measurement' of temperature involved the recording of some temperature-dependent property of a material. Some materials have electrical properties which are measurably temperature-dependent, and so these materials can be employed in the recording of temperature. Let us consider two thermometers which function in terms of their electrical properties.

1. The Resistance Thermometer

It is found that the electrical resistance of a pure metal (that is, its opposition to current flow) increases as its temperature increases. Since this property can be measured very accurately, we have a means of recording temperature very precisely. When platinum is used as the pure metal, a thermometer can

be constructed which is capable of recording temperatures between the limits of −200 °C and 1100 °C. The actual process of recording temperature in terms of resistance requires the use of an electrical bridge circuit for the measurement of that resistance. (The bridge circuit actually used—known as Callendar and Griffiths' Bridge—is a modified form of Wheatstone's Bridge which we shall meet later in our study of electricity.)

An illustration of the platinum resistance thermometer is shown in Fig. 5.7. The copper leads shown are suitable for the recording of temperatures up to about 700 °C. When higher temperatures have to be recorded, these leads are usually replaced by platinum leads. Although this thermometer is extremely accurate—sufficiently so to be taken as a secondary standard for scientific purposes—it is unsatisfactory in so far as it cannot record rapidly-changing temperatures since a considerable time delay is introduced both by the time needed for it to reach the temperature of its surroundings and by the time required for the actual recording procedure.

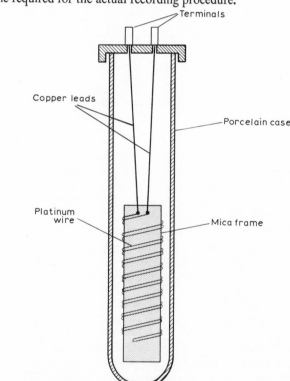

Fig.5.7 The platinum resistance thermometer.

2. The Thermocouple

When two pieces of different metals (usually in the form of wires) are joined at both ends and the junctions maintained at different temperatures, an electric current flows round the circuit formed by the metals. Such a device is known as a thermocouple and a simplified form is shown in Fig. 5.8.

The size and direction of the electric current which flows depends on the nature of the metals employed. More important however, the size of the current depends on the temperature difference between the junctions. It is usual to maintain one junction at 0 °C by placing it in a supply of melting ice, and to record the temperature of the other junction in terms of the reading on a sensitive microammeter which is included in the circuit as in Fig. 5.9.

Thermocouples may be used over the temperature range −200 °C to 1700 °C (depending on the metals used), although they are most frequently used at the upper end of this range in the measurement of oven temperatures and furnace temperatures.

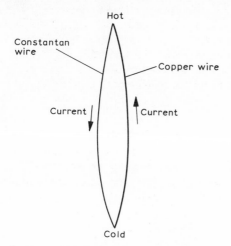

Fig.5.8   A copper-constantan thermocouple.

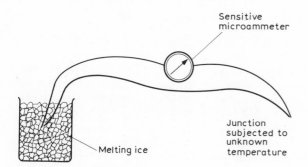

Fig.5.9   Using the thermocouple.

Although current is often taken as a measure of the temperature difference between the junctions, it is much more satisfactory to record the electrical potential difference which is developed between the junctions. The reason for this is that the current which is generated depends on the total resistance of the circuit in addition to the temperature difference between the junctions. Clearly the resistance of the circuit may introduce some errors of observation since it itself is a function of temperature and can thus change when temperature changes. The potential difference between the junctions can be measured accurately by means of a potentiometer—an instrument which we shall meet later in our study of electricity.

Problems

(Where necessary take g as 10 m s^{-2})

1   A 10 gm bullet travelling horizontally at 200 m s^{-1} strikes a sand bag of mass 0·99 kg suspended by a long rope from the branch of a tree. Calculate the original kinetic energy of the bullet, the kinetic energy of the bag and bullet immediately after the collision, and hence the fraction of the original kinetic energy of the bullet which you might expect to appear as heat energy.

2   A piece of lead is pounded fifty times by a stone of mass 1 kg which is raised 1 m above the lead on each occasion and then released. Assuming that all of the original potential energy of the stone is converted to heat energy within the lead each time, calculate the possible rise in temperature of the lead given that its mass is 2 kg and that 130 J of energy are required to raise the temperature of 1 kg of lead by 1 °C. Give two reasons why the actual rise in temperature would be less than this.

3   With what speed would a 0·1 kg cube of ice at 0 °C have to be thrown against a wall so that it would melt completely? (Assume that the cube doesn't shatter on contact, that all of its kinetic energy is converted to heat energy on contact, and that 336 000 J of energy are required to melt 1 kg of ice at 0 °C.)

4   A mountaineer of mass 80 kg can climb 400 m (measured vertically) each hour. How much energy does he store as potential energy in a four hour climb? Assuming that only 25 % of his total energy intake is available to him as useful mechanical energy (the remainder being dissipated as waste heat), calculate the calorific value of the food which he would have to consume before the climb given that 1 calorie is equivalent to 4·2 J.

5   A thermocouple was calibrated by having one junction in melting ice and the other junction subjected to different known temperatures in turn. The potential difference developed between the junctions was noted in each instance, and the results are shown thus:

temperature of hot junction (°C)	0	100	240	300	380
potential difference between junctions (millivolts)	0	0·25	0·60	0·75	0·95

Express these results in the form of a graph, and from your graph predict the temperature of a material which gave rise to a potential difference of 1·125 millivolts.

Chapter 6

The Measurement of Heat

Fig.6.0 Energy in the CO_2 laser beam is being used to raise the temperature of part of the metal plate to its melting point, and then to melt this part of the plate at that temperature. (By kind permission of Ferranti Ltd.)

Fig.6.1 The joulemeter. (By kind permission of Philip Harris Ltd.)

Having shown that heat appears to be a form of energy and different in nature from temperature, we are now in a position to investigate the precise relationship which exists between temperature and heat when a given material is supplied with a certain quantity of heat. Such an investigation will involve considerable experimental discussion, and throughout this discussion, we shall use typical experimental results to facilitate our development of a comprehensive picture of the outcomes of any given heating process. We shall employ electrical heating in our experiments, and to record the number of joules of electrical energy supplied to a given system, (this number being transformed into heat energy within the system) we shall use an instrument called a joulemeter. This instrument (as shown in Fig. 6.1) records the number of joules of electrical energy supplied directly and so eliminates the calculation of energy supplied in terms of electric current, supply voltage, and time of current flow.

6.1 The Specific Heat Capacity of a Substance

We begin our investigation by observing the temperature rise produced when a given mass of water is supplied with a certain amount of heat energy. Using the apparatus shown in Fig. 6.2, it is a simple matter to supply a measured amount of energy to a measured mass of water, and thereafter to observe the resulting rise in temperature. Let us suppose that 10 000 J of energy (as recorded by the joulemeter) is supplied to 0·2 kg of water originally at 20 °C, and that after ample stirring (to ensure a uniform distribution of the energy supplied to the water) the maximum temperature reached by the water is 32 °C. It follows that since

10 000 J of energy supplied to 0·2 kg water raises its temperature by 12 °C,

then   50 000 J of energy supplied to 1·0 kg water raises its temperature by 12 °C,

and   4166 J of energy supplied to 1·0 kg water raises its temperature by 1 °C.

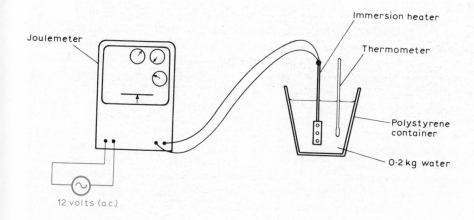

Immersion heater

Thermometer

Polystyrene container

0·2 kg water

12 volts (a.c.)

Fig.6.2 Supplying heat to water.

That is, 4166 J of energy is required to raise the temperature of 1 kg of water by 1 °C.

It is generally accepted that 4200 J of energy is required for this purpose.

If we were to carry out the same type of experiment using 0·2 kg of methylated spirits in the polystyrene container instead of 0·2 kg of water, we would find that *the amount of energy required to raise the temperature of 1 kg methylated spirits by 1 °C is 2300 J*

The quantity of heat energy which is required to raise the temperature of 1 kg mass of a given substance by 1 °C is called the *specific heat capacity* of that substance.

From what we have said already, it follows that the specific heat capacity of water is 4200 J kg^{-1} °C^{-1}, while that of methylated spirits is 2300 J kg^{-1} °C^{-1}. The specific heat capacities of some other common substances are as shown in the following table:

TABLE 6.1

Substance	Specific heat capacity (J kg^{-1} °C^{-1})
water	4200
methylated spirits	2300
ice	2100
aluminium	900
crown glass	670
iron	480
copper	385
silver	235
mercury	140
uranium	115

From this table we see that water has a very high specific heat capacity in relation to other substances. In practical terms, this means that water can store more heat energy per unit mass than any other substance at the same temperature. For this reason, water is a useful fluid for circulation in certain heating and cooling systems. In a domestic central heating system, the rate of circulation of the water need not be high since for a given amount of heat delivered, the fall in water temperature is relatively small. Any other liquid would require to be circulated at a higher rate to transfer the same quantity of heat from one point to another. The same sort of reasoning applies when considering the cooling system of a motor car engine. Water is not always suitable as a coolant however and to provide cooling in large electrical transformers special oils are used whose specific heat capacities are as high as possible. Water is unsuitable in such systems because it is liable to introduce corrosion and provide a possible means of electrical conduction.

Let us now consider a substance whose specific heat capacity is s (J kg^{-1} °C^{-1}). From our definition of specific heat capacity, it follows that

s J are required to raise the temperature of 1 kg of this substance by 1 °C

hence ms J are required to raise the temperature of m kg of this substance by 1 °C

and $ms \, \Delta\theta$ J are required to raise the temperature of m kg of this substance by $\Delta\theta$ °C

We have thus found that the quantity of heat energy, measured in joules, required to raise the temperature of m kg of a substance of specific heat capacity s (J kg^{-1} °C^{-1}) by $\Delta\theta$ °C is given by Q in the expression

$$Q = m \times s \times \Delta\theta \quad \dots\dots\dots\dots \quad (6.1)$$

It is obvious that equation (6.1) could be used to calculate the heat energy which would have to be removed from m kg of a substance of specific heat capacity s (J kg^{-1} °C^{-1}) to lower its temperature by $\Delta\theta\,°C$.

It is perhaps worth pointing out at this stage that the specific heat capacity of a given substance is a variable quantity in as much as it has slightly different values when measured in the locality of different temperatures. When we quote a value for the specific heat capacity of a substance, we are usually quoting a mean value for it—this mean having been estimated over the temperature range with which we are concerned. At ordinary temperatures, the difference between the specific heat capacity of a substance at a given temperature, and the mean specific heat capacity of the substance as estimated between two temperatures (between which the given temperature lies), is usually so small as to be quite insignificant in relation to other relevant uncertainties. When we are referring to the term specific heat capacity in experimental discussion or in calculation, we are therefore usually referring to the term mean specific heat capacity—this mean being relevant over a certain range of temperature within which our interest lies.

When we come to determine the specific heat capacity of a solid experimentally, it is convenient to employ a block of the solid whose mass is 1 kg. It is also convenient to provide the block with two recesses for the purpose of housing an immersion heater and a thermometer (Fig. 6.3). The specific heat capacity of a solid such as copper can thus be determined by using the experimental arrangement illustrated in Fig. 6.4.

The initial temperature of the block is noted, a measured amount of energy is supplied to the block, and the highest final temperature reached is noted. Let us suppose that 10 000 J of energy supplied produce a temperature rise of $26\,°C$. The specific heat capacity of copper can then be calculated from the formula $Q = m \times s \times \Delta\theta$ since we know the values of Q, m, and $\Delta\theta$.

Since
$$Q = m \times s \times \Delta\theta$$

then
$$s = \frac{Q}{m \times \Delta\theta}$$

hence
$$s = \frac{10\ 000}{1 \times 26}$$
$$= 385$$

The specific heat capacity of copper is thus $385\ \mathrm{J\ kg^{-1}\,°C^{-1}}$.

In such an investigation sufficient precautions must be taken to minimise heat transfer to the surroundings. Otherwise the temperature rise produced in the block will be lower than it should have been, and so the calculated value of the specific heat capacity will be higher than it should have been. Hence the reason for the cotton wool insulation surrounding the copper block.

Fig.6.3 A 1 kg copper block used in the determination of the specific heat capacity of copper. (By kind permission of M.L.I. Ltd.)

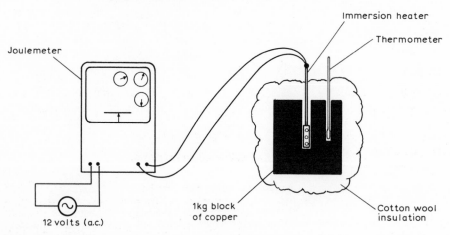

Fig.6.4 Finding the specific heat capacity of copper.

6.2 Exchanging Heat

From our everyday experience we are quite familiar with the fact that when two bodies at different temperatures are brought into contact, the hotter body becomes colder and the colder body becomes hotter until the two reach the same temperature. We can now investigate this phenomenon experimentally.

In this investigation we take a known mass of water at a known temperature and mix it with another known mass of water at a different known temperature. After thorough stirring, the temperature of the mixture is noted. Let us suppose that 0·1 kg water at 70 °C is mixed with 0·2 kg water at 22 °C and that after stirring, the final temperature of the mixture is found to be 38 °C.

The heat gained by the cold water can be calculated from the formula $Q = m \times s \times \Delta\theta$, where $m = 0·2$, $s = 4200$, and $\Delta\theta \, (= 38 - 22) = 16$.

Hence the heat gained by the cold water $= 0·2 \times 4200 \times 16$
$$= 13\,440 \text{ J}$$

The heat 'lost' by the hot water can also be calculated from the formula $Q = m \times s \times \Delta\theta$ where $m = 0·1$, $s = 4200$, and $\Delta\theta \, (= 70 - 38) = 32$.

Hence the heat 'lost' by the hot water $= 0·1 \times 4200 \times 32$
$$= 13\,440 \text{ J}$$

We see therefore that when two substances at different temperatures are mixed, a transfer of heat energy occurs between them until they reach the same temperature. Further, we may say that in the process, the heat given out by the hot body is equal to the heat taken in by the cold body—provided of course that no heat is 'lost' to the surroundings.

This result is a specific instance of the more general law of heat exchange—itself a specific instance of the more general law of conservation of energy. The law of heat exchange states that:

when two or more bodies at different temperatures are placed in contact, heat flows from the warmer bodies to the eooler ones until all are at the same temperature. During this process, the amount of heat given out by the warmer bodies is exactly equal to the amount of heat taken in by the cooler ones, provided that no heat is transferred to the surroundings.

Let us employ this law in the solution of a problem:

Problem 1 A piece of metal of mass 0·10 kg is heated to a temperature of 100 °C and dropped into a copper vessel of mass 0·08 kg containing 0·06 kg of water at 15 °C. After stirring, the final temperature of the system is 20 °C. What is the specific heat capacity of the metal? (Take the specific heat capacities of water and copper as 4200 J kg⁻¹ °C⁻¹ and 380 J kg⁻¹ °C⁻¹ respectively.)

Assuming no heat losses to the surroundings,

$$\frac{\text{Heat given out}}{\text{by metal}} = \frac{\text{Heat taken in}}{\text{by water}} + \frac{\text{Heat taken in}}{\text{by vessel}}$$

If we denote the specific heat capacity of the metal by s and express each heat term above in the usual '$m \times s \times \Delta\theta$' notation, then we have:

$$0·10 \times s \times (100 - 20) = [0·06 \times 4200 \times (20 - 15)]$$
$$+ [0·08 \times 380 \times (20 - 15)]$$
$$\Leftrightarrow 8s = 1260 + 152$$
$$= 1412$$
$$\Leftrightarrow \quad s = 176·5$$

The specific heat capacity of the metal is thus 176·5 J kg⁻¹ °C⁻¹

6.3 The Specific Latent Heat of a Substance

Our investigation of the heat process so far has been concerned with the relationship between heat and temperature. Any heating process has another aspect however and this is revealed by the following experiment.

Some water is poured into a polystyrene cup and an immersion heater placed in the cup supplies heat to the water at a steady rate for say twenty minutes. The temperature of the water is noted before and every minute after heating begins. A graph is drawn of water temperature against heating time and this is similar to that shown in Fig. 6.5.

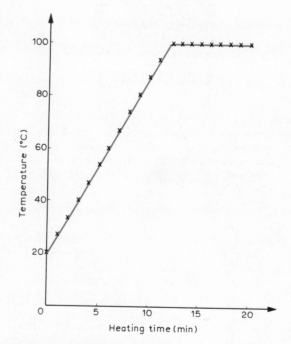

Fig.6.5   A heating curve for water.

We see from this graph that for the first twelve minutes of heating, the temperature of the water rises steadily. After twelve minutes however, the water temperature remains constant, despite the fact that the water is receiving heat at the same rate as previously! The heat supplied from twelve minutes onward is in fact changing the state of the water from liquid to gas at 100 °C. The temperature of the steam would not rise above 100 °C until the conversion was complete—assuming that the steam was somehow retained in the system and heating was continued.

The heat absorbed during boiling is given back when the process is reversed and the steam is condensed. The heat required to boil the water is thus said to be *latent* (or hidden) in the steam.

The quantity of heat energy which is required to change one kg mass of a liquid into gas at the boiling temperature of the liquid is called the *specific latent heat of evaporation* of the liquid.

The change of state from liquid to gas is not the only change in state which can be effected by heating a material however. It is also possible to effect the change of state from solid to liquid by heating.

The quantity of heat energy which is required to change one kg mass of a solid into liquid at the melting temperature of the solid is called the *specific latent heat of fusion* of the solid.

Let us consider a liquid whose specific latent heat of evaporation is L_E. From the definition, it follows that

L_E J are required to change the state of 1 kg of the liquid

hence $2L_E$ J are required to change the state of 2 kg of the liquid

and mL_E J are required to change the state of m kg of the liquid

The quantity of heat, measured in joules,—Q say—required to evaporate m kg of a liquid of specific latent heat of evaporation L_E at its boiling point is therefore given by

$$Q = m \times L_E \quad \dots \dots \dots \dots (6.2)$$

(When the gas formed condenses, the same amount of heat is released.)

Similarly the quantity of heat—Q' say—required to melt m kg of a solid of specific latent heat of fusion L_F at its melting point is given by

$$Q' = m \times L_F \quad \dots \dots \dots \dots (6.3)$$

Towards a molecular interpretation of the nature of latent heat, we consider a solid at some temperature below its melting point. In this condition the molecules of the solid are held in position by their mutual attractions and any molecule of the solid merely vibrates about a given fixed point. When heat is supplied to the solid, its temperature rises, this being an indication of the increased vigour of vibration of the molecules. When the temperature reaches the melting

point of the solid, further heat supplied serves to break down the structure of the solid by separating the molecules from each other without increasing their average energy of vibration. That is, when the melting point is reached, heat supplied does not increase the average kinetic energy of the molecules, but instead increases their average potential energy by doing work in separating them against the action of the binding forces which normally hold them together. The molecules thus separated are relatively free to wander, and constitute the liquid state of the original solid substance. Further heating would increase the average kinetic energy of the molecules in the liquid state, and this would appear as a rise in the temperature of the liquid.

When heating is discontinued, the temperature of the liquid falls until it reaches the solidifying point—equal to the melting point of the original solid. At this temperature, the average potential energy of the molecules is reduced as they re-establish the solid structure. This reduction constitutes the release of a certain amount of heat—equal to the amount which was previously required to melt the solid at this temperature.

Let us now consider the experimental approaches towards determining a value for each of the specific latent heat of evaporation of water, and the specific latent heat of fusion of ice.

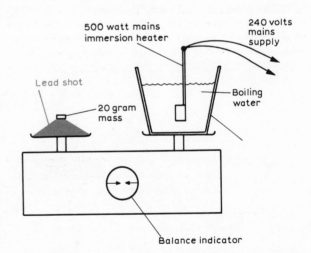

Fig.6.6 Finding the specific latent heat of evaporation of water.

Experiment 1
The apparatus used in the determination of the specific latent heat of evaporation of water is illustrated in Fig. 6.6. The right hand pan of the balance is originally heavier than the left hand pan. Water is then boiled off until the two pans come into balance. At this instant, the 20 gm mass is removed from the left hand pan, and a stopwatch is started. The time

required to restore balance (that is, to boil off 20 gm of water) is recorded on the stopwatch. Knowing the rating of the immersion heater, the energy required to boil off 20 gm of water can thus be found.

Using a 500 watt heater, it is usually found that some 90 seconds are required to boil off the 20 gm of water.

Equation 6.2 tells us that Q is the quantity of heat required to evaporate m kg of a substance of specific latent heat of evaporation L_E

In our experiment, $Q = 500 \times 90$ J $= 45\,000$ J, and $m = 0.02$ kg.

Since $Q = m \times L_E$, then $L_E = \dfrac{Q}{m}$

$$= \frac{45\,000}{0.02}$$

$$= 2\,250\,000$$

The specific latent heat of evaporation of water is thus $2\,250\,000$ J kg^{-1}. *The correct value is usually taken as $2\,260\,000$ J kg^{-1}.*

Experiment 2

The apparatus used in the determination of the specific latent heat of fusion of ice is illustrated in Fig. 6.7. The heater (A) is switched on and switched off after 10 000 J of energy have been recorded on the joulemeter. Before finding the mass of water collected in beaker A, several minutes are allowed to pass to ensure that all the heat supplied has been absorbed by the ice. The mass of water collected in beaker A is then found, and from this is subtracted the mass of water

collected in beaker B. This latter mass is a measure of the mass of water present in A which is due to room heat and not the 10 000 J. The apparatus B is thus a control experiment in this investigation.

In such an investigation it is possible to find 38 gm of water collected in beaker A and 8 gm of water collected in beaker B—depending of course on the temperature of the laboratory in which the investigation is carried out.

Equation 6.3 tells us that Q' is the quantity of heat required to melt m kg of a substance of specific latent heat of fusion L_F.

In our investigation, $Q' = 10\,000$ J, and $m = (38 - 8)$ gm $= 0.03$ kg.

Since $Q' = m \times L_F$, then $L_F = \dfrac{Q'}{m}$

$$= \frac{10\,000}{0.03}$$

$$= 333\,333$$

The specific latent heat of fusion of ice is thus $333\,333$ J kg^{-1}. *The correct value is usually taken as $336\,000$ J kg^{-1}.*

6.4 Worked Example

We conclude this chapter by solving a problem which illustrates the type of situation in which we have to apply all of this chapter's findings.

Problem 2 A mass of 0.3 kg of ice is contained in an insulated copper vessel of mass 0.5 kg with 0.7 kg of water all at 0 °C. If 0.2 kg of steam at 100 °C is condensed in the vessel, what

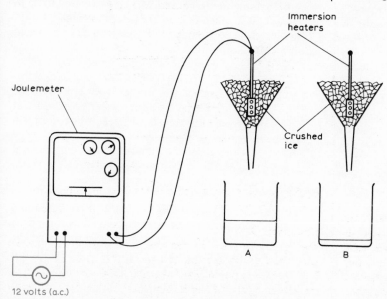

Fig.6.7 Finding the specific latent heat of fusion of ice.

is the final temperature of the mixture? (Take the specific heat capacities of water and copper as 4200 J kg^{-1} °C^{-1} and 380 J kg^{-1} °C^{-1} respectively. Take the specific latent heats of fusion of ice and evaporation of water as 336 000 J kg^{-1} and 2 260 000 J kg^{-1} respectively.)

Let the final temperature be t where $0 < t < 100$ (°C).

Assuming that no heat is transferred to the surroundings, then

$$\begin{matrix} \text{heat given out} \\ \text{by steam} \end{matrix} = \begin{matrix} \text{heat taken in} \\ \text{by vessel} \end{matrix} + \begin{matrix} \text{heat taken in} \\ \text{by water} \end{matrix}$$
$$+ \begin{matrix} \text{heat taken in} \\ \text{by ice} \end{matrix}$$

In giving out heat, the steam will condense to form water at 100 °C, and this water will give out heat as its temperature drops to t °C. In taking in heat, the ice will first melt to form water at 0 °C and this water will then take in heat to raise its temperature to t °C.

The last expression can thus be written symbolically in the form

$$[(m \times L) + (m \times s \times \Delta\theta)]_{\text{steam}} = (m \times s \times \Delta\theta)_{\text{copper}}$$
$$+ (m \times s \times \Delta\theta)_{\text{water}}$$
$$+ [(m \times L)$$
$$+ (m \times s \times \Delta\theta)]_{\text{ice}}$$
$$\text{(in the usual notation)}$$

$$\Leftrightarrow (0{\cdot}2 \times 2\,260\,000) + (0{\cdot}2 \times 4200 \times (100 - t))$$
$$= (0{\cdot}5 \times 380 \times (t - 0))$$
$$+ (0{\cdot}7 \times 4200 \times (t - 0))$$
$$+ (0{\cdot}3 \times 336\,000)$$
$$+ (0{\cdot}3 \times 4200 \times (t - 0))$$

$$\Leftrightarrow 452\,000 + (840 \times (100 - t)) = (190 \times t)$$
$$+ (2940 \times t)$$
$$+ 100\,800$$
$$+ (1260 \times t)$$
$$= (4390 \times t) + 100\,800$$
$$\Leftrightarrow 5230 \times t = 435\,200$$
$$\Leftrightarrow \qquad t = 83{\cdot}2$$

The final temperature of the mixture is thus 83·2 °C.

Problems

(Where necessary, refer to Table 6.1)

1 How much heat is given out when 80 gm of silver cools from 100 °C to 10 °C?

2 A copper vessel of mass 0·06 kg is at a temperature of 30 °C when 0·08 kg of water at 100 °C is poured into it. What is the final temperature of the vessel and its contents? What are you assuming?

3 A piece of metal of mass 0·5 kg is heated to 200 °C and then dropped into 0·05 kg of water at 0 °C contained in a vessel of mass 0·025 kg and specific heat capacity 850 J kg^{-1} °C^{-1}. If the final temperature of the mixture is 50 °C, find the specific heat capacity of the metal. State your assumptions.

4 A copper block contains a heating coil and thermocouple, the whole assembly being equivalent to 25 gm of copper. The block is immersed in liquid oxygen until the thermocouple reading is constant, and then quickly transferred to a tank of water at 0 °C. A coating of ice forms around the block. The heating coil—rated at 25 watts—is now switched on, and after 70 seconds, the ice has all melted. What was the temperature of the liquid oxygen?

(In the following problems, take the specific latent heats of fusion of ice and evaporation of water as 336 000 J kg^{-1} and 2 260 000 J kg^{-1} respectively, where necessary.)

5 How much heat is required to melt 2 kg of ice at 0 °C?

6 How much heat is required to convert 15 kg of ice at −50 °C to water at 20 °C?

7 To what temperature must a piece of iron of mass 0·5 kg be heated in order to convert 0·05 kg of ice at −10 °C to water at 50 °C when the two are placed in contact?

8 How much heat is required to convert 0·02 kg of ice at −10 °C to steam at 100 °C?

9 A light copper can contains 0·1 kg of water at 20 °C. The can is placed in the freezing compartment of a refrigerator which removes heat at the rate of 1000 J per minute. How long will it take before all the water becomes ice at 0 °C? How would this time be affected if the copper can had the same mass as the water?

10 An electric kettle is rated as 1·5 kW. How long would it take for the kettle to boil 'dry' if initially it contains 0·8 kg water at 20 °C? What assumptions are you making?

11 A piece of ice of mass 0·5 kg at −10 °C is contained in a vessel of very low specific heat capacity, and is supplied with heat at the rate of 10^5 J min^{-1}. Assuming that the vessel absorbs no heat, draw a graph of the temperature of the vessel's contents against the time of heating, for the first six minutes of heating. In what respects would the graph differ if the vessel had a reasonably high specific heat capacity, and this were taken into account?

Chapter 7

Gases

Fig.7.0 (By kind permission of the International Telecommunications Union, Geneva, Switzerland.)

In our consideration of heating processes in the last chapter, we confined our attention to those processes in which heat was supplied to solids and liquids. In this chapter, we turn to consider the outcome of supplying heat to gases. We have left this consideration to the last since the behaviour of a gas is in several respects more complicated than the behaviour of most solids and liquids. This complicated behaviour is easily demonstrated in several different ways. While a solid has both definite shape and volume, a liquid has only a definite volume. A gas however has neither definite shape nor volume, and will occupy the volume of its container completely, regardless of the shape of that container. While most solids and liquids show only slight elasticity and change in volume when subjected to compression, most gases show perfect elasticity and considerable change in volume when compressed. This property of gases becomes fairly obvious when we block the nozzle of a bicycle pump and attempt to push the handle inwards. As action at the handle is increased, increased reaction from the gas is experienced—this reaction resulting from a continual bombardment of the pump's piston by the air molecules trapped inside. It is this continual bombardment of a surface by gas molecules which we refer to as *gas pressure*—a property of the gas which is dependent on the volume of the container, on the gas temperature, and the mass of gas involved.

In this chapter we shall first of all define the term pressure fairly rigorously, and then attempt to relate the pressure of a gas to its volume and its temperature. Finally, we shall attempt to explain the relationship between these three quantities in terms of a kinetic theory of gases.

7.1 Pressure

Our discussion of pressure is in connection with fluids which are at rest, as regards their bulk behaviour. The term 'fluid' can be used to describe either a liquid or a gas (since both can flow) and although we are primarily concerned with gases in this chapter, we discuss liquid pressure for a certain degree of completeness.

Pressure is defined as the perpendicular component of force per unit area which a fluid exerts on any surface with which it comes in contact.

Let us consider a surface of area A m² which is acted upon by a force of $\underline{F}$ N at an angle θ to the normal to the surface, as shown in Fig. 7.1. Let a unit vector $\underline{n}$ be drawn normal to the surface as shown.

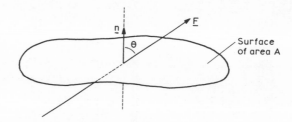

Fig.7.1 Defining pressure.

When we consider the scalar product* of the vectors $\underline{F}$ and $\underline{n}$, then

$$\underline{F} \cdot \underline{n} = F \times n \times \cos \theta \quad \text{(by definition)}$$

Hence
$$\underline{F} \cdot \underline{n} = F \times 1 \times \cos \theta$$
$$= F \cos \theta$$

But $F \cos \theta$ is the component of $\underline{F}$ perpendicular to the surface. This component is therefore a scalar quantity. Since pressure is defined as the perpendicular component of force per unit area, then the pressure P exerted on the surface is given by

$$P = \frac{F \cos \theta}{A}$$

and is therefore a scalar quantity.

In all of our applications, the applied force will be at right angles to the given surface, so that $\theta = 0°$, and

$$\boxed{P = \frac{F}{A}} \tag{7.1}$$

* For a discussion of 'scalar product', see 'Modern Mathematics for Schools' (Book 9) by the Scottish Mathematics Group (Blackie.)

(If the applied force were not at right angles to the surface, then it would have a component parallel to the surface, and this component would cause motion of the fluid.)

From equation 7.1, the unit of pressure is obviously $N\,m^{-2}$. This is sometimes referred to as the Pascal (written Pa).

Let us now consider two important properties concerning pressure within a stationary fluid:

1. *The pressure is the same at all points on the same horizontal plane within a stationary fluid.*

If this were not the case, a horizontal pressure gradient would exist and cause fluid to flow. Hence, for a stationary fluid, the pressure must be the same at all points on the same horizontal plane.

This property can be verified experimentally by setting up the apparatus shown in Fig. 7.2. The j-tubes are immersed in water so that their lower ends are at the same horizontal level, and then turpentine is carefully poured into each until it reaches the lower end. The upper levels in each tube are then found to be equal!

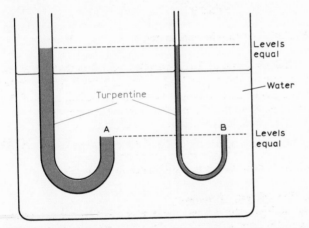

Fig.7.2 When the lower levels are equal, the upper levels are found to be equal too.

Although a larger force is exerted on surface A than on surface B (by virtue of the weight of the larger column of water directly above A), the same force must act on each *unit area* of both surfaces since the turpentine is supported to the same height in each tube. The *pressure* exerted at surface A is thus (by definition) equal to the *pressure* exerted at surface B, so that the pressure is the same at different points on the same horizontal plane within a stationary fluid.

2. *At any point or level in a stationary fluid, the pressure existing is the same in all directions.*

If this were not the case, any small element of fluid surrounding the point would experience a resultant force and so the fluid could not be at rest.

As an experimental check on this property, we can set up the apparatus shown in Fig. 7.3. The tubes are immersed in water so that their lower ends are at the same level, and then turpentine is carefully poured into each until it reaches the lower end. The upper levels are then found to be equal. Since the lower ends of the tubes are at the same depth, we conclude that the pressure at a given depth is transmitted equally in all directions. This is to say that pressure is not exerted in any preferred direction within a fluid, and this may be fairly obvious from the fact that pressure is a scalar quantity by definition.

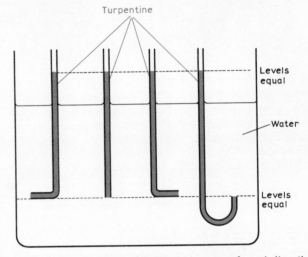

Fig.7.3 Pressure is not exerted in any preferred direction.

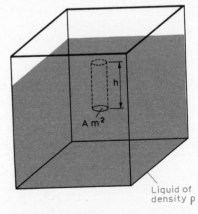

Fig.7.4 Calculating the pressure at a depth h in a liquid.

Having discussed the fact that the pressure is the same at all points on the same horizontal plane within a stationary fluid, we can now attempt to calculate the pressure exerted at a particular depth in a liquid.

Let us consider an area A m^2 at a depth h m below the surface of a liquid of density ρ (kg m⁻³). The pressure exerted on A is due to the weight of the liquid column immediately above A—assuming that no external pressure is exerted on the surface of the liquid. The situation is thus as shown in Fig. 7.4.

The volume of liquid in the column immediately above A is $A \times h$ m³. The mass of liquid in the column is thus $(\rho \times A \times h)$ kg, since the liquid density is ρ(kg m⁻³). The force acting on A is the weight of the column which is $(\rho \times A \times h \times g)$ (where $g = 10$ m s⁻²).

Since the pressure exerted on a surface can be calculated as force/area, the pressure at the depth h in the liquid can be written as P, where

$$P = \frac{\rho \times A \times h \times g}{A}$$

$$\Leftrightarrow \boxed{P = \rho \times h \times g} \ \cdots\cdots\cdots \ (7.2)$$

In most problems we shall meet, the surface of the liquid will be exposed to the atmosphere. If the pressure due to the atmosphere is denoted by P_A, then the total pressure experienced at the depth h below the surface of the liquid can be written as P_h, where

$$\boxed{P_h = P_A + (\rho \times h \times g)} \ \cdots\cdots\cdots \ (7.3)$$

7.2 Measuring Gas Pressure

Although our discussion of pressure within a stationary fluid has been with reference to liquid fluid, it is completely valid as far as the consideration of a given mass of gaseous fluid is concerned. The idea of pressure within a liquid is perhaps more consistent with our first hand experience however.

Having defined and discussed pressure, we now discuss several methods of measuring gas pressure which could be of use to us in our subsequent investigation of how the pressure of a given mass of gas is related to its volume and temperature.

1. The Simple Manometer

The manometer is an instrument which measures an unknown gas pressure in terms of the height of a liquid column which can be supported by the gas. Such an instrument is usually constructed in the form of a U-tube as shown in Fig. 7.5. The tube is filled with a liquid of known density and connected to the sample of gas whose pressure has to be determined. If the unknown pressure is denoted by P, then the pressure at X is P, and so too is the pressure at Y (since both X and Y lie on the same horizontal plane). The pressure at Y can be written as $P_A + (\rho \times h \times g)$, since Y is at a depth h below the surface Z which is exposed to atmospheric pressure P_A. Hence

$$\boxed{P = P_A + (\rho \times h \times g)} \ \cdots\cdots\cdots \ (7.4)$$

If the atmospheric pressure is known, the pressure of the gas sample under test can therefore be determined after measuring the height of the liquid column YZ.

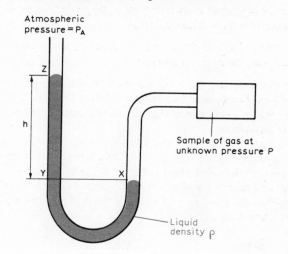

Fig.7.5 The simple manometer.

(If the pressure of the gas sample is less than that due to the atmosphere, the liquid level in the left hand limb will be lower than that in the right hand limb. The pressure of the gas sample can thus be calculated from the equation

$$\boxed{P = P_A - (\rho \times h' \times g)} \ \cdots\cdots\cdots \ (7.5)$$

where h' denotes the new difference in the levels.)

2. The Mercury Barometer

By modifying the simple manometer slightly, we can create an instrument which will enable us to measure the pressure exerted by the *atmosphere* itself. Such an instrument is called a *barometer*. To convert the manometer to a simple barometer, we connect the left hand limb to a vacuum pump and so remove the air above the liquid (in this case mercury) in the left hand limb. The right hand limb is opened to the atmosphere which then becomes the sole source of gas pressure present in the system. The arrangement is thus as shown in Fig. 7.6.

The pressure at A is that due to the atmosphere. This is equal to the pressure at B which is provided by the weight of the mercury column above B. Denoting the density of mercury by ρ, then the pressure at B has the value $(\rho \times h \times g)$, and so the atmospheric pressure can be calculated as $(\rho \times h \times g)$.

The mercury barometer can be constructed more simply, by taking a long straight glass tube of uniform and fairly wide bore which is sealed at one end, and filling this tube with mercury to within a centimetre of the open end. Covering this end with a finger and inverting and reinverting the tube several times provides for the removal of any trapped air pockets in the mercury column. The tube is then 'topped up' with mercury and with a finger over the open end, inverted in a dish of mercury. When the finger is removed under the mercury surface, the mercury drops inside the tube, leaving a vacuum space at the top.

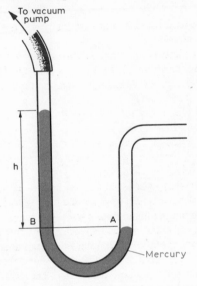

Fig.7.6 Converting the manometer to a barometer.

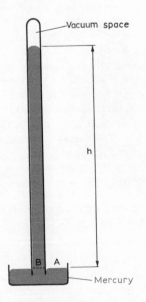

Fig.7.7 A simple mercury barometer.

With reference to Fig. 7.7, the pressure exerted at B is due to the weight of the mercury column above B. Since B is on the same horizontal plane as A, which is subjected to atmospheric pressure, we can calculate the atmospheric pressure as equal to ($\rho \times h \times g$), where ρ is the density of mercury. The atmospheric pressure is said to be normal or standard when the height of the mercury column h is 76 cm or 0·76 m. Taking the density of mercury as 13 600 kg m^{-1}, then normal atmospheric pressure has the value

$$13\ 600 \times 0.76 \times 9.81 \quad \text{(taking the accurate value of } g\text{)}$$

or   101 400 N m^{-2}

(Check the dimensional consistency of this calculation.)

3. The Bourdon Gauge

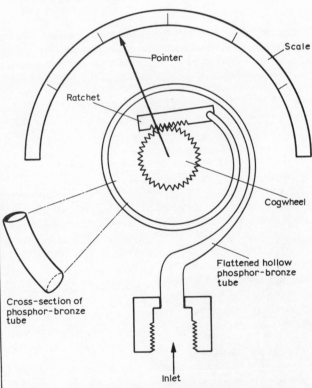

Fig.7.8 The construction of the Bourdon gauge.

The Bourdon gauge is constructed according to the illustration in Fig. 7.8. A flattened hollow phosphor-bronze tube of oval cross section is coiled and sealed at one end. When gas pressure is increased within this tube, the tube uncoils slightly as a result of the slight change in shape of its cross section. The tip of the tube is linked to a ratchet and cogwheel, the combined effect of both causing a pointer to move across a scale. When gas pressure is reduced within the tube, the process is reversed, and the pointer moves back across the scale.

The scale is graduated in N m⁻² in more recent gauges, the gauge having been calibrated against a manometer by its manufacturer. Some of the older gauges are outdated in as far as their scales are graduated in 'lbs wt. in⁻²' and as far as these are concerned a re-calibration is perhaps desirable if they are to be used for a purpose other than demonstration. Figure 7.9 shows an instrument with a dual scale.

Fig.7.9   The Bourdon gauge.

The Bourdon gauge is an instrument which gives a direct reading of pressure rather than an indirect reading in terms of the height of some liquid column. For this reason it is perhaps the most convenient instrument of the three which we have discussed, and so we adopt it for use in our investigation of gas properties.

7.3 The Gas Laws

Having discussed the nature and measurement of pressure, we now turn to consider the relationship between the pressure volume and temperature of a *fixed mass* of gas. If we denote pressure by P, volume by V, and temperature by θ, then clearly we wish to find how each of P, V, and θ is affected by the others. It would be quite meaningless to attempt to interpret changes in say P if both V and θ were allowed to vary simultaneously. Rather we should hold one quantity constant—say V—vary another—say θ—and attribute any

changes in the third (P) to the changes in θ alone. We should then have a relationship between P and θ for the fixed mass of gas at constant volume. Since we can hold any of the three variables constant at any one time, we can therefore conduct three investigations in turn for a fixed mass of gas. These investigations would provide us with relationships between

1   P and θ for constant V

2   V and θ for constant P

3   P and V for constant θ

(In each investigation the mass of gas would have to be held constant. Why?)

Once we derive the three relationships, we may find it possible to incorporate them into a general gas law.

Let us now proceed with the investigations in the order stated.

1) In this investigation we wish to find the relationship between the pressure (P) and temperature (θ) of a fixed mass of gas. Towards that end, we shall hold the volume of the gas constant so that changes occurring in pressure may be attributed to changes in temperature alone.

The apparatus used in this investigation is as shown in Fig. 7.10. The fixed mass of gas is enclosed in a round bottom glass flask which is immersed in water. The temperature of the gas is taken as equal to the temperature of the water. The pressure of the gas is recorded on a Bourdon gauge connected to the flask by a piece of thick walled rubber tubing. (Why must the bore of the tubing be as narrow as possible, and why should the length of tubing be as short as possible?)

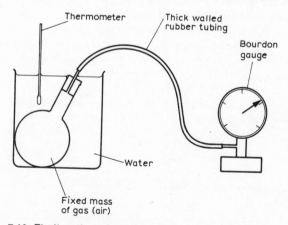

Fig.7.10 Finding the relationship between the pressure and temperature of a fixed mass of gas of constant volume.

The pressure of the gas is noted for different water temperatures and in an attempt to relate the gas pressure and temperature, a graph is drawn using the experimental values of these quantities. This graph might appear as in Fig. 7.11. We note

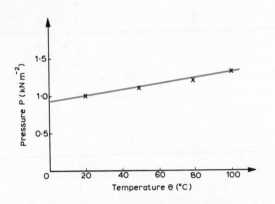

Fig.7.11 The variation of pressure with temperature for a fixed mass of gas of constant volume.

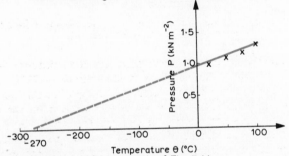

Fig.7.12 Extrapolating the graph of Fig. 7.11.

that the graph is a straight line, but this line does not pass through the origin ($P = 0$, $\theta = 0$). Relating the results to the set of axes set out in Fig. 7.12, we can extrapolate the graph however until it cuts the temperature axis at a point near $-270\,°C$. In actual fact this point should be $-273\,°C$. The graph is then a straight line through $-273\,°C$ so that if we now label this point as the origin, the graph is a straight line through the origin. Hence the pressure of the fixed mass of gas is directly proportional to its temperature, *the latter being measured relative to* $-273\,°C$. If we denote temperature measured relative to $-273\,°C$ by T, then

$$P \propto T$$
$$\Leftrightarrow P = k \times T$$
$$\Leftrightarrow \frac{P}{T} = k$$

The ratio of pressure to temperature measured relative to $-273\,°C$, for our fixed mass of gas at constant volume is therefore constant. We may therefore write

$$\boxed{\frac{P_1}{T_1} = \frac{P_2}{T_2}}$$ (provided V remains constant)

Result 1

Although this result has been derived for air as the gas

under test, it is found to hold true for all gases under the same sort of conditions as those experienced by air in this experiment. The value of the constant k would of course be different for the same masses of different gases, and for different masses of the same gas.

The temperature $-273\,°C$ is often referred to as the *absolute zero of temperature*—written $0\,°A$. Temperatures measured relative to this zero are then referred to as absolute temperatures or Kelvin temperatures (after Lord Kelvin (Fig. 7.0)—a pioneer in this field of study). To convert a Centigrade temperature to an absolute (or Kelvin) temperature, we merely add 273 degrees to the given temperature. Hence $0\,°C = 273\,°A$ ($°K$), $100\,°C = 373\,°A$ ($°K$) etc.

The name *absolute zero* is derived from the idea that at $-273\,°C$ the pressure of the fixed mass of gas would seem to be zero—according to the graph in Fig. 7.12. This would imply that all molecular movement had ceased and so the kinetic energy of the molecules was zero. It would therefore be impossible to cool the gas further since cooling requires the removal of energy.

To adhere to this view too rigidly may be somewhat harmful as regards more advanced studies in physics. It is generally accepted that the idea of absolute zero is a very difficult one, and one which cannot be explained in simple terms. Our derivation of the temperature $-273\,°C$ has involved a geometrical construction and not an actual physical measurement so that such a temperature does not have to be explained in exact physical terms. In referring to this derived temperature we are able to relate the pressure and temperature of a fixed mass of gas *considered under normal temperature conditions*. The temperature $-273\,°C$ is thus a mathematical convenience and not necessarily a physical reality for the given mass of gas.

The physical reality of $-273\,°C$ as a result of our derivation is questionable in as far as temperature on the scale used is somewhat meaningless below $-39\,°C$—the point at which mercury freezes. Further, the gas used in the experiment (air) condenses at low temperatures and is therefore no longer a gas. For satisfaction we would have to postulate an ideal gas which did not condense above $-273\,°C$ and whose temperature could be measured on a scale which operated down to the lowest temperatures likely to be met and which agreed with the mercury scale at ordinary temperatures.

Result 1 is applicable to a fixed mass of ideal gas over a very wide range of temperature and to actual gases over more restricted ranges of temperature (depending on the particular gas considered). Over the restricted range of temperature within which an actual gas obeys Result 1, the gas is said to behave ideally. Under normal laboratory temperatures, (and accepting the limited accuracy of the apparatus usually available), most gases behave ideally, and so the equation in Result 1 describes their behaviour in terms of pressure and temperature.

2) In our second investigation, we wish to find the relation-

ship between the volume (V) and the temperature (θ) of a fixed mass of gas. We shall therefore have to hold the pressure of the gas constant so that changes resulting in volume can be attributed to changes in temperature alone.

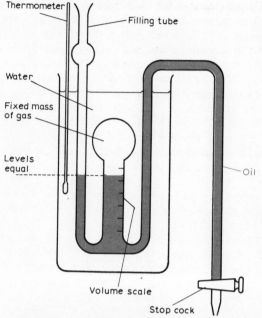

Fig.7.13 Finding the relationship between the volume and temperature of a fixed mass of gas at constant pressure.

The apparatus used in this investigation is as shown in Fig. 7.13. Oil is poured into the filling tube until the right hand limb is filled and the levels in the central and left hand limbs are equal. This being the case, the pressure exerted on the oil in the central limb is equal to that exerted on the oil in the left hand limb which is open to the atmosphere. The fixed mass of gas is thus at a pressure equal to that of the atmosphere. The temperature of the gas is assumed to be equal at all times to that of the water in which the assembly is immersed.

The gas temperature is noted along with the gas volume (the latter being read from the scale on the central limb). The water temperature is raised by heating the beaker, and the new temperature is noted. Before noting the new gas volume, some oil is run from the apparatus until the levels in the central and left hand limbs are again equal—thereby ensuring that the pressure of the fixed mass of gas is still equal to atmospheric pressure. This procedure is repeated several times until the water boils, the results obtained being used to plot a graph of the gas volume against temperature.

Such a graph is found to be a straight line but the line does not pass through the origin 0 °C. Relating the results to the set of axes set out in Fig. 7.14 however, we can extrapolate

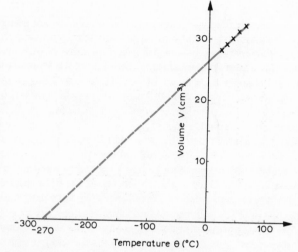

Fig.7.14 The variation of volume with temperature for a fixed mass of gas at constant pressure.

until the line cuts the temperature axis at a point near −270 °C. In actual fact this point should again be −273 °C. The graph can then be considered as a straight line through the point −273 °C so that if we now call this point the new origin as before, the graph is a straight line through the (new) origin. The volume of the fixed mass of gas is therefore directly proportional to its temperature measured relative to the point −273 °C. Denoting temperature measured relative to this point by T as before, then

$$V \propto T$$
$$\Leftrightarrow V = k' \times T \quad \text{where } k' \text{ is a constant}$$
$$\Leftrightarrow \frac{V}{T} = k'$$

The ratio of volume to temperature measured on the absolute or Kelvin scale for our fixed mass of gas at constant pressure is therefore constant. We may therefore write

$$\boxed{\frac{V_1}{T_1} = \frac{V_2}{T_2}} \quad \text{(provided } P \text{ remains constant)}$$

Result 2

This result is known as *Charles' Law* and although it has been derived for air as the gas under test, it is found to hold true for all gases under the same sort of conditions as those experienced by air in this experiment. The value of the constant k' would of course be different for the same masses of different gases, and for different masses of the same gas.

Once again we are confronted with the idea of absolute zero, and so we have to guard against reading too much into the graph of the experimental results. The temptation in this case would be to say that the volume of the gas is zero at absolute zero. However at any given pressure a real substance must condense finally to a finite volume and the idea of going to zero volume is quite absurd—as absurd as extrapolating to find the temperature at which a given quantity of mercury would have zero volume by using the fact that the volume of mercury changes by a factor of 0·00018 for every degree of temperature change over the normal range. (By such thoughtless extrapolation, mercury might seem to have zero volume at about −5500 °C!)

Only an ideal or perfect gas would obey Result 2 over a very wide range of temperature, and real gases obey it over more restricted temperature ranges (when they are said to behave ideally). Once again we have used the temperature −273 °C as a mathematical convenience. We have used it to help us relate the volume and temperature of our fixed mass of gas over a normal range of temperature. We have rejected it however as a possible physical reality for the real gas which we have considered.

3) In this our last investigation, we wish to find the relationship between the pressure (*P*) and the volume (*V*) of a fixed mass of gas. We must therefore hold the temperature of the gas constant so that changes resulting in pressure can be attributed to changes in volume alone.

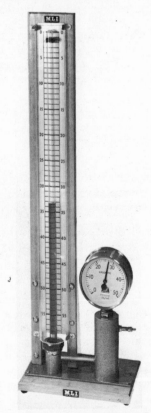

Fig.7.15 Finding the relationship between the pressure and volume of a fixed mass of gas at constant temperature. (By kind permission of M.L.I. Ltd.)

The apparatus used in this investigation is shown in Figs. 7.15 and 7.16. The pressure gauge reading is taken as a measure of the pressure of the fixed mass of gas trapped above the oil in the glass tube. This procedure is somewhat inaccurate in as much as it does not take into account the pressure due to the weight of the oil column. With a low density oil in the tube however, the error involved is acceptably low in value when compared with other errors resulting from experimental observation. The volume of the fixed mass of gas can be read directly from the volume scale which is located behind the tube.

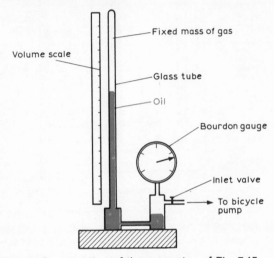

Fig.7.16 Construction of the apparatus of Fig. 7.15.

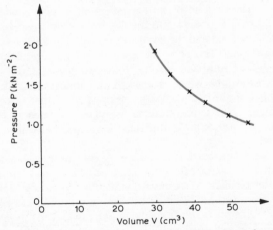

Fig.7.17 The variation of pressure with volume for a fixed mass of gas at constant temperature.

By means of a bicycle pump and the inlet valve, the oil in the tube can be made to rise to different levels—thereby altering the pressure of the fixed mass of gas by changing its volume. The pressure of the fixed mass of gas is noted at each level along with the corresponding volume, and a graph of pressure against volume is drawn. This is as shown in Fig. 7.17.

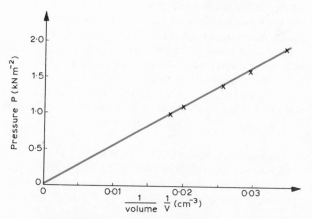

Fig.7.18 The variation of pressure with the reciprocal of volume, for a fixed mass of gas at constant temperature.

This graph of P against V is not particularly interesting. If we draw a second graph, of P against $\frac{1}{V}$, then we find it to be a straight line through the origin, as shown in Fig. 7.18. This second graph provides us with the relationship

$$P \propto \frac{1}{V}$$

$$\Leftrightarrow P = k'' \times \frac{1}{V} \quad \text{where } k'' \text{ is a constant}$$

$$\Leftrightarrow \quad P \times V = k''$$

The product of pressure and volume for a fixed mass of gas at constant temperature is therefore constant, and so we may write

$$\boxed{P_1 \times V_1 = P_2 \times V_2} \quad \text{(provided } \theta \text{ remains constant)}$$

Result 3

This result is known as *Boyle's Law*, named after Robert Boyle (Fig. 7.19) and although we have verified it for only one particular gas, it is found to hold true for all gases under the same sort of conditions as we have met in the experiment: that is, where the values of pressure and volume are not in any way extreme. The value of the constant k'' is of course different for the same masses of different gases, and for different masses of the same gas: k'' would also vary for a fixed mass of a given gas if the experiment were performed at some other constant temperature.

This far, we have investigated the relationship between any two co-ordinates of a fixed mass of gas—the third

Fig.7.19 (By kind permission of The Science Museum, London. Neg. no. 94/60.)

co-ordinate being held constant. In many situations however, we find all three co-ordinates varying simultaneously. For example, let us suppose that the volume of a gas is changing as a result of both its pressure and temperature changing. We can treat such a process as two-stage by first adjusting the original volume to meet the new pressure conditions, and then correcting this 'intermediate' volume for the temperature change. We can break the process down in this way since we are interested only in the final state of the gas as a result of both its pressure and temperature changing, and not in the details of the intermediate stages.

The volume V' produced purely as a result of the pressure of the gas changing from P_1 to P_2 can be written as

$$V' = \frac{P_1 \times V_1}{P_2} \quad \text{(where } V_1 \text{ represents the original volume of the gas.)}$$

When we consider this volume to change to V_2 purely as a result of the temperature changing from T_1 to T_2, then we may write

$$V_2 = \frac{V' \times T_2}{T_1}$$

Writing V' in terms of P_1, P_2, and V_1, then we have

$$V_2 = \frac{\dfrac{P_1 \times V_1}{P_2} \times T_2}{T_1}$$

Hence

$$\boxed{\frac{P_1 \times V_1}{T_1} = \frac{P_2 \times V_2}{T_2}} \quad \ldots\ldots\ldots\ldots \text{(7.6)}$$

This equation tells us that for a *fixed mass* of gas, the

quantity *Pressure × Volume/(absolute) Temperature* is a constant. The equation is known as *The General Gas Equation* and finds wide application in the description of all gases. With it, we can predict the behaviour of a fixed mass of gas whose pressure, volume, and temperature, are all changing simultaneously. Only an ideal gas would obey this equation over the whole conceivable temperature range, but real gases are found to obey it to a high degree of accuracy under non-extreme temperature conditions: that is, at temperatures well removed from the liquefaction point of the particular gas at the pressure being used.

If we consider a quantity of any gas equal in mass to the molecular 'weight' of the gas expressed in kg (this quantity being known as *a kilogram mole* of the gas), then the term $\dfrac{P \times V}{T}$ assumes the value 8317 J (kg mole)$^{-1}$°C^{-1}. This particular universal value is known as the *gas constant* and it is always denoted by R. The letter R must only be used when we are considering *one kilogram mole* of gas.

For one kilogram mole of gas, the general gas equation may therefore be written

$$\frac{P \times V}{T} = R$$

or $\boxed{PV = RT}$ . . . . (7.7)

7.4 A Kinetic Theory of Gases

Finally, in this chapter, we wish to account for the results of our three investigations in terms of a microscopic theoretical model of a gas. The success of this model will depend upon the agreement between its predictions and the evidence which we have already collected from our experiments. In setting up such a model, we shall have to make certain (mainly qualitative) assumptions, and from these, we shall attempt to derive certain quantitative relationships. Agreement between these relationships and our experimental results would afford us considerable satisfaction as regards the validity of our kinetic theory model. Let us then list the assumptions upon which our model is to be built.

1. *Gases consist of particles (called molecules)*
   Depending on the gas considered, each molecule will consist of one atom or a group of atoms. If the gas is pure, all its molecules will be alike.

2. *The size of each molecule is negligible*
   The volume of the molecules themselves is negligible compared to the volume which the gas occupies. This follows from the observations that a gas may be compressed to a tiny fraction of its original volume, and that when a gas condenses, the liquid formed may have a volume thousands of times smaller than the original gas volume.

3. *The number of molecules in a gas is large*
   Experiment has indicated that in the best laboratory vacuum, there are many million molecules remaining in each cubic centimetre of space.

4. *The motion of the molecules is completely random, and such that it can be described by Newton's Laws of Motion*
   We assume that the molecules are continually moving but in a very random fashion. We hope that Newton's Laws will find successful application in the microscopic realm.

5. *Collisions are perfectly elastic*
   We assume that collisions between the molecules themselves and with the walls of the container conserve kinetic energy and momentum. If this were not the case, the kinetic energies of molecules would gradually become smaller so that the gas would eventually condense to a liquid—even if it were contained in a heat-insulated vessel. This has never been observed.

6. *The forces between gas molecules are negligible*
   By this we mean that the molecules exert appreciable forces on one another only during collisions. The forces between widely separated molecules can be ignored completely, while those between molecules close together are very significant. The strong mutual attraction between closely packed particles can be held responsible for the slowness of a liquid's normal evaporation, and for the cohesion within most solids.

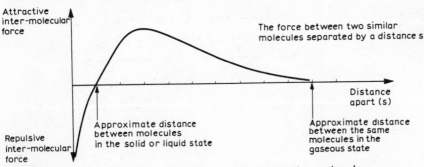

Fig.7.20 The force exerted by one molecule on a similar molecule.

When particles of matter become very crowded, we assume that attractive forces give way to repulsive forces. We must assume this in order to account for the fact that solids and liquids offer great resistance to compression—this resistance increasing with increasing compression. Similarly for the rebounding of two gas molecules in collision.

The force exerted on one molecule by another can thus be plotted against their distance of separation as shown in Fig. 7.20.

Using these six assumptions, we shall now attempt to derive a relationship between the pressure of a gas and the number, mass, and speeds of its molecules. The relationship we are about to investigate was first derived by Joule in 1848. In this investigation, we consider a pure sample of gas which is kept at constant temperature and pressure within a rigid cubical box of side a. Each molecule of the gas has mass m_0, and there are n molecules in the sample.

Let us consider a particular molecule—the ith molecule say—whose velocity is $\underline{v}_i$. We can resolve this velocity into components parallel to the edges of the box along which a set of rectangular axes have been set up as in Fig. 7.21. Vectorially we may write

$$\underline{v}_i = \underline{v}_{Xi} + \underline{v}_{Yi} + \underline{v}_{Zi}$$

The X-component of momentum of this molecule is $m_0\underline{v}_{Xi}$. If the molecule collides with wall A of the box, then its X-component of momentum will become $-m_0\underline{v}_{Xi}$. The change in the X-component of momentum as a result of this collision is therefore $-2m_0\underline{v}_{Xi}$ ($= \Delta \underline{p}$ say).

This change in momentum occurs every time the molecule collides with wall A. That is, every $\dfrac{2a}{v_{Xi}}$ seconds ($= \Delta t$ say).

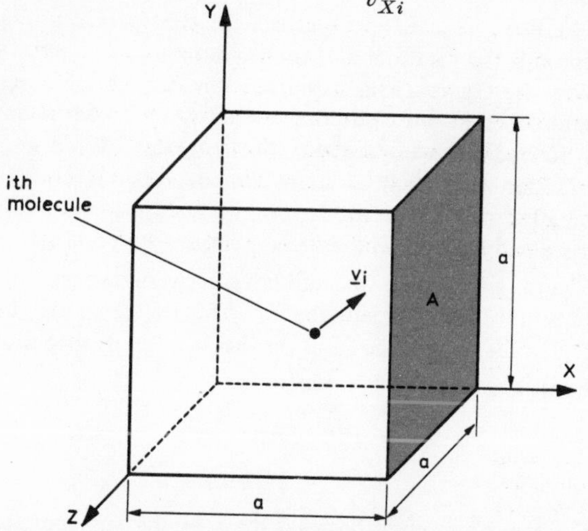

Fig.7.21 The ith molecule in a cubical box of side a.

According to Newton's Second Law, the *average* force exerted on the molecule by wall A is $\underline{f}_i$ where

$$f_i \left(= \frac{\Delta \underline{p}}{\Delta t} \right) = \frac{-2m_0\underline{v}_{Xi}}{\dfrac{2a}{v_{Xi}}}$$

$$= -\frac{m_0 v_{Xi}}{a} \underline{v}_{Xi}$$

According to Newton's Third Law, this average force is equal and opposite to the average force—$\underline{f}_i'$ say—which the molecule exerts on the wall A.

Hence

$$\underline{f}_i' = \frac{m_0 v_{Xi}}{a} \underline{v}_{Xi}$$

Having established that this force is directed in the same sense as the X-component of velocity of the ith molecule (that is, at right angles to wall A), we may now dispense with the vector notation. The size of the average force exerted on wall A by the ith molecule is therefore given by

$$f_i' = \frac{m_0 v_{Xi}{}^2}{a}$$

The size of the total average force exerted on wall A by all n molecules can be written as F where

$$F = \sum_{i=1}^{n} f_i'$$

Hence

$$F = \sum_{i=1}^{n} \frac{m_0 v_{Xi}{}^2}{a}$$

$$= \frac{m_0}{a} \sum_{i=1}^{n} v_{Xi}{}^2$$

$$= \frac{m_0 n}{a} \left(\frac{\sum_{i=1}^{n} v_{Xi}{}^2}{n} \right)$$

Let us now perform a little mathematical analysis to help us grasp the significance of the term $\left(\dfrac{\sum_{i=1}^{n} v_{Xi}{}^2}{n} \right)$.

For the ith molecule, we may write

$$\underline{v}_i = \underline{v}_{Xi} + \underline{v}_{Yi} + \underline{v}_{Zi}$$

The sizes of these vectors may be related by the equation

$$v_i{}^2 = v_{Xi}{}^2 + v_{Yi}{}^2 + v_{Zi}{}^2$$

For all n molecules we may therefore write

$$
\begin{aligned}
v_1{}^2 + v_2{}^2 + \ldots + v_n{}^2 &= (v_{X1}{}^2 + v_{Y1}{}^2 + v_{Z1}{}^2) \\
&\quad + (v_{X2}{}^2 + v_{Y2}{}^2 + v_{Z2}{}^2) + \ldots \\
&\quad + (v_{Xn}{}^2 + v_{Yn}{}^2 + v_{Zn}{}^2) \\
&= (v_{X1}{}^2 + v_{X2}{}^2 + \ldots + v_{Xn}{}^2) \\
&\quad + (v_{Y1}{}^2 + v_{Y2}{}^2 + \ldots + v_{Yn}{}^2) \\
&\quad + (v_{Z1}{}^2 + v_{Z2}{}^2 + \ldots + v_{Zn}{}^2)
\end{aligned}
$$

That is

$$\sum_{i=1}^{n} v_i{}^2 = \sum_{i=1}^{n} v_{Xi}{}^2 + \sum_{i=1}^{n} v_{Yi}{}^2 + \sum_{i=1}^{n} v_{Zi}{}^2$$

and

$$\frac{\sum_{i=1}^{n} v_i{}^2}{n} = \frac{\sum_{i=1}^{n} v_{Xi}{}^2}{n} + \frac{\sum_{i=1}^{n} v_{Yi}{}^2}{n} + \frac{\sum_{i=1}^{n} v_{Zi}{}^2}{n}$$

or

$$\overline{v^2} = \overline{v_X{}^2} + \overline{v_Y{}^2} + \overline{v_Z{}^2}$$

The term $\overline{v^2}$ denotes the average value (calculated for n molecules) of the squares of the molecular speeds, and the term $\overline{v_X{}^2}$ denotes the average value (calculated for n molecules) of the squares of X-components of molecular speeds. The terms $\overline{v_Y{}^2}$ and $\overline{v_Z{}^2}$ are defined in a similar manner.

Since we have assumed the motion to be random, there can be no preferred direction of motion so that

$$\overline{v_X{}^2} = \overline{v_Y{}^2} = \overline{v_Z{}^2}$$

Hence

$$\overline{v^2} = 3\overline{v_X{}^2}$$

or

$$\overline{v_X{}^2} = \tfrac{1}{3}\overline{v^2}$$

Now

$$F = \frac{m_0 n}{a} \left(\frac{\sum_{i=1}^{n} v_{Xi}{}^2}{n} \right)$$

$$= \frac{m_0 n}{a} \overline{v_X{}^2}$$

$$= \frac{m_0 n}{a} \frac{\overline{v^2}}{3}$$

The pressure exerted on wall A by the n molecules in the box can be written as P, where

$$P = \frac{F}{a^2}$$

Hence

$$P = \frac{m_0 n}{a^3} \frac{\overline{v^2}}{3}$$

But a^3 is the volume of the box—V say.

Hence

$$P = \frac{m_0 n}{V} \frac{\overline{v^2}}{3}$$

or

$$\boxed{PV = \tfrac{1}{3} m_0 n\, \overline{v^2}} \quad\cdots\cdots\cdots \quad (7.8)$$

Here we have an equation relating the pressure and volume of a quantity of gas to the number of molecules present, the mass of each, and a new term $\overline{v^2}$. Since each of the n molecules has mass m_0, the product $m_0 n$ represents the total mass of the gas sample which we shall call m. Equation 7.8 thus becomes: $PV = \tfrac{1}{3} m \overline{v^2}$. Using the fact that the density of the gas may be

calculated as its mass divided by its volume, then denoting the density by ρ, we may write finally

$$\boxed{P = \tfrac{1}{3} \rho \overline{v^2}} \quad\cdots\cdots\cdots \quad (7.9)$$

The dimensions of P and ρ are $ML^{-1}T^{-2}$, and ML^{-3} respectively. The dimensions of $\overline{v^2}$ are thus L^2T^{-2}. That is, the dimensions of (speed)^2. By taking the square root of $\overline{v^2}$, we should therefore obtain a quantity which has the dimensions of speed. This quantity, called the *root-mean-square speed* (r.m.s. speed) of the molecules is not the same thing as the ordinary average speed. For example, if we have three speeds 1 m s^{-1}, 3 m s^{-1}, and 5 m s^{-1} then the average speed can be calculated as $\bar{v}$ where

$$\bar{v} = \frac{1 + 3 + 5}{3} = 3 \text{ m s}^{-1}$$

The r.m.s. speed v_{rms} however is calculated as

$$v_{rms} = \sqrt{\frac{1^2 + 3^2 + 5^2}{3}} = 3 \cdot 4 \text{ m s}^{-1}$$

As far as a sample of gas is concerned, it may be shown that the average speed of the molecules ($\bar{v}$) is related to the r.m.s. speed according to the expression

$$\bar{v} = \sqrt{\frac{8}{3\pi}}\, v_{rms}$$

(The derivation of this expression is far in advance of the requirements of our course.)

We have already expressed the General Gas Equation in the form $PV = RT$ for one kg mole of the gas.

Equation 7.8 can be re-written in the form $PV = \tfrac{1}{3} m\overline{v^2}$ where m is the total mass of the gas sample.

Now the General Gas Equation was derived from experimental observation, while the revised form of equation 7.8 was derived from our kinetic theory model. We note with satisfaction that each of these two expressions contains a term 'PV'.

If we can now demonstrate equivalence between the terms 'RT' and '$\tfrac{1}{3} m\overline{v^2}$', then we shall have derived the General Gas Equation from our kinetic theory. This done, we may derive considerable confidence from the theory. Let us then attempt to relate the terms 'RT' and '$\tfrac{1}{3} m\overline{v^2}$'.

Now

$$PV = \tfrac{1}{3} m\overline{v^2}$$

$$= \tfrac{2}{3}(\tfrac{1}{2} m\overline{v^2})$$

Since m represents the total mass of the gas sample, the term $\tfrac{1}{2} m\overline{v^2}$ is equal to the total translational kinetic energy of the gas molecules. Denoting this by E we may write:

$$PV = \tfrac{2}{3} E$$

If we can now show that $E = \frac{3}{2}RT$, then we shall have derived the equation $PV = RT$ as required.

The specific heat capacity of a substance has been defined as the heat per unit mass required to raise the temperature of the substance by one degree. The convenient unit of mass for a gas is the *kg mole* and the corresponding specific heat capacity is called the *molar heat capacity*.

Let us suppose that the molar heat capacity of a gas is c_v when the gas is heated at constant volume. The change in internal energy of the gas (ΔE say) when N kg moles of the gas are heated through $\Delta T\,°$K is given as:

$$\Delta E = N \times c_v \times \Delta T$$

(This change in internal energy refers to a change in kinetic energy of the molecules. It cannot refer to any potential energy since we have assumed that no forces act between molecules except during collisions.)

Hence
$$c_v = \frac{1}{N}\frac{\Delta E}{\Delta T}$$

For one kg mole of the gas:

$$c_v = \frac{\Delta E}{\Delta T}$$

Now the quantity c_v when measured for each of helium gas, argon gas, and mercury vapour has the value 12 550 J(kg mole)$^{-1}$ $°$K^{-1} and this is almost exactly $\frac{3}{2}R$.

That is
$$c_v \left(= \frac{\Delta E}{\Delta T} \right) = \frac{3}{2}R$$

Hence
$$\frac{\Delta E}{\Delta T} = \frac{3}{2}R$$

and
$$\Delta E = \frac{3}{2}R\,\Delta T$$
$$= \Delta(\tfrac{3}{2}RT) \quad \text{since } R \text{ is a constant}$$
$$\Leftrightarrow E = \tfrac{3}{2}RT$$

Now
$$PV = \tfrac{2}{3}E \quad \text{according to our theory}$$

Hence
$$PV = \tfrac{2}{3}(\tfrac{3}{2}RT)$$
$$\Leftrightarrow PV = RT \quad \text{for one kg mole of the gas.}$$

We have thus shown that the relationship $PV = RT$ is quite consistent with our kinetic theory model of a gas. Our basic assumptions concerning the behaviour of the molecules of a gas are thus apparently consistent with the results of our experimental evidence.

In our application of the theory to problems, it is useful to bear the following additional information in mind:

1 One kilogram molecular 'weight' of any substance contains 6×10^{26} particles. This number is called Avogadro's Number (or Constant).

2 For a gas at normal atmospheric pressure and at a temperature of 0 °C, (known as normal or standard temperature), one kg mole occupies a volume of 22·4 m³. This volume is referred to as the kilogram molecular volume of a gas at normal temperature and pressure (n.t.p.)

Let us conclude this chapter by applying our theory in the solution of a typical problem:

Problem 1 Calculate the r.m.s. speed of argon molecules at n.t.p., and estimate the spacing between the molecules under these conditions. (The molecular weight of argon is 40.)

The equation $PV = \frac{1}{3}m_0 n\overline{v^2}$ may be written as
$$PV = \tfrac{1}{3}m\overline{v^2} \quad \text{where } m \text{ is the total mass of the gas}$$

Hence
$$v_{\text{r.m.s.}} = \sqrt{\frac{3PV}{m}}$$

Let us consider one kg mole of argon. Then $m = 40$ (kg) and $V = 22·4$ m³ (since the gas is at n.t.p.). Since the pressure of the gas is normal, P has the value 101 400 N m^{-2}

Hence
$$v_{\text{r.m.s.}} = \sqrt{\frac{3 \times 101\,400 \times 22·4}{40}}$$
$$= 412 \text{ m s}^{-1}$$

One kg mole of any gas at n.t.p. occupies 22·4 m³ and contains 6×10^{26} molecules.

That is 6×10^{26} molecules occupy 22·4 m³

Hence 1 molecule occupies $\dfrac{22·4}{6 \times 10^{26}}$ m³

That is $3·73 \times 10^{-26}$ m³

or $37·3 \times 10^{-27}$ m³

If we now imagine the volume available to each molecule to be in the form of a little cubical box and also each molecule to be at the centre of its box at a particular instant, then the molecules would be separated by a distance equal to the length of the side of the box. This is represented in Fig. 7.22.

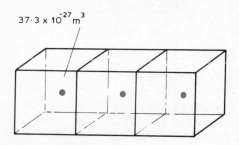

Fig.7.22 See Problem 1 (text).

The length of the side of the box is given as b where

$$b = \sqrt[3]{37 \cdot 3 \times 10^{-27}} \text{ m}$$

Hence the average molecular spacing is approximately $3 \cdot 40 \times 10^{-9}$ m.

It is interesting to note that this calculated spacing is of the order of ten molecular diameters—the argon molecular diameter being approximately $3 \cdot 40 \times 10^{-10}$ m. (Note the consistency between this figure and the diagram in Fig. 7.21.)

Problems
(Assume the values quoted for Avogadro's number and kilogram molecular volume, where necessary)

1 An older type of Bourdon gauge has a scale which is marked 0, 5, 10, 15, 20, 25 'lbs wt in.$^{-2}$'. Using the following information, draw a calibration graph from which the gauge reading could be converted to read in terms of N m^{-2}. 1 lb wt is equivalent to 4·45 N, and 1 in. is equivalent to 2·54 cm.

2 A tyre gauge registers a tyre pressure of 174 kN m^{-2} in the early morning when the temperature is 5 °C. What will it register in the afternoon when the temperature is 25 °C? (Note that the gauge pressure is that in excess of atmospheric pressure which you may take as 101 kN m^{-2}. Assume the tyre volume to remain constant.)

3 A bubble of volume 2 cm^3 is formed at the foot of a loch 50 m deep at which depth the temperature is 5 °C. What is the volume of the bubble when it reaches the surface where the temperature is 25 °C? (Take the density of water as 10^3 kg m^{-3} and the atmospheric pressure as 10^5 N m^{-2}.)

4 Gas is contained in a cylinder below a gas-tight piston which is free to move without friction. This is as shown in Fig. 7.23. If the gas volume is 0·8 m^3 and the weight of the piston is 5×10^4 N, what is the gas pressure given that the atmospheric pressure is 10^5 N m^{-2}.

What force would have to be applied at the piston in order to reduce the height of the gas column to 1 m? (The temperature remaining constant.)

5 The mercury column in an accurate barometer is supported to a height of 76 cm on a day when the mercury column in an identical faulty barometer (one with a little air trapped above the mercury) is supported to a height of 74 cm. On another day, the accurate barometer reads 70 cm and the faulty one 69 cm. What is the height of the top of each barometer tube above the surface of the mercury reservoir?

6 A sample of oxygen gas has a volume of 1 m^3 at 20 °C and at a pressure of 101 400 N m^{-2}. What fraction of a kg mole of oxygen is present?

7 How many oxygen molecules are contained in a cylinder of volume 1 m^3 in which the gas is maintained at a pressure of 10^6 N m^{-2} and stored at a temperature of 20 °C?

8 The speeds of 15 particles are:

$$0, 1, 1, 1, 2, 2, 3, 3, 3, 3, 4, 4, 4, 5, 5 \text{ m s}^{-1}$$

What is their average speed? What is their r.m.s. speed? What is the most probable speed?

9 What is the r.m.s. speed of argon molecules at 20 °C? (Take the gas constant as 8317 J(kg mole)$^{-1}$ °C^{-1} and the molecular 'weight' of argon as 40.)

10 At what temperature will the r.m.s. speed of helium molecules be twice their r.m.s. speed at 30 °C?

11 If the density of helium gas is 0·178 kg m^{-3} at normal temperature and pressure, what is the r.m.s. speed of helium molecules under these conditions? (Take normal temperature and pressure as previously.)

12 The best man-made vacuum can still support mercury to a height of 10^{-14} cm in an evacuated tube. How many molecules remain in 1 cm^3 of such a vacuum? (Take the density of mercury as 13 600 kg m^{-3}.)

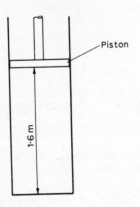

Fig.7.23 See Problem 4.

Chapter 8

Static Electricity

Fig.8.0   The Van de Graaf generator. (By kind permission of M.L.I. Ltd.)

The view which holds that the study of electricity has had the most far reaching consequences within the whole of physics is reflected to a certain extent by the fact that six of this book's twenty chapters are devoted to that study alone. The view is also reflected by the fact that there is hardly any aspect of our daily lives which is not in some way related to electricity. We rely on electricity for heating, lighting, communication, transport, and entertainment. The functioning and control of our bodies is explained in terms of electrical impulses travelling along nerve fibres. Electrical forces are considered responsible for maintaining atomic and molecular structure. Considerations such as these remind us of the all-round importance of electricity, and suggest that a proper understanding of this phenomenon will require a somewhat lengthy and far-reaching study.

The word *electricity* is usually taken to mean *a flow of electric charge*. Before investigating electricity in terms of this definition however, we shall discuss what we mean by electric charges in terms of their behaviour whilst at rest. This will enable us to establish a basis for the more ambitious study of moving charges. This study of electric charges at rest is

known as *electrostatics*: it forms the backbone of this chapter.

8.1 Producing Static Electricity

Let us suppose we have two similar polythene rods X and Y. If we rub the ends A of each rod with a piece of fur, suspend rod X by a piece of silk thread, and bring up the end A of rod Y close to end A of X, then the rods are observed to *repel* each other. This investigation is illustrated in Fig. 8.1.

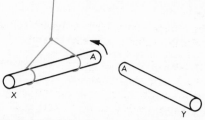

Fig.8.1   Two polythene rods rubbed in a similar fashion will repel each other.

If we replace rod X by a glass rod Z—end A of which has been rubbed with a piece of silk—then an *attraction* is observed between the rods Z and Y as illustrated in Fig. 8.2.

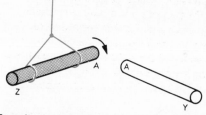

Fig.8.2   Two dissimilar rods rubbed differently may attract each other.

If we now replace rod Y by a second glass rod Z'—end A of which has been rubbed with a piece of silk—then a *repulsion* is observed between the rods Z and Z' as is illustrated in Fig. 8.3.

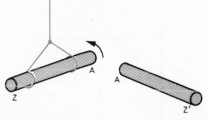

Fig.8.3   Two glass rods rubbed in a similar fashion will repel each other.

In explaining the results of these three simple experiments we say that the ends of the rods which have been rubbed have become *electrified*, or have acquired an *electric charge* in the rubbing process. Further, like rods rubbed in a similar manner will have acquired similar charges. Since these rods repel each other after rubbing, then like charges repel each other. We have also seen that in certain cases attraction is observed. In such cases, we may consider the charges to be unlike—these charges having been produced by rubbing rods of different materials with different types of cloth.

By rubbing rods of many different materials with different cloths or furs, and investigating their effects on each other in this way, we find that electrically charged bodies belong to either of two disjoint sets. The negative set comprises those bodies which when rubbed, will repel polythene rubbed with fur. All members of this set are said to acquire a *negative charge* when rubbed, and any two members of the set will obviously repel each other after being rubbed and brought close together. The positive set comprises those bodies which when rubbed, will repel perspex rubbed with wool. All members of this set are said to acquire a *positive charge* when rubbed, and any two members of the set will repel each other after being rubbed and brought close to each other. Any member of the negative set when rubbed will attract any member of the positive set when rubbed.

8.2 The Atomic View of Charging

Although the production of static electricity was recognised and reported as early as 600 B.C.—Thales of Miletus, a Greek scholar, having observed that a rubbed piece of amber (or 'elektron' in Greek) had the ability to attract small pieces of straw—it is only in this century that a satisfactory theory has emerged which enables us to account in detail for the effects we have observed. This theory is known as the electron theory, and is based on modern atomic theory. Let us summarise its main points.

The atoms of all elements are constructed according to the same general pattern. This pattern involves a central core, or nucleus, round which electrons revolve at high speed. The nucleus contains particles called protons and neutrons, the number of the protons and of the revolving electrons being the same for all atoms of a given element. The electron, with a mass of $9 \cdot 11 \times 10^{-31}$ kg, embodies the smallest possible unit of negative charge, while the proton, with a mass of $1 \cdot 67 \times 10^{-27}$ kg, embodies the smallest possible unit of positive charge. The amounts of charge carried by each electron and each proton are the same in spite of their greatly differing masses. The neutron is equal in mass to the proton, but it is electrically neutral. In any normal atom, the number of protons (called the atomic number of the element represented) equals the number of electrons, so that the atom as a whole is electrically neutral.

In the diagram of Fig. 8.4, the atom of helium which is represented is seen to be mostly empty space. This is in fact the case: if the nucleus of such an atom were represented by a pea, then the radius of the orbiting electrons would be of the order of 150 metres! Heavy atoms are characterised by the same emptiness, both their nuclei and their electrons being packed more tightly—so much so that the nuclear density is of the order of 10^{11} kg cm^{-3}!

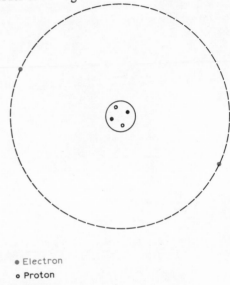

- Electron
- Proton
- Neutron

Fig.8.4   A simple picture of a helium atom.

The atom represented in Fig. 8.4 is electrically neutral—the numbers of protons and electrons being the same. If these numbers are made to differ, then the atom will have a net charge. If the atom were to gain an extra electron, then its net charge would be that due to two protons and three electrons—that is $(+2) + (-3)$, or (-1). If on the other hand, the atom were to lose an electron, its net charge would be that due to two protons and one electron—that is $(+2) + (-1)$, or $(+1)$.

We can thus account for the process of charging negatively in terms of a material gaining extra electrons, and for the process of charging positively in terms of a material losing some electrons. Polythene becomes negatively charged when rubbed by fur because, during rubbing, it gains electrons from the fur. Glass becomes positively charged when rubbed by silk because, during rubbing, it loses electrons to the silk. It is important to discuss charging in terms of an excess or a deficiency of *electrons*, and *not* in terms of an alteration of number of protons. Further, in any charging process, charge is transferred or separated, but never manufactured or destroyed.

8.3 Charging by Induction

The diagram in Fig. 8.5 illustrates two identical metal balls in contact, each supported on a non-metallic stand such as glass. If a negatively charged rod is now brought up close to

A without actually touching it, and the balls are separated in the presence of this rod, then we find that B has the ability to repel a suspended rod charged negatively, while A has the ability to attract such a rod. This investigation is represented step by step in Fig. 8.6.

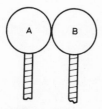

Fig.8.5 Two identical metal balls in contact—each on an insulating stand.

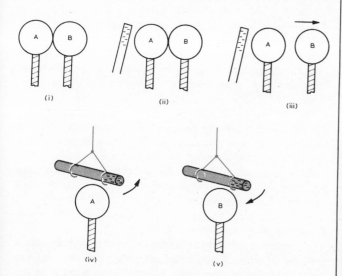

Fig.8.6 The separation of charge by induction.

The metal balls have obviously acquired electrical charges although they have neither been rubbed nor placed in contact with other charged bodies with which they could possibly have shared charge. Negative charge has been induced in ball B, and positive charge in ball A, purely by the influence and presence of the negatively charged rod first introduced in Fig. 8.6(ii).

When this investigation is repeated with non-metallic balls, no charges are found to be induced in the balls. This demonstrates a fundamental difference between metals and non-metals as far as electrical phenomena are concerned. Metals are usually referred to as electrical *conductors*, while

non-metals are referred to as electrical *insulators*. At the atomic level, metallic atoms possess loosely bound electrons, whereas non-metallic atoms do not. In being loosely bound, these electrons within the metal are relatively free to drift through the metal under some suitable electrical influence. That is, negative charge can be transferred through a metal, but not through a non-metal.

The results of the induction experiment now fall neatly into place. When the negative rod was brought up close to the balls, free electrons in A were repelled by the rod and so a net negative charge accumulated in B. Since A had then lost some electrons, it acquired a net positive charge. This state of affairs would have been maintained for as long as the rod was in the position shown in Fig. 8.6(ii). When the balls were then separated in the presence of the rod, the net negative charge in B became stranded, thereby maintaining the electron deficiency (and hence net positive charge) in A. Ball B was thus able to repel the suspended negatively charged rod, while ball A was able to attract it.

While non-metals generally require to be charged by rubbing, metals may be charged somewhat more easily by an induction process which owes its success to the conduction property of the metal concerned.

A device which operates on the induction principle and which is employed when large quantities of charge are required in electrostatic experiments is the *electrophorus* (Fig. 8.7). We shall describe its action both in terms of the diagrams in Fig. 8.8 and the following discussion.

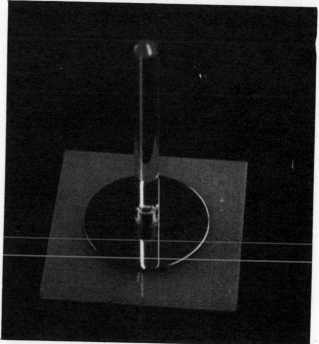

Fig.8.7 The electrophorus.

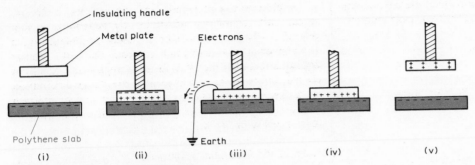

Fig.8.8   Charging an electrophorus.

A polythene slab is placed on the bench and its top surface rubbed with fur so as to provide it with a net negative charge (i). A metal plate, provided with an insulating handle, is then placed on the slab with the result that electrons within the metal tend to migrate to its upper surface—induced to do so by the influence of the negative slab. The lower surface of the metal is then effectively positive (ii). When the metal plate is then earthed momentarily by touching, the displaced electrons are further displaced to earth under the influence of the negative slab (iii). The metal plate, having lost electrons by the momentary earthing, is thus left with a net positive charge (iv). When the plate is removed from the influence of the slab, this net charge distributes itself evenly over the entire surface of the metal (v).

The electrophorus is a particularly useful device in as much as the metal plate may be charged over and over again without our having to recharge the polythene slab.

8.4 The Location of Charge on a Charged Conductor
Since charge is relatively free to move within a conductor, it may be interesting to investigate how a net charge distributes itself on a particular conductor. In such an investigation we shall employ an instrument called the *gold leaf electroscope*, illustrated in Fig. 8.9. The electroscope is an early device used in electrostatic experiments both to detect charge and to measure electric potential. We shall discuss electric potential later in the chapter and employ the electroscope meantime as a means of charge detection on isolated charged bodies.

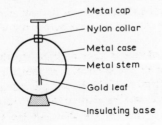

Fig.8.9   The gold leaf electroscope.

When the electroscope acquires a net charge, this charge is detected by a deflection of the gold leaf. The deflection is explained by saying that when a net charge is given to the electroscope cap, this charge distributes itself over the entire metallic surface. Since some of this charge will appear on both the gold leaf and the lower extremity of the stem, the repulsive forces set up between these two will cause the leaf to rise.

In addition to the electroscope, we shall employ a device called the proof plane—a small metal disc which is provided with a long insulating handle. This device is used when we wish to obtain a measure of the surface density of charge (the quantity of charge carried by unit area of the surface), at some point on a given charged conductor. When the disc is held against the surface of the charged conductor, then, being small, it effectively becomes part of that surface and so acquires an amount of charge which is representative of the surface density of charge at that point.

With the aid of the electroscope and the proof plane we can now investigate the distribution of charge on three different charged conductors in turn.

1. The Hollow Conductor
The conductor under test—in this experiment a metal can—is placed on an electroscope cap and given a charge by sharing with a charged electrophorus plate. The deflection of the electroscope leaf is noted and taken as an indication of the total charge which is contained in the system comprising metal can and electroscope. A proof plane is now lowered into the can, touched against its base or side (Fig. 8.10), and then removed. The leaf deflection is found to be unaltered and so we may conclude that no charge has been shared with the proof plane. When the proof plane is touched against the outside surface of the can and then removed, the leaf deflection is found to be slightly smaller than before, and so we may conclude that charge has been shared with the proof plane. Apparently charge resides on the outside surface of the conductor.

This experiment illustrates the general finding that when a hollow conductor is given a net charge, this charge is found to reside on the outside surface of that conductor—even when the conductor is charged by sharing charge with its inside surface.

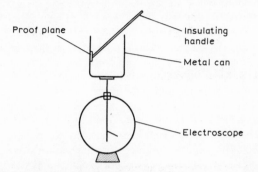

Fig.8.10 Investigating the charge distribution on a hollow charged conductor.

2. The Solid Spherical Conductor

A metal ball supported on a suitable insulating stand is given a charge by several sharings with a charged electrophorus plate. A sample of charge is then taken from the ball by means of a small proof plane being touched against its side. This sample is then communicated to an electroscope by touching the proof plane against the inside base of a metal can standing on the electroscope cap. The leaf deflection produced is then an indication of the size of the charge sampled by the proof plane.

It may seem strange that charge is communicated to the electroscope in this manner. With the can in place, however, we find that the proof plane gives up the *whole* of its sample charge when touched against the can's inside surface! Had the proof plane simply been touched against the electroscope cap without the can in place, it would merely have *shared* its charge with the electroscope while retaining some itself. This property of the metal can was discovered by Michael Faraday in his famous 'ice-pail experiment'—an account of which is given in most text-books of electricity.

Fig.8.11 The charge distribution on a charged solid spherical conductor.

When the leaf deflection has been noted for the first sample of charge, the electroscope is discharged and the procedure is then repeated for a second sample of charge taken from another part of the ball's surface. This sample is communicated

to the electroscope as before, and the new leaf deflection noted. This is found to be almost exactly the same as the first deflection—the very small difference being attributable to the small amount of charge removed from the ball. Similar deflections are obtained when further samples are taken from the ball and so we may conclude that the charge distribution on a charged solid spherical conductor is one of uniform density. A positively charged metal sphere can thus be represented as in Fig. 8.11.

3. The Solid Pear-Shaped Conductor

The pear-shaped conductor, supported on a suitable insulating stand, is given a charge by several sharings with a charged electrophorus plate. With reference to Fig. 8.12 a sample of charge is taken from the sharp end of the conductor (A) by means of a small proof plane and communicated to an electroscope by touching the proof plane against the bottom inside surface of a metal can place on the electroscope cap. The electroscope leaf deflection is noted as an indication of the size of the charge communicated, which is in turn an indication of the surface density of charge at the chosen point on the conductor.

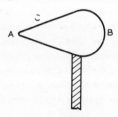

Fig.8.12 A solid pear-shaped conductor.

This procedure is repeated for samples of charge taken from the blunt end (B) and the flat side (C) of the conductor in turn, the electroscope being discharged before receiving each new sample.

When the leaf deflections representing the sample charges taken from the three areas of the conductor are compared, they are found to be significantly different. The fact that the different deflections are *not* due to the small amounts of charge removed from the conductor by successive proof plane contacts, may be verified by making a second contact at A, and observing that the deflection produced is almost exactly the same as that produced with the first contact at A. That is, the amounts of charge removed by the proof plane is quite insignificant.

The sample of charge communicated to the electroscope from the point of the conductor is found to produce the largest leaf deflection while the sample taken from the flat side produces the smallest deflection. The surface density of charge is thus largest at the point of the conductor and smallest at its flat side. A positively charged metal pear-shaped conductor can thus be represented as in Fig. 8.13.

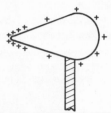

Fig.8.13 The charge distribution on a charged solid pear-shaped conductor.

Because charge tends to accumulate in high concentration at the sharp points of charged conductors, it is liable to escape or stream from such points fairly readily on account of the strong mutual repulsions which must exist in the neighbourhood of any large charge density. As an illustration, we can consider the case of a needle attached to the dome of an electrostatic charge generator (Fig. 8.0). A steady draught is detected as being directed away from the point of the needle when the system is switched on and the dome and needle thereby charged. With reference fo Fig. 8.14 we may say that a high concentration of positive charge will be developed at the point of the needle and the associated strong electrical influence will have the ability to ionise surrounding air molecules. The negative ions (electrons) in being attracted to the point, will neutralise the positive charge there, while the more massive positive ions in being repelled from the point give rise to an 'ion wind'—detected as a steady draught. The net effect is that positive charge is streaming away from the point in the form of positively charged gas molecules thus creating the 'ion wind'.

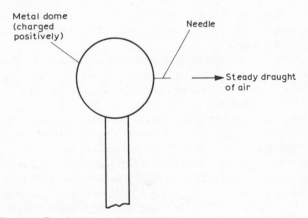

Fig.8.14 Producing an 'ion wind'.

This apparent streaming of charge from a sharp point is the basis of explanation of the principle of operation of a lightning conductor. A lightning conductor is usually pointed, and

connected via a stout copper cable to a large copper plate buried at some depth in the earth. Let us suppose that a thundercloud whose underside has become positively charged (by frictional effects in the internal motions of its water droplets) is positioned above a building fitted with a lightning conductor. Electrons, in being attracted to the top of the conductor, will form a high concentration of charge at the points there. These electrons will then appear to stream from the point towards the underside of the cloud and so gradually neutralise the positive charge there. A violent lightning discharge is then not so liable to occur as it would have been had the charge on the cloud continued to accumulate in the absence of the rod. If lightning does happen to 'strike', then the conductor provides an excellent conducting path to earth and in so doing protects the building to which it is attached. It is important to note that television aerials although pointed and of metallic construction, do not protect a building from lightning damage—the reason being that they are not satisfactorily grounded.

In the experimental investigations which we have discussed, it is quite essential that the apparatus employed should be clean and dry if the results are to be at all consistent. The presence of dampness in the apparatus is perhaps the most frequent cause of failure in electrostatic experiments. To remove dampness in and around the experimental apparatus, it is most advisable to warm all components frequently with the draught from a small warm-air blower such as a hair drier.

8.5 Electric Potential

Earlier in the chapter it was stated that an electroscope had the dual function of detecting electric charge and measuring *electric potential*, although we did not elaborate on the meaning of electric potential at that stage. Let us now attempt to define electric potential before investigating this latter function of the electroscope.

Fig.8.15 Defining electric potential.

Potential energy may be stored with an electric charge which has had work done on it by moving it against an electrostatic force of repulsion. Let us consider a large fixed metal sphere which holds a large positive charge, and a small movable metal ball which holds a small positive charge. With reference to Fig. 8.15, we can say that the ball, originally at B, will experience a force of repulsion at that point. Further, if the ball is moved from B to A, then work has to be done against the repulsive force and hence energy transformed in the process. The energy transformed is now in the form of electric potential energy and is stored with the charge in its new position. If the charge is then released, it will move back to its original position by virtue of the electrostatic repulsion—the electric potential energy it had previously gained being transformed into kinetic energy in the process.

When work is required to move a charge from one point to another in a region of electrical influence or electric field, then these two points are said to differ in electric potential, or a potential difference is said to exist between them.

The potential of any point in an electric field—such as A— is defined as the amount of work required to move a unit of charge from infinity to that point. Since more work would be required to move a unit charge from infinity to A than from infinity to B, we could say that, by definition, point A was at a higher electric potential than point B. As we have already suggested, a charge will flow from a point of high potential to a point of low potential if allowed to do so—in our case from A to B—and this idea is fundamental to our development of current electricity in the next chapter.

If V joules of energy are expended in bringing a unit charge from infinity to some point P in an electric field, then the electric potential at P is V. If, instead of a unit charge, we bring up a charge Q from infinity, then the energy expended (E joules say) will be Q times as great as V. That is,

$$E = Q \times V, \text{ or}$$

$$\boxed{V = \frac{E}{Q}} \quad \cdots\cdots\cdots\cdots\cdots (8.1)$$

The unit of charge is called the coulomb (written as 1 C) and it is such that two like charges, each of magnitude one coulomb, and separated by a distance of one metre, will repel each other with a force of 9×10^9 N.

It follows from equation 8.1 that the unit of electric potential is the joule divided by the coulomb, or 1 JC^{-1}. For brevity, this unit is called the *volt* and is written as 1 V. With reference to Fig. 8.15, let us suppose that $E_{\infty B}$ joules of work are required to bring the charge Q from infinity to B, while $E_{\infty A}$ joules are required to bring the same charge from infinity to A. The potential of point B, V_B say, and the potential of point A, V_A say, are given by the expressions

$$V_B = \frac{E_{\infty B}}{Q} \quad \text{and} \quad V_A = \frac{E_{\infty A}}{Q}$$

The potential difference between these points, which we shall write as V_{AB}, is then given by

$$V_{AB} (= V_A - V_B) = \frac{E_{\infty A}}{Q} - \frac{E_{\infty B}}{Q}$$

$$= \frac{E_{\infty A} - E_{\infty B}}{Q}$$

But $\qquad E_{\infty A} = E_{\infty B} + E_{BA}$

where E_{BA} denotes the amount of work required to move the charge Q from B to A.

Hence $\qquad V_{AB} = \frac{1}{Q}(E_{\infty B} + E_{BA} - E_{\infty B})$

$$= \frac{E_{BA}}{Q}$$

Alternatively we may write

$$\boxed{E_{BA} = Q \times V_{AB}} \quad \cdots\cdots\cdots\cdots (8.2)$$

Having discussed electric potential on a theoretical basis this far, let us conclude our discussion with an experimental investigation concerning our earlier remarks on the role of the electroscope in the measurement of electric potential. In this experiment, we shall reinvestigate the charged pear-shaped conductor of the last section.

The pear-shaped conductor is charged as before and then a fine wire, connected at one end to the cap of an electroscope, is touched against the conductor at its other end. This wire is supported by being wound round an insulating handle as illustrated in Fig. 8.16. The electroscope leaf deflection is noted to be *constant* regardless of the position of the free end of the wire on the conductor surface. The electroscope in this situation is thus indicating and measuring something *other* than charge density, which as we have already found, is far from being uniform.

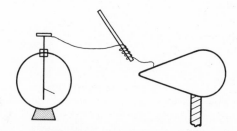

Fig.8.16 In this situation, the electroscope is indicating the potential of the charged pear-shaped conductor.

The possibility that the electroscope is now measuring electric potential becomes acceptable in view of the following discussion.

If the charge distribution on a charged pear-shaped conductor were *uniform* in density as indicated in Fig. 8.17, then less work would be required to bring a unit positive charge from negative infinity to X′, then to bring a similar charge from positive infinity to X. This is because there is effectively more charge at X than at X′. By definition therefore, X is at a higher potential than X′. If this were the case, electrons would begin flowing in the conductor under the electric influence, until the charge distribution became uneven, and the potential of the whole surface the same. The *uneven* surface density of charge on the charged pear-shaped conductor is thus consistent with a *uniform* electric potential over the whole surface.

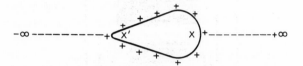

Fig.8.17 This charge distribution would imply that the potential of the conductor surface was non-uniform.

We conclude therefore that when the cap of an electroscope is in *permanent connection* with a charged conductor, the leaf deflection is in fact an indication of the electric potential of that conductor. This result will prove most useful in our investigations of electric capacitance in the following section.

8.6 Capacitance

If we were asked to define the capacity of a motor car tyre for holding air, then we would be incorrect in defining it merely as the internal volume of the tyre. Such a volume is a constant quantity, and in no way describes how much air can be squeezed into the tyre. The capacity of the tyre might be defined more correctly in terms of the mass of air introduced, and the internal pressure produced, necessary to explode the tyre. This definition is of course quite unsatisfactory, and so finally we might decide to define the tyre's capacity in terms of the mass of air which must be introduced in order to raise the internal pressure by a certain amount.

In an analogous situation, the capacity of an electrical conductor for holding charge is correctly defined in terms of the quantity of charge necessary to raise the potential of the conductor by one volt. It would be unsatisfactory to define the capacity of the conductor in terms of its physical size, or in terms of the amount of charge which could be added to it before a lightning discharge resulted from it.

If one coulomb of charge added to a conductor raises its potential by one volt, then its capacity is said to be one coulomb per volt or, for brevity, one farad—written 1 F. The farad is an extremely large unit of capacitance, and we shall find that in practice capacitances are usually dealt with which are of the order of microfarads (10^{-6} F—written μF) or picofarads (10^{-12} F—written pF).

From the definition of the farad it follows that

1 Coulomb of charge is required to raise the potential of a conductor of capacitance 1 F by 1 Volt

hence 2 Coulombs of charge is required to raise the potential of a conductor of capacitance 2 F by 1 Volt

and C Coulombs of charge is required to raise the potential of a conductor of capacitance C F by 1 Volt

also 2C Coulombs of charge is required to raise the potential of a conductor of capacitance C F by 2 Volts

and CV Coulombs of charge is required to raise the potential of a conductor of capacitance C F by V Volts

The charge stored by a conductor of capacity C farads which has been raised to a potential of V volts is thus given by Q where

$$Q = C \times V \quad (Q \text{ in coulombs})$$

Alternatively $\boxed{C = \dfrac{Q}{V}}$ .... (8.3)

Let us now perform a simple experiment which provides us with results consistent with this equation.

Theory: Equation 8.3 states $C = \dfrac{Q}{V}$. This implies that if the charge in a system remains constant, then the capacity and potential of the system are inversely proportional.

Method: Using the apparatus shown in Fig. 8.18, can (i) is given a charge by sharing with a charged electrophorus plate. The can shares this charge with the electroscope, and the leaf deflection provides a 'measure' of the potential of the arrangement, since the two are in permanent connection. When the capacity of the system is increased by dropping a wire connector between cans (i) and (ii), the leaf deflection is observed to fall, indicating a lowering of the potential of the whole system. (The total charge in the system is still the same however.) Similarly, when a second wire connector is dropped between cans (ii) and (iii). That is, the capacity and potential of the system are inversely related—the net charge contained in the system remaining constant.

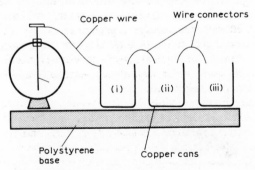

Fig.8.18 Investigating the relationship between capacitance and potential.

The *nature* of the inverse relationship may be investigated by first calibrating the electroscope using the apparatus in Fig. 8.19. The electroscope is connected to a monitored variable E.H.T. supply (0–1000 V), and the leaf deflections (in degrees) noted for different potential differences supplied.

The leaf deflections are then plotted against potential on a graph, so that the exact potential of the capacitive system (of which the electroscope will form a part) may be easily found. (This calibration exercise is most easily performed with a projection type electroscope.)

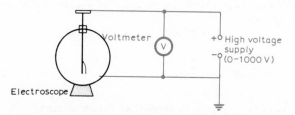

Fig.8.19 Calibrating a gold leaf electroscope.

The experiment is then repeated as we have described it, the potential of the system being noted when its capacity is one, two, and three units (cans). A graph of capacitance (number of cans) against potential may then be drawn, but this graph is not particularly meaningful. The results are more meaningful when a second graph is drawn of capacitance against (potential)$^{-1}$. This graph is of a straight line nature, the straight line being inclined to each axis, but not necessarily passing through the origin. (Why not?).

By re-defining the origin as required (having explained the reason for doing so), the graph assumes the nature of 'a straight line through the origin', and so we may conclude that the capacity and potential of a system of conductors are inversely proportional, provided their total charge remains constant. This is quite consistent with equation 8.3.

In this experiment we have taken the physical size of the conductors, or their arrangement, as a measure of capacitance although we decided against this procedure in defining capacitance. In the experiment however, we have been concerned with the relative capacitances of two or more arrangements and not with their absolute capacitances. In such a situation the physical size of a conductor is a sufficiently acceptable guide to its capacitance—especially as identical conductors are being used.

Finally in this section, let us consider the principle of construction of devices to store charge in electric circuits. Such devices are called *capacitors* (Fig. 8.20) and are quite different in form from the copper cans we have been employing in the development of our discussion this far. A practical capacitor is a combination of conducting plates separated by sheets of insulator. Let us construct a capacitor in this way and investigate its features.

Suppose that a metal plate is connected to an electroscope and given a net negative charge as shown in Fig. 8.21. The plate will share its charge with the electroscope, and the leaf deflection will give a measure of the potential of the charged plate since it is in permanent connection with the electroscope.

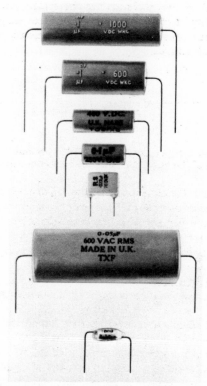

Fig.8.20 A selection of practical capacitors. (By kind permission of R. S. Components Ltd.)

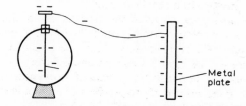

Fig.8.21 A charged metal plate connected to an electroscope.

We find that when an earthed plate is brought close and parallel to the charged plate, the leaf deflection falls, indicating that the potential of the system has been reduced. Further, the leaf deflection continues to fall as the separation of the plates is continually reduced, assuming that the plates are never brought into direct contact.

Since the amount of negative charge has remained constant we may say that the capacity of the system has been increased. This may be explained as follows, with reference to Fig. 8.22. Some free electrons in the second plate are repelled to earth by the influence of the net negative charge on the first plate. A positive charge is thus induced on the second plate and so a certain attractive force is brought to bear on the first plate.

Because of this force, less work would be required to place additional negative charge on the first plate—that is, its potential has been reduced. A greater charge can thus be placed on the first plate to bring its potential back to the original value—that is, its capacity has been increased since more charge is now required to raise its potential to the required value.

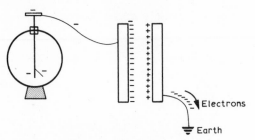

Fig.8.22 When a second earthed plate is brought up close to the first plate, the leaf deflection falls.

If either of the parallel plates illustrated in Fig. 8.22 is moved into or out of the paper, so that their effective area of overlap is reduced, the electroscope leaf deflection is observed to increase, thereby indicating that the potential of the system has been raised, or alternatively, that its capacity has been reduced—since the net negative charge has remained constant. Can you account for this?

When the two plates are set parallel, with the overlap area at a maximum, the leaf deflection is observed to fall if a sheet of insulating material such as polythene is introduced between the plates. The introduction of a dielectric or insulating sheet between the plates thus serves to reduce the potential of the system and so to increase its capacity—since its net charge remains constant. The explanation of this result is that a phenomenon known as electric polarisation takes place within the dielectric material when it is introduced between the plates. This polarisation results in an electric field being set up within the material and in *opposition* to the original electric field between the plates. The original field is thus reduced in value and so too is the potential difference between the plates. The capacity of the system is therefore increased.

We have seen therefore that the factors contributing to the maximum possible capacity of a parallel plate capacitor are:

i)   One of the plates should be earthed,
ii) The separation of the plates should be at a minimum,
iii) The overlap area of the plates should be at a maximum,
iv) A dielectric sheet should be introduced between the plates.

If we denote the capacity of such a system by C, the separation of the plates by d, and the area of plate overlap by A, then fuller investigation shows that

$$C \propto \frac{A}{d}$$

or

$$C = \frac{k \times A}{d} \quad \dots \dots \dots \dots (8.4)$$

where k is a constant related to the type of dielectric material introduced between the plates. Can you suggest the units of k, given that C is measured in farads, A in (metres)^2, and d in metres?

A practical capacitor which is constructed according to minimum plate separation, maximum plate overlap, and the central dielectric sheet, is the common paper capacitor. Its plates are two strips of aluminium foil separated by a dielectric of paper impregnated with paraffin wax. The assembly is rolled up so as to enclose the maximum possible amount of metal foil within the minimum possible volume. The construction of this capacitor is shown in Fig. 8.23.

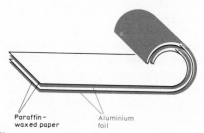

Fig.8.23 The composition of a paper capacitor.

Such a capacitor is inexpensive to manufacture and can be made to have a capacity in the range 0·001 μF to 8 μF. The paper dielectric is now being replaced by a thin layer of polystyrene which gives rise to smaller energy losses than paper.

In electrical circuit diagrams, the capacitor is represented by the symbol shown in Fig. 8.24.

Fig.8.24 The symbol for a capacitor in an electrical circuit diagram.

8.7 The Determination of the Charge and Mass of the Electron

We stated earlier in the chapter that electrons are fundamental constituents of every type of atom—always having the same charge and mass. Because the electronic charge and mass are fundamental atomic constants which appear in many physical formulae, it is obviously important to have accurate measurements of their values. In this the last section of the present

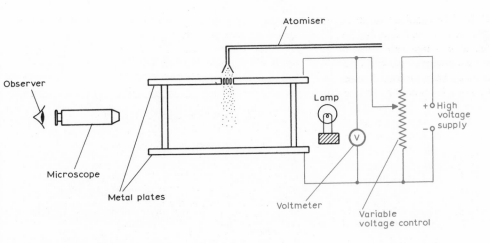

Atomiser

Observer

Lamp

+ o High voltage supply
− o

Microscope

Metal plates

Voltmeter

Variable voltage control

Fig.8.25 Apparatus used in the determination of the electronic charge.

chapter, we review the theoretical principles underlying the performance of one historically important experiment—the determination of the electronic charge by Robert Millikan in 1909.

The ratio of charge to mass for the electron had been determined earlier by J. J. Thomson, and so following Millikan's determination of the electronic charge, the electronic mass could be easily calculated.

The method employed by Millikan was a modification of that of an earlier experiment carried out by H. A. Wilson (the inventor of the Wilson cloud chamber). Millikan's apparatus is illustrated in Fig. 8.25.

A pair of optically-flat circular metal plates are set parallel with optically-flat identical glass separators. The upper plate has fine holes drilled near its centre which allow fine droplets of oil to be sprayed into the observation chamber from an atomiser (or perfume spray). These droplets (illuminated by a light beam) appear like tiny bright golden stars when viewed through the microscope.

The oil droplets are found to be charged (presumably by frictional effects in the spraying process) and this charge is usually negative. This would imply that the droplets have gained one or more excess electrons during spraying. Since the metal plates are connected to a variable high voltage supply (whose value is recorded at all times by a voltmeter connected across it), the electric field between the positively charged upper plate and the negatively charged lower plate may be varied in strength. Any negatively charged droplet may then be held stationary between the plates—attracted to the upper plate, repelled by the lower plate, and pulled downward by gravity.

Consider a typical droplet of mass m, which carries an excess negative charge Q. Suppose that this droplet remains stationary between the plates when the voltmeter records a potential difference of V between them. Since the droplet is stationary, there can be no net force acting on it, and so

$$W = F$$

where W is the weight of the droplet, and F is the force which it experiences (upwards) in the electric field between the plates.

Suppose the droplet had been held at the upper plate and then moved vertically downward against the electric force F. If the plate separation is d, then the work done is Fd. This work would appear as potential energy stored with the droplet and of an amount QV (according to equation 8.2). Hence:

$$Fd = QV \quad \text{or} \quad F = \frac{QV}{d}$$

Writing the weight of the droplet as mg, then

$$mg = \frac{QV}{d}$$

and so

$$\boxed{Q = \frac{mgd}{V}} \quad \dots\dots\dots\dots\dots \text{(8.5)}$$

The charge on the droplet could thus be calculated.

This calculation neglects the effect of the force of air buoyancy on the oil droplet.

To determine the mass of the droplet we must first calculate the drop radius. This calculation is complicated and is based on observation of the droplet under free fall in the absence of the electric field. A complete account of the theoretical aspects of the problem may be found in *Physics of the atom* by M. Wehr and J. Richards (Addison-Wesley Publishing Company).

In the course of his experiments, Millikan measured the charges on thousands of oil droplets, with a most satisfactory result. Every droplet studied was found to have a charge equal to a small integral multiple of a basic quantity of charge—q say. Droplets were observed to have charges q, $2q$, $3q$, $4q$, and so on, but never for example $1 \cdot 1q$, $4 \cdot 7q$, or any other non-integral value. Millikan concluded therefore that q was the smallest unit of electric charge available in nature and that this corresponded to the charge embodied in an electron. If a droplet had charge q, then it had acquired one extra electron during spraying. If it had charge $3q$, then it had acquired 3 extra electrons. The value of q, the electronic charge, was found to be $1 \cdot 6 \times 10^{-19}$ C.

J. J. Thomson had previously found the ratio of charge to mass for the electron to be $1 \cdot 76 \times 10^{11}$ C kg^{-1}. It followed then that the electronic mass was $9 \cdot 11 \times 10^{-31}$ kg.

For his work on the determination of the electronic charge, Robert Millikan received the Nobel Prize in Physics in 1923.

Problems

(Where necessary, take the electronic charge as $1 \cdot 6 \times 10^{-19}$ C, and g as 10 m s^{-2}.)

1 An electroscope may be charged positively by induction according to the diagrams shown in Fig. 8.26. Describe and explain each stage of the process redrawing the diagram to show complete charge distributions at each step. Suggest how another electroscope might be charged negatively by induction.

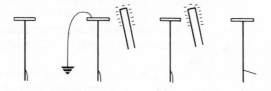

Fig.8.26 See Problem 1.

2 A negatively charged rod is brought close to the cap of a negatively charged electroscope and the leaf deflection increases. Why? What would have happened if a positively charged rod had been brought up close to the cap instead? Why?

3 A positively charged rod is held close to a small light uncharged metal ball suspended by a silk thread. The ball is attracted to the rod and makes contact with it. Immediately after contact, however, the ball is repelled from the rod. Explain the initial attraction and the final repulsion in detail.

4 A charged metal can rests on a polystyrene sheet. How might you show that its charge is confined to its outside surface given a proof plane and an uncharged electroscope fitted with a metal can on its cap?

5 A force of $0 \cdot 04$ N is necessary to move a charge of 25 μC between two points 25 cm apart in an electric field. What potential difference exists between the two points?

6 In atomic physics we often meet the unit of energy called the *electron volt* (written ev). This is the energy acquired by an electron (initially at rest) on being accelerated across a potential difference of one volt. What is the relationship between electron volts and joules? What would be the speed of an electron of energy 1 ev? (the electronic mass is $9 \cdot 1 \times 10^{-31}$ kg.)

7 What charge is stored in a $0 \cdot 5$ μF capacitor which is connected to a 100 V battery?

8 Two parallel plates separated by 3 mm of air have a capacitance of 50 pF. These are connected to a 100 V battery. What charge does the capacitor then hold? The plates (still connected to the battery) are now separated by a further 2 mm. What is the new charge on the capacitor? What has happened to the work required to effect the separation?

9 In a Millikan experiment an oil drop is balanced when a potential difference of 400 V is maintained between the plates which are separated by 2 cm. If the drop carries four surplus electrons, what is its mass?

Chapter 9

Current and Resistance

Fig.9.0   The resistance box. This piece of apparatus is used frequently in the experimental determination of electrical resistance. (By kind permission of Griffin & George Ltd.)

In our discussions of electrostatic phenomena in the last chapter, we were concerned to a large extent with the forces resulting from the interaction of electric charges and the distributions of charges brought about by the actions of these forces. We noted that as far as metallic materials were concerned, electric charges were able to re-arrange themselves within the material whenever it was introduced into an electric field such as that surrounding a charged rod. (This re-arrangement of charge was in fact transforming the interior of the metallic material into a field-free region in which the electric potential was constant.)

Having classified metals as electric conductors because of the presence of 'free' electrons which allow for re-arrangement of charge, we now discuss the motion of charge in a conductor when an electric field is maintained within the conductor.

9.1 Current

The motion or flow of electric charge constitutes an *electric current*. Any currents we have come across as yet have been *transient* currents—that is, currents of extremely short duration resulting from the rearrangement of charge within a conductor which has been introduced into an electric field. If we can arrange to maintain a steady electric field within a conductor by setting up a constant potential difference between its ends, then the resulting current will be continuous rather than transient, and will be known as *direct*. (If the potential difference between the ends of the conductor is reversed in sense periodically, the current flowing within the

conductor is known as *alternating*.)

As a source of constant potential difference, we shall employ the familiar dry cell—a device whose terminals are maintained at different electric potentials as the result of chemical activity within the cell. When a conductor is connected across the terminals of a cell, a constant potential difference will be maintained between the ends of the conductor and a continuous motion of charge (electrons) will take place within it. From our discussion of electric potential we may say that a free negative charge will flow from a point of high negative potential to a point of lower negative potential— that is, to a point of greater positive potential. It follows then that when a conductor is connected across the terminals of a cell, the direction and sense of electric current will be from the negative terminal of the cell towards its positive terminal. (In most older physics text books, electric current is regarded as flowing from positive to negative. This 'conventional current'—as it is known—is the unfortunate result of an arbitrary choice made years ago.) This is as indicated in Fig. 9.1 in which the symbol for an electric cell is introduced for the first time.

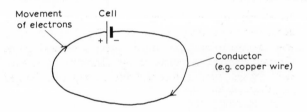

Fig.9.1   Current flowing in an electric circuit.

An electric current is correctly defined as the rate of flow of charge through any perpendicular cross section of a conductor in an electric circuit.

If a quantity of charge Q passes a given cross section of a conductor in a time t, then the average current in the circuit can be calculated as I where

$$I = \frac{Q}{t} \quad \dots\dots\dots\dots\dots\dots (9.1)$$

Further, if the rate of flow of charge through the given cross section is one coulomb per second, then the current in the circuit is said to be one *ampere* (after the French scientist André Marie Ampère, 1775–1836)—written 1 A. In equation (9.1) therefore, I is in amperes or amp (A) when Q is in coulombs (C), and t is in seconds (s).

9.2 The Relationship between Current and Potential Difference

Having introduced and defined electric current, we can now attempt to establish a relationship between the current in a material, and the potential difference which exists between its ends.

Such a relationship can be established by setting up the simple circuit illustrated in Fig. 9.2. The conductor under test is a one metre length of 32 gauge manganin wire. The current in the circuit and hence in the manganin is recorded on the ammeter, and the potential difference between the ends of the manganin is recorded on the voltmeter. (A discussion of these instruments will have to be left until the next chapter.) The potential difference between the ends of the manganin is varied by altering the number of cells in the battery, and the corresponding current is noted in each case.

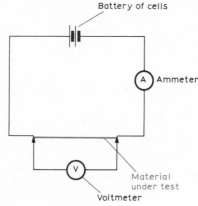

Fig.9.2 Investigating the relationship between current and potential difference.

The results of such an investigation are likely to appear similar to those in the following table.

potential difference V — (volts)	current I — (amp)	$\dfrac{V}{I}$
1·5	0·21	7·0
3·0	0·43	7·0
4·5	0·64	7·0
6·0	0·86	7·0

We see from the table that the ratio of potential difference to current is constant for the material under test, so that as the potential difference between the ends of a conductor increases, the current in the material increases proportionately.

In symbols we can say

$$I \propto V$$

$$\Leftrightarrow I = kV \quad \text{where } k \text{ is a constant}$$

The constant k is known as the electric *conductance* of the piece of material under test: it has the same value for any value of V, provided the temperature remains constant.

This result was discovered early in the nineteenth century by Georg Simon Ohm (1787–1854), and it is generally known as *Ohm's Law*.

It is more convenient, as a rule, to talk of the *resistance* of the piece of material rather than of its conductance. The resistance is simply the inverse of the conductance. That is,

$$\text{resistance } (R) = 1/\text{conductance } (k)$$

It follows that

$$I = \frac{V}{R}$$

or

$$\boxed{V = I \times R} \quad \ldots\ldots\ldots\ldots (9.2)$$

The resistance of a material is said to be one *ohm* (written 1 Ω), when a potential difference of one volt applied between its ends causes a current of one amp to flow in it. In equation 9.2 therefore, R is in ohms (Ω), when V is in volts (V) and I is in amp (A).

All materials can be characterised by a certain resistance to the flow of electrons, whether they be conductors or insulators. Copper, because of its abundance of free electrons, is an excellent electric conductor, but it still offers a little resistance to the surge of electrons through it. This resistance is sufficiently low that it may be neglected in most electric circuits however, and copper wire is used therefore to connect the various components in any given circuit. In circuit diagrams connecting leads are represented by continuous lines, whereas components offering significant resistance are represented by the symbol ⌐\/\/\/⌐. Such components are often referred to as resistors and they have appreciable and definite resistances to electron flow.

9.3 Combining Resistors

Having identified and defined the resistance of a piece of material, we can now attempt to calculate the net resistive effect of several resistive components in an electric circuit. If we can calculate the net resistance in the circuit, then, given the potential difference of the source or battery, we shall be able to calculate the current which will be drawn from that source.

If the current drawn from the source is confined to a single conducting path, then the circuit is referred to as a *series circuit*. If however separate conducting paths are available to the current, then the circuit is referred to as a *parallel circuit*. Let us investigate in turn the net resistive effects of resistors arranged in series, and resistors arranged in parallel.

1. Resistors in Series

The circuit diagram in Fig. 9.3(a) shows three resistors R_1, R_2, and R_3 arranged in a series combination. The potential difference of the cell is V. Since there is but one conducting path, the same current must flow through each of R_1, R_2, and R_3—otherwise charge would accumulate at different points in the circuit and, from our studies in electrostatics, we have seen that charge can only be accumulated on an *isolated* conductor.

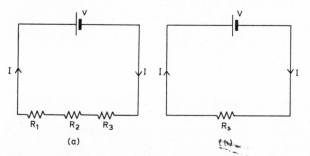

(a)

Fig.9.3 Combining resistors in series.

Since current flows through each resistor, there must be a potential difference between the ends of each, and further, since potential difference in the circuit is provided ultimately by the cell, the sum of the potential differences across each of the resistors must equal the potential difference of the cell. If the potential differences across R_1, R_2, and R_3 are denoted by V_1, V_2, and V_3 respectively, then we may write

$$V = V_1 + V_2 + V_3$$

From Ohm's Law, the potential difference between the ends of a component may be written as the product of its resistance and the current flowing in it. If the current flowing in the circuit is I, then

$$V = IR_1 + IR_2 + IR_3$$
$$= I(R_1 + R_2 + R_3)$$

If the same current I was drawn from the cell when the resistors R_1, R_2, and R_3 were replaced by a single resistor R_s, as in Fig. 9.3(b), then we should write

$$V = I \times R_s$$

But
$$V = I(R_1 + R_2 + R_3)$$

Hence
$$\boxed{R_s = R_1 + R_2 + R_3} \ldots \ldots \ldots \ldots (9.3)$$

(R_s, R_1, R_2, and R_3 all measured in ohms).

Since R_s alone gives the same effect as R_1, R_2, and R_3 in series, we can say that the effective or total resistance in a series circuit is calculated as the sum of the resistances of the individual components.

2. Resistors in Parallel
The circuit diagram in Fig. 9.4(a) shows three resistors R_1, R_2, and R_3 arranged in a parallel combination. The potential difference of the cell is V. Since there are several available conducting paths, the current I drawn from the cell will divide as indicated, so that currents I_1, I_2, and I_3

flow in the resistors R_1, R_2, and R_3 respectively. Since charge can neither be created nor destroyed, it follows that

$$I = I_1 + I_2 + I_3$$

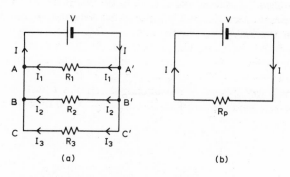

(a)   (b)

Fig.9.4 Combining resistors in parallel.

According to Ohm's Law, the current flowing in a resistor may be calculated as the potential difference between the ends of the resistor divided by its resistance. Since the points A, B, and C of the circuit in Fig. 9.4(a) are connected to the positive terminal of the cell and the points A′, B′, and C′ are connected to the negative terminal, the full potential difference of the cell is developed between the ends of each resistor. Hence

$$I = \frac{V}{R_1} + \frac{V}{R_2} + \frac{V}{R_3}$$
$$= V\left(\frac{1}{R_1} + \frac{1}{R_2} + \frac{1}{R_3}\right)$$

If the same current I was drawn from the cell when the resistors R_1, R_2, and R_3 were replaced by a single resistor R_p, as in Fig. 9.4(b), then we should write

$$I = \frac{V}{R_p}$$

But
$$I = V\left(\frac{1}{R_1} + \frac{1}{R_2} + \frac{1}{R_3}\right)$$

Hence
$$\boxed{\frac{1}{R_p} = \frac{1}{R_1} + \frac{1}{R_2} + \frac{1}{R_3}} \ldots \ldots \ldots (9.4)$$

(R_p, R_1, R_2, and R_3 all measured in ohms)

Since R_p alone gives the same effect as R_1, R_2, and R_3 in parallel, we can say that the effective or total resistance in a parallel circuit is calculated as the reciprocal of the sum of the reciprocals of the resistances of the individual components.

It is very seldom that an electric circuit is purely series or purely parallel in its construction. We are far more likely to encounter a complex circuit or network in which some components are in series while others are in parallel. The reader may care to attempt the following problem before proceeding with the topic of electric heating.

Problem 1 Compute the effective resistance of the network shown in Fig. 9.5, and hence determine the current drawn from the cell. (Ans. 1 A).

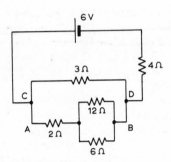

Fig.9.5   See Problem 1 (text).

9.4 Electric Heating

If it were possible to observe a 'free' conduction electron in a metal between the ends of which a steady potential difference was being maintained, we should find that the motion of the electron was a series of accelerations each of which was terminated whenever the electron collided with one of the atoms of the metal. The electron's kinetic energy before the collision would be transferred to the atom on colliding, and would thus serve to set the atom into vibration. It is this internal vibrational energy of atoms which we have previously referred to as heat energy.

Let us then attempt to derive the rate at which heat is developed in a conductor as the result of an electric current flowing in it. We consider a portion XY of a conductor in which the potentials of the points X and Y are V_x and V_y respectively. If the current in the conductor is I, then in a time Δt, the quantity of charge which enters this portion of the conductor at X is ΔQ, where

$$\Delta Q = I \times \Delta t$$

In the time Δt, this same quantity of charge must leave the portion of the conductor at Y. Otherwise, charge would accumulate within this portion of the conductor. The amount of charge ΔQ is therefore transferred between the points X and Y in a time Δt. To move this quantity of charge from potential V_y to potential V_x would require an amount of work ΔW to be done such that

$$\Delta W = \Delta Q \times (V_x - V_y) \quad \text{(from equation 8.2)}$$

The energy given up by the charge ΔQ (presumably as heat) in transferring from the potential V_x to V_y can therefore be written as ΔW.

That is
$$\Delta W = \Delta Q \times (V_x - V_y)$$
$$= I \times \Delta t \times V_{xy} \qquad \text{where } V_{xy} \text{ denotes the potential difference between X and Y.}$$

The rate at which heat is developed within the conductor can then be written as P where

$$P\left(= \frac{\Delta W}{\Delta t}\right) = I \times V_{xy}$$

We have previously referred to the *rate* of transfer of energy as *power*, and so it seems that the power dissipated in an electric component may be calculated in terms of the current in this component and the potential difference between its ends. If a potential difference V exists between the ends of a conductor when a current I flows in the conductor, then the power dissipated as a result is P where

$$\boxed{P = I \times V} \quad \ldots\ldots\ldots\ldots\ldots \text{(9.5)}$$

If the current I is measured in amp and the potential difference V in volts, then the unit of power P is given as

$$1 \text{ amp} \times 1 \text{ volt}$$

or
$$1 \frac{\text{coulomb}}{\text{second}} \times 1 \frac{\text{joule}}{\text{coulomb}}$$

or
$$1 \frac{\text{joule}}{\text{second}}$$

or
$$1 \text{ watt}$$

Our present system of units thus shows a most satisfactory consistency with that of our previous discussions.

By combining Ohm's Law with equation 9.5, it is possible to express the power dissipated in a conductor in terms of its resistance and the current flowing in it, or in terms of its resistance and the potential difference between its ends. As the conductor has its temperature raised as a result of power being dissipated, its resistance is liable to change, so that the power being dissipated is also liable to change. If the average resistance of the conductor is R over the temperature range concerned, then the average power dissipated in the conductor, P say, is given as

$$\boxed{P = I^2 \times R} \quad \ldots\ldots\ldots\ldots\ldots \text{(9.6)}$$

(where I is now the average current flowing in the conductor over the temperature range considered).

Also,
$$\boxed{P = \frac{V^2}{R}} \quad \ldots\ldots\ldots\ldots\ldots \text{(9.7)}$$

(where V is the potential difference between the ends of the conductor).

In most examples we shall encounter, the temperature range involved will be sufficiently small for us to regard the resistance of the conductor as constant and hence the power dissipated within the conductor as constant.

Let us now solve a problem dealing with the heating effect of an electric current.

Problem 2 A 6 V cell is connected in series with coils of wire whole resistances are 1, 2, and 3 ohms. The 2 ohm coil is immersed in a liquid of specific heat capacity 2400 J kg^{-1} °C^{-1}. One minute after switching on, the temperature of the liquid has risen by 1 °C. What would be the rise (per minute) in the liquid's temperature if the 1 and 3 ohm resistors were re-connected in parallel in the circuit?

The diagram in Fig. 9.6 shows the original circuit.

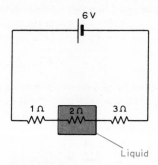

Fig.9.6   See Problem 2 (text).

The total resistance of this circuit is clearly 6 Ω. The current flowing in each resistor is therefore 1 A. The power dissipated in the 2 Ω resistor is thus ($1^2 \times 2$) watts—that is, 2 watts, or 2 J s^{-1}. In one minute, the heat developed in the 2 Ω resistor is therefore 120 J.

This heat raises the temperature of the liquid of specific heat capacity 2400 J kg^{-1} °C^{-1} by 1 °C. The mass of this liquid is thus 0·05 kg.

The diagram in Fig. 9.7 shows the final circuit.

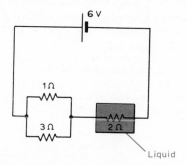

Fig.9.7   See Problem 2 (text).

The effective resistance of the 1 and 3 ohm resistors is given by R where

$$\frac{1}{R} = \tfrac{1}{1} + \tfrac{1}{3} = \tfrac{4}{3}$$

Hence

$$R = \tfrac{3}{4} \ \Omega$$

The total resistance of the circuit is thus $2\tfrac{3}{4}$ Ω. The current in the circuit and hence in the 2 Ω resistor is therefore given as $\frac{6}{2\tfrac{3}{4}}$ A—that is, $\tfrac{24}{11}$ A. The power dissipated in the 2 Ω resistor is thus [$(\tfrac{24}{11})^2 \times 2$] watts—that is 9·6 watts or 9·6 J s^{-1}. In one minute the energy supplied to the liquid is therefore 576 J. Since the mass of the liquid is 0·05 kg, and its specific heat capacity is 2400 J kg^{-1} °C^{-1} this amount of energy will serve to raise the temperature of the liquid by 4·8 °C in the one minute period.

Although the fundamental unit of electrical energy is the joule, it is often convenient—especially where large quantities of energy are concerned—to employ a larger unit called the kilowatt hour. This is the energy dissipated when an electric power of 1000 watts operates over a period of 1 hour. Since the watt is expressed as one joule per second, it follows that the joule may be expressed as one watt second. Since one kilowatt is equivalent to 1000 watts, and one hour equivalent to 3600 seconds, it follows that one kilowatt hour is equivalent to 3 600 000 watt seconds or 3 600 000 joules.

Our domestic consumption of electricity is calculated as the number of kilowatt hours of electric energy which we use. The kilowatt hour is usually referred to as a Board of Trade Unit (B.T.U.), or simply a 'unit' of electricity. The number of units of electrical energy which are consumed by a particular electric appliance can be calculated quite simply by multiplying the power rating of the appliance (in kilowatts) by the number of hours for which it has been in use.

9.5 Further Means of Measuring Resistance

We now turn to criticise our experimental verification of Ohm's Law earlier in the chapter, and then to discuss some perhaps more satisfactory approaches towards a more accurate determination of electric resistance.

Let us re-consider the experimental circuit of section 9.2. This is redrawn in Fig. 9.8.

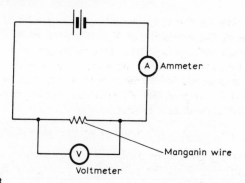

Fig.9.8

Our assumptions regarding this experiment were that the ammeter would record the current flowing in the manganin wire while the voltmeter would record the potential difference between its ends. The voltmeter is only activated however when some small current flows throught it. In other words, some of the current recorded by the ammeter actually flows through the voltmeter rather than through the manganin wire. If the resistance of the voltmeter is very high compared to that of the material under test, then the voltmeter will draw but a very small fraction of the total current in the circuit so that the test material will draw almost all of the current recorded by the ammeter. If on the other hand, we had used this circuit for the investigation of a test material of high resistance—as high as the resistance of the voltmeter say—then only about half of the current recorded by the ammeter would in fact be flowing in the material under test. The current recorded as flowing in the test material would then be in error by the order of 50 % so that the error in the calculated resistance of the test material would be of the same order.

To determine the resistance of a material of high resistance accurately and by means of an ammeter/voltmeter experiment, we should have to modify the circuit of Fig. 9.8 slightly to the form shown in Fig. 9.9.

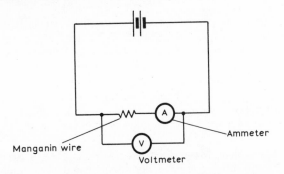

Fig.9.9 The accurate determination of high resistance.

In this arrangement, the ammeter records the exact current flowing in the test material since it is immediately in series with the material. In this arrangement however, the voltmeter records the potential difference between the extremities of the test material and the ammeter. An ammeter is an instrument whose resistance is very small so that the ammeter will offer little or no resistance to the current it is intended to measure. Because it has a very small resistance, only a very small potential difference will exist between its terminals when a given current flows through it. The material under test is now assumed to have a very high resistance so that a large potential difference will exist between its terminals when the same current as that in the ammeter flows in it. That is, although the voltmeter is in fact recording the potential difference between the ends of the series combination of material and ammeter, it can be regarded as measuring the

potential difference between the ends of the test material alone—provided the resistance of this material is very much greater than that of the ammeter.

The circuit of Fig. 9.9 would be quite unsuitable for the determination of the value of the resistance of a low resistance material. If a material were inserted whose resistance was of the same size as that of the ammeter, then the potential difference developed across it would be of the same order as that developed across the ammeter and so the voltmeter would record about twice the potential difference which it really should record.

The ammeter-voltmeter experiments appear reasonably acceptable provided that the order of the resistance of the material under test is known beforehand, so that the more suitable circuit may be selected. If, as often happens, the order of resistance is completely unknown, then these experiments are quite unsatisfactory. Equally well, neither circuit is acceptable if the resistance of the material has an intermediate value, being neither very high, nor very low.

Let us now consider several alternative approaches towards the determination of electrical resistance.

1. The Substitution Method

The substitution method of determining resistance requires the use of the *resistance box* (Fig. 9.0). Brass plugs are inserted between gaps in a bar of thick brass so that with all plugs in place, the box offers effectively no resistance. Below and across each gap, however, is connected a small standard resistance coil so that, when a plug is removed from the box, the coil bridging the gap created introduces resistance to the circuit into which the box has been inserted. If several plugs are removed from the box, the total resistance offered by the box is equal to the sum of resistances of the coils introduced, since these coils are arranged in series within the box. The construction of the resistance box is shown in Fig. 9.10.

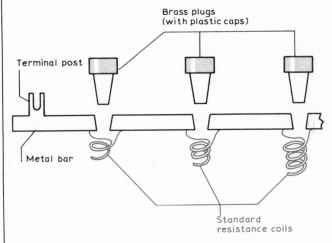

Fig.9.10 Construction of the resistance box.

To determine the resistance of a test resistor by the method of substitution, we place the resistor—R say—in the circuit of Fig. 9.11, and note the current in the circuit on the ammeter. We then replace the resistor R by a resistance box. Initially, several plugs must be removed from the resistance box; otherwise the box would offer near zero resistance, and a very large current would flow—possibly destroying the ammeter. Plugs are now changed in the box until the ammeter records as nearly as possible the same current as before. The resistance offered by the box is now as close as we can get to the resistance of the test resistor. This is found by counting the resistances operating in the box in terms of the labelled plugs which have been removed.

Fig.9.12 The variable resistor. (By kind permission of Griffin & George Ltd.)

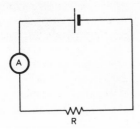

Fig.9.11 The circuit used in the method of substitution.

Since in this approach we are comparing an unknown resistor with standard resistors, the question concerning the means by which the ammeter has been calibrated is of no significance. The approach is not necessarily exact however since most resistance boxes might only introduce resistance to the nearest ohm. This means that a resistance of say 14·4 ohms would be determined as either 14 ohms or 15 ohms—unless of course additional and more sensitive resistance boxes are available for insertion in the circuit in series with the original box.

2. Wheatstone's Bridge

The Wheatstone network known as the 'Wheatstone Bridge' provides an accurate and widely used approach towards the determination of electric resistance. This network includes four resistors R_1, R_2, R_3, and R_4 which form a closed circuit in a diamond pattern. A cell is connected across two opposite corners of the network for the purpose of supplying it with current, and a centre-zero galvanometer and variable resistor (Fig. 9.12) are connected in series across the opposite corners. The arrangement thus appears as in Fig. 9.13.

In general, the galvanometer will show some deflection to one side or to the other. It is found however that a null deflection may be obtained by altering the value of one or more resistors in the network. When such a null deflection has been achieved, the bridge is said to be balanced, and a relationship between the values of the four resistors can then be derived as follows.

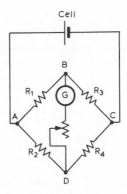

Fig.9.13 Wheatstone's Bridge circuit.

When the galvanometer shows no deflection, no current is flowing in the line BD of the circuit of Fig. 9.13. That is, the points B and D must be at the same potential. Hence the potential difference across each of the resistors R_1 and R_2 must be the same. Further, the potential difference across each of R_3 and R_4 must be the same. Let us suppose that, at balance, the currents flowing in the lines ABC and ADC of the circuit are I and I' respectively. Then since the potential difference across each of R_1 and R_2 is the same, it follows that

$$I \times R_1 = I' \times R_2$$

Further, since the potential difference across each of R_3 and R_4 is the same, it follows that

$$I \times R_3 = I' \times R_4$$

Dividing these two equations, we have

$$\frac{R_1}{R_3} = \frac{R_2}{R_4}$$

and so

$$\boxed{\frac{R_1}{R_2} = \frac{R_3}{R_4}} \quad \dots\dots\dots\dots (9.8)$$

This equation provides us with the condition of balance for the bridge circuit.

In the experimental situation, it is usual to have the resistors R_3 and R_4 of known values. The resistor R_2 is a resistance box, and R_1 is the resistor whose value is to be determined. When the circuit is set up, the variable resistor is set so as to offer maximum resistance, thereby ensuring that any current which does flow in the galvanometer line is such that it will not overload the meter. The resistance of the resistance box is now varied by removing plugs until a balanced state is almost achieved. The variable resistor is then set to offer minimum resistance so that the balance point may be achieved with much greater sensitivity. When the balance point has finally been reached, the value of R_2 is found in terms of the labelled plugs which have been removed from the box. Since the values of R_3 and R_4 are known, it is then but a simple exercise to calculate the value of R_1 using equation 9.8.

A simple form of Wheatstone bridge which allows for the determination of an unknown resistance in terms of one known resistance is called the metre bridge. The circuit of this bridge is illustrated in Fig. 9.14.

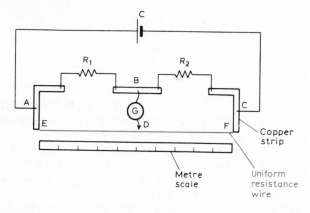

Fig.9.14 The metre bridge circuit.

A metre length of uniform resistance wire is stretched between two thick strips of copper. Between these two strips is a third strip, and in the gaps formed between the strips resistors R_1 (of unknown value) and R_2 (of known value) are connected. Current is supplied to the resistors and to the resistance wire by means of a cell C, connected as shown.

A centre-zero galvanometer is connected with one terminal to the terminal B on the centre copper strip, and with its other terminal to a sliding contact or 'jockey' (Fig. 9.15) which can be moved back and forth along the resistance wire. The deflection of the galvanometer pointer is found to vary from one side of the zero to the other as the sliding contact is moved from one end of the wire to the other, a null deflection being recorded when the slider is at some point D on the wire. When this point D is found, the lengths of the wire ED and DF are measured on a cm and mm scale which lies alongside the wire.

Fig.9.15 (By kind permission of Griffin & George Ltd.)

Let us suppose that the lengths ED and DF are L_1 and L_2 respectively, and that the resistance of the uniform wire is ρ ohms per cm length. It follows that the resistances of the portions ED and DF are ρL_1 and ρL_2 ohms respectively. Since balance has been achieved, then applying equation 9.8, we may say

$$\frac{R_1}{R_2} = \frac{\rho L_1}{\rho L_2}$$

or

$$\frac{R_1}{R_2} = \frac{L_1}{L_2}$$

Since the value of R_2 is known, the values of R_1 may be calculated in terms of R_2 and the ratio of the two measured lengths of wire.

Again it may be wise to incorporate a variable resistor in the apparatus in series with the galvanometer so that the meter may be protected during the initial attempt at finding the balance point. When the approximate balance point has been found, the resistance of the variable resistor may be reduced to its minimum value so that the full sensitivity of the meter may be employed in finding the exact balance point.

9.6 The Electromotive Force and Internal Resistance of a Cell

If we set up the circuit illustrated in Fig. 9.16, we note that the ammeters 1, 2, and 3 each record the same current. That is, the current passing through the cells themselves is equal to the current supplied to the circuit by these cells. Since current is actually passing through the cells, we may conclude that each cell has a certain internal resistance across which a certain internal potential difference is developed whenever the cell is delivering current.

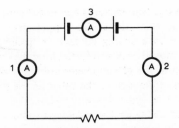

Fig.9.16 The current is the same at all points of a circuit.

If we consider the circuit of Fig. 9.17(a), then obviously a certain amount of energy is required to drive each coulomb of charge through the resistor R. The potential difference between the ends of the resistor, a measure of this energy, could be measured by connecting a voltmeter in parallel with the resistor, and hence in parallel with the cell, as in Fig. 9.17(b). The voltmeter is then giving a measure of the external potential difference of the cell, or the energy which the cell is able to supply to drive each coulomb of charge through an external circuit not including itself.

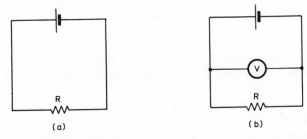

Fig.9.17 The voltmeter measures the external potential difference of the cell.

A certain amount of energy is also required to drive each coulomb of charge through the cell itself, this energy being a measure of the internal potential difference which must exist within the cell whenever it delivers this particular current.

The total energy available within a cell is thus available to drive current through an external circuit and through an internal circuit too. This *total* amount of energy available to drive each coulomb of charge is called the *electromotive force* (e.m.f.) of the cell, and it is usually denoted by E. Since the electromotive force is a measure of energy per coulomb of charge, or 'joules per coulomb', it is measured in volts. It is in effect the total available 'voltage' of the cell.

If the voltmeter in Fig. 9.17(b) records a potential difference V, then the e.m.f. of the cell E, may be written as

$$E = V + v \quad \text{where } v \text{ is the}$$
potential difference
developed internally
when the cell is
supplying current.

If a current I flows in the circuit of Fig. 9.17(a), it follows that

$$E = IR + Ir \quad \text{Where } r \text{ is the}$$
internal resistance
of the cell

Hence $\boxed{E = I(R + r)}$ . . . . (9.9)

If a cell is on open circuit—that is, isolated from any component—it gives no current and so no potential difference is developed within it. Its e.m.f. could therefore be determined by measuring the potential difference between its terminals. To do this satisfactorily, a voltmeter of infinite resistance would have to be employed, and so it would have to be of an electrostatic type. A voltmeter of the moving coil type which is activated only when a small current flows in it is not strictly suitable for the measurement of a cell's e.m.f. Why?

One very suitable instrument for the determination of e.m.f. or the comparisons of e.m.f.'s is the potentiometer. The potentiometer is also usefully employed in the determination of the internal resistance of a cell. Let us consider its principle of operation.

The circuit diagram of Fig. 9.18 shows the potentiometer in its simplest form.

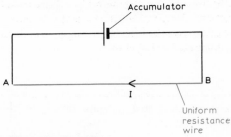

Fig.9.18 The potentiometer.

An accumulator is connected to a uniform resistance wire AB whose resistance is $\rho\ \Omega$ per cm length. Let us suppose that a current I flows in the wire as shown.

If a test cell of e.m.f. E is now connected along with a centre zero galvanometer as shown in Fig. 9.19, then no current will flow through the test cell as long as the sliding contact X is not touching the wire AB.

Since no current is flowing in the line AX, the e.m.f. of the cell is equal to its terminal potential difference which is in turn equal to the potential difference between the points A and X, since these are connected to the terminals of the cell by non-current-carrying conductors. Let X now touch the wire at Y, where the potential of Y is more negative than that of X. Current will flow in the line AX in the sense X to A. The galvanometer will thus show a deflection to one side. If however the potential of the point Y is less

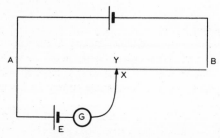

Fig.9.19 The e.m.f. of the test cell may be balanced against the potential difference across a certain length of potentiometer wire.

negative than that of X, current will flow in the line AX and in the sense A to X. The galvanometer will then show a deflection to the opposite side. If however the point Y is at exactly the same potential as X, no current will flow in the circuit of the test cell so the galvanometer will register no deflection. When this point Y is found, such that the galvanometer registers no deflection, then the potential difference between A and Y on the resistance wire is equal to the potential difference between A and X on the test cell circuit. Since no current is passing through the test cell, this latter potential difference is in fact equal to the e.m.f. of the test cell.

If $AY = L$ cm when the galvanometer deflection is zero, then

$$E = I \times \rho \times L$$

The e.m.f. of a cell can thus be balanced against the fall in potential along a uniform current-carrying resistance wire. Let us employ this principle in the determination of the e.m.f. of a test cell.

The e.m.f. of such a test cell is usually determined in terms of the known e.m.f. of a standard cell, using the circuit illustrated in Fig. 9.20.

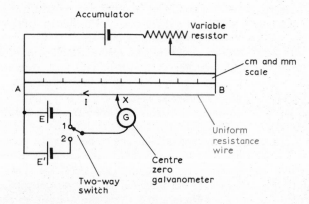

Fig.9.20 Determining the e.m.f. of a test cell in terms of the e.m.f. of a standard cell.

Let the e.m.f. of the test cell be E, and that of the standard cell be E'.

With the two-way switch at position 1, a balance point is found by moving the sliding contact X along the wire until the centre zero galvanometer registers a null deflection. Let us suppose that this balance point is at a distance L cm (as measured on the metre scale) from the point A. Then

$$E = I \times \rho \times L$$

where, as before, I and ρ are the assumed values of the current in the resistance wire and the resistance of this wire per cm length, respectively.

With the two-way switch at position 2, a balance point is then found following the same procedure for the standard cell. Let this balance point be measured on the scale as being L' cm from A. Then

$$E' = I \times \rho \times L'$$

Dividing the last two equations, it follows that

$$\frac{E}{E'} = \frac{L}{L'}$$

Hence
$$E = E' \times \frac{L}{L'}$$

Knowing the e.m.f. of the standard cell, the e.m.f. of the test cell can thus be calculated quite simply.

In performing such an investigation, it is essential that the current I flowing in the potentiometer wire should be steady in value. Otherwise the balance points will be liable to wander and thus difficult to determine accurately. For this reason it is advisable to use an accumulator rather than any other cell for the generation of the current I in the wire.

Why is it essential that the terminal potential difference of the accumulator should always be greater than the e.m.f. of the cell under test?

Can you suggest two reasons why the variable resistor might be inserted in the circuit diagram of Fig. 9.20?

What steps might you take to protect the galvanometer during the initial attempts to find a balance point?

Now we may consider an experiment to determine the internal resistance of a test cell. The experiment makes use of the circuit illustrated in Fig. 9.21. Suppose that the e.m.f. of the test cell is E, and that its internal resistance is r. A resistor of known resistance R is connected across the test cell through a switch as shown.

With this switch open, the sliding contact X is moved along the wire until the centre zero galvanometer registers a null deflection. Let the balance point thus achieved be at a distance L along the resistance wire from A. Then

$$E = I \times \rho \times L \quad \text{— in the usual notation.}$$

With the switch now closed, the sliding contact is again moved along the resistance wire until the meter registers a

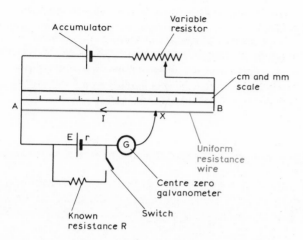

Fig.9.21 Determining the internal resistance of a test cell.

null deflection. Let this new balance point be at a distance L' from A. It will be found that $L' < L$ because, with the switch closed, the test cell is delivering current to an external circuit (in this case the resistance R) and so it is its terminal potential difference rather than its e.m.f. which is being balanced against the potential difference across a length of current-carrying resistance wire. Denoting the terminal potential difference of the cell by V, then

$$V = I \times \rho \times L'$$

Dividing the last two equations, we have

$$\frac{E}{V} = \frac{L}{L'}$$

If the current supplied by the test cell to the resistance R is i, then we may write

$$E = i(R + r)$$

and

$$V = iR$$

Hence

$$\frac{E}{V} = \frac{R + r}{R}$$

and so

$$\frac{R + r}{R} = \frac{L}{L'}$$

Thus

$$R + r = R \times \frac{L}{L'}$$

$$\Leftrightarrow r = \left(R \times \frac{L}{L'} \right) - R$$

That is

$$r = R\left(\frac{L}{L'} - 1\right)$$

Since the value of the resistor R is known, the internal resistance of the cell can easily be calculated.

Problems

1 A capacitor of capacitance 100 μF is charged to a potential of 25 V. What charge does it hold? If it is discharged in a time of 2 ms by connecting a piece of wire between the plates, what is the average current in the wire during this time?

2 What is the average current flowing in a wire if 10·8 C of charge pass a given point in 3 hours?

3 Three resistors, having resistances 8 Ω, 5 Ω, and 10 Ω, are connected in parallel in an electrical circuit. If the current in the 5 Ω resistor is 0·8 A, what are the currents flowing in the other two?

4 Four resistors are connected as shown in Fig. 9.22. What is the effective resistance across (i) AC (ii) AD?

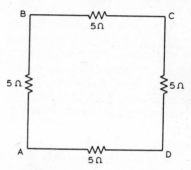

Fig.9.22 See Problem 4.

5 Two resistors connected in parallel have an effective resistance of 10 Ω. When connected in series, their effective resistance is 72 Ω. What are their values?

6 A lamp carrying a current of 0·5 A is immersed in 0·2 kg of water at 20 °C, and after one minute the temperature of the water is 26 °C. Stating your assumptions, find the potential difference between the terminals of the lamp. (The specific heat capacity of water is 4200 J kg⁻¹ °C⁻¹.)

7 The following table shows a list of household appliances, their power ratings, and the average time for which they are used each day. If the cost of electricity is 2·9p for each of the first 124 units consumed, and 0·8p for each unit thereafter, calculate the cost of operating these appliances for 90 days.

Appliance	Cooker	Immersion Heater	Kettle	T.V.	Fire
Power rating (kW)	10	3	2	0·2	3
time in use (hours)	2	2	1	5	6

8 Equation 9.9 is often referred to as Ohm's Law for a complete circuit; why?

9 A current of 0·25 A is drawn from a cell when a resistance of 4 Ω is connected across the terminals. When this resistance is replaced by one of 10 Ω the current falls to 0·125 A. What is the e.m.f. of the cell?

10 When a platinum resistance thermometer is included in the circuit shown in Fig. 9.23, and immersed in water at 0 °C, the ammeter reads 5 mA. The thermometer is then immersed in hot oil and the current in the circuit falls to 3 mA. Calculate the temperature of the oil, given that the resistance of the platinum coil at temperature θ °C (R_θ) is related to its resistance at 0 °C (R_0) by the equation

$$R_\theta = R_0(1 + 0\cdot0038 \times \theta)$$

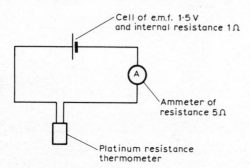

Cell of e.m.f. 1·5 V and internal resistance 1 Ω

Ammeter of resistance 5 Ω

Platinum resistance thermometer

Fig.9.23 See Problem 9.

11 In the bridge circuit shown in Fig. 9.24 the resistors in the arms have the values shown. Show that when the meter registers no current, $q = \sqrt{p \times r}$. Show further, that when this is achieved, the current drawn from the battery is given by I where

$$I = \frac{2(p + 2q + r)}{(p + q)(q + r)}$$

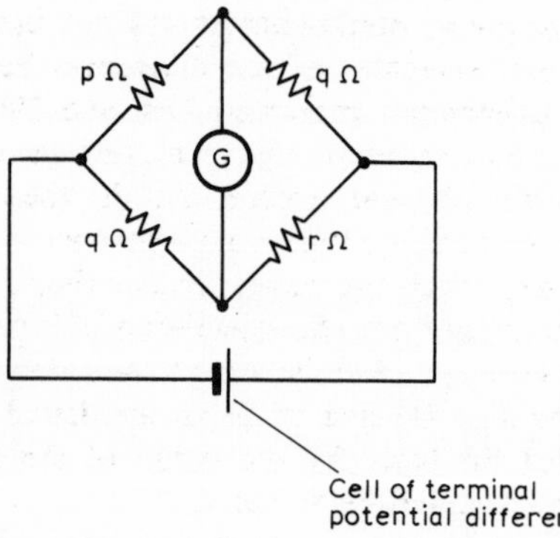

p Ω   q Ω

G

q Ω   r Ω

Cell of terminal potential difference 2 V

Fig.9.24 See Problem 11.

12 The circuit of Fig. 9.25 is used to find the internal resistance of the test cell labelled E. A 75 cm length of potentiometer wire is required to balance the e.m.f of the test cell alone, while a 70 cm length is required to balance the potential difference between the terminals of the cell when a 10 Ω resistor is connected across the cell. What is the internal resistance of the cell?

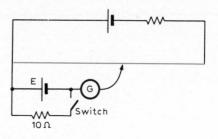

E

G

Switch

10 Ω

Fig.9.25 See Problem 12.

Chapter 10

Electromagnetism

Fig.10.0 The Cruachan 'pumped-storage' hydro-electric scheme. (By kind permission of the North of Scotland Hydro-Electric Board.)

Most of us have some knowledge regarding magnets and their effects—this knowledge being derived perhaps from childhood experience with magnetic toys, or from studying the basic properties of magnets in the early school years. We are perhaps already acquainted with the facts that the naturally occurring black oxide of iron called magnetite (Fe_3O_4) has the ability to attract unmagnetised iron or steel, and that such a piece of steel, after being held close to or being rubbed by a piece of magnetite, can itself become a fairly permanent magnet. We may know that, when a bar magnet is immersed in iron filings and then removed, the filings tend to cling to the ends or *poles* of the magnet. Further, a bar magnet when floated on a cork in water will always rotate until one pole (called the *North pole*—denoted by N) points northwards, and the other pole (called the *South pole*—denoted by S) points southwards. And perhaps most fascinating of all, like magnetic poles repel each other while unlike poles attract each other.

A knowledge of such elementary magnetic properties in no way suggests any connection between magnetic and electric phenomena however and Sir William Gilbert (about 1580) had been among the first to emphasise the striking *differences* between these phenomena. The main difference was that static electric charges interacted only with each other as did static magnetic poles; static charges did not interact with static poles. An awareness of the differences between the two types of phenomena prompted 17th and 18th century investigators to develop electricity and magnetism as separate disciplines within physical science, but in these separate developments it was noted that some experimentally derived laws looked very much the same whether they referred to electricity or to magnetism. So scientists of this period were faced with a seeming contradiction. It was not until 1820 that Hans Christian Oersted made an accidental discovery which provided the basis for the union of electricity and magnetism into a composite discipline.

Oersted happened to place a current-carrying wire parallel to a small pivoted compass needle, and quite unexpectedly observed the needle to rotate until it was at right angles to the wire. When he reversed the sense of current flow in the wire, the needle again took up a direction at right angles to the wire, but this time pointing in the opposite sense. Oersted's discovery is usually referred to as accidental in as much as it is believed that he was actually intending to demonstrate the lack of interaction between an electric current and a magnet. Following his discovery, however, there began a feverish campaign of research into this new branch of physics by many of the eminent physicists of that time.

10.1 The Magnetic Field of an Electric Current

It is evident from the results of Oersted's experiment that a magnetic field is generated in the region of a current-carrying wire—the direction of this field being constant but its sense being dependent on the sense in which current flows in the wire. Following Oersted's experiment, the French physicist Ampère investigated the shape of this magnetic field and found it to encircle the wire carrying the current responsible for it. Ampère's result may be verified by using the apparatus of Fig. 10.1(a).

The small power pack can supply either direct current (d.c.) or alternating current (a.c.), depending on which of its terminals are selected. In this experiment, a stout piece of copper wire is connected to the d.c. terminals of the pack such that an electron current will flow in the upward sense relative to a piece of cardboard which has been fixed with its plane at right angles to the direction of the wire. (The power supply has a sufficiently high internal resistance to allow a continuous short circuit current to flow—as in this case—

without any damage resulting to the unit due to overloading.)

With no current in the wire, the needles of the little plotting compasses all point in the north-south direction. When the current is switched on, however, the needles arrange themselves in a circular formation, all pointing in the same sense. This sense is reversed if the sense of the current flow is reversed. The experiment suggests therefore that the current-carrying wire is surrounded by effective circular lines of magnetic force in its immediate vicinity.

The distribution of these effective lines of force can also be demonstrated by removing the plotting compasses from the platform, and sprinkling the platform with fine iron filings. When the current is switched on and the platform tapped gently, the filings arrange themselves in concentric circles round the wire.

The sense of the effective lines of magnetic force relative to the sense and direction of the electron flow can be recalled conveniently in terms of Ampère's 'left hand rule' for a straight current-carrying conductor. This rule states that when the conductor is grasped in the left hand with the thumb extended in the sense of flow of the electron current, the fingers will then encircle the conductor pointing in the same sense as that of the effective lines of magnetic force. The rule is represented diagrammatically in Fig. 10.1(b).

When a current-carrying wire is wound in the form of a long circular coil, then a magnetic field can be detected in and round the coil by the directions of plotting compass needles—the plotting compasses being placed on a horizontal card through which the coil has been wound, as in Fig. 10.2. The

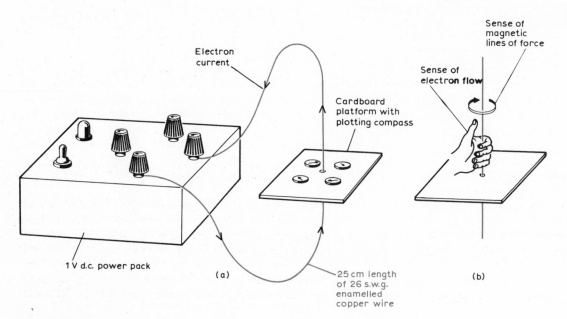

Fig.10.1 Investigating the magnetic field around a straight current-carrying wire.

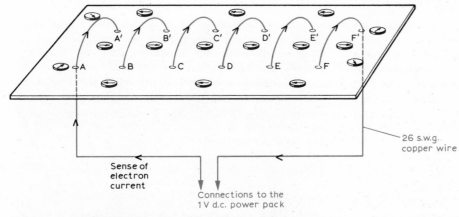

Fig.10.2   Investigating the magnetic field in and around a current-carrying coil. '

needles assume the pattern shown in Fig. 10.2 only for as long as current flows in the coil. The sense of the pattern is reversed if the sense of flow of the electron current is reversed.

The pattern assumed by the compass needles can be explained by applying Ampère's left hand rule to those small elements of the coil which are at right angles to the plane of the card—that is, the small elements emerging from and entering the holes at ABCDEF and A'B'C'D'E'F' respectively. The field round each such element is circular and in a plane at right angles to the element—that is in the plane of the card. It is perhaps fairly obvious that the total magnetic field within the circular coil due to the contributions of all current elements must be three dimensional in form. By placing a card in the coil, we have sampled the magnetic field in one plane only.

When a second piece of cardboard is placed over a small bar magnet, and plotting compasses placed on the card, the needles of the compasses are observed to assume the same pattern as those in Fig. 10.2, so that the magnetic field pattern surrounding the bar magnet appears similar to that shown in Fig. 10.3.

It would seem therefore that, when a coil of wire is carrying a current, a magnetic field similar to that of a bar magnet is set up in the vicinity of the coil, so that the coil is provided with an effective north pole at one end, and an effective south pole at the other end. The 'existence' of such poles may be verified by setting up the apparatus shown in Fig. 10.4. It is found that the bar magnet is either attracted into or repelled out of the air space of the coil—depending on the sense of the electron current supplied to the coil.

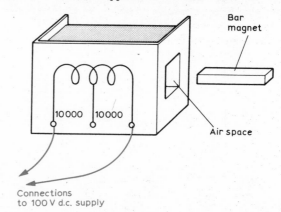

Fig.10.4   Demonstrating the existence of magnetic poles in a current-carrying coil.

Consideration of the diagrams in Fig. 10.2 and 10.3 would seem to suggest that an effective north pole has been formed at the right hand side of the coil in Fig. 10.2. The position of the effective north pole set up within a current-carrying coil can be remembered in relation to the sense of flow of the electron current in the coil in terms of a second 'left hand rule'. If we imagine the coil to be grasped in the left hand

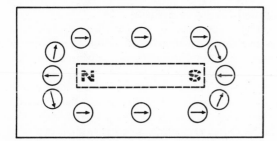

Fig.10.3   The magnetic field of a bar magnet.

with the fingers curled and pointing in the sense of flow of the electron current, then the thumb when extended will point to the position of the effective north pole. This rule is represented diagrammatically in Fig. 10.5. It is sometimes referred to as Ampère's left hand rule for a coil or solenoid.

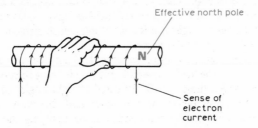

Fig.10.5   Ampere's left hand rule for a current-carrying coil.

It is found that when a bar of unmagnetised iron is placed within a current-carrying coil, then the bar becomes magnetised—a pole being formed at each end—for as long as current is maintained in the coil. The strength of this *electromagnet* depends on the type of iron inserted in the coil (soft iron being more suitable than cast iron), the number of turns of wire on each cm length of the coil, and on the size of the current flowing in the coil. It is possible to construct a strong electromagnet with a small electric current strength provided a large number of turns are present in the coil

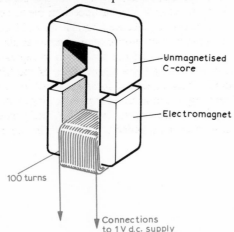

Fig.10.6   A demonstration electromagnet.

A demonstration electromagnet may be constructed by winding say 100 turns of 26 s.w.g. copper wire round a laminated C-core, and connecting the ends of the wire to the 1 V d.c. terminals of the small power pack. Although the electromagnet once constructed will lift a wide variety of iron or steel objects, its strength is only truly realised when a second unmagnetised C-core is brought up close, as in Fig. 10.6, and allowed to make contact. Considerable effort is then required to separate the cores (Fig. 10.7).

Fig.10.7

10.2 The Current-carrying Conductor in an External Magnetic Field

In Oersted's experiment, a wire fixed between two posts was positioned above and parallel to a pivoted compass needle. When current was passed in the wire, the needle rotated until it was directed at right angles to the direction of the wire. Presumably the current in the wire had caused a magnetic force to be exerted on the compass needle. According to Newton's third law, an equal and opposite magnetic force should have been exerted on the wire by the compass needle, but because the wire was fixed, it showed no motion. It seems likely that had the wire been free to rotate and the compass needle been fixed, then the wire would have rotated relative to the compass needle whenever current was flowing.

Since the compass needle is small magnet, it seems likely that there exists the possibility for the motion of a current-carrying conductor whenever it is introduced to the field of a fixed magnet. This prediction can be tested on setting up the apparatus shown in Fig. 10.8.

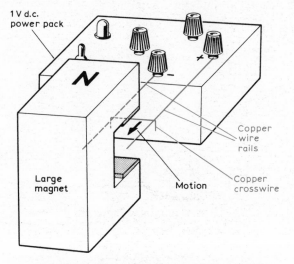

Fig.10.8   The motion of a current-carrying conductor in an external magnetic field.

Three pieces of 26 s.w.g. copper wire are stripped bare and arranged as shown, connections being made to the 1 V d.c. terminals of the small power pack. When the current is switched on and a strong magnetic field introduced (provided by an "Eclipse Major" magnet), the cross wire is observed to move along the 'rails' in the sense shown in the diagram. When the sense of either the current or the magnetic field is reversed, the sense of motion of the cross wire is also reversed.

The diagram in Fig. 10.9(a) relates the sense of motion of the cross wire, the sense of electron current flow in the cross wire, and the sense of the magnetic field, all to a three dimensional set of rectangular axes. Conveniently, we may relate these three senses by the use of a right hand rule, illustrated in Fig. 10.9(b). The thumb and first two fingers of the right hand are opened and held at right angles to each other, forming a right handed set of axes, each element being ascribed one particular sense.

Given the sense and direction of each of the electron current in a wire and the field into which this wire is being introduced, then provided these two are directed at right angles to each other, we may determine the sense and direction of the subsequent motion of the conductor by applying the right hand rule.

It is found that when a current carrying wire is introduced to a magnetic field, the size of the force which it experiences, F say, is proportional to the size of the current in the wire, I say, the density of the effective lines of magnetic force, B say, and to the length of the wire actually present in the magnetic field, L say. By a suitable choice of units, we may write

$$F = I \times B \times L$$

It is perhaps an interesting exercise to perform vector addition regarding the densities of effective lines of magnetic force for each of the current carrying wire and the external magnetic field into which it was introduced in the last experiment. The net pattern of effective magnetic lines of force may help us to understand why motion should occur at all.

In Fig. 10.10(a), lines of force are drawn to represent the uniform field as existing between the poles of the 'Eclipse' magnet. In Fig. 10.10(b), lines of force are drawn surrounding a current-carrying wire in which current is flowing in the sense out of the plane of the paper. In Fig. 10.10(c), these two field patterns have been added vectorially—in the loosest

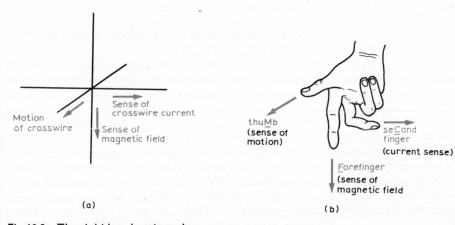

(a)

(b)

Fig.10.9   The right hand motor rule.

possible sense of the word, since neither of the magnitudes of the external magnetic field strength and electron current have been stated.

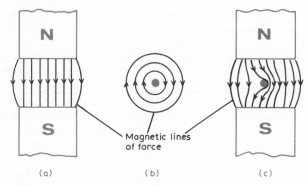

Fig.10.10 The interaction of magnetic fields.

Since the wire would in fact be projected out of the external magnetic field horizontally and in the sense right to left—according to the right hand rule—it would seem that the distorted lines of force to the right of the wire in Fig. 10.10(c) act as do rubber bands in a catapult. The increased density of lines in deformation shows or implies the presence of potential energy stored in the magnetic field. Further, this energy is transformed into kinetic energy of the wire (assuming the magnet to be fixed) if the wire is free to move within the field.

10.3 Applications of the Motor Effect
Having discussed and analysed the force exerted by a magnetic field on a straight current carrying wire, we now consider two simple devices which operate according to this motor effect. These devices are the moving coil meter, and the d.c. motor.

1. The Moving Coil Meter
The moving coil meter is essentially an instrument used for the detection and measurement of electric current. Its main features are illustrated in the diagram in Fig. 10.11. In such a meter, a small coil of fine copper wire wound on a light aluminium former is mounted so that it can rotate about a vertical axis between the poles of a permanent magnet. The jewel bearings, between which the coil is pivoted, provide minimal frictional resistance to its rotation and also allow the instrument to operate in any position.

When the current under test is introduced to the instrument, equal and opposite forces are exerted on the vertical sides of the coil and so it rotates about the vertical axis in the clockwise sense. This rotation can be deduced by applying the right hand rule to each vertical side of the coil in turn—taking the sense of current flow as downward in the near side of the coil, and upward in the far side, as indicated in the diagram.

The rotation of the coil is increasingly opposed however by the coiling of a pair of hairsprings (which also act as current leads), until an equilibrium is achieved between the forces of magnetic interaction on the coil on one hand, and the forces of opposition of the hairsprings on the other. The pointer is then stationary at some point on the scale.

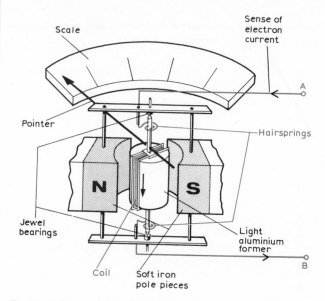

Fig.10.11 The construction of the moving coil meter.

Since the soft-iron pole pieces attached to the permanent magnet are cylindrical, the coil in rotating encounters a magnetic field which is everywhere uniform and at right angles to its vertical sides. The side thrusts on the coil are therefore always perpendicular to its plane, and of the same magnitude for a given steady current. This means that the final angular deflection of the coil, as recorded on the scale by the position of the pointer, is directly proportional to the current in the coil. The scale of the meter is therefore linear; that is, equal changes in current produce equal changes in deflection.

Obviously the coil and its leads obey Ohm's Law since they are metallic conductors. This being the case, the current which flows in the coil at any time will be proportional to the potential difference between the input terminals A and B. In other words, the deflection of the pointer of the instrument is not only proportional to the current flowing in the instrument, but also to the potential difference between its terminals. For this reason, it is possible to calibrate the instrument for use as a voltmeter as well as an ammeter.

An ammeter is an instrument which is inserted in series in a circuit so as to provide for the measurement of current in that circuit. Obviously its resistance must be as low as possible in order that its introduction in the circuit should result in the least possible interference with the current already flowing in the circuit. When we realise that the resistance of the moving coil may be of the order of 20 Ω, and further, that it is wound of very fine gauge wire which would melt quickly if a current of the order of one or two amp were introduced, it seems that the moving coil meter is severely limited in its possible application. However, by inserting a very low resistance in parallel with the coil, it is possible to reduce the effective resistance of the instrument considerably, and further, to render it capable of accepting a large current (of the order of one or two amps). Most of such a large current would then bypass the delicate coil through the shunt resistance, only a small, but representative fraction of the total current flowing in the meter coil, thereby activating the instrument. The reading on the instrument can then be taken as representative of the total current in the system.

By way of example, let us consider the possibility of converting a typical moving coil meter for use as a low resistance ammeter capable of recording currents up to 5 A. Let us suppose that the resistance of the coil is 20 Ω and that the pointer shows a full scale deflection when a current of 5 mA flows in the coil. The diagram in Fig. 10.12 shows the meter with a low resistance *shunt* in parallel with it. A current of 5 A flows through the meter shunt combination, and so if this is to cause a full scale deflection of the pointer, 5 mA must flow in the coil, and 4·995 A in the shunt. Let the resistance of the shunt be R.

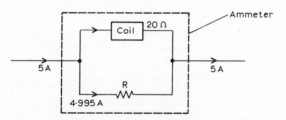

Fig.10.12 Converting the moving coil meter for use as an ammeter.

Since the potential difference across each of the shunt and the meter coil is the same, then according to Ohm's Law,

$$0·005 \times 20 = 4·995 \times R$$

$$\Leftrightarrow R = 0·02 \ \Omega \quad \text{to a close approximation}$$

That is, in order that a current of 5 A should cause the meter to register a full scale deflection, a shunt of resistance 0·02 Ω would have to be connected in parallel with the meter.

We have said already that when a low resistance shunt is connected in parallel with the meter coil, the resistance of the whole instrument is considerably less than that of the coil alone. The resistance of the ammeter as a whole can be calculated as R', say, where

$$\frac{1}{R'} = \frac{1}{0·02} + \frac{1}{20}$$

$$\Leftrightarrow R' = 0·02 \ \Omega \quad \text{to a close approximation}$$

The meter and shunt combination thus provides us with a very low resistance instrument requiring a fairly large current for its full scale deflection.

What total current would be flowing in the circuit in which the meter and shunt combination was inserted if the meter deflection was observed to be 2 mA?

In contrast to an ammeter, a voltmeter is an instrument which is inserted between two points in a circuit in such a way as to be in parallel with any component which may connect them. Its presence enables the potential difference between the two points to be determined. When the moving coil meter which we have been discussing shows a full scale deflection, the potential difference between its terminals is very small; 0·1 V in fact for a current of 0·005 A flowing in the 20 Ω coil. If we were to connect the meter between two points across which the potential difference was of the order of volts, the meter, because of its comparatively low coil resistance, would draw more current than the coil could sustain. To complicate the issue further, the drawing of a fairly large current by the meter—assuming that it could sustain such a current—would alter the total flow of current in the circuit, and hence alter the potential difference between the two points in question.

The problem can be solved however by connecting a large resistance in series with the meter so that current flowing in the meter is kept at a sufficiently low value whenever the combination of meter and resistance is connected between two given points in a circuit. Further, because the instrument now has a high resistance as a whole, its connection across a circuit component (whose resistance we can regard as being very low in comparison) should have very little effect on the effective resistance of that component, so that the current in the circuit is almost unaffected. This being the case, the potential difference across the component will be almost unaffected by the introduction of the voltmeter—as required.

By way of example, let us consider the conversion of the moving coil meter of the last example for use as a voltmeter capable of recording potential differences up to 5 V so that a full scale deflection of the meter pointer will correspond to the existence of a potential difference of 5 V between the terminals of the modified instrument; that is, across the combination of meter and high resistance.

The diagram in Fig. 10.13 shows the meter and a high resistance or *multiplier* in series with it—this resistance being of such a value that when a potential difference of 5 V is applied between the combination, the meter shows a full scale deflection. That is, the value of the resistance will be chosen such that a current of 5 mA will flow in the meter and multiplier whenever a potential difference of 5 V exists across their series combination. Let the value of the multiplier required be R''.

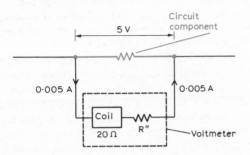

Fig.10.13 Converting the moving coil meter for use as a voltmeter.

Since a potential difference of 5 V is to exist across the coil and multiplier for a current of 5 mA flowing in each, then according to Ohm's Law,

$$5 = (0{\cdot}005 \times 20) + (0{\cdot}005 \times R'')$$
$$= 0{\cdot}005(20 + R'')$$
$$\Leftrightarrow R'' + 20 = 1000$$
$$\Leftrightarrow R'' = 980 \ \Omega$$

Hence, by connecting a resistance of 980 Ω in series with the moving coil meter, we have produced an instrument which is capable of recording potential differences of up to 5 V. The resistance of the voltmeter as a whole is 1000 Ω and it draws a current of only 0·005 A when the potential difference between its terminals is 5 V. Such an instrument is particularly useful when we wish to measure accurately the potential difference between the ends of a circuit component of low resistance—that is $\ll 1000 \ \Omega$.

2. The d.c. Motor

The simple electric motor is illustrated in principle in the diagram of Fig. 10.14. This diagram shows a rectangular loop of wire mounted on a horizontal spindle so that it may be rotated between the curved pole pieces of a permanent magnet. The ends of the loop are permanently connected to the two halves of a copper split ring or *commutator* against which two spring loaded carbon *brushes* are caused to press lightly. It is found that when a cell is connected to the brushes as shown, the coil rotates in the clockwise sense.

The sense of rotation may be deduced by considering the loop to be lying horizontally when the current is first switched on. Applying the right hand rule we see that side AB is caused to move upward and side CD downward. The loop therefore begins to rotate clockwise. When it completes one quarter of a revolution, it is in the vertical plane and the brushes are no longer in contact with the commutator

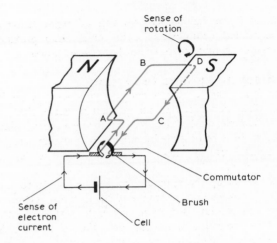

Fig.10.14 The d.c. motor.

segments. The momentum of the loop acquired during this quarter cycle carries it beyond the vertical position however, so that the brushes then come in contact with the opposite commutator segments. Side CD is then forced to move upward, and side AB downward. The rotation of the loop thus continues for as long as current is supplied.

A d.c. motor when constructed using components from the laboratory electromagnetic kit (Fig. 10.15), is neither powerful nor efficient. Improvements in its performance are observed when many loops of wire are wound rather than one loop, when the supply current is increased in strength, and when the strength of the magnet is also increased. Each of these possible improvements is considerably limited however, so that the simple laboratory motor can never reach the standards required in heavy industrial practice.

Fig.10.15 A simple laboratory d.c. motor. (Can you label its parts?)

In larger and more successful motors, a horizontally mounted soft-iron cylinder serves as an armature and it is provided with a series of longitudinal slots into which coils of wire are wound—each coil having its own pair of segments on a multi-segmented commutator. This elaboration provides for a smooth running motor of much increased power.

10.4 Electromagnetic Induction

Having found that a current-carrying conductor is set in motion when introduced to an external magnetic field, it seems reasonable to ask if the process is in any way reversible. That is, might it be possible by moving a conductor relative to a magnetic field to generate or induce current to flow in that conductor?

When we set up the apparatus shown in Fig. 10.16 and move the bar magnet down into the 10 000 turn coil, the meter registers a momentary deflection. When the magnet is withdrawn from the coil, a momentary deflection of the meter is again observed, but this time in the opposite sense. No deflection of the meter is observed while the magnet is held stationary inside the coil.

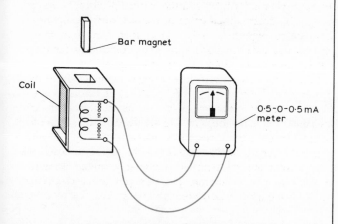

Fig.10.16 Demonstrating electromagnetic induction.

When this investigation is repeated with a 20 000 turn coil, the results follow the same pattern except that the momentary meter deflections are somewhat larger. It is also found that larger meter deflections may be produced either by introducing two magnets (bound together as in Fig. 10.17) to the coil rather than one, or by moving a single magnet into or out of a given coil at greater speed.

Fig.10.17 A greater induction effect is achieved using a stronger magnet.

(Although in these experiments the magnet has been moving relative to a stationary coil, exactly the same results are obtained if the coil is moved relative to a stationary magnet, so that the relative motion between the two is the same as before. The induced electrical effect is apparently dependent on the *relative motion* of circuit and magnet rather than on the particular motion of either.)

We have shown therefore that current may be induced to flow in a circuit whenever that circuit is in relative motion to an external magnetic influence. It is more correct however to say that an *e.m.f.* has been induced in the circuit, because the induced current can be altered in size by altering the resistance of the circuit. Provided the size of the circuit, strength of the magnet, and speed of relative motion are all held constant, it is found that the product of induced current and circuit resistance is always the same—that is, the same e.m.f. is generated when the same size of circuit is moved relative to the same magnet and at the same speed, regardless of the resistance of that circuit.

When discussing the principle of the induced e.m.f., the essential point to be borne in mind is that such an e.m.f. is generated if, and only if, the electrical circuit and the magnetic influence are in relative motion. This point is further demonstrated when we set up the apparatus shown in Fig. 10.18.

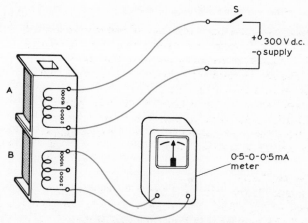

Fig.10.18 Demonstrating electromagnetic induction using the magnetic field of a current-carrying coil.

On closing the switch S, the meter registers a momentary deflection. On opening the switch, the meter again registers a momentary deflection, but this time in the opposite sense.

These results may be understood when we consider that in closing the switch, the current in coil A increases quickly but not instantaneously to its steady value. The magnetic field of this current thus grows in intensity round coil A and since this growth implies a certain change or movement of magnetic influence relative to coil B, then it is quite reasonable to expect an induced current to flow in B. When the current in A has reached its final steady value, so too has its associated magnetic field. Since this magnetic field is then no longer changing, no further current is induced to flow in B. When the switch is re-opened, the current in coil A decays and so too does its associated magnetic field. This changing of the magnetic influence relative to coil B then gives rise to an induced e.m.f. and hence a current in B.

The investigation may be extended by closing the switch and then lifting coil A clear of coil B. The meter registers a momentary deflection because the magnetic field of coil A is being moved relative to coil B. When coil A is replaced on coil B, the meter again registers a momentary deflection, but this time in the opposite sense. These momentary meter deflections may be increased in size by increasing the speed at which the coils are separated or replaced.

The principle of the induced e.m.f. was discovered almost simultaneously, but quite independently, by Faraday and Henry, although the credit is generally given to Faraday (Fig. 10.19). Henry alone discovered that while the current in a coil is increasing, (after the switch connecting it to a cell has been closed) an e.m.f. is induced in the same coil acting in the opposite sense. The effect of this e.m.f. is to prolong the time required for the current to reach a steady value. Further, when the current in a coil is decreasing (after the switch connecting it to a cell has been opened), a small e.m.f. is induced in the coil in the same sense as the decaying current— thereby prolonging the time required for it to reach its zero value. In the experiment of Fig. 10.18 we were able to demonstrate the *mutual inductance* arising between two coils in close proximity, but in terms of Henry's work, it would seem that any coil has a certain *self inductance*. The self inductance of a coil can be understood to some extent by considering that when the current in a coil is changing (for example growing), the associated changing (growing) magnetic field implies magnetic movement relative to the coil which in turn implies the induction of an e.m.f. and hence a change in the current in the coil.

Fig.10.19 (By kind permission of the Science Museum, London. Neg no 64163.)

That the self-induced current in a coil tends to flow in a sense which tends to oppose the change causing it, illustrates a particular instance of the more general Lenz's Law. Lenz was a Russian physicist who, while investigating electromagnetic phenomena at the same time as Faraday and Henry, deduced a law as equally important in electromagnetic theory as the Faraday principle of the induced e.m.f. Lenz's Law is itself a recognition of the principle of conservation of energy in the context of electromagnetic induction, and it states that the *sense* of the induced e.m.f., and hence of the current is always such as to ensure that its own magnetic field opposes the motion or change causing it.

As an illustration let us consider the apparatus shown in Fig. 10.20.

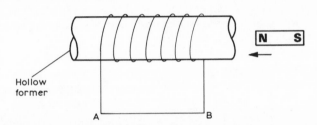

Fig.10.20 The sense of the induced e.m.f. is such as to oppose the motion causing it.

If the bar magnet is thrust inside the coil former as shown, then, according to Lenz's Law, current must be induced to flow in the coil in such a sense as to oppose the motion causing it. That is, current must flow in such a sense as to generate an effective north pole at the right hand end of the coil. According to our earlier left hand rule for a coil, current would therefore be induced to flow in the sense B to A. This sense of induced current flow is found to be correct if a sensitive ammeter is inserted between A and B. Can you explain, with reference to Lenz's Law, why the current induced in the coil flows in the opposite sense whenever the magnet is withdrawn from the coil former?

In terms of the conservation of energy, it is obvious that work is required to transfer the magnet from outside the former into the former, and that this work appears somehow as energy of the induced current flowing in the coil. If the current were induced in such a sense that an effective south pole was created at the right hand end of the coil, then the magnet would be attracted into the coil and so move faster relative to the coil, thereby inducing a larger current in the coil and hence a larger magnetic field which would attract the magnet inside with an even greater force so that a still larger current would be induced in the coil, the whole process building up and up. This process would therefore be self-perpetuating and a huge current would be induced in the coil with no work being done by an outside agent—clearly a violation of the principle of conservation of energy.

Lenz's Law proves to be most useful in the explanation of the phenomenon of *eddy currents*, which usually gives rise to embarrassing and unwanted energy losses in certain electromagnetic induction processes. Eddy currents may be identified as regards their effect using the apparatus illustrated in Fig. 10.21(a). A triangular aluminium plate supported on a relatively frictionless horizontal axis, is set swinging with its lower edge in the region between the poles of a powerful magnet. It is found that the plate rarely executes more than one complete oscillation—it behaves as if moving in a highly viscous fluid. Such damped motion can largely be eliminated however by cutting the lower edge of the pendulum as in Fig. 10.21(b).

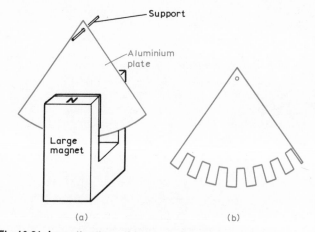

Fig.10.21 Investigating eddy current damping.

The damping effect may be explained when we consider that the plate, in swinging, is moving relative to the magnetic influence, and so, according to the Faraday principle, induced currents will be caused to flow within the plate. Each of these currents will have its own associated magnetic field which according to Lenz's Law will interact with the field of the large magnet in such a way as to oppose the motion responsible for the induction. These currents are envisaged as flowing in small loops within the metal—the sense of current flow in any given loop being such as to produce effective magnetic poles in the metal which will interact with the external magnetic poles so as to bring motion to a halt as quickly as possible. Thus in the diagram of Fig. 10.22 (in which two eddy current loops are shown), the left hand loop has that current sense which generates an effective north pole on the nearside of the metal, thereby opposing the motion of that part of the metal into the magnetic field. The right hand loop however has that current sense which generates an effective south pole on the nearside of the metal, thereby opposing the motion of that part of the metal out of the magnetic field. This kind of interference between the effective poles due to the eddy current loops and the actual poles of the permanent

magnet is such as to bring the motion to an abrupt end.

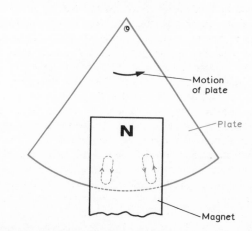

Fig.10.22 Typical eddy current loops.

Although the induced e.m.f. is usually quite small, the eddy currents may themselves be very large since they are induced in a solid sheet of conductor whose resistance will be quite small. These large eddy currents react strongly with the permanent magnetic field so that a large damping effect is produced. Eddy currents are normal induced currents produced in sheets or blocks of metal instead of in a piece of wire.

By cutting the lower edge of the plate as in Fig. 10.21(b) much of the metal available for the induction of eddy currents is removed so that the eddy current damping is reduced to a more acceptable level.

10.5 The Production of Alternating Current

The principle of the induced e.m.f. is fundamental to our present day large scale programme of electricity production and distribution. This principle, by which mechanical energy may be transferred into electric energy, is in many respects far superior to that by which chemical energy is converted to electric energy.

Our domestic electricity supply is of the alternating current (a.c.) type as opposed to the direct current (d.c.) type which we discussed in Chapter 9. The generation of a.c. electricity is achieved by a device known as an alternator in which a coil or loop of wire rotates about a horizontal axis which is perpendicular to a uniform magnetic field. The ends of the coil are connected to slip rings which are concentric with the axis of the coil and rotate with it, but are insulated from each other. Spring loaded brushes bearing against these rings connect the coil to the load which is required to be supplied with electricity. The alternator thus appears as in Fig. 10.23. (Can you suggest several mechanical means by which the coil might be rotated?)

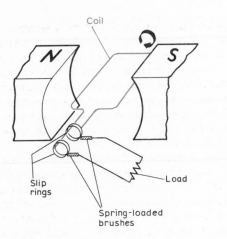

Fig.10.23 The alternator.

The photographs in Fig. 10.24 show the machines which have been installed in the Cruachan Hydro-Electric Scheme. These machines serve as water pumps as well as electricity generators (alternators), depending on the sense of the change-over switches.

(a)

Fig.10.24 (a) The Cruachan machine hall. (b) A model of one of the pump generator machines. (By kind permission of the North of Scotland Hydro-Electric Board.)

For a steady speed of rotation of the coil, the size of the e.m.f. induced in it varies sinusoidally with time, so that a graph of e.m.f. against time would take the form shown in Fig. 10.25. This e.m.f. applied to a resistive load would give rise to a current in that load such that this current would also vary sinusoidally with time.

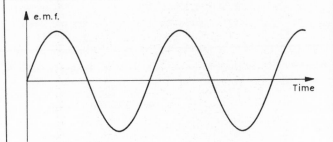

Fig.10.25 Alternating e.m.f. in relation to time.

The form of the graph of alternating e.m.f. against time may be checked by connecting the mains e.m.f. to the input terminals of an oscilloscope (an instrument which we shall consider in some detail in Chapter 12) as in Fig. 10.26. By suitable adjustment of the time base and stability controls,

(b)

he trace of alternating e.m.f. against time can be made to appear stationary.

Fig.10.26 The nature of the mains e.m.f.

A.c. electricity may be generated simply in the laboratory for the purpose of demonstration rather than consumption by setting up the apparatus illustrated in Fig. 10.27.

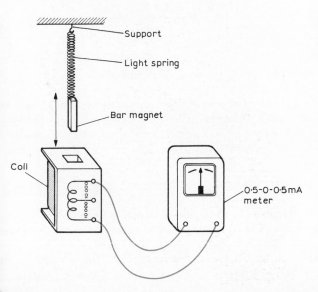

Fig.10.27 The production of low frequency alternating e.m.f.

A small bar magnet suspended on a light spring is made to oscillate along the axis of a large coil. The current induced

to flow in the coil is monitored on a sensitive centre zero ammeter. If the amplitude of oscillation of the magnet is the same on each side of the centre of the coil, the pointer of the meter is observed to move to one side of the scale, and then to the other side by an equal amount. This continues for as long as the oscillation of the magnet is continued. Can you explain why the pointer of the meter shows its maximum deflection (to one side or the other) when the magnet is passing through the central region of the coil?

The e.m.f. induced in the coil may be observed to be of a sinusoidal form in relation to time by connecting the terminals of the coil to the input terminals of an oscilloscope and making suitable adjustments to the time base and stability controls.

The frequency of this alternating e.m.f. is a function of the stiffness of the spring. Obviously a stiff spring will have a shorter period of vibration than a slack spring of the same dimensions, and so will give rise to an alternating e.m.f. of higher frequency than the latter. Although we can employ stiffer and stiffer springs, it would be somewhat impossible to generate large quantities of a.c. electricity at the frequency of the mains supply—50 Hz—by this laboratory approach.

An alternating e.m.f. generator is represented by the symbol —(~)— in circuit diagrams.

10.6 Transformers

We have already demonstrated the existence of mutual induction between two coils in close proximity. Let us suppose that two coils are placed as in Fig. 10.18, and that an alternating e.m.f. is applied between the terminals of one of the coils. It follows that the magnetic field within this coil will be continually changing. Since the coils are in close proximity, this continually changing magnetic field will be responsible for the induction of an alternating e.m.f. in the second coil. The size of this induced e.m.f. will of course depend on the size of the second coil, and so herein lies the possibility of transferring and transforming alternating e.m.f.'s from one coil or circuit to another. With the coils placed relative to each other as in Fig. 10.18, the process would be rather inefficient due to the leakage of the magnetic lines of force into the air surrounding the coils, but were we to arrange the coils on the same bar of iron, then the effect would be greatly enhanced since most of the magnetic lines of force would be contained within the volume of the iron—leaving only a very small leakage at the ends of the bar. The situation could be improved further by joining the ends of the bar by bending it into the form of a continuous loop.

Let us extend this discussion to the experimental situation.

The diagram in Fig. 10.28 shows two C-cores from the electromagnetic kit clipped together. On each core is wound 10 turns of 26 s.w.g. insulated copper wire. An alternating e.m.f. of 1 V is applied to one of the coils—called the primary—and a voltmeter capable of recording alternating e.m.f. is connected between the ends of the other coil—called the secondary. It is found that the size of the e.m.f. induced in the secondary is also 1 V! When the experiment is repeated for different numbers of turns in the primary and secondary coils, results similar to those in the following table are found.

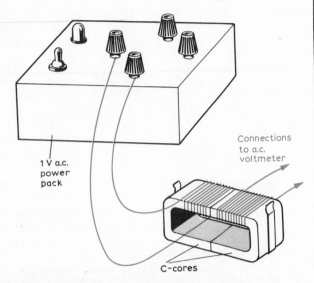

Fig.10.28 Investigating the properties of a transformer.

primary turns (N_p)	secondary turns (N_s)	turns ratio $\left(\dfrac{N_p}{N_s}\right)$	primary volts (E_p)	secondary volts (E_s)	volts ratio $\left(\dfrac{E_p}{E_s}\right)$
10	10	1	1	1	1
10	20	$\frac{1}{2}$	1	2	$\frac{1}{2}$
10	50	$\frac{1}{5}$	1	5	$\frac{1}{5}$
50	10	5	1	$\frac{1}{5}$	5

We see from this table that e.m.f. can either be 'stepped up' or 'stepped down' by adjusting the sizes of the windings of the primary and secondary coils of the apparatus. This apparatus is known as a *transformer* and is represented by the symbol shown in Fig. 10.29 in circuit diagrams.

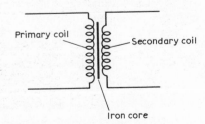

Fig.10.29 The symbol for an iron core transformer.

Also from the table of results we see that the ratio of

primary turns to secondary turns is exactly equal to the ratio of primary e.m.f. to secondary (induced) e.m.f. That is,

$$\boxed{\frac{N_p}{N_s} = \frac{E_p}{E_s}} \quad \ldots\ldots\ldots\ldots (10.1)$$

This may be explained by saying that, since a closed core is employed, a complete magnetic circuit exists, and this in turn almost guarantees that all of the primary magnetic field links the secondary coil. Because the same field links both primary and secondary coils, the same e.m.f. is induced per secondary turn as existed for each primary turn.

In actual fact however, not all of the primary magnetic field links the secondary coil, since not all of it is confined to the iron core—some of the field exists in the air surrounding the coil and core. The field which links both coils, by being contained within the core, is known as the mutual field or flux. That part linking only the primary coil is called the primary leakage field or flux, and that part linking only the secondary coil is called the secondary leakage field or flux. The diagram in Fig. 10.30 illustrates the instantaneous magnetic field patterns in a typical iron core transformer.

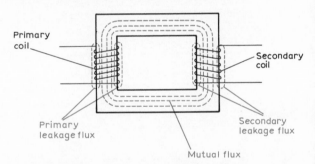

Fig.10.30 The flux patterns in a transformer core.

Although the transformer is a highly efficient device, it does suffer some energy losses between its input and output—one source of losses being that which we have just discussed in the form of leakage flux. Other sources of energy losses are:

1 Heat being developed in the windings of the coil as a result of the intrinsic resistance of the wire.
2 'Hysteresis'—energy losses resulting from the continuing reversal of the magnetic field within the core. This gives rise to some heating in the core.
3 The generation of eddy currents within the core. These currents take the form of closed loops and circulate in planes at right angles to the direction of the magnetic field. They waste energy by opposing the changes which cause them and so their reduction is of the utmost importance. This is achieved by laminating the core—the laminations taking the form of thin metal sheets with

insulating surfaces, constructed and set in planes parallel to the magnetic flux, so that the eddy currents generated are caused to flow at right angles to the laminations, thus having to cross many interfaces of high resistance which greatly reduce their magnitude.

Despite the energy losses which we have listed, the transformer is still a most efficient device. In general, transformer efficiences are usually well over 90 %, and some may reach as high as 99 %. Let us consider a perfect transformer in which there are no energy losses (this is almost the case for the very high efficiency transformers). If a load is connected across the secondary coil so that a current I_s flows in the secondary circuit, then we may write

energy generated in the primary circuit per second = energy generated in the secondary circuit per second

that is   primary power = secondary power

(a)

(b)

Hence $I_p \times E_p = I_s \times E_s$ where I_p is the primary current drawn when I_s flows in the secondary circuit. E_p and E_s as before.

Hence

$$\boxed{\frac{E_p}{E_s} = \frac{I_s}{I_p}}$$ .... (10.2)

It follows then that when we step up the e.m.f. using a transformer, we automatically step down the current. We are liable to think that by using a transformer we are in fact getting something for nothing when we consider its step up role for e.m.f.'s. The fact that current is simultaneously stepped down proves that there can be no power or energy gain with the transformer, or for that matter, with any machine.

The photographs in Fig. 10.31 show some practical transformers. Photograph (a) shows a small mains transformer with a multitude of secondary windings. Photograph (b) shows a laboratory demonstration transformer. Photograph (c) shows one of the main oil-immersed, water cooled transformers in the Cruachan Hydro-Electric Scheme.

(c)

Fig.10.31 (a) By kind permission of R. S. Components Ltd. (b) By kind permission of Philip Harris Ltd. (c) By kind permission of the North of Scotland Hydro-Electric Board.

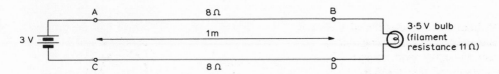

Fig.10.32 Transmitting low voltage d.c. electricity.

10.7 The Transmission of Electrical Energy

What has often been described as the 'victory' of a.c. electricity over d.c. electricity is that the former may be transformed from one voltage to another with a minimum loss of energy in the process. It was realised from an early stage that d.c. electricity was unsuitable for transportation over long distances if the project was to be economically viable. About 1890 however, electrical engineers realised that by using a.c. electricity and transformers, the electricity could be transformed to high voltage and then transmitted over long distances with a minimum loss of power. This implied that the long range transmission of electrical energy could be economically viable and so electricity could be manufactured wherever the necessary fuels such as coal or water were to be found. Let us investigate this discussion experimentally.

The circuit diagram of Fig. 10.32 represents some apparatus which may be used to simulate the transmission of d.c. electricity. The transmission lines consist of one metre lengths of 32 s.w.g. Eureka wire, and each has resistance 8 Ω. Such high resistance represents that which may be produced when very long lengths of good conducting material (such as copper) are used in transmitting practice. The bulb represents some distant electrical installation which is to be supplied with electricity.

It is found that when the circuit is completed, the bulb fails to light. That is, energy is not being transmitted satisfactorily over the long distance. The equivalent circuit of Fig. 10.32 is drawn in Fig. 10.33.

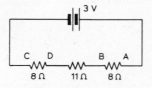

Fig.10.33 The equivalent circuit of Fig. 10.32.

The total resistance of the system we see is 27 Ω. The current flowing in the bulb is thus $\frac{1}{9}$ A, so the power being dissipated in the bulb is $\frac{11}{81}$ watt, or 0·136 watt. The power being developed at the source is ($\frac{1}{9} \times 3$) or $\frac{1}{3}$ watt—that is, 0·333 watt. It would seem therefore that more than half of the energy being developed at the source is being 'lost'—presumably in the form of heat in the transmission lines.

When the battery of cells in Fig. 10.32 is replaced by an alternating e.m.f. of 3 V, the same unsatisfactory results are to be found—that is, the bulb does not light.

On setting up the apparatus represented in Fig. 10.34 however, we find that the bulb lights fairly brightly. Let us attempt to analyse the success of this arrangement by assuming first of all that the source is generating electrical energy at the rate of 1 watt. If we assume further that both transformers are as near 100% efficient as makes little difference, then energy is being developed across the secondary coil of the step up transformer at the rate of 1 watt. Further, since the e.m.f. being developed across this secondary coil is 300 V (according to equation 10.1) then the current flowing in the transmission lines must be $\frac{1}{300}$ A. The potential difference developed across each of AB and CD will therefore be $\frac{8}{300}$ V or 0·027 V, and so the e.m.f. appearing across the primary coil of the step down transformer will be (300−0·054) V. That is, 299·946 V. The e.m.f. being developed across the secondary of the step down transformer is thus as near 3 V as makes little difference, and so the bulb is caused to light brightly.

We see therefore that by transmitting the electrical energy at high voltage, very little potential difference is developed across the transmission lines themselves, and so little energy is 'lost' in the form of heat being developed in these lines.

Exercise Repeat the last analysis assuming the transformers to be 90% efficient

In this country, electricity is generated at 11 000 V and then stepped up to 132 000 V for transmission on the grid system. In some areas of the country however, the step up

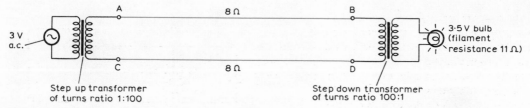

Fig.10.34 Transmitting a.c. electricity at high voltage.

voltage is at present 375 000 V, and it is intended that this 'super' grid voltage should eventually be in used throughout the whole country. The present 132 000 V grid voltage is stepped down in stages at the distant end first to 66 000 V, then to 6600 V, and finally to 240 V for domestic consumption.

Problems

1 Why is it essential that the ticker timer (described in Chapter 2) should be operated from an a.c. supply rather than from a d.c. supply?

2 The diagram in Fig. 10.35 illustrates the construction of an electric bell. Explain how its vibrational action is achieved using a d.c. supply.

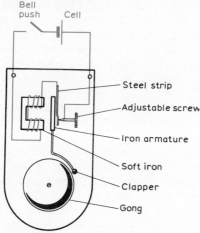

Fig.10.35 See Problem 2.

3 An ammeter has a coil resistance of $0 \cdot 1$ Ω and reads up to 1 A. How can it be converted to a voltmeter capable of reading up to 40 V?

4 A meter of coil resistance 30 Ω shows a full scale deflection for a current of 1 mA. How can this meter be converted to read currents up to 10 A? What is now the effective resistance of the meter?

5 The pointer of a meter of coil resistance 10 Ω registers 12 scale divisions when a current of 5 mA flows through the meter. How can this meter be adapted for use as a voltmeter in which one scale division corresponds to one volt?

6 A 600 Ω resistor and a 400 Ω resistor are connected in series across a 90 V supply. When a voltmeter is connected across the 400 Ω resistor, it records a potential difference of 30 V. What is the resistance of the voltmeter?

7 When the switch in the circuit shown in Fig. 10.36 is closed, the $3 \cdot 5$ V filament bulb glows but the neon bulb (which requires about 70 V to 'strike') doesn't. When the switch is opened however, the neon flashes for an instant. Explain why this should happen.

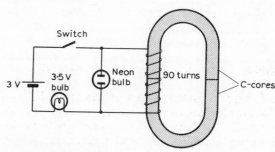

Fig.10.36 See Problem 7.

8 Aluminium is a metal which is normally unaffected by a magnet. Yet when an aluminium ring is suspended from a twisted fibre and the fibre allowed to untwist, so that the ring rotates, its rotation can be halted abruptly by bringing a powerful magnet up close to the ring. Why should this happen?

9 Why is transformer action impossible with d.c. electricity?

10 With reference to Fig. 10.37, discuss the readings on the centre zero voltmeter when the switch is closed and then re-opened.

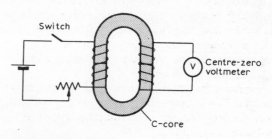

Fig.10.37 See Problem 10.

11 The diagram in Fig. 10.38 shows a simple transformer circuit. If the transformer is 100 % efficient, calculate
 i) the e.m.f. developed across the secondary circuit with the switch open.
 ii) the primary current when the switch is closed and a current of 4 A flows in the secondary circuit.

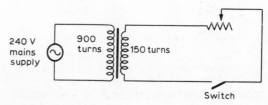

Fig.10.38 See Problem 11.

12 A 10 Ω heating coil is connected across the secondary coil of a step down transformer and immersed in 0·5 kg of paraffin as shown in Fig. 10.39. If the transformer is 100 % efficient calculate

   i) The e.m.f. developed between the ends of the coil.

   ii) The heat energy given to the paraffin per second.

   iii) The time required to raise the temperature of the paraffin by 5 °C assuming no heat losses to the surroundings and taking the specific heat capacity of paraffin as 2200 J kg^{-1} °C^{-1}.

   iv) The current flowing in the primary circuit of the transformer during heating.

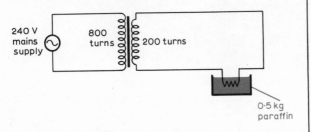

Fig.10.39 See Problem 12.

13 Electricity is generated at the rate of 1000 kW and at 250 V (a.c.) in a small power station. If it is transmitted to where it is required by means of transmission lines whose total resistance is $\frac{1}{50}$ Ω, how much power will be 'lost' in the lines themselves? What would the power loss be if the energy had been fed into the primary of a step up transformer (of turns ratio 1:40) first of all?

Chapter 11

Alternating Current Circuits

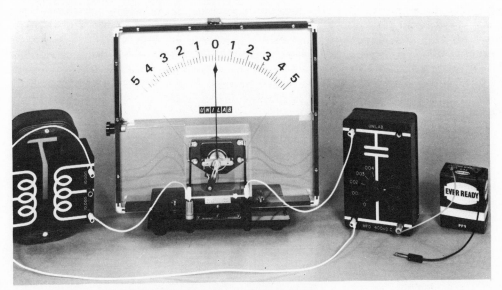

Fig.11.0 Apparatus used in the detection of damped electrical oscillations. (By kind permission of Unilab.)

Having introduced the ideas of the capacitor, the resistor, and the coil (or inductor), in the preceding three chapters, we evaluate the roles of these three components in a.c. circuitry in this present chapter. This evaluation will serve as a useful foundation for our subsequent employment of the components in that branch of electricity which is commonly referred to as *electronics* and which we shall develop in Chapters 12 and 13. Before proceeding with our investigations however, let us define the concept of a.c. more rigorously by deciding on what is to be regarded as the effective value of any given a.c. quantity.

11.1 The Relationship between the Peak Value and Effective Value of an a.c. Quantity

In our discussions of transformers in the last chapter, we made several references to such terms as say '250 V a.c.' and '1 A a.c.'. But what exactly do we mean by an alternating current of one ampere? Do we mean that the peak value of the current corresponds to one ampere, or that its average value corresponds to one ampere? No. An alternating current is said to be one ampere in value if it gives rise to the same heating effect as a direct current of one ampere.

The effective value of any alternating quantity (whether it be current or voltage) is defined as the d.c. quantity which gives rise to the same heating effect.

Let us consider the two circuits shown in Fig. 11.1.

If both bulbs are lit with equal brightness, then assuming these bulbs to be identical, we may decide that the same heating effect is taking place in the filament of each. We stated in Chapter 10 that the size of an alternating e.m.f. varied

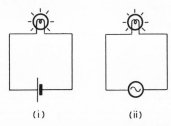

Fig.11.1 The same heating effect is taking place in each bulb.

sinusoidally with time and so it is reasonable to expect that the size of the current in the circuit (ii) will vary sinusoidally with time. Let us write this current as I' where

$$I' = I_0 \sin \theta$$

In this equation, I_0 denotes the peak value of the current and θ is some measure of time.

Since the bulbs are lit with equal brightness, we may deduce that the steady heating effect in circuit (i) is equal to the average heating effect in circuit (ii). Denoting the steady current in the first circuit by I and the filament resistance of each bulb (when hot) by R, then

$$I^2 \times R = \text{average value of } (I'^2 \times R)$$
$$= R \times \text{average value of } I'^2$$

That is,
$$I^2 = \text{average value of } I'^2$$
$$= \overline{I'^2} \text{ say}$$

Hence
$$I = \sqrt{\overline{I'^2}}$$

Now by definition, the effective value of the alternating

current I' is the direct current which produces the same heating effect. Hence the effective value of I' is $\sqrt{\overline{I'^2}}$. Alternatively, the effective value of the alternating current is its *root-mean-square* (r.m.s.) value. But how is this related to the peak value?

Since $I' = I_0 \sin \theta$, then $I'^2 = I_0^2 \sin^2 \theta$

Further, since I_0 is a constant quantity,

$$\overline{I'^2} = I_0^2 \overline{(\sin^2 \theta)} \quad \text{where the bar again denotes an average value}$$

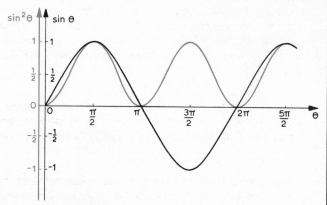

Fig.11.2 Graphs of $\sin \theta$ and $\sin^2 \theta$ against θ. The average value of $\sin \theta$ is zero, but the average value of $\sin^2 \theta$ is $\frac{1}{2}$.

The graphs in Fig. 11.2 show the variations of $\sin \theta$ and $\sin^2 \theta$ with θ. As we can see the average value of $\sin \theta$ is 0, but the average value of $\sin^2 \theta$ is $\frac{1}{2}$.

It follows then that

$$\overline{I'^2} = I_0^2 \times \tfrac{1}{2}$$

and so

$$\sqrt{\overline{I'^2}} = \frac{I_0}{\sqrt{2}}$$

Hence the effective or r.m.s. value of an alternating current may be calculated as $\dfrac{1}{\sqrt{2}}$ times its peak value. Similarly, the effective values of an alternating e.m.f. may be calculated as $\dfrac{1}{\sqrt{2}}$ times its peak value. When we speak of an alternating e.m.f. of 240 V, we imply that the r.m.s. or effective value of this e.m.f. is 240 V. The peak value of the e.m.f. is of the order of 350 V however.

11.2 Measuring Alternating Current

If an alternating current is introduced to a suitably shunted moving coil meter, the pointer of the meter shows no move-

ment. This is because the inertia of the pointer prevents it from following the rapid alternations of current. The current flowing in such a meter is thus responsible for the generation of heat within the meter. Clearly, if alternating current is to be measured successfully, and in terms of its effective value, then some instrument will have to be found whose pointer movement will be determined by the heating effect of the alternating current. Since the heating effect of such a current is independent of the sense of current flow, it follows that the pointer deflection will be in the same sense for a direct current flowing through the instrument in either sense—that is, the instrument will be *idiostatic*.

The *hot wire ammeter* is an instrument whose action depends on the heating effect of a current and so may be used to determine the effective value of an alternating current once it has been calibrated in terms of a direct current. The meter is represented diagrammatically in Fig. 11.3.

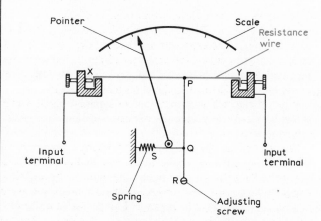

Fig.11.3 The construction of a hot wire ammeter.

A fine piece of resistance wire XY (usually a platinum alloy) is supported as shown. When current is passed through this wire, heating of the wire results, and an associated expansion takes place. The slight sagging resulting from expansion is responsible for a reduction in tension in the wire PR so that the spring is able to enforce a slight movement in the thread SQ. This thread in being looped round the pulley, causes the pulley to rotate slightly and hence the pointer to move across the scale. The deflection of the pointer is found to depend on the rate at which heat is developed in the wire XY—as required.

Such a meter has often been described as sluggish since the movement of its pointer is slow to reach a final deflection, but this characteristic is not always unwelcome and in some situations it may even be a decided advantage.

(Explain why the meter is best calibrated by the use of direct current and hence why the meter can thereafter be used to measure either direct or alternating current.)

11.3 The Capacitor in an a.c. Circuit

Any capacitor has a certain blocking effect when introduced to a d.c. circuit, and so it is not at all obvious that the same capacitor may be able to pass an alternating current. The blocking effect in the d.c. circuit may be demonstrated by setting up the circuit illustrated in Fig. 11.4.

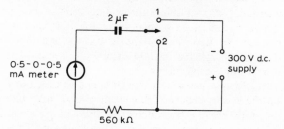

Fig.11.4 Demonstrating the blocking effect of a capacitor in a d.c. circuit.

When the switch is closed at position 1, the meter shows a quick deflection and then a slow return to zero. That is, current flows in the capacitor and battery circuit for as long as is required to charge the capacitor to that value where the potential difference between its plates is equal to the e.m.f. of the battery. Thereafter, direct current is blocked.

When the switch is then closed at position 2, the meter shows a quick deflection to the opposite side and then a slow return to zero.

We can explain the charging and discharging processes in the following way. When the switch is closed at 1, electrons flow from the battery to the right hand plate of the capacitor and simultaneously, electrons flow from the left hand plate of the capacitor to the battery. The plates thus acquire negative and positive charges, so the potential difference between the plates increases and the electron current falls to zero when the potential difference between the plates equals the battery e.m.f. When the battery is disconnected by closing the switch at 2, electrons flow from the right hand plate of the capacitor towards the left hand plate until the positive charge thereon is completely neutralised. Current thus flows for as long as charges exist on the plates, but this current steadily decreases as the charges neutralise each other.

The idea that a capacitor passes alternating current can be easily demonstrated by setting up the apparatus shown in Fig. 11.5.

Whenever the switch is closed, the bulb lights continuously, showing that current is flowing in the circuit, and thereby suggesting that alternating current is being passed by the capacitor. In actual fact, the capacitor is continually being charged, discharged, recharged with the opposite polarity, discharged, recharged with the original polarity etc., as a result of the application of alternating e.m.f. in the circuit. The instantaneous current flowing in the circuit is therefore that current which is either charging or discharging the

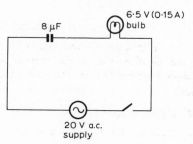

Fig.11.5 The capacitor appears to pass a.c. current.

capacitor.

Let us attempt to relate the current in the circuit to the e.m.f. of the source at any given time. For simplicity, let us eliminate the bulb from the circuit so that the potential difference between the capacitor plates is equal to the source e.m.f. at any time. Since the applied e.m.f. is a sinusoidal function of time, we may write its instantaneous value E at time t as

$$E = E_0 \sin \omega t$$

where E_0 is the peak value of the e.m.f., and ω is a constant related to the frequency of the supply. If the capacitor has capacitance C, and holds charge q at time t, then we may write

$$q = CE_0 \sin \omega t$$

The current to or from the capacitor is calculated as the rate of flow of charge to or from the capacitor. If a charge Δq flows in a time Δt, then the average current flowing in the time Δt, is given as $\dfrac{\Delta q}{\Delta t}$. The instantaneous current is the limiting value of this expression as $\Delta t \to 0$. That is, the instantaneous current is the derivative of q with respect to t and we shall write this as $\dfrac{dq}{dt}$. Denoting the instantaneous current by i, then

$$i \left(= \frac{dq}{dt} \right) = \frac{d}{dt} (CE_0 \sin \omega t)$$

$$= C\omega E_0 \cos \omega t$$

$$= C\omega E_0 \sin \left(\omega t + \frac{\pi}{2} \right)$$

$$= i_0 \sin \left(\omega t + \frac{\pi}{2} \right) \quad \text{say}$$

where i_0 ($= E_0 \omega C$) represents the peak value of alternating current in the capacitor circuit.

This last expression would seem to suggest that the current in the circuit is $\dfrac{\pi}{2}$ radians, or one quarter of a cycle *ahead of* the e.m.f. applied to the capacitor plates! A combined graph of circuit current and applied e.m.f. against time would thus appear as in Fig. 11.6.

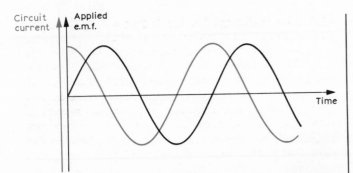

Fig.11.6 The current in the circuit leads the e.m.f. applied between the capacitor plates by one quarter of a cycle.

We can explain this apparent anomaly by realising that at time zero (with respect to the graph), the capacitor plates are uncharged, since at that instant, no potential difference exists between them. As the applied e.m.f. increases however, current will flow in the circuit to charge the capacitor, and since the plates are initially uncharged, this initial current will assume a maximum value. As the potential difference between the plates tends to a maximum value however, the charging current will fall to zero, since the capacitor will then be fully charged. As the e.m.f. applied between the plates then decreases, current will build up in the opposite sense so that when the applied e.m.f. is zero (at the end of the first half cycle) the rate at which the electrons can leave the capacitor is greatest. That is, the current has reached a maximum value in the opposite sense. The second half cycle of the process is similar but in the reverse sense.

This out-of-phase relationship between the alternating e.m.f. applied to a capacitor and the alternating current which flows as a result, may be satisfactorily demonstrated by setting up the apparatus indicated in Fig. 11.7, in which the alternating supply (Fig. 11.8) has a frequency of 0·1 Hz.

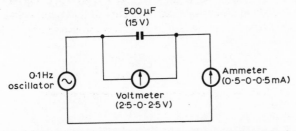

Fig.11.7 Demonstrating the out-of-phase relationship between current and applied e.m.f. in the capacitive a.c. circuit.

The pointer of the ammeter is observed to perform the same oscillatory motion as that of the voltmeter, but its action leads that of the voltmeter by exactly one quarter of a cycle.

Fig.11.8 A very low frequency electrical oscillator (0·1 Hz). (By kind permission of Unilab.)

Another interesting outcome of the presence of a capacitor in an a.c. circuit is that the size of the current in the circuit is then related to the *frequency* of the a.c. supply. This is easily demonstrated by using the apparatus of Fig. 11.9, and noting the current in the circuit over a range of different frequencies, while keeping the e.m.f. of the source at a steady value. A suitable source is that shown in Fig. 11.10. The results of such an investigation attract greater interest when displayed in graphical form; Fig. 11.11 being typical of the results obtained.

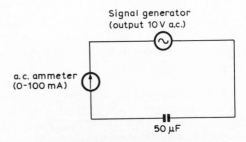

Fig.11.9 Investigating the relationship between capacitor current and the frequency of the a.c. supply.

Fig.11.10 A 0–40 V signal generator. (By kind permission of Advance Electronics Ltd.)

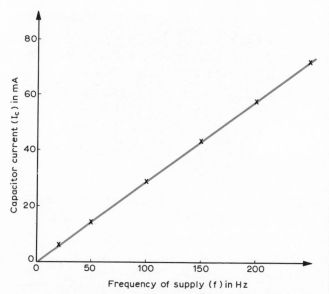

Fig.11.11 The relationship between capacitor current and the frequency of the a.c. supply.

From this graph we see that the capacitor current is a function of the frequency of the alternating current supply. The opposition to current in the circuit of Fig. 11.9 due to the presence of the capacitor is non-resistive since no power is dissipated in the capacitor which does not become hot. This opposition is given the name *capacitive reactance*, and it is denoted by the symbol X_C. The unit for its measurement is the ohm.

Denoting the frequency of the supply by f and the capacitor current by I_C, then referring to Fig. 11.11, we see that at $f = 0$, $I_C = 0$. This implies that $X_C = \infty$ at $f = 0$. Further as $f \to \infty$, then $I_C \to \infty$. This implies that $X_C \to 0$ as $f \to \infty$.

Using this information, we can deduce the graphical relationship between capacitive reactance and frequency to be that which is illustrated in Fig. 11.12.

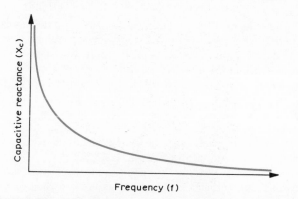

Fig.11.12 The relationship between capacitive reactance and the frequency of the a.c. supply.

11.4 The Inductor (or Coil) in an a.c. Circuit

An inductor, unlike a capacitor, has no blocking effect as far as the passage of direct current is concerned. This is perhaps fairly obvious since the inductor is usually made from conducting wire such as copper. If the inductor or coil has an appreciable self inductance however, a d.c. potential applied across it will produce a d.c. current which rises steadily in value to its final maximum: it does not reach this maximum instantaneously. This property can easily be demonstrated using the apparatus illustrated in Fig. 11.13.

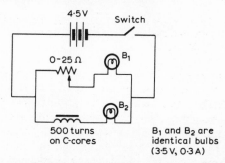

Fig.11.13 B₂ takes an appreciable fraction of a second to reach the same brightness as B₁ following the closing of the switch.

Whenever the switch is closed, the bulb B_1 is observed to light an appreciable fraction of a second before the identical bulb B_2. This may be explained when we consider that as current begins to flow in the lower branch of the network, a magnetic field is set up within the coil. As the current grows, this magnetic field changes and so an e.m.f. is induced across the coil, such as to oppose the current. This *back* e.m.f. due to the self inductance of the coil thus opposes the growth of current in the lower branch and so makes the growth gradual.

Assuming the variable resistor to be set such that its resistance is equal to that of the coil, then the growth of current in each of the upper and lower branches of the circuit could be sketched against time and in graphical form as in Fig. 11.14.

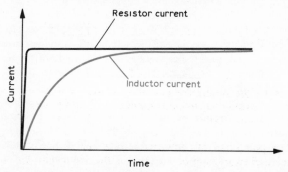

Fig.11.14 The growth of current in a resistor and in a coil of the same resistance.

This demonstration shows how the self inductance of a coil opposes current changes in that coil. It is therefore fairly obvious that a coil of relatively high self inductance will oppose an alternating current, since such a current and its associated magnetic field are continually changing. This 'choking' effect of a coil—as far as the passage of alternating current is concerned—may easily be demonstrated by the circuit of Fig. 11.15. The bulb does not light.

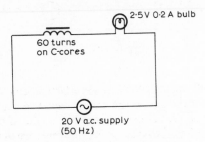

Fig.11.15 Demonstrating the choking effect of a coil.

Further, the choking effect is dependent on the *frequency* of the alternating supply of e.m.f. That is, as the frequency of the supply is increased, then assuming the size of the e.m.f. of the supply to be constant, the current flowing in the coil becomes less and less. This effect may be investigated experimentally using the apparatus of Fig. 11.16.

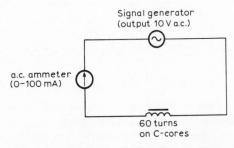

Fig.11.16 Investigating the relationship between coil current and the frequency of the a.c. supply.

The current in the circuit is noted over a range of different frequencies while the e.m.f. of the supply is maintained at a steady value. Again, the results of such an investigation are easier to understand when displayed as a graph such as that of Fig. 11.17 which is typical.

From this graph we see that the inductor current is dependent on the frequency of the alternating supply. The opposition to current flow in the circuit of Fig. 11.16 is not absolutely non-resistive however, since the current approaches a finite value at $f = 0$. This is because the conducting wire of which the coil is made must have some small but finite resistance. That part of the opposition which is due to the effect of the

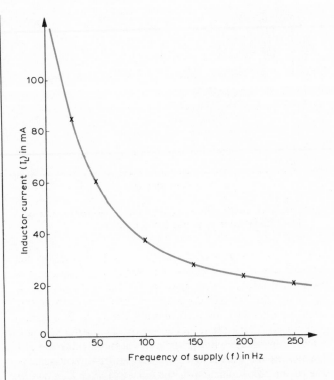

Fig.11.17 The relationship between coil current and the frequency of the a.c. supply.

inductor alone however is referred to as the *inductive reactance*, and is denoted by the symbol X_L. The unit for its measurement is the ohm.

The presence of the small but finite resistance of the coil is responsible for the finite value of current which is found to flow in the circuit of Fig. 11.16 at supply frequency zero. Were we able to eliminate this resistance, say by cooling the inductor to extremely low temperatures, then the result might be to create an extremely large current in the coil—then the opposition to current flow would be non-resistive and so purely reactive.

Denoting the frequency of the supply by f and the inductor current by I_L, then referring to Fig. 11.17 and bearing in mind the distinction between the resistive and reactive components of opposition to current flow, we see that at $f = 0$, $I_L \to \infty$, for a coil whose opposition to current flow is purely reactive. This would imply that at $f = 0$, $X_L = 0$. Further, as $f \to \infty$, then $I_L \to 0$. This implies that $X_L \to \infty$ as $f \to \infty$. Using this information, we can deduce the graphical relationship between inductive reactance and frequency to be that which is illustrated in Fig. 11.18.

We noted earlier that whenever a capacitor was inserted in an a.c. circuit, an out-of-phase relationship existed between the potential difference being developed across the capacitor plates at any time and the current flowing in the circuit at that

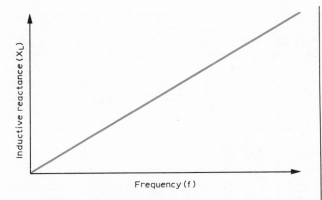

Fig.11.18 The relationship between inductive reactance and the frequency of the a.c. supply.

time. It seems reasonable therefore to ask whether or not such an out-of-phase relationship might exist between the potential difference being developed between the ends of a coil at any time and the current flowing in the coil at that time, whenever the coil is inserted in an a.c. circuit. The sketch graph of Fig. 11.14 might lead us to expect some out-of-phase relationship although this graph refers to the effect of the coil in a d.c. circuit. This sketch graph suggests that the current is slow to reach its maximum value considering that the full source potential difference was developed across the coil at the closing of the switch—that is, at time zero.

Before investigating the possibility of the out-of-phase relationship experimentally, let us consider the mathematical aspects of the problem in the hope that they might provide us with some preliminary ideas.

A coil is said to have self inductance one henry (1 H) if current when changing at the rate of one ampere per second in the coil induces a back e.m.f. of one volt across the coil. It follows therefore that if an average back e.m.f. of $\bar{E}$ is induced across the coil by a change of current Δi occurring in a time Δt, the self inductance of that coil—L say—is given as

$$L = \frac{\bar{E}}{\frac{\Delta i}{\Delta t}}$$

or

$$\bar{E} = L\frac{\Delta i}{\Delta t}$$

It follows that the instantaneous back e.m.f.—E say—is the limiting value of the average back e.m.f. as the time interval Δt tends to zero. That is

$$E = L\frac{di}{dt} \quad \text{in the usual notation}$$

Let us suppose now that the coil of self inductance L is connected to an alternating e.m.f. whose instantaneous value

E' is at time t given by the expression

$$E' = E_0 \sin \omega t$$

where E_0 is the peak value of the e.m.f. and ω is a constant related to the frequency of the supply. The situation is thus as represented in Fig. 11.19.

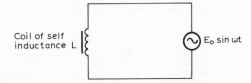

Coil of self inductance L

$E_0 \sin \omega t$

Fig.11.19

Clearly the potential difference which causes current to flow in the circuit is at any instant equal to the algebraic sum of the applied e.m.f. and the back e.m.f. If a current i flows in the circuit, then assuming the resistance of the circuit to be due to the windings of the coil alone and to have the value R, we may write

$$E_0 \sin \omega t - L\frac{di}{dt} = i \times R$$

If we choose a coil whose resistance is almost zero, then it follows that

$$L\frac{di}{dt} = E_0 \sin \omega t$$

and so

$$\frac{di}{dt} = \frac{E_0}{L} \sin \omega t$$

The current in the circuit is therefore found as

$$i = \frac{E_0}{L} \int \sin \omega t \, dt$$

$$= -\frac{E_0}{L\omega} \cos \omega t$$

$$= \frac{E_0}{L\omega} \sin\left(\omega t - \frac{\pi}{2}\right)$$

$$= i_0 \sin\left(\omega t - \frac{\pi}{2}\right) \quad \text{say}$$

where $i_0 \left(= \frac{E_0}{L\omega}\right)$ represents the peak value of alternating current in the coil.

This last expression would seem to suggest that the current in the circuit is *lagging* the e.m.f. applied between the ends of the coil by $\frac{\pi}{2}$ radians or one quarter of a cycle. A combined graph of circuit current and applied e.m.f. against time would thus appear as in Fig. 11.20.

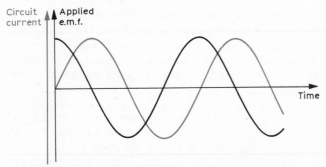

Fig.11.20 The e.m.f. applied to the coil would seem to lead the current in the coil by one quarter of a cycle.

The out-of-phase relationship between the alternating e.m.f. applied across the ends of a coil, and the alternating current flowing as a result may be demonstrated by setting up the apparatus indicated in Fig. 11.21. Due to the finite resistance of the coil however, the current lags the applied e.m.f. by somewhat less than one quarter of a cycle. As the resistance of the coil increases, the phase lag becomes smaller and smaller so that in ideal circumstances only (that is, where the coil resistance is zero) would we find the current in the coil trailing the applied e.m.f. by exactly one quarter of a cycle.

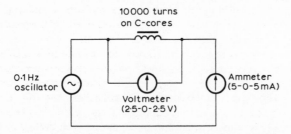

Fig.11.21 Demonstrating the out-of-phase relationship between e.m.f. and current in the inductive a.c. circuit.

11.5 The Resistor in an a.c. Circuit

When a circuit is purely resistive, there is no back e.m.f. generated in that circuit as a result of the circuit being supplied with alternating current. Consequently, we should not expect to find any out-of-phase relationship between the current flowing in the resistor at any time and the e.m.f. being developed between its ends at that time.

If an alternating e.m.f.—E say—is applied to a resistance R where $E = E_0 \sin \omega t$ as before, then the current i in the resistance is given as

$$i = \frac{E}{R} \qquad \text{at any instant}$$

Hence

$$i = \frac{E_0}{R} \sin \omega t$$

or

$$i = i_0 \sin \omega t \quad \text{say}$$

where $i_0 \left(= \dfrac{E_0}{R} \right)$ represents the peak value of alternating current in the resistance.

This last expression suggests that the current in the resistance is *exactly in phase* with the applied e.m.f. A combined graph of circuit current and applied e.m.f. against time would thus appear as in Fig. 11.22.

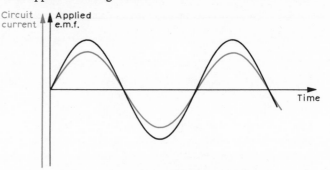

Fig.11.22 The e.m.f. applied to the resistor would seem to be in step with the resistor current.

The in-phase relationship between the applied e.m.f. and resulting current is easily demonstrated by setting up the apparatus indicated in Fig. 11.23. The pointers of both the voltmeter and ammeter are observed to move exactly in step.

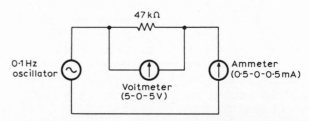

Fig.11.23 Demonstrating the in-phase relationship between e.m.f. and current in the resistive a.c. circuit.

11.6 Electrical Oscillations

Having investigated the behaviour of each of the capacitor, the inductor, and the resistor in an a.c. circuit, we are now in a position to investigate the introduction of combinations of these components into such a circuit. Before doing so however, let us demonstrate and discuss a most interesting and important result—that which is obtained when a charged capacitor is discharged through an inductor. In section 11.3 we discussed the discharge of a capacitor through a resistor. The discharge through a coil provides us with a much more interesting situation however.

If we connect a very large coil (mounted on an iron core) to a capacitor which as previously been charged, and include a centre zero ammeter in the circuit, we observe the pointer of the meter to oscillate, with decaying amplitude, following the completion of the circuit. This investigation may be performed using the apparatus of Figs. 11.24 or 11.0 (observe the conventional symbol for the coil mounted on an iron core). The switch is held momentarily at position 1 during which time the capacitor is charged from the battery. When the switch is closed at position 2, the capacitor discharges through the coil. The oscillatory nature of the current in the coil and capacitor circuit may be represented graphically in relation to time as in Fig. 11.25.

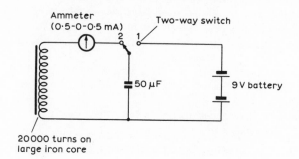

Fig. 11.24 The production of a damped electrical oscillation.

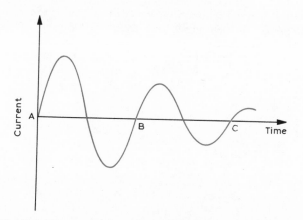

Fig. 11.25 The damped current oscillation in relation to time.

By connecting the input terminals of an oscilloscope across the capacitor, we may study the potential difference between its plates in relation to time. This study, as we might expect, reveals a decaying oscillatory pattern, and graphing it as a function of time, we should obtain a close resemblance to the form of the graph in Fig. 11.25.

But how can we account for and explain the decaying alternating current in the inductor-capacitor circuit of Fig. 11.24? The diagram in Fig. 11.26(a) represents a charged capacitor, a switch, and a coil. Whenever the switch is closed, the capacitor begins to discharge since the coil offers a conducting path between its plates. The flow of current in the coil will give rise to a magnetic field in and around the coil as in Fig. 11.26(b). Once the capacitor is fully discharged, the magnetic field will begin to collapse, and so, according to Faraday's principle, an induced e.m.f. will be developed across the coil. Further, the sense of this e.m.f. will be such as to oppose the motion or change causing it—according to Lenz's Law. The induced e.m.f. will thus give rise to a flow of current in the same sense as before, so that the capacitor will become charged but this time in the opposite sense. This stage is represented in Fig. 11.26(c). The process now repeats itself in the opposite sense until the capacitor is re-charged as initially. The whole cycle of events then begins again.

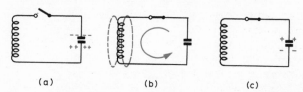

Fig. 11.26 Explaining the processes involved in the damped oscillation.

We have indicated in Fig. 11.26(c) that the charge on the capacitor is somewhat less than the initial charge as in Fig. 11.26(a). This 'loss' of charge is consistent with the continually diminishing amplitude of the oscillation and can be accounted for in terms of energy losses during the operation of the circuit. Energy is released from the circuit whenever current flows in the coil. The coil has a finite resistance and so heat is generated in and lost from the coil whenever current flows in it. Electrical energy is also released from the circuit in the form of electromagnetic radiation, but this effect becomes pronounced only at higher frequencies. It is because energy is released from the circuit during each cycle that the electric oscillation eventually dies out as indicated in Fig. 11.25.

Reference to this figure also indicates that the duration of each cycle is exactly the same. That is, AB = BC. This duration is known as the *period* of the oscillation and its value is determined by the values of each of the coil and the capacitor. This may be verified by inserting different values of components into the original circuit and observing changes in the rate at which the pointer of the meter oscillates.

The number of complete oscillations or cycles of the system occurring in one second is known as the natural frequency of oscillation of the circuit, and it may be calculated as f where

$$f = \frac{1}{2\pi\sqrt{LC}} \text{ (Hz)}$$

L and C denote the values of the inductance (in henries) and the capacitance (in farads) respectively.

The production of a damped oscillation in this way is in many respects analogous to the production of a damped oscillation in a simple mechanical system such as a simple pendulum. Let us consider the pendulum illustrated in Fig. 11.27. If the bob of the pendulum is pulled aside to B, it is given potential energy, so that when it is released, this energy is transformed from the potential form to the kinetic form as the bob swings through its lowest point A. The bob does not stop at this lowest point however, but overswings to some point B′—its kinetic energy at A being transformed eventually into potential energy at B′. The bob will then swing back in the opposite sense towards B, and the whole cycle of events will begin over again. Due to the presence of air resistance, and friction at the pendulum support, the amplitude of each successive oscillation will decrease slightly until the bob is finally at rest. Although the amplitude of oscillation is continually decreasing however, the period of the oscillation is unaffected and remains constant for as long as the oscillation continues.

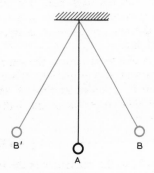

Fig.11.27 A mechanical analogy.

From this short discussion, we can draw parallels between:
1 the potential energy of the mass at the positions B and B′ in the mechanical situation, and the electric potential energy stored in the capacitor when it is fully charged in one sense or the other, in the electrical situation.
2 The maximum kinetic energy and zero potential energy of the mass at the position A in the mechanical situation, and the maximum flow of current (or maximum kinetic energy of electrons) in the circuit when the capacitor is fully discharged, in the electrical situation.
3 The independence of period and amplitude of oscillation in the mechanical situation, and the independence of period and amplitude of oscillation in the electrical situation.

This pendulum analogy may help us to understand the nature of the damped electric oscillation a little more fully.

As far as a pendulum is concerned, we are well aware that if the minute amount of energy lost in each swing could be replaced at the end of that swing, then the pendulum could be kept swinging. This is the principle on which the grandfather clock operates successfully. In view of the close connections between the natural oscillation of a pendulum

and the natural oscillation of an inductor-capacitor circuit, it seems likely that an electric oscillation could be maintained in a circuit by feeding in a minute amount of energy to the circuit in step with each half cycle of the otherwise damped oscillation. We shall investigate this possibility further in Chapter 13 when we have learned something about the principles underlying the action of the transistor.

11.7 Electric Resonance

Having found that the inductor-capacitor circuit has its own natural frequency of free oscillation, we now consider the behaviour of such a circuit when an alternating signal is imposed on it, so that oscillations set up therein are in fact forced oscillations. Clearly the inductors and capacitors can be arranged either in series or in parallel (although we considered the parallel arrangement in the last section), and so, for completeness, we shall investigate each possibility in turn.

1. *The Series Combination of Inductance and Capacitance in an a.c. Circuit*

Since any inductor has a finite resistance, we are in fact setting up an a.c. circuit in which the components are inductance, capacitance, and resistance. We find that on setting up such a circuit, the current flowing in it is frequency dependent—assuming the size of the e.m.f. of the source to remain constant. The dependence of current on frequency may be investigated experimentally by using the apparatus of Fig. 11.28, and noting the current in the circuit over a range of different frequencies while keeping the e.m.f. of the source constant. The results of a typical experiment are shown in Fig. 11.29.

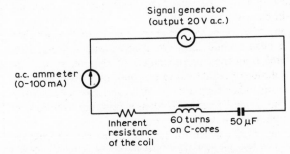

Fig.11.28 Investigating the series resonance effect.

From this graph, we see that the current in the circuit reaches a maximum value at a frequency of 100 Hz. That is, the frequency 100 Hz is the 'ideal' frequency for the passage of alternating current in that series circuit whose components have the values shown in Fig. 11.28. This frequency is known as the *resonant frequency* of the circuit, and at this frequency, *electric resonance* is said to be occurring. If we suppose the

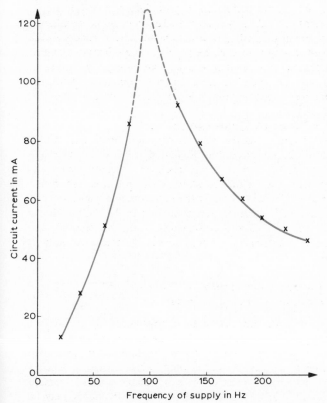

Fig.11.29 Typical results for a series resonance investigation.

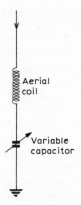

Fig.11.30 A series resonant circuit may be used in an aerial tuning circuit.

series combination of components to have its own natural frequency of oscillation, then it is perhaps reasonable to expect that when a signal is imposed on the circuit at a frequency equal to this assumed natural frequency, a resonant effect will be produced.

In terms of a mechanical analogy, we are well aware that when we push a child on a swing at a frequency equal to the natural frequency of oscillation of the swing, then a large amplitude of oscillation can be built up. If we push the swing at any other frequency,—say at a frequency of three that of the natural frequency—then a very jerky motion of small amplitude will result.

The series circuit which we have described can be used to advantage in an aerial tuning system for a radio receiver. This system is illustrated in Fig. 11.30. A radio signal reaching the aerial induces a small e.m.f. across it. By altering the value of the variable capacitor, the resonant or natural frequency of the system may be adjusted to equal that of the incoming signal, so that a maximum current is induced to flow in the aerial.

Let us attempt to analyse the series resonant circuit in mathematical terms by considering the potential difference being developed across the inherent resistance of the inductor,

the inductor itself, and the capacitor. Let us denote the values of the three components by R, L, and C respectively, and the potential difference across each component by V_R, V_L, and V_C respectively.

Since the circuit is of a series nature, the same current will flow in each component at any instant. If we denote this current by i (where $i = i_0 \sin \omega t$ at time t), then we may write the potential differences across the individual components at any time as

$$V_R = iR, \qquad V_L = iX_L, \qquad V_C = iX_C$$

where X_L and X_C refer to the reactances of the inductor and the capacitor respectively.

We are aware that the potential difference across the resistor is in step with the current flowing in it, and that the potential differences across each of the inductor and the capacitor are out of step with the current flowing by $\frac{\pi}{2}$ radians or 90° (in angular measure). The potential difference across the inductor leads the current flowing in it by 90°, while the potential difference across the capacitor lags the current flowing in it by 90°. It is perhaps fairly obvious that we can only relate these potential differences meaningfully by referring to vector methods. If we represent the potential differences across the components by the vectors (or *phasors* as they are more commonly referred to in electricity) $\underline{V}_R$, $\underline{V}_L$, and $\underline{V}_C$, then choosing the direction and sense of $\underline{V}_R$ to be that of the positive X-axis, the directions and senses of the three vectors would appear as in Fig. 11.31.

Fig.11.31 Representing voltages by vectors.

If we denote the e.m.f. of the source by a vector $\underline{E}$, then since the components are in series, it follows that

$$\underline{E} = \underline{V}_R + \underline{V}_L + \underline{V}_C$$

Let us suppose that V_L is greater than V_C. Then the size and direction (or phase relationship) of $\underline{E}$ could be found from the vector addition performed as in Fig. 11.32.

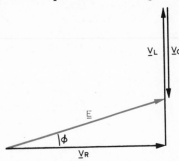

Fig.11.32 Adding voltages vectorially in the series resonant circuit.

We see from this diagram that the e.m.f. of the source leads the potential difference across the resistive component of the inductor by some time-related quantity ϕ (called the phase angle). What this really means is that the current in the circuit (which remember is in step with the potential difference across the resistive component) lags the e.m.f. of the source by an amount ϕ—that is, by $\dfrac{\phi}{360}$ of a cycle.

From Fig. 11.32, it follows that

$$E^2 = V_R{}^2 + (V_L - V_C)^2$$

But $\quad V_R = iR, \quad V_L = iX_L, \quad$ and $\quad V_C = iX_C$

Hence $\quad E^2 = i^2R^2 + (iX_L - iX_C)^2$

$$= i^2(R^2 + [X_L - X_C]^2)$$

Hence $\quad \boxed{i = \dfrac{E}{\sqrt{R^2 + (X_L - X_C)^2}}} \dots\dots\dots\dots(11.1)$

Note also that

$$\tan \phi = \frac{X_L - X_C}{R}$$

We found earlier that inductive reactance increased with increasing frequency, whereas capacitive reactance decreased with increasing frequency. It is reasonable to assume that there will exist some frequency at which the inductive reactance will equal the capacitive reactance—for the two components present in our circuit. At this frequency $X_L = X_C$, and so according to equation 11.1

$$i = \frac{E}{R}$$

Clearly, this is the maximum value which the current i can attain. Further, when this value is attained, the opposition to current flow is purely resistive so that the current flowing in the circuit is in phase or in step with the applied e.m.f.

We might conclude then that the resonant frequency of a series inductor-capacitor circuit is that frequency at which the inductive and capacitive reactances are equal so that the net reactance of the circuit is zero.

The term $\sqrt{R^2 + (X_L - X_C)^2}$ in the equation (11.1) is called the *impedance* of the circuit, and is usually denoted by Z. Impedance is the name given to the joint opposition of reactance and resistance to the current in an a.c. circuit. It is measured in ohms.

2. *The Parallel Combination of Inductance and Capacitance in an a.c. Circuit*

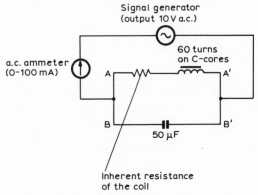

Fig.11.33 Investigating the parallel resonance effect.

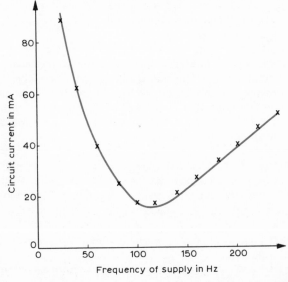

Fig.11.34 Typical results for a parallel resonance investigation.

When an inductor and a capacitor are connected in parallel and an alternating e.m.f. is applied as in Fig. 11.33, the current recorded by the meter is found to vary as the frequency of the supply is varied—the e.m.f. of the supply remaining constant. This variation is expressed graphically, using the components shown in the circuit of Fig. 11.33, in Fig. 11.34.

From this graph, we see that the current in the circuit reaches a minimum value at a frequency of 105 Hz. This suggests that the impedance of the parallel circuit has reached a maximum value at the frequency 105 Hz. This effect is known as *parallel resonance* and once more, the frequency 105 Hz is the *resonant frequency*. The reason why the impedance of the circuit should be a maximum at resonance might be somewhat obscure, so we shall perform a short circuit analysis to bring out the fuller implications of the parallel resonant effect. A proper analysis of the circuit is very complicated, and so, for simplicity, we shall consider the approximate solution which is obtained when the inherent resistance of the inductor is ignored.

Since the same potential difference exists across each of the parallel branches, it follows that the current in the inductive branch lags the applied e.m.f. by 90° while the current in the capacitive branch leads the applied e.m.f. by 90°. The currents in the two branches will thus be 180° or ½ cycle out of step with each other.

Clearly the total current being drawn from the supply can only be deduced vectorially being the vector sum of the currents in the two branches. If we denote the inductor and capacitor currents by I_L and I_C respectively, then these currents will have the same direction vectorially, but the opposite sense. If we choose the positive X axis as a reference vector, along which we might choose to describe the applied e.m.f. vectorially, then the currents could be represented vectorially as in Fig. 11.35.

Fig. 11.35 Representing currents by vectors.

Now $$I_C = \frac{E}{X_C} \quad \text{and} \quad I_L = \frac{E}{X_L}$$

where E denotes the e.m.f. of the source, and X_C and X_L denote the capacitive reactance and inductive reactance respectively. As before, for any given inductor and capacitor, there will exist some frequency at which the inductive reactance and capacitive reactance are numerically equal. When this frequency is reached, then the currents flowing in the branches of the parallel circuit will also be numerically equal,

but since they are out of step by 180°, their vector sum will be zero at this frequency. That is the net current in the circuit will be zero (ideally). It is at this frequency that parallel resonance is said to be occurring.

In the ideal case of parallel resonance which we are discussing here, we have the interesting result that at the resonant frequency, significant or even large currents flow in each of the inductor and the capacitor, and no current is being drawn from the source! (This would not of course be the case in a practical situation in which some finite resistance would be present in the circuit.) At resonance, the parallel circuit is in fact oscillating. The capacitor charges and discharges through the inductor and the energy of the system is alternately stored in the electric field of the capacitor when charged, the current being zero, and in the magnetic field of the inductor when the capacitor is discharged the current being a maximum. Since no resistance is present, according to our assumptions, no energy is dissipated. This situation has been likened to a frictionless pendulum after it has been given an initial push.

The fact that significantly large currents are flowing in the branches of a parallel resonant circuit at resonance, while the current in the main supply line of the circuit is very small, may be verified by connecting two additional a.c. meters in the circuit of Fig. 11.33—one in each of the branches AA′ and BB′.

The parallel inductor-capacitor circuit is used to advantage in the reception of radio signals. If the circuit is tuned by means of varying the capacitance of the capacitor, then its impedance can be made a maximum at a variety of frequencies—each determined by the setting of the capacitor. Thus by varying the capacitance in the circuit, the circuit may be made to resonate at the frequency of any given incoming signal. The potential difference across the circuit is proportional to its impedance, so that a maximum potential difference is developed for the purposes of amplification of the signal, by a voltage amplifying system. We shall consider the use of the parallel inductor-capacitor circuit in the reception of radio signals in Chapter 13.

Problems

1 What is the peak value of an alternating e.m.f. of 440 V r.m.s.? What peak current would flow in a 2·2 kΩ resistor if it were connected across this supply?

2 The instantaneous potential difference across a reactive component is given as v where $v = 16 \sin(100\,\pi t)$, where t refers to time. The instantaneous current in the component is given as i where $i = 8 \sin\left(100\,\pi t - \frac{\pi}{2}\right)$. What are the peak values of current and potential difference? What is the phase relationship between current and potential difference?

What is the nature of the component?

3 Can you form a theory as to why an alternating current tends to confine itself to the outer 'skin' of a wire as the frequency of the supply is continually increased?

4 In what respects does the oscillation of a mass on a vertical spring compare with the damped oscillation which may be set up in an inductor-capacitor circuit? Is the mass analogous to the inductor or to the capacitor?

5 An alternating e.m.f. of 10 V and frequency (f) 50 Hz is applied across a coil of inductance (L) 10 H whose resistance is 300 Ω. Find the size of the current flowing in the circuit and also that fraction of a cycle by which it lags the applied e.m.f. (The reactance of the coil may be calculated as $2\pi fL$.)

6 An alternating e.m.f. of 10 V and frequency (f) 50 Hz is applied to an 8 μF capacitor (C) in parallel with a 500 Ω resistor. Find the size of the current drawn from the supply, and also its phase relationship with the applied e.m.f. (The reactance of a capacitor may be calculated as $\dfrac{1}{2\pi fC}$).

7 With reference to the formulae quoted in the last two problems, calculate the inductive reactance of a 2 H inductor at 50 Hz, and also the capacitive reactance of a 50 μF capacitor at the same frequency. At what frequency would these two reactances be equal in magnitude? Draw graphs (on one sheet of graph paper) of the reactances of each of the components as a function of frequency.

8 How could you demonstrate a mechanical resonant effect given a magnet, a spring, a coil of wire, and a variable frequency source of alternating e.m.f.?

9 An a.c. voltmeter records 45 V when connected across an inductor, 60 V across a capacitor, and 8 V across a resistor—these three components being connected in series in an a.c. circuit. What would the voltmeter record if placed across the whole circuit?

Chapter 12

Thermionics

Fig.12.0   The Maltese Cross tube in operation.

This far, our dealings with electricity have been concerned mainly with the concept of electrons flowing in solid conducting materials as a result of maintaining differences in potential between different points in these materials. It is also possible for electrons to flow through a vacuum space however, whenever a difference in electric potential exists across that space.

The flow of electrons through vacuum tubes is responsible for some forms of lighting, the generation of X-rays, the detection of shipping and aircraft, and the operation of television. It is the study of this phenomenon of the passage of electrons in vacuum which is frequently referred to as *electronics*, although electronics has been defined more fully as

that field of science and engineering which deals with electron devices and their utilisation

The *electron devices* referred to are such that

electrical conduction is principally by electrons moving through a vacuum, gas, or semiconductor.

The study of electrical conduction by electrons moving through a vacuum we shall refer to as *thermionics*, and this study will constitute the material of this present chapter. The study of the principles underlying conduction in semiconductor materials we shall encounter in some detail in the next chapter.

12.1 Early Thermionic Investigations

During the course of his experiments on electric lamps, Thomas Edison (Fig. 12.1) observed that after a period of time the inner surface of the glass bulb became coated with a thin black deposit. It is reported that he attributed this deposit to particles having been ejected from the lamp filament during its heating. Further, he observed that by sealing a metal plate inside the lamp near its filament, the clouding of the inner glass surface could be stopped. More important still, Edison observed that an electric current flowed between the lamp filament and the metal plate when the lamp was connected as in Fig. 12.2(a) but not when the connection was as in Fig. 12.2(b). (Can you explain this?)

Fig.12.1   (By kind permission of the Science Museum, London, Neg. no. 493/55.)

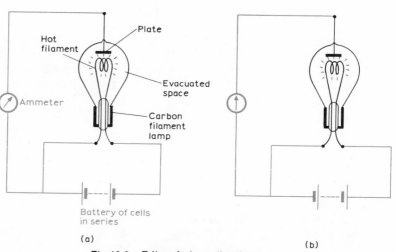

Fig.12.2   Edison's investigations.

Although Edison detected the thermionic emission of electrons in 1883, he was not the first person to do so. It is reported that as early as 1859, Julius Plücker, a German physicist, constructed an evacuated tube in which an aluminium Maltese cross was maintained at a high positive potential relative to a heated filament (or cathode). Plücker observed a sharp shadow of the cross to be cast on the end of the tube and concluded that some radiation (other than light) was proceeding in a straight line manner from the cathode towards the cross (or anode). This 'radiation' we now know to be streams of fast moving electrons which have been ejected from the heated cathode and accelerated towards the positive anode. At that time however, the nature of the radiation was uncertain and it was named *cathode rays* by another German physicist Eugen Goldstein.

The diagram in Fig. 12.3 illustrates the operation of a more up-to-date Maltese cross tube than that of Plücker. In addition to the Maltese cross, this more modern tube incorporates a hollow anode which provides for the divergence as well as the acceleration of the electrons following their liberation from the hot cathode. Most of these electrons travel through the region of the hollow anode and proceed towards the Maltese cross which is maintained at the same potential as the anode. Many of the electrons are stopped by the presence of the cross, but the others proceed to strike the fluorescent screen thereby causing it to glow green. The result is to produce a distinct shadow of the Maltese cross on a bright green background. The distinct nature of this shadow is sufficient to indicate that the cathode rays travel in straight lines from the cathode of the apparatus.

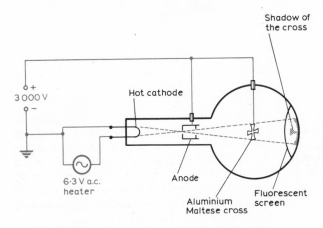

Fig.12.3 The operation of the Maltese Cross tube.

A most interesting effect may be observed by bringing a magnet close to the side of the tube beyond the cylindrical anode—the effect being to distort the form and alter the position of the fluorescent shadow. When the shadow is interfered with in this way however, an identical but fainter

shadow of the cross is still observed in place on the screen. This shadow is produced by light from the white hot cathode travelling from that cathode and being obstructed by the Maltese cross. This shows that the cathode rays are quite unlike light radiation in as much as they can be deflected by the presence of a magnetic field. Light is an electromagnetic radiation, and as such its propagation is unaffected by the presence of a magnetic field or of an electric field.

The displacement of a cathode ray beam in a magnetic field is described perfectly by the right hand rule which we discussed in Chapter 10 for the motion of a current-carrying conductor in a magnetic field. Moving charges in a conductor set up their own magnetic fields as do moving charges in vacuum, and the interaction of these fields with an external field results in a displacement of either the current—carrying conductor or the cathode ray beam as the case may be. The fact that the displacement of the cathode ray beam may be described by the right hand motor rule provides us with substantial grounds for believing that cathode rays are in fact electrons.

The fact that the cathode rays carry negative charge was satisfactorily demonstrated by Professor Jean Perrin of the University of Paris in 1895. His studies employed an evacuated tube, an up-to-date form of which is represented in operation in Fig. 12.4.

The anode of this tube has a small hole to allow only a narrow beam of cathode rays to enter the spherical chamber. When the apparatus is switched on, a green spot is observed on the centre of the fluorescent screen, thereby indicating that the cathode rays are travelling in a straight line path through the apparatus. If a magnet is now brought up close to the tube just beyond the anode, the cathode ray beam may be manoeuvred into the small Faraday cylinder, by suitably delicate adjustment of the magnet's position. When the beam enters the cylinder, the leaf of the electroscope rises, thus showing the instrument to be charged. If the filament heater supply is then switched off, the electroscope is observed to remain charged. Also, when a negatively charged rod is brought up close to the cap of the electroscope, the leaf rises further, thereby indicating that the charge on the instrument is negative. We may conclude from this experiment, as Perrin did, that the cathode rays must be small electrically-charged particles rather than some wavelike radiation. It is accepted that if the cathode rays were wave-like radiations, then the electroscope would lose its charge when the radiations from the heated filament were terminated. We are thus provided with more convincing evidence regarding the identical nature of cathode rays and electrons.

Having identified the nature of the cathode ray beam, it is fairly obvious that such a beam will be affected by the presence of an electric field. This is easily demonstrated by setting up the vacuum tube and associated apparatus illustrated in Fig. 12.5.

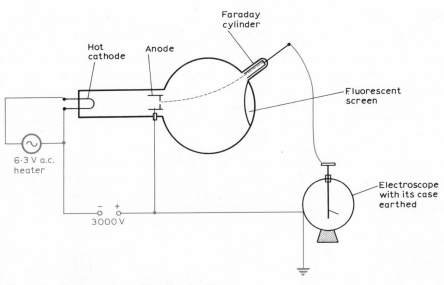

Fig.12.4 The operation of the Perrin tube.

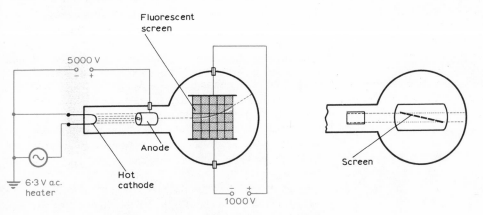

Fig.12.5 The operation of the electrostatic deflection tube.

The fluorescent screen is mounted in the vertical plane but it is turned so as to be at a slight angle to the path of the incident beam. This results in the beam being made visible along the entire length of the screen. When a large potential difference is applied between the deflecting plates in the sense shown, the beam is observed to deflect upwards thereby showing that its path is affected by the presence of an electric field. The upwards sense of deflection also provides us with confirmatory evidence as regards the nature of the electric charge carried by the components of the beam.

Using this technique of electrostatic deflection of the cathode ray beam along with that of magnetic deflection, J. J. Thomson succeeded in measuring the ratio of charge to mass for the cathode rays in 1897. For this determination, he received the Nobel Prize for Physics in 1906.

From the results of the early investigations, it was gradually realised that the cathode rays were in fact electrons—always having the same properties regardless of the nature of the cathode employed. The realisation was given added support when in 1899, J. J. Thomson showed conclusively that the Edison effect was due to electron transport. The fact that electrons could be generated by thermionic emission was thus established by the end of the 19th century.

The principles of thermionic emission of electrons and electrostatic deflection of an electron beam are inherent in the operation of one of the most versatile instruments available to modern electrical science—the cathode ray oscilloscope (C.R.O.). With the developmental background of cathode ray or electron physics in mind, we now consider the construction of this instrument.

12.2 The Construction of the Cathode Ray Oscilloscope

The cathode ray oscilloscope is somewhat similar in appearance to a small television set endowed with a large number of controls (Figs. 12.6, 12.7). Although there are many similarities between the two instruments, the purpose of using each is quite different. The oscilloscope is an instrument which can be used as a voltmeter, as a means of determining the frequency of alternating electric signals, and as a means of displaying electric signals in picture form.

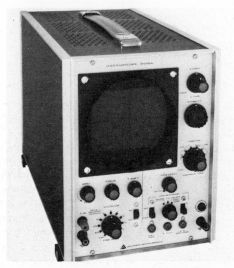

Fig.12.6   (By kind permission of Advance Electronics Ltd.)

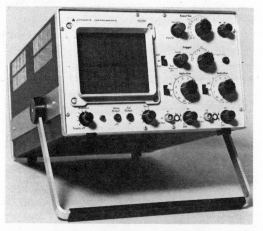

Fig.12.7   (By kind permission of Advance Electronics Ltd.)

The construction of the instrument is as illustrated in Fig. 12.8. As can be seen, the cathode ray oscilloscope is no more than a simple cathode ray tube with an electron gun at one end, a fluorescent screen at the other end, and a beam deflection system between the two ends.

The electron gun consists of a series of cylindrical electrodes. The cathode is usually in the form of a metal disc or cylinder, coated with barium oxide, heated indirectly by a fine current-carrying tungsten wire which is located behind it. The control grid is a slightly larger cylinder surrounding the cathode to some extent; its potential may be varied in a manner which leaves it always negative with respect to the cathode. It therefore has the effect of repelling the electrons liberated from the cathode. The more negative the grid potential is made, the fewer electrons pass through the grid aperture and so the fainter the spot on the fluorescent screen becomes. The potential of the grid electrode is varied by means of a small rheostat or potentiometer, the sliding contact of which constitutes the *brightness* control of the oscilloscope. The three diagrams in Fig. 12.9 illustrate the repelling action of the control grid when its potential is (a) the same as that of the cathode, (b) slightly negative with respect to that of the cathode, and (c) largely negative with respect to that of the cathode.

Figure 12.9 also indicates that when the electron beam passes through the aperture of the control grid, it has a tendency to diverge as a result of the mutual repulsions between the electrons in the beam. Were this tendency to continue unchecked, then we would find a diffuse patch of light on the fluorescent screen rather than a desired well defined spot. Focussing of the electron beam is achieved by incorporating two anodes into the electron gun rather than one. The first anode is at a lower potential than the second so that each contributes to the overall acceleration of the beam. The difference in potential between the two anodes gives rise to the presence of an electric field between them and this field changes the nature of the beam from that of divergence to convergence. The amount of focussing may be varied by altering the potential of the first anode thereby altering the potential difference between the anodes and so the pattern of the electric field between them. The potential of the first anode is varied by means of a small rheostat whose sliding contact constitutes the *focus* control of the oscilloscope. The focussing effect of the two anodes is similar to the focussing of a light beam by a convex lens, and so the two anodes are sometimes referred to as an *electron lens*. The diagram in Fig. 12.10 gives some idea of the nature of the electron beam between cathode and screen when the brightness and focus controls have been suitably adjusted.

The screen of the oscilloscope is usually coated with zinc silicate—a substance which glows green under impact from an electron beam. All fluorescent materials give rise to some 'afterglow'—this phenomenon depending on the nature of the material used for the screen coating. Zinc silicate is known as a short persistence material since it gives rise to only a slight afterglow of the order of 50 ms. A long persistence material such as calcium phosphate with dysprosium may give rise to an afterglow of the order of 2 s. An oscillo-

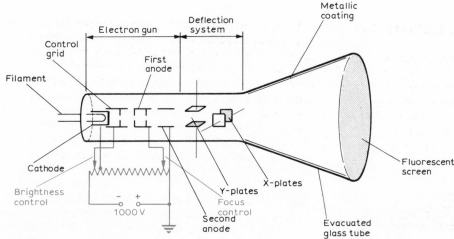

Fig.12.8   The construction of the cathode ray oscilloscope.

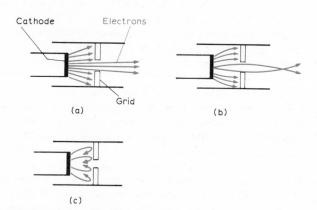

Fig.12.9   The action of the control grid.

scope with a long persistence tube is particularly useful when a transient phenomenon (one which lasts only a very short time) has to be observed. As an example, we might quote the rapid discharge of a capacitor. An oscilloscope with a short persistence tube on the other hand is particularly useful when the trace on the screen is to be photographed, in which case any afterglow might give rise to a blurring effect.

The metallic coating is present on the tube wall to absorb electrons ejected from the fluorescent screen when the electron beam strikes it. These electrons ejected in this way are known as secondary electrons, and it is estimated that they are ejected in numbers equal to those of the impinging electrons. Were it not for this phenomenon of secondary emission, a net negative charge would build up on the fluorescent screen so that the beam would suffer a certain repulsion. The metallic coating is connected to an internal earthing point on the oscilloscope so that secondary electrons striking it are conducted to earth and thereby prevented from giving rise to a net negative charge on the tube walls which, depending on its distribution, might distort the electron beam.

The deflection system of the oscilloscope consists of two pairs of parallel plates referred to as X-plates and Y-plates. By applying electric signals to these sets of plates, the electron beam is deflected accordingly, and the path traced out by the spot on the screen then represents these signals visually.

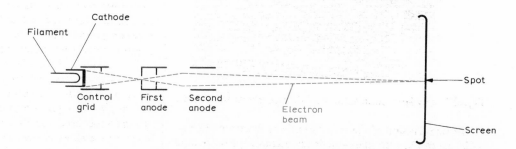

Fig.12.10   The effects of the brightness and focus controls when properly adjusted.

Herein lies the beauty and simplicity of the oscilloscope. It will be more instructive perhaps to consider the function of each pair of deflecting plates in context when we consider each of the three applications of the oscilloscope—as a voltmeter, as a signal display unit, and as a means of measuring the frequency of a given alternating electric signal. Let us consider each application in turn.

12.3 The Oscilloscope as a Voltmeter

The cathode ray oscilloscope is frequently used as a voltmeter. In this capacity it is of special value since there is no movable part whose inertia would prevent an immediate response to any rapid change in the potential difference being measured. The only movable part of the oscilloscope is the electron beam, the inertia of which can be regarded as effectively zero.

When the oscilloscope is to be used as a voltmeter, only the Y-deflection plates are used, and the potential difference to be measured is applied between the Y-input terminals of the instrument—the effect being to deflect the beam, and hence the spot on the screen, vertically. Let us consider the case of a steady direct potential difference being applied between the Y-deflection plates such that the upper plate is positive with respect to the lower plate. It follows that the spot will be deflected vertically upwards as a result of the beam being attracted towards the upper plate and repelled from the lower plate. More interesting still, the displacement of the spot on the screen from its zero position is *directly proportional* to the size of the unknown potential difference applied between the plates, so that the calibration of the instrument as a voltmeter is a very simple exercise. We can prove this relationship quite simply using the notation shown in Fig. 12.11.

The diagram shows the electron beam having left the second anode with speed v and entering the region of the Y-plates between which an unknown potential difference V has been applied. The dimensions of those parts of the tube in question are as shown.

When the electrons enter the region of the plates, each is subjected to a force acting vertically upwards. According to Newton's second law, each will therefore experience an acceleration vertically upwards, for as long as it is within the region of the plates. Since no force acts on the electrons horizontally (their horizontal acceleration having been completed at the second anode), then according to Newton's first law, their horizontal speed will remain unchanged. The motion of the electrons in the region of the Y-plates is thus analogous to that of a horizontally projected body in the Earth's gravitational field. (In this discussion we are neglecting the effects of gravity on the electron beam. This is a perfectly legitimate procedure which the reader may verify for himself in problem 2 at the end of the chapter.)

Let us consider the motion of any one electron of mass m and charge q in the region of the deflection plates. Since the horizontal speed of the particle is constant, then the time it spends between the plates is t where

$$t = \frac{x}{v}$$

The net force acting on the particle is that due to the presence of the electric field. Denoting this force by F, then

$$F = \frac{qV}{d}$$

Since this is the net force acting on the particle (neglecting its weight), then we may relate this force to the vertical acceleration of the particle—a say—by the equation

$$ma = \frac{qV}{d}$$

Hence

$$a = \frac{qV}{md}$$

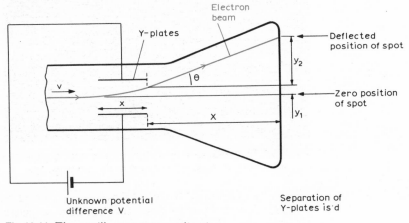

Fig.12.11 The oscilloscope as a voltmeter.

The vertical displacement of the electron on leaving the region of the plates may be calculated as s where

$$s = ut + \tfrac{1}{2}at^2$$

where u is the initial vertical speed of the electron (on entering the region of the plates), a is its vertical acceleration, and t is the time it spends between the plates. Since the electron is travelling horizontally on reaching the region of the plates, u is zero. Hence

$$s = \tfrac{1}{2}at^2$$
$$= \tfrac{1}{2}\left(\frac{qV}{md}\right)\left(\frac{x}{v}\right)^2$$
$$= \frac{qVx^2}{2mdv^2}$$

That is
$$y_1 = \frac{qVx^2}{2mdv^2}$$

Beyond the region of the plates, the electron experiences no net force, and so its trajectory will be a straight line, the slope of this line making some angle θ with the original direction and sense of motion.

The value of θ may be deduced by considering the direction of the electron's velocity as it leaves the region of the plates. This velocity has two components—v horizontally, and $\left(\frac{qV}{md}\right)\left(\frac{x}{v}\right)$ vertically (the latter being derived from the equation $v = u + at$ applied to the vertical motion). These two velocities may be compounded by adding vectors drawn as in Fig. 12.12.

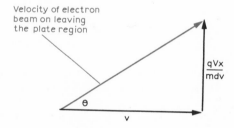

Velocity of electron beam on leaving the plate region

$$\frac{qVx}{mdv}$$

θ

v

Fig.12.12 Finding the velocity of the beam on leaving the region of the Y-plates.

The value of θ is then given by the equation

$$\tan\theta = \frac{qVx}{mdv^2}$$

Now the vertical displacement of the electron beam as a result of travelling between the Y-plates and the screen is given by the equation

$$y_2 = X\tan\theta$$

Hence
$$y_2 = \frac{XqVx}{mdv^2}$$

The net vertical displacement of the spot on the screen as measured from its zero position is calculated as $y_1 + y_2$. Denoting this by y, then we may write

$$y = \frac{qVx^2}{2mdv^2} + \frac{XqVx}{mdv^2}$$
$$= \frac{qx}{mdv^2}\left(\frac{x}{2} + X\right)V$$

Since q, x, m, d, v, and X are constants of the electron and of the instrument, then we may write

$$y = kV \quad \text{where } k \text{ is some composite constant}$$

That is
$$y \propto V$$

The net vertical displacement of the spot from its zero position on the screen is thus directly proportional to the potential difference applied between the Y-plates of the instrument. A single measurement of deflection produced by a known potential difference is therefore sufficient to calibrate the oscilloscope for use as a voltmeter.

When an alternating potential difference is applied between the Y-plates of the oscilloscope, the electron beam, and hence the spot on the screen, is made to oscillate vertically about the undisturbed zero position. If the frequency of the applied signal is fairly high—say 50 Hz—then the eye sees a vertical line on the screen rather than a moving spot (Fig. 12.13). This is because the spot is moving too quickly for the eye to follow. The length of this line represents twice the peak value of the applied alternating potential difference.

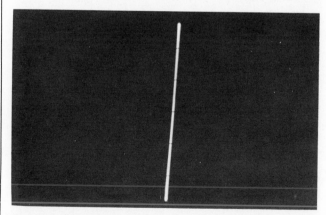

Fig.12.13 The effect of applying an alternating potential difference to the Y-plates of the oscilloscope.

We have suggested that the oscilloscope is a very satisfactory voltmeter in as much as the electron beam has a negligible inertia. In fact the oscilloscope offers many advantages as a voltmeter, the principal ones being listed below.

1 The oscilloscope is capable of recording both direct and alternating potential differences—the latter up to and including frequencies of the order of 10^6 Hz!

2 It is impossible to overload the instrument by applying a large unknown potential difference to the Y-plates. A very large potential difference would serve to deflect the beam into the Y-plates themselves, thereby doing no harm.

3 The resistance of the oscilloscope is infinite to direct current. This means that the instrument will draw no current from any circuit in which it is placed to measure potential difference. Its reactance to alternating current is also very high.

4 The oscilloscope incorporates a valve amplifier whose gain may be altered to allow for the measurement of very small potential differences which would produce negligible deflections on their own. When the gain of the amplifier is changed, the oscilloscope must be re-calibrated.

12.4 The Oscilloscope as an Oscillograph

So far we have considered the case of applying a potential difference between the Y-plates of the oscilloscope. We noted that if this potential difference was of an alternating nature, the spot on the screen would oscillate vertically, giving rise to a continuous vertical line trace (for a sufficiently high frequency signal). The length of this line gives information as to the peak value of the applied alternating signal but no information about its amplitude at times between the peaks. By the simultaneous use of both pairs of deflection plates however, the oscilloscope may be used to display the potential difference applied to the Y-plates as a function of time, as on a graph. This may be achieved by applying a potential difference between the X-plates which will sweep the spot across the screen at steady speed, so that when the potential difference under investigation is applied between the Y-plates, a picture or graph of this quantity is obtained in relation to time. The potential difference applied to the X-plates, giving rise to the effective time axis or *time base* is usually referred to as a *time base voltage*, and is supplied by an internal circuit of the oscilloscope known as the time base generator. The nature of this potential difference is displayed itself in relation to time in the sketch graph of Fig. 12.14.

We note that the time base voltage starts at a maximum negative value. By this we mean that the potential of the X-plate corresponding to the left hand side of the screen (viewed from the front) is made very negative with respect to the other X plate which is maintained at earth potential. The potential of this first plate then drops to a minimum negative (or maximum positive) value, after which it returns to its original value. Were a steady potential difference applied between the X-plates, then the spot would be observed to accelerate across the screen. Since the potential difference

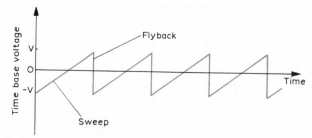

Fig.12.14 The nature of the time base voltage in relation to time.

between the plates rises linearly (from maximum negative) with respect to time, the speed of the spot across the screen does not rise linearly with respect to time. That is, the spot traverses the screen at steady speed, and in the sense left to right. If the sweep of the spot were not at steady speed, the horizontal deflection of the spot would not be proportional to time, and so the screen trace would not be a simple graph of potential difference against time.

If the potential difference being applied between the Y-plates is of a periodic nature—such as that of the (stepped down) mains supply—then one complete cycle of the signal will appear on the screen when the frequency of the time base voltage is equal to the frequency of the applied signal. If the frequency of the time base voltage is a simple fraction of that of the applied signal—say $\frac{1}{2}$, $\frac{1}{3}$, $\frac{1}{4}$ etc., then a corresponding integral number of complete cycles of the applied signal will appear on the screen—2, 3, 4 etc. When such a relationship between frequencies is not achieved, the traces from successive sweeps are not superimposed on previous traces, and the result is a continually moving picture. The diagram in Fig. 12.15 illustrates the appearance of the screen trace when a stepped down mains potential difference has been applied to the Y-plates of the oscilloscope and the frequency of the time base voltage has been set at 25 Hz.

In order to achieve a continuous graphical trace rather than a transitory trace, it is necessary that the spot should continually sweep the screen horizontally. Further, the time interval between sweeps should be zero so that perfect synchronisation is achieved between the time base signal and the applied signal. This implies that the return movement of the spot from right to left, known as the flyback motion, should be as rapid as possible. This is the reason for the time base voltage being of a sharp saw-tooth nature as in Fig. 12.14. Further, since the flyback bears no relation to the signal under observation, it is desirable that the return motion should not be seen. For this reason many oscilloscopes are now equipped with a suppressing circuit which has the effect of making the grid of the electron gun more negative than usual during the flyback period so that electrons are strongly repelled and never reach the screen during that period.

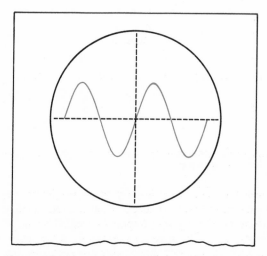

Fig.12.15 The trace obtained when the frequency of the time base voltage is equal to half the frequency of the applied signal.

12.5 The Oscilloscope as a Means of Determining Frequency

In the next chapter we shall consider the construction of an electronic oscillator. When such a device is constructed, it is desirable to know its frequency of oscillation, and although this frequency may be calculated in terms of the values of the circuit's components, it is easily and accurately measured using the oscilloscope. When the oscilloscope is being used to determine the frequency of a regular sinusoidal alternating signal, the time base control of the instrument is switched off, and the test signal is applied between the X-plates. The alternating sinusoidal signal from a calibrated signal generator is then applied between the Y-plates of the instrument, and the frequency of this signal adjusted until some stable pattern is observed on the oscilloscope screen. A careful examination of this pattern enables us to deduce the frequency of the signal under test.

The pattern obtained on the screen in this way is called a Lissajou Figure, after the French mathematician and physicist Jules Lissajou (1822–1880). The nature of the Lissajou Figure obtained depends on the frequencies and amplitudes (or peak values) of the two signals being supplied to the oscilloscope. If the two frequencies are exactly the same, a simple figure such as a straight line, a circle, or an ellipse is obtained. The frequency of the unknown signal is then taken as equal to that read off from the dial of the signal generator. That two signals of the same frequency can give rise to three simple geometrical figures is due to the possibility that these two signals might not be reaching the sets of plates exactly in phase. That is, although the frequencies of the two signals may be exactly the same, there exists the possibility that one reaches its set of plates say $\frac{1}{4}$ cycle before the other

reaches its plates. When the frequencies of the two signals are the same and their phase difference is zero, the resulting Lissajou Figure is a straight line. Further, if the peak value of each signal is the same, the straight line is inclined at 45° to the screen's X-axis. When the frequencies of the two signals are the same and the phase difference between the signals is between zero and 90°—that is, the two signals arrive at their respective plates out of step by less than $\frac{1}{4}$ cycle—the Lissajou Figure produced is an ellipse (Fig. 12.16). The angle between the screen's X-axis and the major axis of this ellipse is a measure of the phase difference between the signals. When the frequencies of the two signals are equal and the signals are out of step by exactly 90°, the Lissajou Figure produced is an ellipse whose major axis is observed to lie along either the X-axis or Y-axis on the screen, depending on which of the signals has the greater amplitude. By altering the amplitude of either signal until the two amplitudes are equal, the ellipse may be reduced to a circle (Fig. 12.17).

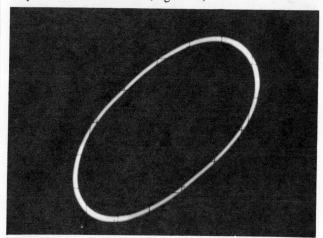

Fig.12.16

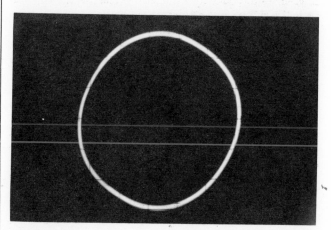

Fig.12.17

When the frequencies of the two signals applied to the oscilloscope are such that one is exactly twice the other, the Lissajou Figure produced is a figure eight. If the signal applied to the X-plates has a frequency equal to half that of the signal applied to the Y-plates, the figure eight appears on its side thus: ∞ (Fig. 12.18). If on the other hand the frequency of the signal applied to the X-plates is twice that of the signal applied to the Y-plates, the figure eight appears normal thus: 8. Once the frequency of the unknown signal has been determined from the observation of the simple Lissajou Figure, it is a useful exercise to vary the frequency of the calibrated signal until a figure eight pattern is obtained on the screen. This serves as a satisfactory check on the first result.

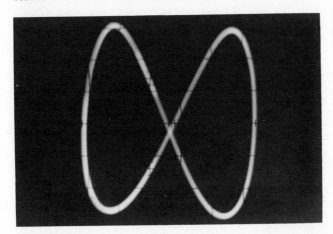

Fig.12.18

Can you draw the form of the Lissajou Figure which would be observed when the frequency of the test signal (applied to the X-plates) was equal to one third that of the calibrated signal (applied between the Y-plates)?

12.6 The Thermionic Diode and Rectification of an Alternating Potential Difference

When Edison carried out the investigation which we discussed in section 12.1, he was in fact investigating a crude form of that device known today as the thermionic diode. The diode is a simple device which permits electric current to flow in one sense only, and we may demonstrate its action with the circuit of Fig. 12.19.

When the switch in this circuit is closed, the ammeter indicates that a small current of the order of milliamperes is flowing in the circuit and hence through the vacumn tube. When the high tension supply is reversed however, so that the right hand plate of the tube is electrically negative with respect to the left hand plate, the meter registers no current at all. The diode is thus an asymmetric device in as much as

it permits electron current flow in one sense only.

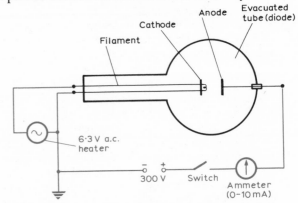

Fig.12.19 The operation of the demonstration diode.

The diode is also somewhat unusual in that it does not obey Ohm's Law when conducting current. Were we to vary the size of the potential difference between the anode (right hand plate) and cathode (left hand plate), connected as in Fig. 12.19, and to note the current flowing between the two as a result, we should find the relationship between current and potential difference to be that indicated by the sketch graph of Fig. 12.20.

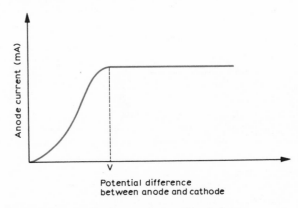

Fig.12.20 The diode does not obey Ohm's Law.

We may explain the nature of this relationship by saying that when the filament is heated by an electric current, electrons are 'boiled' from it by thermionic emission. These electrons constitute a small current as they drift across the tube under the influence of the potential difference between anode and cathode. Further, as the value of this potential difference is increased (between 0 and V), the attractive influence of the anode becomes greater, and so more of the thermionic electrons in the region immediately surrounding the cathode are included in the current. The strength of the tube current thus increases but according to a three halves power law, and not linearly as in the case of a metallic conductor which obeys Ohm's Law.

When a particular value of tube potential difference is reached, (V), we see that the tube current reaches a maximum or saturated value. This condition is achieved when the anode potential is sufficiently high to sweep electrons across the tube as soon as they are liberated from the hot filament. The size of the saturation current is limited by the number of electrons liberated from the filament per second, and so increasing the anode potential beyond this particular value V cannot possibly increase the current strength. The tube current may of course be raised above the saturation value of Fig. 12.20 by liberating more electrons from the filament each second, and this may be achieved by increasing the filament temperature by raising the potential difference of the heater supply.

Unusual as the characteristics of the diode may be, its action is of great importance in many electric circuits. The process of obtaining a direct current from a circuit to which an alternating potential is applied is known as *rectification*. The diode achieves this objective and is therefore known as a *rectifying device*.

The rectifying action of a thermionic diode may be demonstrated by using the circuit of Fig. 12.21 in which we introduce the conventional symbol for the thermionic diode for the first time.

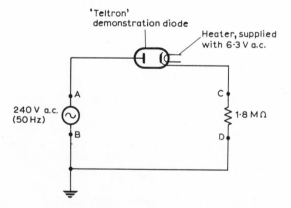

Fig.12.21 Investigating the rectifying action of the thermionic diode.

When an oscilloscope is connected between the points A and B and its time base control adjusted to give a stationary trace on the screen, the trace appears similar to that which is shown in Fig. 12.22(a). In the interpretation of this trace, we can say that it represents a graph of the potential difference of the source against time. Actually, since side B of the source is earthed, the trace is a graph of the potential of point A (and hence the anode of the diode) against time.

When the oscilloscope is then connected between the

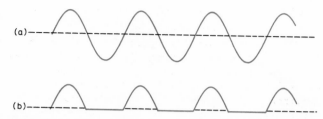

Fig.12.22 The signal before and after half-wave rectification.

points C and D—its time base control set as before—the trace on the screen appears similar to that shown in Fig. 12.22(b). From this trace we see that the potential difference developed across the 1·8 MΩ resistor is direct although not steady in value. Further, since point D is at earth potential this trace is a graph of the potential of point C against time.

Comparing the traces (a) and (b) of Fig. 12.22, we see that the negative half cycles produced at the source do not appear across the load resistance CD. That is, the alternating potential difference of the source has been rectified by the presence of the thermionic diode. This type of rectification, in which alternate half cycles of potential difference are eliminated, is referred to as *half-wave rectification*.

We can explain the rectifying action of the diode by considering that during that half cycle in which the potential of point A varies positively relative to that of point B (zero volts) the potential of the anode of the diode varies positively relative to that of the cathode. The diode thus conducts, and current therefore flows in an anticlockwise sense in the circuit. This means that current flows in the sense D to C through the load resistor, so that point C varies positively relative to point D (at zero volts). During the following half cycle in which the potential of point A varies negatively relative to that of point B (zero volts), the potential of the anode varies negatively relative to that of the cathode. The diode does not conduct therefore, so that no current flows in the circuit and hence no potential difference is developed between points C and D. Point C is thus at the same potential as point D (zero volts) during negative half cycles.

It appears rather wasteful to eliminate half of the alternating signal by this process of half-wave rectification. By employing two diodes and a centre-tapped transformer however, *full-wave rectification* (a process in which the negative half cycles of the source are developed as positive half cycles across the load resistor in addition to the original positive half cycles) may be obtained. An example of this is given in problem 9 as the end of the chapter.

As we have noted from the trace in Fig. 12.22(b), the potential of the point C is direct but its value is far from steady. The mean value of the potential of the point C may be increased, and the variation in its value smoothed, by the introduction of a large reservoir capacitor in the circuit of Fig. 12.21, so that it appears as in Fig. 12.23.

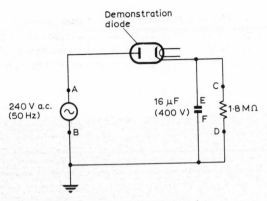

Fig.12.23 Introducing a reservoir capacitor.

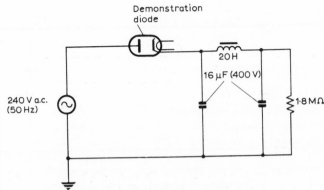

Fig.12.25 Introducing a simple filter circuit.

When the oscilloscope is then connected between the points C and D of the modified circuit, (time base setting as before), then by increasing the oscilloscope's input gain control, the 'smoothed' trace may be examined in the detail of Fig. 12.24. From this trace we see that the variation in the potential of point C has been smoothed considerably in relation to its original form (indicated by the dotted line in the diagram).

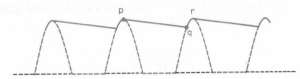

Fig.12.24 The smoothing action of the reservoir capacitor.

In Fig. 12.24, the point p represents the beginning of the capacitor's slow discharge through the resistor. This slow discharge continues while the potential across the diode is in the 'reverse' direction and the diode is not conducting. When the potential of A rises above that of E (on the next positive half cycle)—at the point q—the diode will conduct again, thereby charging the capacitor to its maximum value again, at the point r. The larger the capacitance of EF and the higher the resistance of CD, the slower will be the fall along pq and the smaller the residual ripple.

The ripple in the potential of point C can be further reduced, in an attempt to produce a steady potential, by the introduction of a filter circuit consisting of an inductor and a second capacitor, arranged as shown in Fig. 12.25.

We recall from Chapter 11 that the reactance of an inductor is $2\pi fL$ (in the usual notation). Since the single diode provides for half-wave rectification, 50 ripples (of the type shown in Fig. 12.24) will be generated per second, so that the ripple frequency is 50 Hz. The reactance of the coil shown in Fig. 12.25 is thus $(2 \times 3 \cdot 14 \times 50 \times 20)$ Ω or 6000 Ω (approx-

imately). Further, the reactance of a capacitor is $\dfrac{1}{2\pi fC}$ (in the usual notation), so that the reactance of the second capacitor is approximately 200 Ω. The reactance of the inductor is thus of the order thirty times as large as that of the capacitor, and since the two are in series, only about one part in thirty of the *ripple* component of the signal represented in Fig. 12.24 will appear across the second capacitor in Fig. 12.25. The full value of the direct component of the signal of Fig. 12.24 will be passed by the coil (since its d.c. resistance is effectively zero) so that this d.c. component will appear unaltered across the second capacitor and hence across the load resistor. This resistor is thus finally supplied with an acceptable steady direct current.

Problems
(Where necessary, take the electronic charge as $1 \cdot 6 \times 10^{-19}$ C, the electronic mass as 9×10^{-31} kg, and g as 10 m s^{-2}.)

1 Write a short essay on the early investigations which led to the idea that cathode rays were in fact electrons.
2 Explain why it is a legitimate procedure to neglect the weight of an electron when discussing its vertical deflection between horizontal parallel metal plates 5 cm apart and between which exists a potential difference of 400 V.
3 An alternating potential difference is supplied to the Y-plates of an oscilloscope whose time base control has been switched off. The result is to produce a vertical line 4 cm long on the screen. If the oscilloscope construction is such that 5 V (d.c.) deflects the spot on the screen 1 cm vertically, what is the r.m.s. value of the applied alternating signal?
4 In the electron gun of an oscilloscope, the potential difference between the cathode and the final anode is 1000 V. With what speed will the electrons in the beam emerge from this anode?
5 Electrons accelerated as in the last problem then enter a vertical deflection region whose characteristics are as shown in Fig. 12.26.

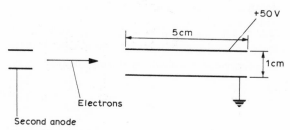

Fig.12.26 See Problem 5.

Calculate the time each electron spends between the plates, and hence find the vertical deflection of the beam on leaving the plates. Find also the velocity of the beam leaving the plates, and hence calculate the deflection of the spot on the oscilloscope screen from its zero position, given that the right hand edges of the deflection plates are 10 cm distant from the screen.

6   A simple time base circuit may be constructed according to the circuit diagram of Fig. 12.27.

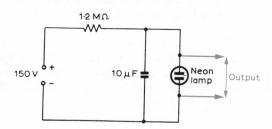

Fig.12.27 See Problem 6.

When the Y-plates of an oscilloscope are connected to the output terminals of this circuit, a screen trace similar to that illustrated in Fig. 12.28 is produced.

Fig.12.28 See Problem 6.

Explain the processes contributing to this trace, and discuss the limitations in its form for use as a time base voltage.

7   Given a source of alternating potential difference, a resistor, a capacitor, and an oscilloscope, how might you demonstrate that a phase difference of $\frac{1}{4}$ cycle exists between the potential differences developed across the two components resistor and capacitor when they are connected in series across the alternating supply?

8   Figure 12.29 shows the oscilloscope trace obtained when alternating signals of different frequencies were applied to the X-plates and Y-plates of the instrument simultaneously.

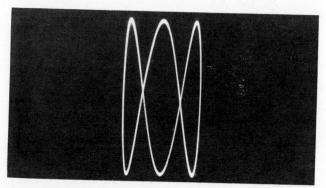

Fig.12.29 See Problem 8.

If the frequency of the signal applied to the Y-plates was 50 Hz, what was the frequency of the signal applied to the X-plates?

9   The diagram in Fig. 12.30 illustrates a circuit which gives rise to full wave rectification.

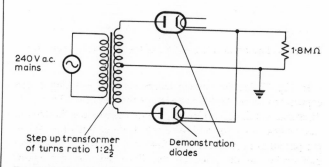

Fig.12.30 See Problem 9.

When the Y-plates of an oscilloscope are connected across the ends of the load resistor, the screen trace appears as in Fig. 12.31.

Fig.12.31 See Problem 9.

Explain what this trace really indicates and why it should assume this form.

10 Sketch the form of the oscilloscope trace (originally as in Fig. 12.31) obtained after a large reservoir capacitor has been connected in parallel with the load resistor of Fig. 12.30.

Calculate the approximate reduction in the ripple appearing in the potential difference across the load resistor if an additional filter circuit is connected, in which the coil has inductance 2 H (and negligible resistance) and the capacitor has capacitance 25 μF—the filter circuit being connected in a similar manner to that in Fig. 12.25.

Chapter 13

Semiconductor Devices and their Applications

Fig.13.0 Three 'driver' transistors from the wide range of Mullard semiconductor devices, shown in relation to matchsticks. (By kind permission of Mullard Ltd.)

In this chapter we shall discuss two devices which are fabricated from materials which, as far as the conduction of electricity is concerned, lie between the metals and the insulators. These materials are known as the *semiconductors*. The study of the properties of semiconductor materials has led to enormous advances in the field of electronics, and it seems likely that semiconductor devices will replace all remaining thermionic devices in the not too distant future.

Although there is now a wide variety of semiconductor devices which can perform a multitude of electrical tasks with high efficiency and reliability, we shall limit ourselves in this chapter to the study of two of the earliest devices—the junction diode and the junction transistor.

It has been suggested that the first significant contribution to semiconductor research was made by Michael Faraday as early as 1833. In that year, Faraday observed that the resistance of silver sulphide varied *inversely* as its temperature, and so established the idea of a negative temperature coefficient of resistance which is now found to be characteristic of all semiconductor materials. Faraday's observation did not initiate a feverish research campaign however, and it was not until 1948 that the transistor was invented. Whether or not the field of semiconductor research was slow to develop, its progress from 1948 has done much to influence and often improve our lives. Transistors by virtue of their size have found application in hearing aids, heart 'pacemakers', and telephone systems. The production of semiconductor devices has to a large extent revolutionised home entertainment as far as radio, television, and stereophonic sound are concerned. Modern commerce and industry seem unable to survive without the assistance of electronic computers—these computers becoming larger and more and more sophisticated as new and more elaborate semiconductor devices become available (Figs. 13.1, 13.2).

It would be quite wrong to assume that semiconductor technology has reached its final limit of advancement in terms of the devices now available. Progress is becoming more rapid as new materials become available and new techniques are developed towards the micro-miniaturisation of the semiconductor devices (Fig. 13.3). Although the

Fig.13.1 The IBM System 370 (Model 135) Computer. (By kind permission of IBM Ltd.)

Fig.13.2　The computer in Fig. 13.1 employs many tiny integrated circuits of the type shown here. One 9 × 13-inch circuit board carries 1152 arrays to provide 524 288 bytes (characters). (By kind permission of IBM Ltd.)

ultimate advancement in devices is unforseeable, the limit to miniaturisation has long been recognised as the finite size of the atom itself. The successful operation of all semiconductor devices is very dependent on the atomic structure of the semiconductor materials, and it is with this structure we begin our discussions.

13.1 Pure and Impure Semiconductors

Semiconductor devices are fabricated from many semiconductor materials, but the most popular of these materials at the present time are germanium and silicon, both of which are hard, brittle, and crystalline in nature. The atoms of each of these two materials have four electrons in the outer orbit (or valence band), and adjacent atoms in the crystal lattice are linked according to a co-valent bonding scheme. Since germanium is the more versatile material in terms of transistor action, we shall make reference to its lattice structure from now on, and represent this structure as in Fig. 13.4. The structure of the crystal is of course three dimensional but it is more convenient to represent it in two dimensions as shown. In the diagram we have shown only the valence shell of each atom in addition to its nucleus, although each atom has in fact 32 electrons, arranged in four orbits. We have shown only the valence shell since it is the nature of this shell which figures largely in the determination of the element's properties; it is the electrons of the valence shell which are engaged in chemical reactions. As far as electrical conduction is concerned, it is only electrons in the valence shell which can contribute to the conduction process—electrons in the inner shells being more tightly bound to the atomic nucleus, and hence more difficult to dislodge from their orbits.

Assuming that the structure shown in Fig. 13.4 represents a pure or perfect sample of a germanium crystal, we can see that in the pure crystalline form, every atom is equidistant from four other atoms, and all the co-valent bonds are intact. This being the case, no electrons are free to drift through the crystal if an electric field is applied to it, so that such a stable and perfect crystal would seem to be a perfect electrical insulator. Electrical conduction can become possible only if

(a)

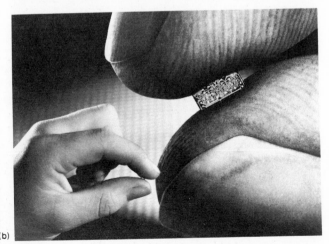

(b)

Fig.13.3　A complete electronic counting circuit containing over 120 components is shown in relation to (a) a no. 5 sewing needle and 40-gauge sewing cotton, and (b) the fingers of an adult hand. (By kind permission of Mullard Ltd.)

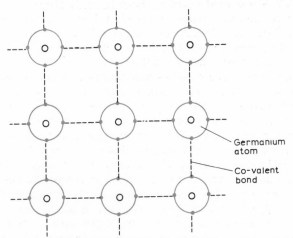

Fig.13.4 The pure germanium crystal lattice represented in two dimensions.

some of the co-valent bonds are broken.

It is accepted that in heating the perfect crystal, some of its electrons acquire sufficient energy to leave their valence bands and thus become available for electrical conduction. The amount of energy required towards this end is known as the *ionisation energy* of the process. When an atom loses an electron in this way, it acquires both a net positive charge, and a 'hole'—the latter being available to accept an electron from some neighbouring atom in the crystal. Let us suppose that atom A has lost an electron by ionisation so that it is left with a hole and of course a net positive charge. If atom A somehow receives an electron from neighbouring atom B, then the hole and the associated positive charge appears to have moved from A to B, although an electron has actually moved from B to A.

When a steady potential difference is applied to a pure semiconductor at room temperature (this temperature being sufficient to give rise to some electron-hole pairs within the lattice), the *free* electrons produced by ionisation are constrained to flow in one sense, while the holes formed are constrained to flow in the opposite sense. Since the movement of a hole is accompanied by an effective transfer of positive charge, it is necessary to regard the total current flowing in the semiconductor material as the sum of the free electron current in one sense and a positive hole current in the opposite sense.

Although there must be equal numbers of electrons and holes in a pure germanium crystal, it is unlikely that the two types of current flowing under a steady potential difference should be equal in size. The reason for this is that, while a free electron can drift between the atoms in the lattice at a steady pace, a given hole is restricted to a series of short movements from atom to atom.

The total current which can be generated in a pure or intrinsic semiconductor as a result of the application of a small potential difference is referred to as the *intrinsic current* of the material, and its size is usually of the order of micro-amps when the potential difference applied to the crystal is of the order of a few volts. As the temperature of the material is increased, more electron-hole pairs are generated thereby adding to the number of available charge carriers in the material. This implies that since a larger intrinsic current can now be generated by the application of the same potential difference, the resistance of the semiconductor material has decreased with increasing temperature.

The electrical conductivity of a semiconductor material can also be increased by adding controlled amounts of chemical impurities to the crystal during its growth. The theory behind such chemical doping is that an impurity material may be chosen such that the valence bands of its atoms contain more than or less than the number of electrons present in the valence band of the normal crystal atoms. A large increase can thus be effected in the number of free charge carriers (electrons or holes, depending on the impurity) present in the semiconductor. The semiconductor, once doped, is thereafter referred to as an *impurity semiconductor* rather than an *intrinsic semiconductor*.

If an impurity element with five valence electrons is introduced to a germanium crystal, only four of these five valence electrons of each impurity atom can be contained in the co-valent bonding scheme of the crystal so that one electron per impurity atom is free within the crystal lattice. It is not free as a result of ionisation, but rather as a result of redundancy in relation to bonding so that the crystal is electrically neutral following doping and not negatively charged as is sometimes wrongly assumed. Germanium doped in this way is referred to as *n-type germanium*—the 'n' denoting the nature of the free charge carriers present and not to some net electrical charging.

Such n-type material may be obtained by introducing *arsenic* to the crystal as an impurity at concentrations of one part in several million—arsenic atoms having five electrons in their valence bands. The diagram in Fig. 13.5 shows part of the crystal lattice in which one of the germanium atoms has been replaced by an arsenic atom, and, as we can see, one electron is relatively free to move through the lattice and thereby to take part in electrical conduction.

In donating free electrons to the crystal lattice in this way, arsenic is referred to as a 'donor' impurity, the free electrons donated constituting the majority current carriers in the crystal. As such, they resemble the free electrons present in a metallic conductor. Since a small number of holes will be present in the crystal as the result of some ionisation occurring within the crystal at room temperature, these will also be available for electrical conduction but in the role of minority current carriers.

It is found that by doping a sample of semiconductor to

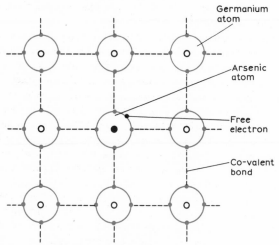

Fig.13.5   Producing *n*-type semiconductor.

the order of one part impurity in one million, the electrical resistance of the sample is of the order of one hundred times less than that of an otherwise identical intrinsic sample.

If an impurity element with three valence electrons is introduced to a germanium crystal, each of these electrons will be contained in the co-valent bonding scheme, and a hole will be introduced to the lattice for every impurity atom present. Again we must emphasise that the hole is not present as the result of ionisation, but rather as the result of impurity introduction, the crystal lattice remaining electrically neutral as a whole. Germanium doped in this way, is referred to as *p-type germanium*—the 'p' referring to the nature of the free charge carriers. We recall that when an electron from a neighbouring atom fills the hole, it leaves a hole behind it, and in addition, a net positive charge, so that a positive hole appears to have detached itself and moved freely from one atom to another.

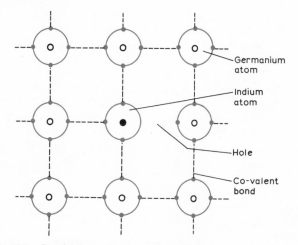

Fig.13.6   Producing *p*-type semiconductor.

A p-type material may be obtained by introducing *indium* to the crystal lattice as an impurity of one part in several million—indium atoms being characterised by three valence electrons in their valence bands. The diagram of Fig. 13.6 shows part of the crystal lattice in which one of the germanium atoms has been replaced by an indium atom, and it is clear that a hole exists in the lattice which can take part in electrical conduction.

Since the impurity atoms in this case are available to accept electrons from neighbouring atoms, the impurity is referred to as an 'acceptor' impurity, and the holes it introduces to the lattice constitute the majority current carriers in the crystal. Free electrons will also be available for electrical conduction but only as minority current carriers since they are produced by a low level of thermal ionisation within the crystal at room temperature.

13.2 The Semiconductor Diode
When a crystal of germanium is grown such that one half of it is p-type in nature and the other half is n-type, the final product has most useful rectifying properties and is known as a p-n junction diode.

When the junction between the p-type and n-type materials is formed in the growth of the crystal, some of the free electrons from the n-type material, diffuse across the junction to neutralise some of the holes on the other side, while some of the holes in this same region, diffuse across the junction to combine with free electrons in the n-type material. Obviously the n-type region, in losing electrons to the p-type region, is becoming positively charged in the vicinity of the junction, while the p-type region, in the vicinity of the junction, is becoming negatively charged, as a result of losing some holes. An effective potential difference (called a *barrier potential difference*) is therefore established across the junction. When this potential difference reaches a certain value of say 0·1 V, it will oppose any further diffusion of charge carriers across the junction. The situation is then as represented as in Fig. 13.7, in which the effective barrier potential difference is indicated by a dotted line. The regions over which the barrier potential difference extends, having lost their charge carriers by diffusion across the junction, constitute what is known as the *depletion layer*.

If a cell whose e.m.f. is greater than the barrier potential difference is now connected across the p-n junction as shown in Fig. 13.8, the free charge carriers in each of the p-type and n-type materials are repelled towards the region of the junction, there to neutralise the electric charges which have built up in the depletion layer. The barrier potential difference is therefore reduced to zero and thereafter, the charge carriers cross the junction—holes from left to right, electrons from right to left. The current thus constituted in the device is then found to increase as the e.m.f. of the cell is increased.

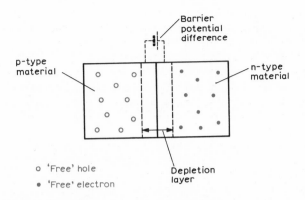

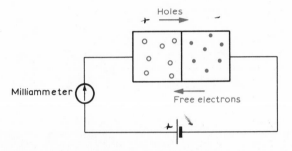

Fig.13.7   Combining *n*-type and *p*-type materials.

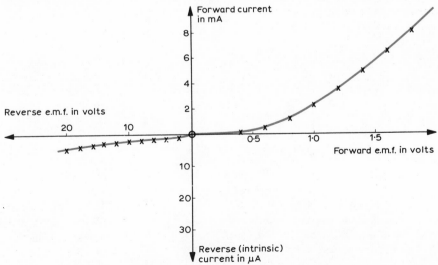

Fig.13.8   The *p–n* junction forward biassed.

When the junction and an external cell are connected in this way so that current flows in the circuit formed, the device is said to be *forward biassed*. As such, it is able to pass a current of several milliamps when the e.m.f. of the external cell is of the order of one or two volts. We shall regard the resistance of the device in the forward biassed configuration as fairly low.

If the same cell is now connected across the p-n junction in the opposite sense, as is shown in Fig. 13.9, the holes in the p-type material are attracted away from the junction and towards the negative pole of the cell, while the free electrons in the n-type material are attracted away from the junction and towards the cell's positive pole. The effect is therefore to increase the electrical charge separation in the depletion layer shown in Fig. 13.7, so that an increased barrier potential difference is established. Current is thus restricted from flowing as far as the majority carriers are concerned, but it is found that a small current may flow as a result of transfer of the minority carriers in the materials. The size of this current is dependent on temperature rather than the applied potential difference since it is limited by the concentration of the minority carriers, which are thermally generated.

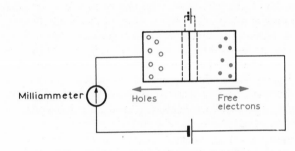

Fig.13.9   The *p–n* junction reverse biassed.

When the junction and an external cell are connected in this way, such that only a very small intrinsic current flows

Fig.13.10 The characteristics of the *p–n* junction.

in the circuit formed, the arrangement is said to be *reverse biassed*. As such, the intrinsic current which flows is of the order of several microamps when the e.m.f. of the external cell or battery is of the order of ten or twenty volts.

The electrical characteristics of a p-n junction may be shown graphically as in Fig. 13.10. These characteristics may be determined using a variable voltage supply, a voltmeter, an ammeter, and a p-n junction such as that of the OA91 diode.

From Fig. 13.10 we see that the effective resistance of the p-n junction is of the order of hundreds of ohms when the junction is connected in the forward biassed arrangement. The effective resistance is of the order of megohms however when the junction is connected in the reverse biassed arrangement. The junction thus exhibits the rectifying property of being able to pass current effectively in one sense only, and it is for this reason that it is usually referred to as the p-n junction diode. It is unlike the thermionic diode however in as much as its current carriers are both positive and negative while those of the thermionic diode are purely negative. Further, the junction diode exhibits a small degree of conduction in the reverse sense—an effect which is not observed with the thermionic diode. A more significant difference between the two types of diode is that the rate of flow of charge carriers in the p-n junction is far less than that in the thermionic device so the semiconductor diode is likely to be somewhat inefficient as regards its response to high frequency signals applied to it.

The semiconductor diode is represented in circuit diagrams by the symbol shown in Fig. 13.11—the symbol being explained by the labels on the diagram. In practice, the n-type end of such a diode is usually identified by a coloured ring (red or black) at that end.

(p-type region)   (n-type region)

Fig.13.11 The symbol for the semiconductor diode.

It follows that when a semiconductor diode is connected in a circuit as in Fig. 13.12(a), it will conduct since it is then forward biassed. When connections are made as in Fig. 13.12(b) however, the diode will not conduct since it is then reverse biassed.

The semiconductor diode may be used to demonstrate half wave rectification when it is included in the circuit of Fig. 13.13. When an oscilloscope is connected between the points A and B of this circuit, and its time base control adjusted to give a stationary trace on the screen, that trace appears similar to that which is shown in Fig. 13.14(a). Following our discussions of the last chapter, this trace represents the

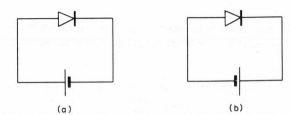

(a)   (b)

Fig.13.12 Biassing the diode in (a) the forward, (b) the reverse sense.

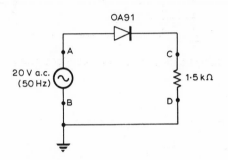

Fig.13.13 Investigating the rectifying action of the semi-conductor diode.

potential of the p-type side of the diode in relation to time.

When the oscilloscope is then connected between points C and D, its time base control being adjusted as before, the screen trace then resembles that shown in Fig. 13.14(b). This trace represents the potential of point C in relation to time.

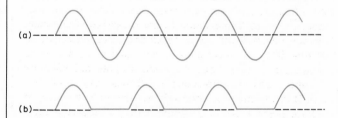

(a)

(b)

Fig.13.14 The signal before and after half-wave rectification.

We see therefore that the insertion of the semiconductor diode in the circuit has suppressed those half cycles of negative e.m.f. generated at the source. An unsteady but direct potential difference has thus been derived from an alternating one.

It is possible to demonstrate full-wave rectification of an alternating e.m.f. when four semiconductor diodes are arranged as shown in the circuit of Fig. 13.15. When an oscilloscope with suitably adjusted time base control is connected between points A and B of this circuit, the screen trace appears similar to that shown in Fig. 13.16(a). When the oscilloscope is then connected between points C and D in the circuit, the screen trace appears similar to that shown in Fig. 13.16(b), assuming the time base control to be unaltered.

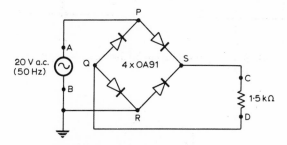

Fig.13.15 Investigating the bridge rectifier circuit.

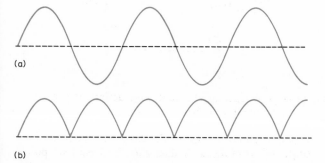

(a)

(b)

Fig.13.16 The signal before and after full-wave rectification.

Since point B of the supply is at earth potential, the trace of Fig. 13.16(a) is a graph of the potential of point A against time. Assuming the forward resistance of each of the four diodes to be small in relation to the resistance of the load, then the potential difference developed across each will at any time be small in comparison with that being developed across the load at that time. Assuming the potential difference developed across that diode in arm QR to be very small, then point D of the circuit is effectively at earth potential, and so the trace of Fig. 13.16(b) is a graph of the potential of point C against time.

We see that the insertion of the four diode network—called a *bridge rectifier*—in the circuit, has provided for the reversal of those half cycles of negative e.m.f. generated at the source, thereby giving rise to the process of full-wave rectification.

We can analyse the full-wave rectification process as follows. During the first half cycle of events, the potential of point A is varying positively with respect to that of B (zero volts). This implies that the potential of the n-type side of the diode in PQ is varying positively throughout this half cycle, so that this diode is effectively reverse biassed during this time. The diode in PS is effectively forward biassed during this first half-cycle however. Also during this time, the potential of the p-type side of the diode in RS is in effect negative,

thereby biassing this diode in the reverse sense. Since the n-type side of the diode in QR is in effect negative during the first half cycle, that diode is forward biassed during this interval. Electron current can therefore flow in the sense $B \rightarrow R \rightarrow Q \rightarrow D \rightarrow C \rightarrow S \rightarrow P \rightarrow A$ during this first half cycle of events. Since the current flows in the sense $D \rightarrow C$ through the load resistor, the potential difference developed across the load as such that C is varying positively with respect to D.

During the second half cycle of events, the potential of point A is varying negatively with respect to that of B (zero volts). In terms of the discussion of the last paragraph, it follows that the diodes in PS and QR are reverse biassed, while those in PQ and RS are forward biassed. Electron current can therefore flow in the sense $A \rightarrow P \rightarrow Q \rightarrow D \rightarrow C \rightarrow S \rightarrow R \rightarrow B$ during this second half cycle. Again, since the current flows in the sense $D \rightarrow C$ through the load resistor, the potential difference developed across the load is such that C is varying positively with respect to D.

Potential difference is thus developed across the load resistor for every half cycle of e.m.f. developed at the source, but in such a way as to be unidirectional. While a varying but unidirectional potential difference is developed across the load resistor fifty times per second in the case of the half-wave rectification process, the same type of potential difference is developed across the load resistor one hundred times per second in the case of full-wave rectification. This latter process thus allows for easier smoothing of the varying but direct output. The filter circuits to be used are then designed with regard to a ripple frequency of 100 Hz rather than one of 50 Hz.

13.3 The Junction Transistor

The junction transistor is essentially a semiconductor sandwich formed when two p-n junctions are arranged back to back in a single piece of semiconductor material. Obviously the two p-n junctions can be arranged so as to form a p-n-p arrangement or an n-p-n arrangement—these arrangements being known as p-n-p and n-p-n transistors respectively. Although the operation of the p-n-p transistor is somewhat more difficult to explain than that of the n-p-n type, the p-n-p transistor is more easily manufactured and hence more popular in electronic circuits. We shall thus concern ourselves with this device.

The diagram in Fig. 13.17(a) shows a suitably labelled representation of the p-n-p transistor for the purposes of our discussion, while the diagram of Fig. 13.17(b) gives a more realistic impression of the actual construction of the transistor.

As is suggested by Fig. 13.17(b) the transistor is a very small device, and this size has enabled it to find widespread application in computers, satellites, and elaborate telephone systems—projects in which compactness and neatness are essential requirements. Associated with its size, the transistor

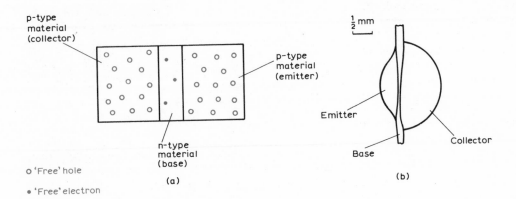

Fig.13.17 The construction of the *p–n–p* transistor.

requires a low voltage supply for its operation—nine volts often being sufficient. This is much more acceptable than the high tension supplies which have to be provided for the successful operation of the more clumsy vacuum tube amplifying devices.

With these introductions to the junction transistor, let us now consider its action in some detail.

In Fig. 13.18, we have shown the p-n-p transistor with connections to two cells arranged such that the emitter-base region is forward biassed, while the base-collector region is reverse biassed.

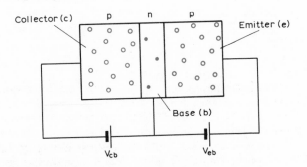

Fig.13.18 Biassing the *p–n-p* transistor.

If the concentration of free holes in the emitter region has been made very large in comparison with that of free electrons in the base region, then the current flowing in the forward biassed emitter-base region will be due almost entirely to the movement of holes from emitter to base. Further, on reaching the base region, only a small number of these holes will recombine with the free and widely spaced electrons in that region. Since the base region is extremely thin and the collector area is large (as can be seen from Fig. 13.17(b)), almost all of the holes are attracted into the collector region under the influence of the potential difference V_{cb} which has been applied between the base and collector regions. The

current flowing into the collector I_c is thus almost equal to the current flowing from the emitter I_e. The difference in size between these currents may be accounted for in terms of the small amount of recombination of holes and electrons which has taken place in the base region. To replace these base electrons, electrons must flow from the emitter-base cell thereby giving rise to a small base current I_b such that

$$I_b = I_e - I_c$$

or

$$\boxed{I_e = I_c + I_b} \quad \ldots \ldots \ldots \ldots (13.1)$$

In practice with a typical low power p-n-p transistor, suitably biassed, it is found that when the emitter current is say 1 mA, the collector current is 0·98 mA, and the base current is 0·02 mA.

If we define α—the current amplification factor (sometimes called the current transfer ratio) of the transistor—as the ratio of the change in collector current (ΔI_c), produced by a change in emitter current (ΔI_e) to this change in emitter current, then we may write

$$\alpha = \frac{\Delta I_c}{\Delta I_e}$$

In our discussion,

$$\alpha = \frac{0·98}{1·00}$$

$$= 0·98$$

This suggests that the transistor is somewhat inefficient in as much as it amplifies current by a factor less than one.

Let us examine the situation more closely. We have suggested that a current of 1 mA flows between the emitter and base regions, the resistance between which is of the order of say 100 Ω, since the junction between these regions is forward biassed. Further, it seems that a current of 0·98 mA flows between the base and collector regions, the resistance between which is of the order of 10^6 Ω, since the junction between these regions is reverse biassed. On calculating the power dissipation at each junction, it would seem that 10^{-4} watts of power is dissipated between the emitter and base, while 0·96 watts is dissipated between the base and collector. The action of the transistor therefore seems to have been successful as regards the amplification of power. The action of the transistor has allowed for the passage of a given current through a large resistor almost unaffected. This idea of current transfer through a resistor gave rise to the coining of the name trans-istor or transistor.

Regarding the input to the transistor as being constituted by those connections existing between the emitter and base regions, and the output from the device as constituted by those connections between base and collector, we see that the base terminal is common to both input and output circuits as far as our discussion has been concerned this far. When the transistor is considered in this way, we say that it is connected in the *common base configuration*. The diagram of Fig. 13.19 illustrates the circuit diagram for the investigation of this configuration, and in this diagram we introduce the conventional p-n-p transistor symbol for the first time.

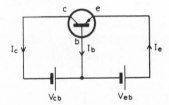

Fig.13.19 The *p–n–p* transistor in the common base configuration.

The transistor may be employed to achieve amplification of current if an input is fed between its base and emitter, and an output taken from between the emitter and collector. The transistor is then said to be connected in the *common emitter configuration*, as shown in Fig. 13.20.

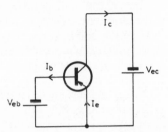

Fig.13.20 The *p–n–p* transistor in the common emitter configuration.

In the case of the common base configuration, we defined the amplification factor of the transistor by the equation

$$\alpha = \frac{\Delta I_c}{\Delta I_e}$$

In the case of the common emitter configuration however, it becomes necessary to define β—the current amplification factor (sometimes called the current transfer ratio) in the common emitter configuration—by the equation

$$\beta = \frac{\Delta I_c}{\Delta I_b}$$

Here ΔI_c is the change in collector current resulting from a change in base current ΔI_b.

Now according to equation (13.1)

$$I_e = I_c + I_b$$

so that

$$\Delta I_e = \Delta I_c + \Delta I_b$$

and

$$\frac{\Delta I_e}{\Delta I_c} = 1 + \frac{\Delta I_b}{\Delta I_c}$$

Hence

$$\frac{1}{\alpha} = 1 + \frac{1}{\beta}$$

$$\Leftrightarrow \beta = \frac{1}{\frac{1}{\alpha} - 1}$$

$$\Leftrightarrow \beta = \frac{\alpha}{1 - \alpha}$$

If the transistor referred to in Fig. 13.20 is the same as that referred to before, then $\alpha = 0·98$ and so

$$\beta = \frac{0·98}{1 - 0·98}$$

$$= 49$$

That is, a change in current of say 10 μA in the emitter-base circuit of the transistor considered should give rise to a change in current of 0·49 mA in the emitter-collector circuit of the transistor.

Having discussed the rather theoretical aspects of the transistor's functioning this far, let us now extend our discussions to consider some practical applications of the device. We shall conclude this chapter by considering three interesting and practical applications of the transistor in everyday use.

13.4 The Common Emitter Amplifier

Although the transistor can be connected in any of three configurations, of which we have so far considered two, the common emitter configuration is by far the most successful and frequently used for the purposes of amplification of audio information. We discussed the fact that in the common emitter configuration, a definite current amplification was obtained—the amplified current appearing in the collector circuit. When information is amplified however, it is more easily extracted from the amplifying system in the form of a potential difference than in the form of a current, and such extraction is usually accomplished by inserting a resistive load in the collector circuit. The potential difference developed across this load is at all times representative of the amplified collector current flowing through it. In our practical transistor amplifier therefore, the circuit of Fig. 13.20 will be modified by inserting a resistor between the transistor's collector and the negative pole of the cell in the collector-emitter circuit.

When audio information is supplied, this information is in the form of an alternating signal. This signal, characterised by an alternating potential difference is applied between the base and emitter terminals of the transistor when the latter is arranged in common emitter configuration. The signal will only be amplified successfully—that is, as a faithful but enlarged replica of the original signal—if the transistor has been set at its correct operating conditions as far as the direct currents in the base and collector regions are concerned. This means that the d.c. biassing arrangements must be chosen wisely with regard to the characteristics of the particular transistor, and the value of the resistive load.

The output characteristics of an OC71 transistor (now being replaced by the AC126 transistor) connected in common emitter configuration, may be obtained by setting up the circuit shown in Fig. 13.21, setting the base current to a particular value, and noting changes in collector current resulting from changes in the potential difference applied between collector and emitter. This procedure may be repeated for different base currents so that a family of output characteristic curves may be obtained for this transistor in this arrangement. Such a family of curves appears in Fig. 13.22.

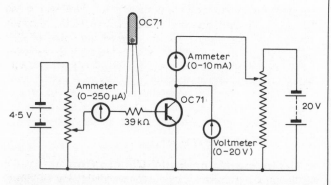

Fig.13.21 Investigating the characteristics of a *p–n–p* transistor in common emitter configuration.

If this transistor is now connected with a 4·7 kΩ resistor in its collector circuit, and a 12 V battery is connected between the two as in Fig. 13.23, then obviously the maximum possible current which the transistor can draw from the supply (when

a suitable current flows in the base circuit) is given as I_c where

$$I_c = \frac{12}{4\cdot7 \times 10^3} \text{ A}$$

$$= 2\cdot55 \text{ mA}$$

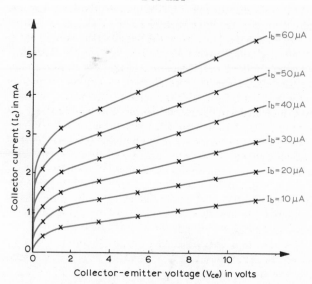

Fig.13.22 The output characteristics of an OC71 (AC126) transistor.

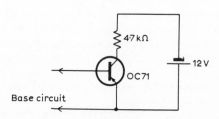

Fig.13.23 Introducing a load resistor.

The introduction of the load resistor may be related to the characteristics of the transistor by drawing the *load line* on the output characteristic curves. This line is drawn by joining the points on the graph representing the maximum potential difference which could possibly exist between the transistor's emitter and collector terminals (in this case 12 V— when the base current is zero and the collector current is in turn almost zero), and the maximum current which could possibly flow in the collector circuit with the load resistor in place (in this case 2·55 mA). The load line is thus drawn between the points ($V_{ce} = 12, I_c = 0$) and ($V_{ce} = 0, I_c = 2·55$) on the output characteristics of Fig. 13.22. This is left as an exercise for the reader.

Having drawn the load line, it is usual to choose the operating point of the transistor midway along the load line—

in our case at the point ($V_{ce} = 6$, $I_c = 1.28$). When the transistor is set to operate at this point, then small input signals which cause the transistor currents to vary over a small portion of the load line, are amplified without distortion.

With reference to Fig. 13.22, and with the load line now drawn, we see that if we wish to set the collector current to approximately 1·25 mA, then the base current would have to be adjusted to approximately 15 µA. When this adjustment is made, it follows that if an alternating signal is injected into the base circuit which causes the base current to alternate by not more than 15 µA on either side of the operating point, then this signal will cause the collector current to alternate by not more than 1·25 mA on either side of the operating point. Signals in this category are then amplified linearly. That is, the output signal is free from distortion. If however the input signal causes a variation in base current of more than 15 µA, then the collector current will be cut off at one extremity, and saturated (at 2·55 mA) at the other. That is, the collector current will be unable to follow the variation in base current satisfactorily, so the output signal will be distorted.

We have thus established the operating conditions of the OC71 transistor with a 4·7 kΩ load in its collector circuit. But how do we know to choose 4·7 kΩ as a suitable value of load resistor in the first place? Why is 4·7 kΩ suitable whereas 10 Ω and 27 kΩ are both unsuitable?

A suitable value for the load resistor may be deduced as follows. If we decide to use a 12 V supply to the transistor then at the operating point (regardless of the value of the load resistor) a potential difference of 6 V will be developed across each of the load and the transistor. From the manufacturer's specifications for the particular transistor, we can find its recommended power dissipation—P say. The collector current which will give rise to this power dissipation—I_c say—will then be calculated as

$$I_c = \frac{P}{6}$$

Since this current must also flow through the load resistor, and since 6 V is developed across the load resistor under the optimum operating conditions, then the most suitable value for the load resistor is given by R where

$$R = \frac{6}{I_c}$$

This value of resistor is usually such as to be of the order of several thousand ohms for a low power transistor such as the OC71 operating from a battery of the order of 10 or 12 volts.

As far as obtaining the necessary base current for the transistor is concerned (in our case 15 µA) it is usual to connect the base of the transistor to the supply potential difference via a large resistor as is indicated in Fig. 13.24.

Also in this diagram we have shown two coupling capacitors—whose function is explained later—as well as input and output terminals. This diagram is in fact a practical transistor amplifier circuit.

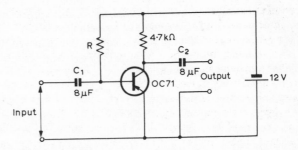

Fig. 13.24 A simple method of producing a suitable base current.

Since the resistance of the emitter-base junction of the transistor is very small, it follows that a very small potential difference will be developed across this junction. This means that the potential difference developed across the resistor R is almost 12 V. If the current flowing in R (and hence to the transistor base) is to be 15 µA, it follows that

$$R = \frac{12}{15 \times 10^{-6}}$$

$$= 800\ 000\ \Omega$$

Since the nearest value to this resistance manufactured is 820 kΩ, this latter value would have to be inserted as the necessary base limiting resistor.

The capacitor C_1 is inserted to block any d.c. component present in the input signal, and thereby to guard against the upsetting of the d.c. potential of the base as established by the presence of the 820 kΩ resistor. Since the value of this capacitor has been chosen as 8 µF, it follows that its reactance to an input audio signal of frequency say 300 Hz is small. The reactance at this frequency—X_c say—is

$$X_c = \frac{1}{2\pi f C}$$

$$= 70\ \Omega\ \text{approx.}$$

The presence of the capacitor C_2 serves the same function as that of C_1, if a second stage is to be added to the amplifier.

A transistor amplifier like that in Fig. 13.24 is rather unsatisfactory in as much as it does not provide for d.c. stabilisation in relation to temperature changes. That is, as the temperature of the transistor changes as a result of current flowing in it, some of the transistor parameters are altered, thereby changing the operating point of the device. This lack of stabilisation is often referred to as thermal runaway, and results from the release of electrons from the crystal lattice following a rise of temperature. These electrons give rise to a larger current in the transistor, which gives rise to a greater rise in temperature, which liberates more electrons from the lattice, which gives rise to a larger current, which causes a greater rise in temperature . . . and so on. If this process is allowed to avalanche unchecked, the transistor is eventually damaged to the point of becoming useless.

A certain measure of stabilisation can be achieved by re-connecting the circuit as shown in Fig. 13.25, but this circuit too has its limitations.

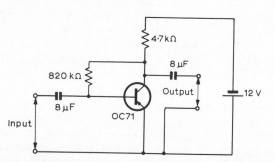

Fig.13.25 A more reliable method of producing a suitable base current.

The idea here is that should the collector current increase for some reason, then the potential difference between collector and emitter should fall. Since one end of the 820 kΩ resistor is now at the falling collector potential, the potential difference across this resistor, and hence the current to the base, should fall. If the base current falls, the collector current should in turn fall too, thereby counteracting the effect of thermal runaway.

Since a certain leakage current is present in the emitter collector-circuit (by virtue of the presence of minority carriers), even when no base current flows, then the stabilisation afforded by the circuit of Fig. 13.25 can only be partly effective because the leakage current itself increases with increasing temperature.

The most successful method of achieving stabilisation in the d.c. working conditions of the amplifier is that which incorporates a *potential divider and emitter resistor stabilisation circuit*. The effect of introducing this extra set of components is firstly to make the potential of the transistor base independent of changes in base current (which might arise from heating in the transistor), and secondly, to introduce a certain amount of negative feedback into the emitter circuit, so that a counteracting effect to thermal runaway is then present. The amplifier circuit corrected in this way thus appears as in Fig. 13.26.

The presence of the emitter resistor R_e ensures that if the current in the collector-emitter circuit increases (with increasing temperature), then the potential difference across R_e

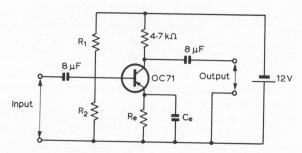

Fig.13.26 A stable amplifier.

will also increase (since R_e is constant), so that the potential of the emitter will decrease. The presence of the potential divider formed by R_1 and R_2 ensures that the base potential is kept constant and unaffected by changes in base current. That is, as the current in the emitter-collector circuit increases, the potential difference between emitter and base decreases. This results in a decrease in base current, and finally in a decrease in emitter current. The avalanche effect is thus averted. An emitter resistor of around 1 kΩ is sufficient to provide the necessary negative feedback effect for the OC71 transistor which we are using here.

The potential divider provides for a steady base potential by allowing a current to flow through itself (R_1 and R_2) such that this current is of the order of ten times the value of the optimum base current. Any variation in the base current will then have little or no effect on this larger current, so that the base potential is determined by the potential divider. Let us find suitable values for R_1 and R_2.

If the potential difference across the base and emitter terminals is to be 0·2 V when the transistor is operating successfully, and the emitter current is approximately 1·25 mA, then the potential difference across the 1 kΩ emitter resistor is 1·25 V. The potential difference across R_2 should therefore be (1·25 + 0·20) V, or approximately 1·5 V.

If the current in the potential divider is chosen to be ten times the value of the base current, then it follows that the value of R_2 is given by

$$R_2 = \frac{1\cdot5}{150 \times 10^{-6}}$$
$$= 10\,000 \; \Omega$$

Further,
$$R_1 + R_2 = \frac{12}{150 \times 10^{-6}}$$
$$= 80\,000 \; \Omega$$

so that
$$R_1 = 70\,000 \; \Omega$$

The nearest value to this resistance manufactured is 68 kΩ. The potential divider is thus made up of resistors whose values are 68 kΩ and 10 kΩ.

In the circuit diagram of Fig. 13.26, we have included a capacitor (C_e) in parallel with the emitter resistor. The value of this capacitor is large—usually of the order of 100 μF so that it offers little or no reactance to the incoming alternating audio signal. The reactance of such a capacitor (100 μF) to a signal of frequency 300 Hz is approximately 5 Ω.

The emitter resistor is therefore effectively short circuited for a.c. by the presence of this large capacitor, and so the input signal appears directly between the emitter and base of the transistor. No loss therefore results in the gain of the system by the presence of the emitter resistor.

The completed amplifier circuit thus appears as in Fig. 13.27.

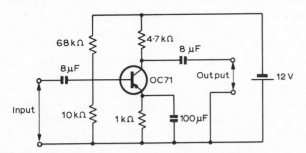

Fig.13.27 A low level amplifier showing typical component values.

13.5 The Transistor Oscillator

In Chapter 11, section 6, we discussed how damped free electrical oscillations were set up in a circuit consisting of an inductor and a capacitor in parallel. In that section we concluded 'it seems likely that an electrical oscillation could be maintained in a circuit by feeding back a minute amount of energy to the circuit in step with each half cycle of the otherwise damped oscillation', and decided to investigate this possibility after studying the operational principles of the transistor. We therefore wish to employ the transistor to replace that small amount of energy lost during each half cycle of the oscillation set up in the inductor-capacitor circuit.

Although there are many transistor circuits capable of oscillating, perhaps one of the simplest is that in Fig. 13.28.

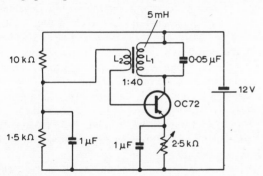

Fig.13.28 A simple transistor oscillator circuit.

This circuit is essentially that of a common emitter amplifier with a tuned circuit for its collector load. Since the inductor of this circuit forms one winding of a transformer (L_1), part of the alternating signal in the tuned circuit can be fed back to the input circuit of the transistor via the second transformer winding (L_2).

When the circuit is switched on, current flowing in the 10 kΩ–1·5 kΩ potential divider establishes the operating potential of the transistor base. The base current does not build up to its full value immediately however, since a small inductor is present in the base lead. The growing base current in this inductor (L_2) sets up a changing magnetic field in the transformer core, which in turn induces an e.m.f. across the winding L_1. This induced e.m.f. charges the 0·05 μF capacitor. When the base current has reached its full value, no more charging of the capacitor will take place, and its oscillatory discharge through L_1 will begin. The alternating potential difference across the collector load will then give rise to an alternating collector current. A fraction of this alternating potential difference is transferred to appear across the emitter-base junction of the transistor, following the transformer action, so that an amplified alternating collector current results, thereby enlarging and sustaining the original alternating collector current. The alternating potential difference across the collector load is thus sustained. Continuous feedback in this way increases (and hence sustains) the amplitude of the collector signal, until it is finally limited in size by the power of the supply and the values of the other circuit components.

The alternating potential difference across the collector load may be examined by connecting the Y-plates of an oscilloscope across the 0·05 μF capacitor, and adjusting the time base and the setting of the emitter variable resistor until a good sinusoidal waveform is obtained.

The oscillation is sustained for as long as the signal fed back to the load is in step or in phase with the original signal. If the signal fed back was out of step by half a cycle with the original, the oscillation would quickly cease and the process would be an example of negative feedback. The oscillation is only sustained as a result of positive feedback, and the positive feedback in this oscillator involves two changes of phase, each of one half cycle, so that the two signals being mixed finally are exactly in step. The transformer introduces a phase change of one half cycle, as is consistent with Lenz's Law in relation to the induced e.m.f.'s—when a positive voltage pulse is developed across one transformer winding, a negative voltage pulse is generated in opposition across the other transformer winding. The transistor connected in common emitter configuration also introduces a phase change of half a cycle, as can perhaps be deduced with reference to Fig. 13.23. If an input signal causes the base to become more negative, then larger base and hence collector currents will flow. This will result in a larger potential difference being developed across the constant load resistor, so that the collector of the transistor becomes more positive. That is, the input and output of the common emitter transistor circuit are in antiphase.

These two phase changes thus provide for the signal fed back to be in step with the existing signal. The oscillation therefore continues.

Note that the $1 \cdot 5 \, k\Omega$ and $2 \cdot 5 \, k\Omega$ resistors are effectively short circuited by the $1 \, \mu F$ capacitors. The presence of these capacitors ensures that the e.m.f. developed across the component L_2 appears only between the base and emitter of the transistor, so that no loss in gain is suffered as a result of the presence of these resistors in the system.

The output of the circuit shown in Fig. 13.28 is quoted as having a frequency of 10^4 Hz and 20 milliwatts of power. This output may be heard as a high pitched whine when connected to a power amplifier and then to a loudspeaker. The same type of circuit as that of Fig. 13.28 may also be used to generate radio frequency signals when the tuned circuit shown is replaced by another containing a smaller inductor and a smaller capacitor, and when the OC72 transistor is replaced by a higher frequency type such as an OC44. We shall discuss the role of such a radio frequency oscillator in the next and final section of the chapter.

13.6 Radio Communication

Radio communication is a process whereby information may be transmitted between two points in a negligible fraction of a second—regarding these two points as being earthbound at present. If a given system is to be effective in the transmission of information, then that system should provide certain essential components for the communication process. We can list these components as follows.

1. *The system must provide a carrier device in which the information can be transmitted.* In the case of telephone communication for example, the direct current in the wires is the carrier on which the information is impressed.

2. *The system must provide a means of modulation at its transmitter.* That is, it must have some means of varying the carrier in a way related to the required information. In a telephone system modulation of the current is achieved by the microphone in the telephone's mouthpiece.

3. *The system must also provide a means of demodulation at its receiver.* That is, it must have some means of extracting or recognising the information impressed on the carrier. In the telephone system demodulation of the current is achieved by the electro-magnetic effect in the earpiece.

4. *When long distance communication is necessary, the system must provide a means of amplification of the incoming signal.*

5. *If different messages are being conveyed, the system must provide for the selection of any one of these.* That is, it must

be able to tune into any one message. In a telephone system 'tuning' is achieved by operating a space division network, in which separate pathways exist for separate calls, or by operating a time division network in which many calls may be carried on one pathway as a result of a rapid switching technique.

In radio communication, the *carrier* is an electromagnetic wave generated by developing the amplified signal from an electrical oscillator (as discussed in the last section) between the poles of an antenna. The frequency of this wave is particularly high—of the order of hundreds of kilohertz—and so it is not itself recognised by the human ear (which can detect signals in the approximate frequency range 25–20 000 Hz) after reception.

The information to be communicated—for example, a pure musical note of frequency 300 Hz—is converted to an electrical signal by a microphone, amplified, and thereafter superimposed on or mixed with the carrier wave in an electronic mixing device known as a modulator amplifier. The carrier wave has now been modulated with the necessary information, and its amplitude now varies at the frequency of the audio frequency signal.

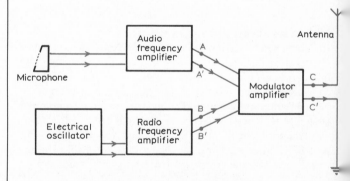

Fig.13.29 The process of radio transmission.

The radio transmission process can thus be represented in terms of the block diagram shown in Fig. 13.29. The potential difference against time graphs for the signals developed at various parts of the system are as shown in Fig. 13.30, and these could be observed in turn by connecting an oscilloscope between the points AA′, BB′, and CC′, assuming the frequency of the time base of the oscilloscope to be sufficiently high to match that of the radio frequency signal.

The electromagnetic waves radiated from the antenna are characteristic of the final graph of Fig. 13.30, and since these waves travel at the same speed as light (3×10^8 m s^{-1}), the information contained is propagated to the receiving system almost instantaneously.

At the receiving system, the modulated carrier wave is picked up as a result of its varying electric and magnetic fields inducing a varying but representative e.m.f. between the poles of the receiving antenna. Each broadcasting station sends out its information on a carrier wave of one particular

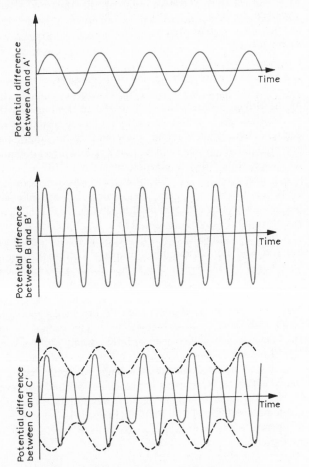

Fig.13.30 The signals developed at different parts of the transmission system.

frequency—this frequency being different for different stations. Further, the signals from the different stations induce corresponding e.m.f.'s between the poles of the receiving antenna simultaneously, so that when the information conveyed by one particular signal is required, the receiver must possess the facility for tuning to that particular signal. Once the required signal has been accepted by the tuning circuit and thereby filtered from the other signals, it is amplified by a radio frequency amplifier (since the e.m.f. induced is usually very small) before the information is extracted from it in demodulation. The demodulation device is in fact a simple semiconductor diode. The information extracted is then amplified in an audio amplifier whose output is connected to a loudspeaker.

The reception process can thus be represented in terms of the block diagram shown in Fig. 13.31. The potential difference against time graphs for the signals developed at the various parts of the system we shall examine as we discuss further the component details of the receiver.

The tuned circuit of the radio receiver is, in its simplest form, a parallel circuit consisting of inductor and variable capacitor, as was noted in section 11.7. Recall that the impedance of such a circuit reaches a maximum value at the resonant frequency, so at this frequency the potential difference developed across the circuit is also at its maximum value. If the resonant frequency of the circuit is adjusted (by means of the variable capacitor) so as to be equal to that of the incoming signal, then this signal will drive the circuit into resonance, so that a maximum varying potential difference (representative of the incoming signal) will be developed for amplification.

After the incoming signal has been selected and amplified as required, it is fed to the demodulator or detector which is a simple semiconductor diode. Such a diode, as we have seen, conducts only during 'positive' half cycles of an alternating signal so that in fact only the 'positive' half cycles of the incoming radio frequency signal are developed at the next

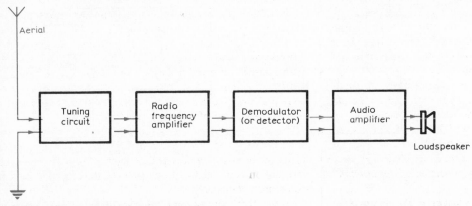

Fig.13.31 The process of radio detection.

stage of the receiver. This rectification is required because neither the audio amplifier nor the cone of the loudspeaker is able to vibrate at radio frequency. Each is thus unable to respond to the exact variations carried by the radio frequency signal. Both the audio amplifier and the loudspeaker cone respond to the average value of the radio frequency signal, but since the average value of the incoming signal is zero, no response would be forthcoming from either. By rectifying the incoming signal however, the average value of its 'positive' aspect can be interpreted both by the audio amplifier and the

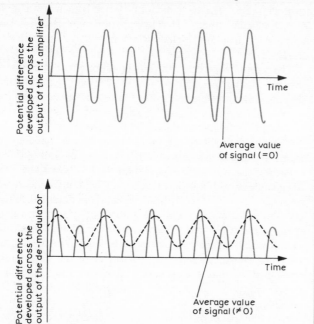

Fig.13.32 The signals developed at different parts of the detection system.

loudspeaker, so that after the demodulation process, the signal becomes meaningful.

By connecting an oscilloscope with a high frequency time base control across the outputs of the radio frequency amplifier and demodulator in turn, traces would be obtained which would represent the variation in potential difference of the received signal as a function of time. These traces are represented as in Fig. 13.32.

As can be seen from the second of these traces, the average value of the demodulated signal has a frequency equal to that of the original information fed to the microphone at the transmitter. As can also be seen, the average value of the demodulated signal may be interpreted as an alternating potential difference superimposed on a certain direct potential difference. Since this direct potential difference carries no information, and is likely to upset the operating conditions at the input of the audio amplifier, it may be removed effectively by connecting a large capacitor between the demodulator and the input to the audio amplifier.

A simple but practical form of radio receiver which utilises our common emitter amplifier (properly stabilised) is represented in Fig. 13.33. In this simple receiver no provision has been made for radio frequency amplification.

This circuit should enable the user to tune to one or two stations in areas of good signal strength, provided a good long aerial and short earth are connected. The output of the amplifier will be insufficient to operate a small loudspeaker.

Improvements can be made by adding a small radio frequency amplifier section before the diode, this section being as shown in Fig. 13.34. Further improvement is found by adding an identical audio amplifier section at the output of the existing audio amplifier. The output might then be just sufficient to operate a small loudspeaker in areas of excellent signal strength.

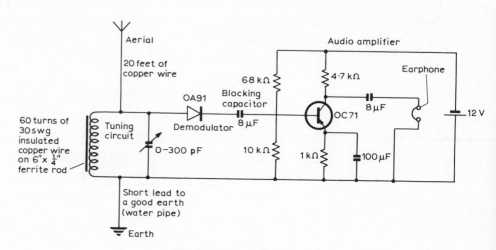

Fig.13.33 A simple radio receiver.

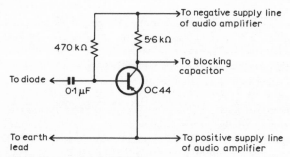

Fig.13.34 A simple r.f. amplifier section.

Problems

1 Can you suggest two reasons why an impurity semiconductor offers an advantage over an intrinsic semiconductor?

2 What is meant by the terms (a) thermally produced electron-hole pairs, (b) hole movement, (c) acceptor, (d) minority carrier, (e) depletion layer in a junction diode?

3 Draw a sketch graph representing the forward and reverse characteristics of an OA91 diode at room temperature. Also on this graph sketch the same characteristics after the temperature of the diode has been raised significantly.

4 When a junction diode is forward biassed by a potential difference of 0·4 V, it passes a current of 12 mA. How could you arrange for the diode to pass the same current if only a 9 V battery was available?

5 When the switch in the circuit of Fig. 13.35 is closed, the ammeter reads 0·5 A. What would the reading be if the battery was reversed? Take the forward and reverse resistances of the diode as 100 Ω and 10^6 Ω respectively?

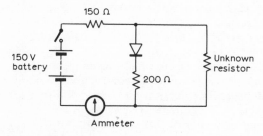

Fig.13.35 See Problem 5.

6 Devise a circuit which would enable you to determine the current transfer ratio of an OC71 transistor connected in the common base configuration. Using this circuit what measurements would you make, and from these how would you evaluate the ratio?

7 With reference to Fig. 13.22 draw a graph of the transfer characteristics of the OC71 transistor at a collector-emitter potential difference of 4·5 V, by plotting the collector currents against base currents at this voltage. From the linear region of your graph, estimate the current amplification factor of the transistor at $V_{ce} = 4·5$ V.

8 With reference to Fig. 13.22, calculate the power dissipated by the transistor at its operating point. What value of load resistor would be required if this power was to be dissipated when the supply potential difference was 9 V?

9 Derive a means of constructing a transformer to the exact specifications of that shown in Fig. 13.28 using a small ferrite rod. The fact that the resonant frequency of a series inductor (L)-capacitor (C) circuit may be calculated as f_0 where

$$f_0 = \frac{1}{2\pi\sqrt{(LC)}}$$

may be useful.

10 The diagram of Fig. 13.36 represents a very simple radio receiver. Label (a) the tuned circuit (b) the detector (c) the audio amplifier.

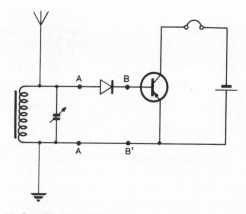

Fig.13.36 See Problem 10.

Draw graphs of how the potential differences developed between AA′ and BB′ vary with time.

11 What are the disadvantages of the amplifier circuit shown in Fig. 13.34?

Bibliography 'Transistor Pocket Book'. R. G. Hibberd (Published: Newnes, 1968).

Chapter 14

Wave Motion

Fig.14.0 The ripple tank and accessories. The tank is essential for the study of water waves. (By kind permission of M.L.I. Ltd.)

It has been suggested that the role of mechanics in physics is analogous to the role of the skeleton in the human body, in as much as mechanics is that branch of physics upon which other branches may successfully be built. Reflecting on our studies this far and on the order in which we have conducted them, the suggestion seems quite acceptable. Had it not been for our study of mechanics in Chapters 1, 2, 3, and 4, we should have been unable to provide a quantitative kinetic theory of gases in Chapter 7, a theoretical approach towards the determination of the electronic charge in Chapter 8, and an analysis of the oscilloscope beam deflection in Chapter 12.

However, the study of mechanics alone provides for a somewhat incomplete 'skeleton' on which to erect the remaining branches of physics—particularly with regard to those branches contributing to what is known as 'modern physics'. It is found that the system of mechanics encountered in Chapters 1 to 4—commonly referred to as Newtonian mechanics—is somewhat inadequate for an accurate description of subatomic phenomena: for an accurate description of these phenomena, the system is rejected in favour of what is

known as relativistic mechanics. Further, in the sub-atomic world, it is found that what we have previously called particles do not necessarily behave like particles, exhibiting rather, certain wave-like characteristics.

To help complete our picture of classical physics and to establish a basis for the notion of a wave-particle view of matter, we now begin a study of wave phenomena. If we regard wave phenomena as being divorced from Newtonian mechanics in as much as the latter doesn't account for and predict the former, then a knowledge of both of these branches of physics must surely provide us with a more complete skeleton.

But what exactly is a wave, and what do we mean by wave motion? We are surrounded by many examples—radio waves, light waves, water waves, sound waves, radar waves—but these examples do not necessarily reveal the nature of wave motion. We are aware of the existence of water waves by observing disturbances on a water surface, but in such a case we are observing water and perhaps not waves. Wave motion is a means of *energy* transfer and not a means of *material* transfer. The exact nature of wave motion is somewhat intangible, and only described properly in mathematical terms. In this chapter, however, we shall keep mathematical discussions to a minimum and attempt to gather some knowledge of wave behaviour by observing wave properties. It is to be hoped that this will prove more rewarding than attempting to answer the philosophical question relating to what a wave really is.

14.1 Mechanical Waves

A wave motion is essentially a regular periodic energy-carrying disturbance which is unusual in as much as the energy is transmitted without material being transferred too. If the wave motion travels through an elastic material substance such as water, then the waves are known as *mechanical waves*. According to this definition, light—which we later hope to consider as a wave motion—is most certainly not a mechanical wave, for the simple reason that it is transmitted through a vacuum. Such transmission is not easily understood since it is perhaps natural, in view of our first hand acquaintance with water waves, to expect or require a material medium for light to 'wave' in. For this reason we shall concentrate our attention on mechanical waves for the present, in an attempt to establish the basic properties of acceptable wave motions. We shall then be in a position to investigate light as a wave motion in the next chapter.

14.2 Pulses

To begin our study of mechanical waves, let us consider an elastic material medium simpler and less troublesome than water. Let us consider a coil spring or 'slinky'. Since a wave motion is by definition a regular succession of disturbances or pulses, let us simplify the problem by analysing first of all

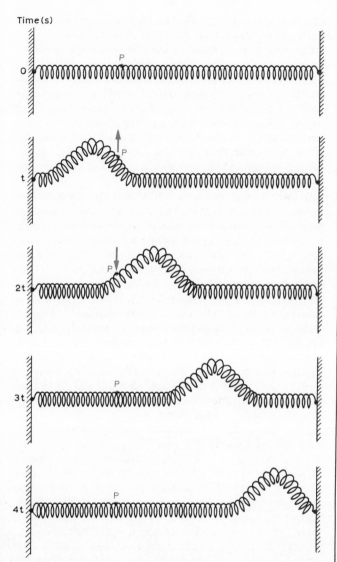

Fig.14.1 The motion of a transverse pulse in an elastic medium.

and also, that any particular portion of the slinky—for example, that portion marked P—executes a flick at right angles to the direction in which the pulse is travelling, as the pulse moves through the region of P. For this reason, such a pulse is referred to as *transverse* in nature.

The diagram in Fig. 14.2 shows successive 'snapshots' of the slinky, following the release of a compression formed by gathering several coils together at one end. We see from this diagram that the pulse again travels undistorted and at constant speed from left to right, (following the release of the original compression) and also that any particular portion

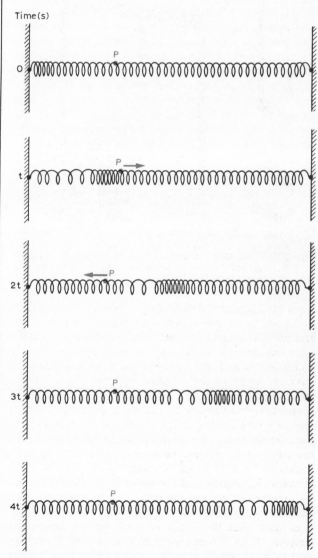

Fig.14.2 The motion of a longitudinal pulse in an elastic medium.

the behaviour of a single pulse.

Let us consider a slinky to be lying horizontally on a table top between two fixed supports. The slinky can be disturbed either by pulling a portion of it out of alignment—at right angles to this alignment so as to form a symmetric crest—and then releasing, or by gathering several coils together in compression at one end, and then releasing. The diagram in Fig. 14.1 shows successive 'snapshots' of the slinky, following the release of the symmetric crest formed by pulling a portion out of alignment. We see from this diagram that the disturbance or pulse travels undistorted and at constant speed from left to right (following the release of the original crest), of the slinky—for example that marked P—executes a flick parallel to the direction in which the pulse is travelling, as the pulse moves through the region of P. For this reason, such a pulse is referred to as *longitudinal* in nature.

We note therefore that, in the cases of a transverse pulse and a longitudinal pulse travelling in an elastic medium, it is the disturbance which is propagated through the medium, and not the actual particles of the medium. The particles of the medium serve to pass on the disturbance by their elastic displacements. Let us now examine the characteristics of transverse pulses more thoroughly, since it is with transverse waves we shall be concerned both in this, and in the next chapter.

Since, in any real situation, we are likely to encounter waves interacting with other waves, let us consider pulses interacting with other pulses. In particular, let us consider two pulses approaching each other along the same rubber tube, one in the sense left to right, and the other in the sense right to left. Let us suppose that the amplitude or height of the left hand pulse is more than that of the right hand pulse, and that the shapes of the pulses are slightly different. The diagram in Fig. 14.3 shows what would be seen on a series of frames on a film from a high speed camera photographing an experiment such as we have just described. We see from this series of recordings that the two pulses pass through each other unaltered, and that on meeting, the amplitudes of the pulses add numerically.

The fact that the amplitudes of any two interacting pulses add algebraically rather than numerically may be demonstrated by sending two pulses towards each other along the same rubber tube, one pulse on each 'side' of the tube, and observing the result of the interaction in terms of a series of successive 'snapshots' of the events. The diagram in Fig. 14.4 shows such a series of events in a rubber tube—before, during, and after the time in which two unequal and unlike pulses interact. In referring to this diagram, as well as to that in Fig. 14.3, we see that there exists a certain *superposition principle* for wave phenomena. We could formulate this principle by saying that it is possible for two wave motions to pass through each other without either being altered as a result. Further, during the period of interaction, the net waveform at any time may be calculated as the algebraic sum of the individual waveforms which are interacting.

Also in any real situation, we are likely to encounter waves interacting with media other than that in which the wave is travelling, and so we must consider the possibilities of reflection of the wave motion at the boundary between the two media, or of onward transmission of the wave into the second medium—or perhaps, a little of both. Let us therefore consider the changes which are likely to occur in the nature of

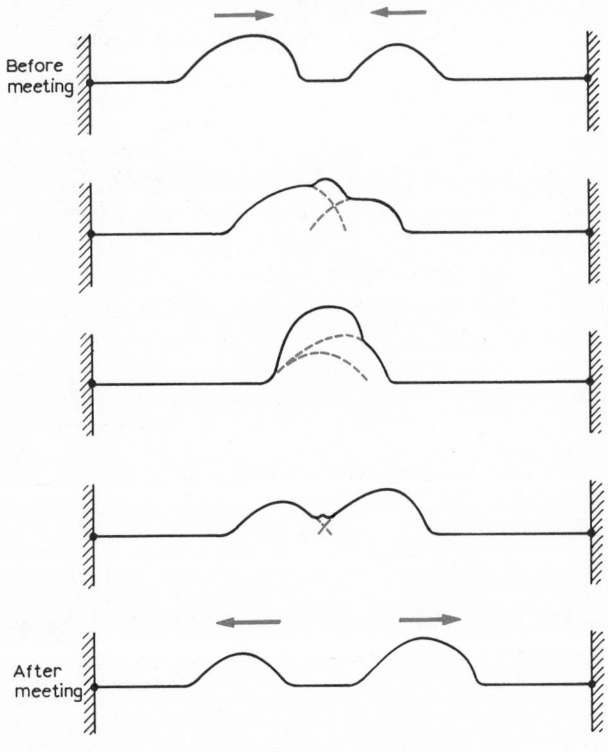

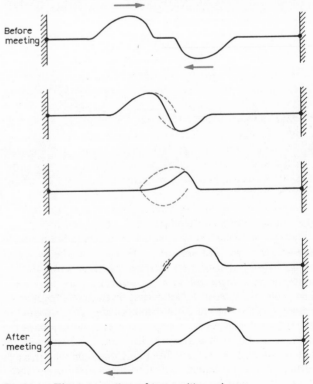

Fig. 14.3 The interaction of two like pulses.

Fig. 14.4 The interaction of two unlike pulses.

a pulse travelling in an elastic string whenever that string is:
  i)   free to move at its far end
  ii) fixed at its far end
  iii) attached to a heavier string at its far end
  iv) attached to a lighter string at its far end.

  (i) The diagram in Fig. 14.5(a) shows a transverse pulse travelling along a taut elastic string in the sense left to right. The far (right hand) end of the string we shall regard as free, since it is connected to a small slip-ring whose motion along the smooth vertical rail is assumed to be frictionless. When the pulse reaches the ring, the ring is caused to rise, and then to fall. This motion is responsible for the generation of a reflected pulse on the same side of the string as the incident pulse, so that the reflected pulse appears as in Fig. 14.5(b).

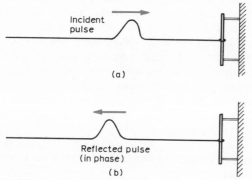

Fig.14.5 The motion of a transverse pulse in an elastic string which is 'free' at one end.

  (ii) The diagram in Fig. 14.6(a) shows a transverse pulse travelling along a taut elastic string, again in the sense left to right. The far (right hand) end of the string may now be regarded as fixed, since it is tied to a rigid fixture. When the leading edge of the pulse reaches the fixture, it applies an upward force to it. According to Newton's third law therefore, the fixture applies an equal and opposite (downward) force to the string, so that a reflected pulse is generated in the opposite phase to the incident pulse, as in Fig. 14.6(b).

  (iii) The diagram in Fig. 14.7(a) shows a transverse pulse travelling along a taut elastic string in the usual sense left to right. The far (right hand) end of the string is in this case attached to a much heavier material—a piece of rope say. Had we merely attached a second piece of elastic string to the far end of the first, instead of a piece of rope, then we might expect the whole pulse to be transmitted from the first piece of string to the second piece, unaffected in any way. By attaching a piece of rope, however, we are in effect creating a boundary at the far end of the string, and this boundary is neither entirely free nor totally immovable. On the arrival of the pulse at the boundary, the string exerts an upward force on the rope. Since the rope is heavy however, it moves

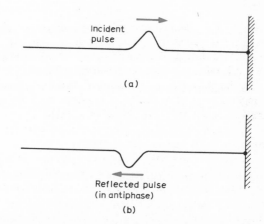

Fig.14.6 The motion of a transverse pulse in an elastic string which is fixed at one end.

only a limited amount and exerts a downward force on the string which generates a reflected pulse in antiphase. Also since the end of the rope does in fact move a little upwards, this will cause a transmitted pulse to move along the rope. This deduction is in keeping with experimental observation, and is represented in Fig. 14.7(b).

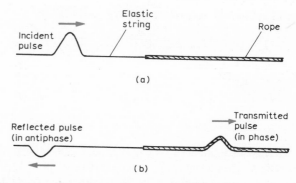

Fig.14.7 The motion of a transverse pulse in an elastic string joined to a piece of rope.

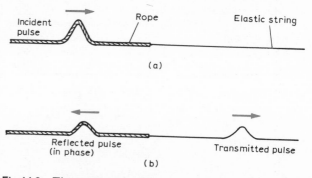

Fig.14.8 The motion of a transverse pulse in a rope joined to an elastic string.

(iv) When the last situation is in effect reversed so that a transverse pulse is travelling along a heavy material (a rope) towards the junction with a light material (string), again in the sense left to right and as in Fig. 14.8(a), it is found that part of the incident pulse is transmitted, while the remainder is reflected in phase with the incident pulse. This result is represented in Fig. 14.8(b). Can you account for it?

14.3 Travelling Waves

The pulses which we have been considering until now represent isolated disturbances travelling in a material medium. Each transverse pulse is generated by moving one end of the medium—a rubber tube say—up and then down. When this motion is repeated regularly and evenly a series of similar pulses is generated in the medium, and these pulses constitute a periodic travelling transverse wave. Such a wave may be generated by setting up the apparatus shown in Fig. 14.9, so that the wave motion is generated in the horizontal plane of the support board.

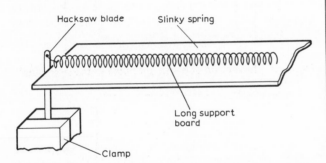

Fig.14.9 The generation of a transverse wave in a slinky.

The type of vibration made by the hacksaw blade is referred to as simple harmonic motion, a characteristic of this motion being that the displacement of the blade from its rest position is a sinusoidal function of time. Since one end of the slinky is attached to the tip of the blade, it follows that the profile of the wave motion in the slinky is sinusoidal in its appearance. The slinky would therefore appear as in Fig. 14.10 when viewed from above. This sinusoidal profile has been redrawn in Fig. 14.11, and its important features labelled.

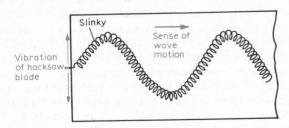

Fig.14.10 The profile of a transverse wave.

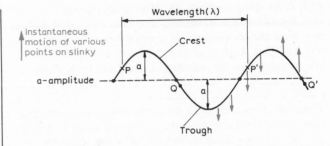

Fig.14.11 The profile of a transverse wave labelled.

Pairs of particles such as P and P′, Q and Q′, are said to be *in phase* with one another since each of P and P′ is performing exactly the same motion at the same time. The distance between any two consecutive points in phase is defined as the wavelength of the wave motion and is usually denoted by the Greek symbol λ (lambda). The wavelength of any wave is of course measured in metres. The natural frequency of vibration of the hacksaw blade determines the frequency of the wave motion—that is, the number of complete waves (crest and trough) generated each second is equal to the frequency of the source. The frequency of the wave motion is usually denoted by f and measured in cycles per second or hertz. Any wave motion is observed to have a finite speed in a given transmitting medium. In the case of a transverse wave motion in a slinky, the finite speed of that wave motion is determined by the tension in the slinky and by its mass per unit length. The speed of a wave motion is denoted by v and measured in metres per second. The speed of the wave motion is measured by the forward movement (per unit time) of any point on the wave profile.

Let us suppose that two complete waves are generated in a slinky each second, and that the wavelength of each is 3 m. Obviously the speed of the wave motion is 6 m s^{-1} since 6 m of 'wave' are effectively being transmitted each second. It follows therefore, and in more general terms, that if the frequency of a wave motion is f, and its wavelength is λ, then the speed of the motion is v, where

$$v = f\lambda \dots \dots \dots \dots \quad (14.1)$$

This expression is a fundamental wave equation and holds true for all types of waves, whether they be transverse or longitudinal in nature.

A final point to be noted from Fig. 14.11 is that the amplitude of the wave motion is the maximum displacement of the transmitting medium from its rest position, in one sense or in the other. It is not the perpendicular distance between crest and trough as is sometimes wrongly assumed. The maximum displacement or amplitude of the wave motion is determined by the amount of energy being transported by the motion. The energy being transported is in fact proportional to the square of the wave amplitude.

14.4 The Properties of Wave Motions

It is found in the study of wave behaviour that certain properties are common to all types of wave motion. These properties are known as reflection, refraction, diffraction, and interference. We shall familiarise ourselves with each of these properties in this section so that, in future, we shall be able to analyse any suspected wave motion in the context of the four properties, and thereby confirm or deny the suspicion. To enable us to study the properties of waves simply, we shall concern ourselves with water waves since they are easily generated, slow moving, and such that they may be projected on a screen as a result of the transparency of water. Surface water waves are usually observed in the laboratory with the aid of a ripple tank, illustrations of which appear in Figs. 14.0 and 14.12. The tank is provided with a glass bottom so that a surface wave pattern may be projected on a white screen below the tank by the light from an overhead lamp. The wave pattern is projected because each crest of the motion acts as an effective converging or focussing lens for the light from the lamp, while each trough acts as a diverging or defocussing lens. In any projected water wave pattern therefore, the wave crests should be recognised by bright regions or bands, and the wave troughs by dark regions or bands.

A straight pulse may be generated in the ripple tank by dipping the edge of a ruler into the water surface. Such a pulse will be observed to travel away from its source at constant speed, always parallel to the source, and in a direction at right angles to its length. The straight pulse could thus be represented as in Fig. 14.13. A circular pulse may be generated in the ripple tank by dipping a point source —such as a pencil point—into the water surface. Such a pulse is observed to travel away from its source at constant speed, and in a continually enlarging circle. The motion of such a pulse is therefore radial, since each segment of the pulse is outwardly directed along the radius of the circle. The circular pulse could thus be represented as in Fig. 14.14.

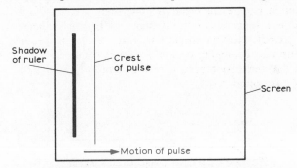

Fig.14.13 The motion of a straight pulse in the ripple tank.

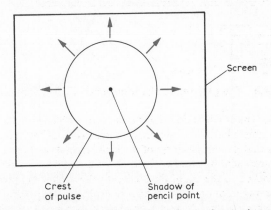

Fig.14.14 The motion of a circular pulse in the ripple tank.

Although the reflection of water waves is easily demonstrated with the ripple tank, the reflection of a single pulse gives a much clearer picture of the reflection process and the law which governs it. Let us suppose that in Fig. 14.13, a second ruler is immersed in the ripple tank, parallel to the direction of the first ruler, thus forming a straight barrier to the pulse as it reaches the far end of the tank. After striking the barrier, the pulse is observed to travel back across the ripple tank in the opposite sense. When the direction of the barrier is altered however, so that it is no longer parallel to the length of the advancing pulse, the reflected pulse is then

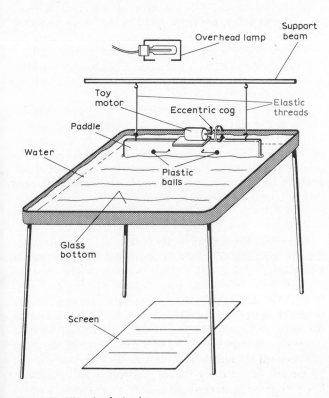

Fig.14.12 The ripple tank.

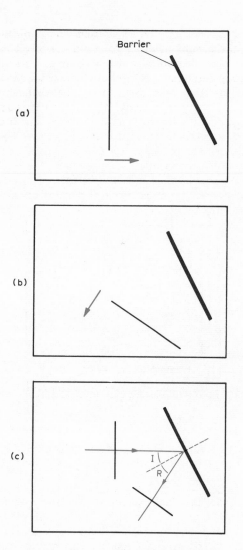

Fig.14.15 The reflection of a straight pulse from a straight
barrier in the ripple tank.

observed to travel in a direction quite different from that of
the incident pulse. The diagram in Fig. 14.15(a) shows the
straight pulse incident on the oblique barrier, while that in
Fig. 14.15(b) shows the reflection of that pulse from the
barrier. The reflection process as observed in terms of these
two diagrams may appear somewhat disordered until we
consider it in relation to the constructions of Fig. 14.15(c).
In this diagram, the directions of motion of the incident
and reflected pulses have been drawn along with a reference
line—called a normal—at right angles to the direction of the
barrier. The angle between the direction of the incident
pulse and the normal (marked 'I' in the diagram), is referred
to as the *angle of incidence* of the pulse on the barrier. The

angle between the direction of the reflected pulse and the
normal (marked 'R' in the diagram), is referred to as the
angle of reflection. Measurement of these two angles in this
last diagram will reveal that $\hat{I} = \hat{R}$. That is, the angle of
incidence of the pulse equals its angle of reflection. This
beautifully simple result is known as the (second) *law of
reflection* for waves, and although we have verified it with
reference to isolated pulses, it is fairly obvious that each of a
succession of pulses constituting a wave motion would be
reflected in exactly the same way.

The reflection of a circular pulse from a straight barrier is
best described in terms of the diagram of Fig. 14.16. The
reflected pulse is observed to be an arc of a circle, the apparent
or virtual centre of which is located as far behind the barrier
as the actual centre of the incident pulse is in front. We shall
meet an analogous situation to this in Chapter 16, when, in
our study of optics, we consider the image of a point source of
light placed in front of a plane mirror.

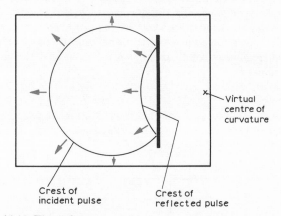

Fig.14.16 The reflection of a circular pulse from a straight
barrier in the ripple tank.

Can you account for the nature of the reflected circular
pulse in Fig. 14.16 by referring to the law of reflection for
waves? (Hint: consider tiny segments of the pulse incident
on the barrier, treating each segment as though it were
straight.)

When we come to consider the phenomenon of refraction,
it is more instructive to consider the behaviour of a travelling
wave motion than that of a single pulse. A periodic straight
wave motion may be generated in the ripple tank of Fig.
14.12 by dipping the lower edge of the paddle in the water
surface, and setting the paddle in regular vibrational motion
by rotating the toy motor at a steady frequency. This steady
frequency is achieved by applying a constant potential
difference between the terminals of the motor. The eccentric
motion of the cog attached to the spindle of the motor
provides the paddle with its regular vibrational motion.
This motion is *not*, as is usually assumed, restricted purely

to the vertical plane so the resulting water wave motion is not purely transverse. The motion of the paddle is more correctly described as slightly rocking in and about the vertical plane, so the resulting wave motion possesses a slight longitudinal component as well. The profile of a periodic straight wave motion in the ripple tank is therefore not perfectly sinusoidal and is in fact similar to that shown in the diagram of Fig. 14.17.

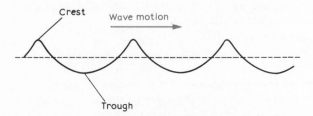

Fig.14.17 The true profile of a periodic straight wave motion in the ripple tank is not exactly sinusoidal.

When projected on a screen below the ripple tank by light from an overhead source, the periodic straight waves produced by the motion of the paddle appear as in Fig. 14.18. Again, wave crests are recognised by bright lines or bands in the projected pattern, while wave troughs are recognised by the dark regions or bands between the crests. The perpendicular distance between any two successive crests is of course the wavelength of the wave motion.

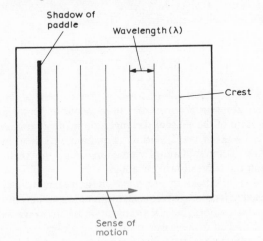

Fig.14.18 Periodic straight waves in the ripple tank.

For all wave motions it is found that the speed of the wave motion is determined ultimately by the properties of the medium through which the wave is passing. In the case of waves travelling in a coil spring, the speed of the wave motion is determined by the tension in the spring. In the case of water

waves, the speed of the wave motion is determined by the depth of the water in which the waves are travelling. This may be easily demonstrated in the ripple tank by placing a glass plate in the tank with its edge parallel to the length of each approaching wave crest. It is found that on entering the shallow region of the tank—that is, the region above the glass plate—the wavelength of the wave motion is changed abruptly to a smaller value as in the diagram of Fig. 14.19.

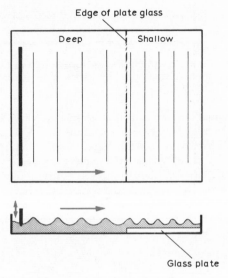

Fig.14.19 Periodic straight waves travelling from a deep to a shallow region in the ripple tank. (Normal incidence.)

When the ripple tank is set up so as to give a wave motion as in Fig. 14.19 and this motion is then observed with the aid of a hand stroboscope, it is found that when the stroboscope is turned at that frequency necessary to 'stop' the motion in the deep region of the tank, then the motion in the shallow region is 'stopped' also. That is, the frequency of the wave motion in both sections of the tank is the same, and so is unaffected by the change in depth. It follows therefore, from equation (14.1), that the change in wavelength occurring when the waves pass from the deep region to the shallow region is a result of a change in wave speed alone. Since the wavelength has decreased in the shallow region, the speed of the wave motion must also have decreased.

When the glass plate is adjusted in position so that its edge is no longer parallel to the approaching wave crests, we find that the change in wavelength produced at the interface of the deep and shallow waters is now accompanied by a change in the direction of the advancing crests. This bending of a wave motion at an oblique interface between two propagation media is known as *refraction*, and is illustrated for this case, in Fig. 14.20.

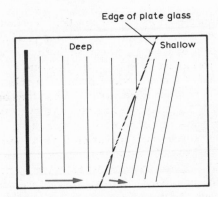

Fig.14.20 Periodic straight waves travelling from a deep to a shallow region in the ripple tank. (Oblique incidence.)

The amount of refraction occurring as the waves pass from one medium to another depends on the size of the change in speed, and so to measure the degree of refraction, it is useful to define a quantity called the *index of refraction* of waves passing from one medium to another, as the ratio of the wave speeds in the two media. If the wave motion has speed v_1 in the deep region of the tank, and speed v_2 in the shallow region, then the index of refraction for water waves passing from deep to shallow waters is defined as n where

$$n = \frac{v_1}{v_2} \qquad (14.2)$$

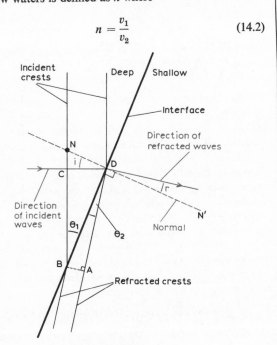

Fig.14.21 An analysis of refraction.

Let us, with reference to Fig. 14.21, attempt to relate this index to the actual change in direction which occurs in the process of refraction. In Fig. 14.21 we have drawn the normal to the refracting surface and labelled the angle of incidence—defined as the angle between the direction of the incident wave motion and the normal to the surface—as 'i'. The angle of refraction—defined as the angle between the direction of the refracted wave motion and the normal to the surface—we have labelled as 'r'. In the diagram we have shown two wave crests undergoing refraction. Since the perpendicular distance between these is a measure of wavelength, it follows that the wavelength of the waves in the deep region—λ_1 say—is measured as CD, while that in the shallow region—λ_2 say—is measured as AB. Now

$$n = \frac{v_1}{v_2} \quad \text{and} \quad v_1 = f\lambda_1, \quad v_2 = f\lambda_2$$

where f is the frequency of the wave motion. Hence

$$n = \frac{f\lambda_1}{f\lambda_2} = \frac{\lambda_1}{\lambda_2}$$

Now $$\lambda_1 = \text{CD} = \text{BD} \sin \theta_1$$
and $$\lambda_2 = \text{AB} = \text{BD} \sin \theta_2$$

Hence $$\frac{\lambda_1}{\lambda_1} = \frac{\sin \theta_1}{\sin \theta_2}$$

That is, $$n = \frac{\sin \theta_1}{\sin \theta_2}$$

Since triangles NCD and NBD are similar, it follows that $\theta_1 = i$. Further, since $\theta_2 + \hat{ADN'} = 90°$, and $r + \hat{ADN'} = 90°$, then it follows that $\theta_2 = r$. Hence

$$\boxed{n \left(= \frac{v_1}{v_2} \right) = \frac{\sin i}{\sin r}} \qquad \ldots \ldots \ldots (14.3)$$

The index of refraction, which is found to be a constant quantity for two given media, may therefore be calculated as the ratio of the sines of the angles of incidence and refraction for a given wave motion. Equation 14.3 is a specific instance of Snell's Law of refraction, a law we shall meet again in the two following chapters.

Having observed that a wave motion may be bent or refracted in its passage from one medium to another, it is also interesting to note that the propagation of any wave motion may be altered to some extent by placing a barrier containing a slit in the path of the waves. When periodic straight waves in the ripple tank are incident on a slit formed by placing two separate barriers in the tank, it is found that the waves on emerging from the far side of the slit are not necessarily straight in nature. If the width of the slit is of the same order of size as the wavelength of the incident waves, then the emerging waves are observed to be of a circular nature and therefore expanding in all forward directions! This flaring out of a straight wave motion at a gap in a barrier placed before it is known as *diffraction*.

When the slit width is altered in relation to the wavelength of the incident wave motion, then the shape of the diffracted waves will be altered too. We observe that, as the slit width is increased relative to the wavelength of the wave motion, the circular parts of the emerging waves are restricted to the edge regions—an effect which is almost negligible if the slit width is very much greater than the wavelength of the incident waves. The diagrams of Fig. 14.22 illustrate the diffraction effects which may be observed with straight waves in a ripple tank when a slit of width (a) one wavelength (b) three wavelengths (c) five wavelengths, is introduced to the tank.

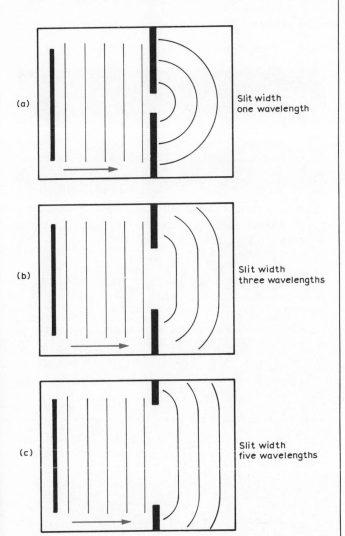

Slit width
one wavelength

Slit width
three wavelengths

Slit width
five wavelengths

Fig.14.22 The diffraction of periodic straight waves in the ripple tank.

The phenomenon of wave diffraction implies that it is almost impossible to isolate a narrow and parallel train of straight waves by placing a narrow slit in front of a broader straight wave motion. If we know exactly where a wave is at a given instant of time it is very helpful to be able to deduce where it will be at some later instant. A construction for this purpose was suggested by Christian Huygens in the seventeenth century as part of his wave theory of light. Huygens' construction states that all points on a given wave at some instant of time must be considered as sources of new secondary wavelets. These wavelets spread out as circles in the forward direction of travel with the speed of the wave in the given medium. In three dimensions, of course, the wavelets will be spherical. At any later instant of time, the position of the new wave is given by the line which is tangential to all these secondary wavelets. Such a line is called the envelope of the family of lines which is made up of the secondary wavelets.

The diagrams in Fig. 14.23 show a circular wavefront and a straight wavefront, and on each, a series of points have been marked. Each point, according to Huygens, is a source of circular secondary wavelets, and these secondary wavelets have been included in the diagrams. By drawing the envelope of the wavelets—as has been done in red—we find the new positions of the original wavefronts a short time later.

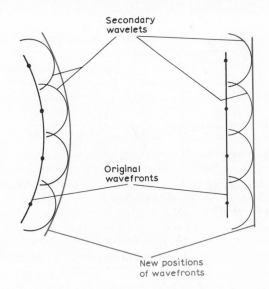

Secondary
wavelets

Original
wavefronts

New positions
of wavefronts

Fig.14.23 The progression of a circular and a straight wavefront.

It is clear from the diagrams that, in general, a circular wave is propagated as a circular wave and a straight one as a straight one. The points at each end of a straight wavefront must, in their generation of secondary wavelets, give rise to a spreading of the wavefront at its ends as it progresses. Further, this effect must become increasingly pronounced as the length of the straight wavefront is reduced. Hence in the case of a very small straight wavefront—as might be produced by directing straight waves towards a very narrow slit of width about one wavelength—we should expect to find the generation of almost perfectly semicircular wavefronts. This is quite consistent with the diagram of Fig. 14.22(a). In the case of a fairly long straight wavefront however—as might be produced by directing straight waves towards a slit of width tens of wavelengths—we should expect to find the progression of almost perfectly straight wavefronts beyond the slit— these wavefronts exhibiting only a slight curvature at their ends.

The diffraction patterns shown in Fig. 14.22 are not entirely correct and we shall return to a fuller investigation in the next chapter. In the meantime, the picture which we have developed is that which you will be able to see quite clearly in the ripple tank.

In our study of pulse properties earlier in the chapter, we observed that when two pulses meet they effectively pass through each other, each continuing as if the other were not present. The disturbance of the medium at the time of meeting was the algebraic sum of the disturbances due to the separate pulses. When we consider the superposition of wave trains rather than of individual pulses, the effect produced is known as *interference*, and the interference property of waves is accepted as the most important in as much as it provides the ultimate evidence of their existence. Let us investigate these effects by superposing two wave trains.

The interference of two wave trains may be demonstrated very satisfactorily by generating two sets of periodic circular waves of the same frequency and phase in the same ripple tank. A pattern of interference is then observed. In order to generate two wave trains so that they have the same wavelength and are exactly in step with each other, the wooden paddle in Fig. 14.12 is raised clear of the water surface, and the two plastic balls on swivel mounts attached to the paddle are turned down until each ball touches the water surface and penetrates it to the same shallow depth—as in Fig. 14.24. When the motor is switched on, a vertical rocking motion of the paddle results, and two circular wave trains are produced in the tank, one from each vibrating plastic ball. This pattern is shown projected on the screen below the tank in Fig. 14.25, and it has been drawn, as seen from vertically above, in Fig. 14.26. This diagram indicates lines of cancellation or calmness, which extend outwards from between the point sources, and are known as *nodal lines*. Between these regions of calm water, there exist regions in which crests and troughs are propagated but such that these crests and troughs are (in places) of twice the amplitude of those originating from either source. These lines or regions of reinforcement are known as *antinodal lines*, and, together with the nodal lines,

they constitute a two-source interference pattern. Let us attempt to account for this pattern with reference to Fig. 14.27.

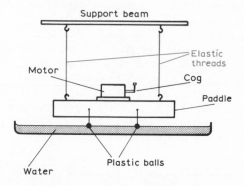

Fig.14.24 Producing two sets of circular waves in phase.

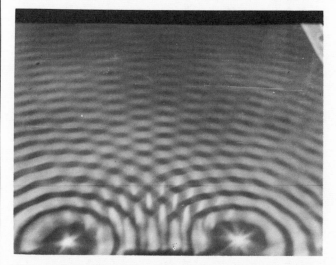

Fig.14.25 The interference pattern as it appears when projected on the screen. Lines of cancellation can be seen spreading out from between the sources.

The diagram of Fig. 14.27 represents two sets of periodic circular waves generated by the point sources S_1 and S_2 which are vibrating with the same frequency, and in phase (or in step). The diagram obviously accounts for only that half of the wave motion forward of the paddle, but a consideration of this half will prove sufficient for our purposes. The line marked A_0 joins three points of intersection of wave crests emanating from each source. We recall that when two like disturbances meet, they add together algebraically to produce a larger disturbance of the same kind. Also on the line A_0 we have points of coincidence of wave troughs emanating from each source, although these are unmarked. These points of course lie midway between the points of intersection of the crests on the line A_0. Along this line A_0

therefore, we should expect to find constructive interference and hence a reinforced wave motion. A_0 is referred to as the central antinodal line of the interference pattern. Can you account for and explain the origins of the first antinodal lines of the pattern which are marked as A_1 and A_1'?

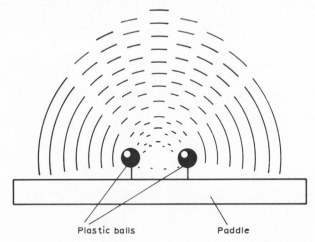

Fig.14.26 The interference of two sets of circular waves in phase.

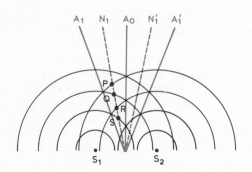

Fig.14.27 The nodal and antinodal lines in interference.

The points P, Q, R, and S, through which is drawn the line N_1, are each such that they lie on a crest emanating from one source, and also midway between crests (that is, on a trough) emanating from the other source. For example, P lies on a crest from S_2 but also on a trough from S_1. We recall that when two unlike disturbances meet, they add together algebraically so that in the special case where their amplitudes are equal, their region of superposition is one of calm. At the points P, Q, R, and S, and hence along the line N_1, we should therefore expect to find destructive interference and a resulting calmness of the water surface. The lines N_1 and N_1' are referred to as the first nodal lines of the interference pattern.

Considerations such as these provide us with results which would seem to be quite consistent with the wave pattern which we have previously observed in Fig. 14.25. Although such

an interference pattern may be projected on the screen below the ripple tank satisfactorily, it is always much more fascinating to look along the surface of the water in the ripple tank and actually observe the lines of undisturbed water extending from between the sources. Between these lines of calmness, one may observe travelling wave motions where crests reinforce crests, and troughs reinforce troughs.

Along the lines N_1 and N_1' in Fig. 14.27, we conclude that there would exist complete destructive interference and hence complete calm. Since this implies that the water surface is motionless in these regions, then we must infer that there is a complete lack of energy in these regions. This seems somewhat strange, for surely each of the two sets of interfering waves was carrying energy? Where has this energy gone? The total energy of the two sets of waves is of course unchanged in its total amount, but in this situation of interference, the energy of the system has been re-distributed and concentrated in the regions of constructive interference.

14.5 An Analysis of Interference

In our discussions of interference in the last section, we concerned ourselves with the explanation of why nodal and antinodal lines should be produced in the interference situation. Let us now take the interference situation a little further by investigating the beautiful relationships which exist between the location of the nodal and antinodal lines, and the wavelength of each of the two sets of interfering waves.

The diagram of Fig. 14.28 shows two point sources of circular waves S_1 and S_2 generating waves of the same wavelength and in phase. Let the wavelength of these waves be λ. Also on this diagram we have drawn the central and first antinodal lines, A_0 and A_1, as well as the first nodal line N_1'.

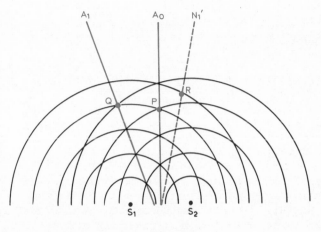

Fig.14.28 An analysis of interference.

line of interference	A_0	$\begin{pmatrix} A_1 \\ A_1' \end{pmatrix}$	$\begin{pmatrix} A_2 \\ A_2' \end{pmatrix}$	$\begin{pmatrix} A_3 \\ A_3' \end{pmatrix}$	$\begin{pmatrix} A_r \\ A_r' \end{pmatrix}$	$\begin{pmatrix} N_1 \\ N_1' \end{pmatrix}$	$\begin{pmatrix} N_2 \\ N_2' \end{pmatrix}$	$\begin{pmatrix} N_r \\ N_r' \end{pmatrix}$
path difference between the sources and any point on the line	0	λ	2λ	3λ	$r\lambda$	$\frac{1}{2}\lambda$	$\frac{3}{2}\lambda$	$(r - \frac{1}{2})\lambda$

If we choose some point P on the central antinodal line and measure the distance S_1P and S_2P by inspection, then we find these to be the same and equal to 4λ. There is thus no *path difference* between the sources S_1 and S_2 and the point P on the central antinode. This is true regardless of the position of the point P, as the reader may verify for himself.

If we choose some point Q on the first antinodal line and measure the distances S_1Q and S_2Q by inspection, then we find these differ by λ. In this case, $S_1Q = 4\lambda$, $S_2Q = 5\lambda$, and so $S_2Q - S_1Q = (5\lambda - 4\lambda) = \lambda$. The path difference between the sources S_1 and S_2 and the point Q on the first antinode is therefore one complete wavelength. This, as the reader can check, is true for all positions of Q.

If we now choose some point R on the first nodal line and measure the distances S_1R and S_2R by inspection, then we find these to differ by $\frac{1}{2}\lambda$. In this case, $S_1R = 5\lambda$, $S_2R = 4\frac{1}{2}\lambda$, and so $S_1R - S_2R = (5\lambda - 4\frac{1}{2}\lambda) = \frac{1}{2}\lambda$. The path difference between the sources S_1 and S_2 and the point R on the first nodal line is therefore one half wavelength. This will clearly be true for all positions of R.

By a similar approach, we find the path difference between the sources and any point on the second antinodal line to be 2λ, while that between the sources and any point on the second nodal line is $\frac{3}{2}\lambda$. The full results of such an analysis as this are conveniently summarised in the table above.

If we were now asked to predict what would be observed at some point X in the vicinity of coherent sources* S_1 and S_2 (as in Fig. 14.29) which generate waves of wavelength λ, then by measuring the path lengths S_1X and S_2X and finding the size of the path difference $|S_1X - S_2X|$, we could say whether X would lie on an antinodal line (when $|S_1X - S_2X|$ was an integral number of wavelengths), or on a nodal line (when $|S_1X - S_2X|$ was a half-integral number of wavelengths).

This analytical approach to interference will prove useful

---

* Sources emitting waves in phase. (A discussion of coherence follows in section 15.3.)

in our development of a wave theory of light in the next chapter.

Fig.14.29 Deducing the nature of the waveform in the vicinity of two coherent sources of waves.

14.6 Stationary Waves

When a continuous train of transverse waves is generated in an elastic cord fixed at one end, then a continuous train of waves is reflected from the fixed end, and interference of the incident and reflected waves results. The resulting wave pattern in such a situation is such that no progressive wave appears to move in either direction, but instead, the cord appears to be divided up into a certain number of segments (Fig. 14.30). Points of maximum disturbance in these segments are referred to as *antinodes*; points of zero disturbance are referred to as *nodes*. Any point on the cord executes an oscillatory motion of a specified amplitude at right angles to the cord. This amplitude is zero at a node, and a maximum at an antinode.

The generation of stationary wave patterns is dependent on achieving sympathy or resonance between the frequency of vibration at the free end of the cord and the tension along its length. When the frequency 'fits in' with the tension in the cord, then the cord is said to be in resonance with the vibrator (Fig. 14.31), and responds vigorously—the segments having maximum amplitude. When the frequency does not 'fit in', the cord responds less vigorously and in a very disordered manner.

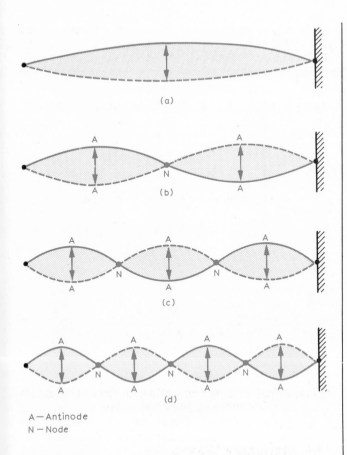

Fig.14.30 Stationary wave patterns.

A — Antinode
N — Node

Fig.14.31 An electric vibrator used in the generation of stationary waves. (By kind permission of Advance Electronics Ltd.)

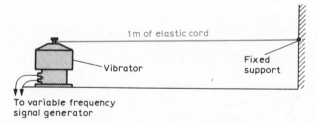

Fig.14.32 Producing stationary wave patterns.

Stationary wave patterns such as those shown in Fig. 14.30 may be established by setting up the apparatus shown in Fig. 14.32, and adjusting the frequency control of the signal generator from say 15 Hz to 100 Hz. Provided that the tension in the cord is not too great, it is possible to observe the stationary wave patterns illustrated in Fig. 14.30. These patterns are observed in turn by slowly increasing the frequency of the signal generator output through the required range.

A study of any one of these stationary wave patterns— (c) say—reveals that the positions of antinodes and nodes are fixed along the length of the cord. Both the antinodes and the nodes are equally spaced, and the ends of the cord are always nodes although the left hand end is not a true node in the strict sense of the word. Further, as far as any one segment is concerned, all 'particles' contained within it vibrate exactly in phase. Any two adjacent segments of the cord are observed to vibrate in antiphase however, although this is perhaps not always obvious—especially if the frequency of vibration is sufficiently high that the eye cannot follow the exact movement of the cord. Some insight may be gained here however by setting up a standing wave pattern such as that in Fig. 14.30(c), switching out all the lights in the laboratory, and illuminating the vibrating cord with the light from a flashing stroboscope—the flashing rate of which has previously been set equal to the frequency of the signal generator output when producing this particular pattern. The motion of the cord may then be observed as 'stopped' and thereby observed instantaneously—as we might observe it with the aid of a photograph. The cord would then appear as in Fig. 14.33, indicating that adjacent segments of the standing wave pattern are vibrating in antiphase.

If the flashing rate of the stroboscope is set very slightly different from the frequency of the signal generator output, the cord is observed to 'snake' backwards and forwards thus reproducing its true movement in slow motion.

Unfortunately the use of the stroboscope gives us no visual information of the fact that two wave motions are

Fig.14.33 'Stopping' the motion of the cord with the aid of a flashing stroboscope.

traversing the cord in opposite directions. Perhaps a reasonably satisfactory approach towards this end is for the reader to draw two identical wave trains on separate pieces of tracing paper, move these across each other each at the same speed and along the same axis (but in opposite senses), and to project the added displacements of the two interfering trains on a selected region of a fixed background sheet of paper. The resultant displacement in this region of the background sheet should then be observed to behave like a boundary to one of the segments of the stationary wave patterns we have already discussed—moving at right angles to the common axis from maximum, through minimum, towards maximum.

Problems

1 A downward pulse is moving along an elastic cord in the sense left to right. How does a tiny knot in the cord behave when the pulse reaches it? Does it move up then down, or down then up? What would have been its motion if an upward pulse had been moving from right to left instead?

2 Two pulses are travelling along an elastic cord as shown in Fig. 14.34, each with speed 4 cm s^{-1}. Sketch the shape of the cord $\frac{1}{2}$ s, 1 s, 1$\frac{1}{2}$ s, and 2 s later. Would it be possible for these pulses to travel at different speeds along this same cord?

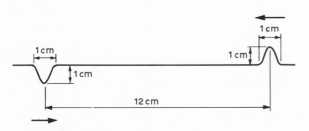

Fig.14.34 See Problem 2.

3 Draw the resultant waveform produced when two sinusoidal waveforms of amplitudes 1 cm and 2 cm, and out of step by $\frac{1}{4}$ cycle, are superposed.

4 In a 50 m swimming pool, a wave machine makes one wave every 2 s. If the wave crests are 2 m apart, how long will any one crest take to travel the length of the pool?

5 Can you devise an experiment which would enable you to measure the speed of water waves in a ripple tank?

6 Periodic straight waves in a ripple tank are incident upon a curved barrier as illustrated in Fig. 14.35. With reference to the law of reflection, and by drawing, find the reflected wave pattern.

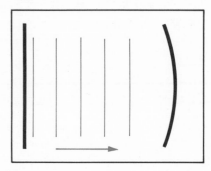

Fig.14.35 See Problem 6.

7 Sound waves travel at 330 m s^{-1} in air, and at 1485 m s^{-1} in water. A sound wave from an underwater explosion is incident on the surface of a loch at an angle of incidence of 30°. At what angle will this sound wave emerge into the air?

8 Periodic straight waves in a ripple tank are incident on two slits, each of width one wavelength, positioned in the ripple tank as shown in Fig. 14.36. Describe carefully why an interference pattern like that shown in Fig. 14.25 is observed in the tank beyond the region of the slits. In what way might this interference pattern be altered if the incident waves were not normal to the direction of the barriers. Would this alteration be due to the interfering waves being out of phase, or having different wavelengths?

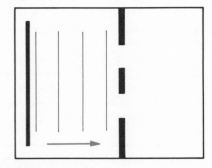

Fig.14.36 See Problem 8.

9 Construct an interference pattern for two sources of circular waves of different wavelengths. In what respects does the pattern of nodal lines differ from that in Fig. 14.25?

10 The fact that sound is a wave motion may be demonstrated by setting up an interference pattern using two sources of sound. Two loudspeakers fed from the same signal

generator gave rise to an interference pattern as indicated in the diagram of Fig. 14.37. An observer walking across the room parallel to the line joining the loudspeakers detected antinodes at A, B, C, D, and E. The distances L_1D and L_2D were found to be 3 m and 2·35 m respectively At what frequency was the signal generator set?

(the speed of sound in air $= 330$ m s^{-1})

11 Do you think that it might be possible to generate standing waves by superposing two wave motions of equal amplitude but of different wavelengths, travelling in the same cord in opposite senses?

12 How might you generate and recognise standing wave patterns in (a) a circular ripple tank (b) a rectangular ripple tank?

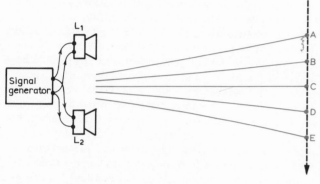

Fig.14.37 See Problem 10.

Chapter 15

The Wave Properties of Light

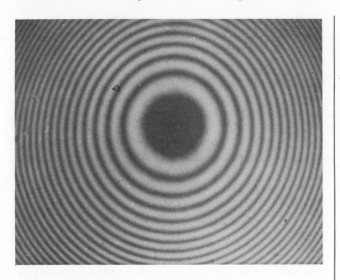

Fig.15.0 The interference of light is illustrated in this 'Newton's Rings' pattern as circles of reinforcement and cancellation.

The word *light* refers to that radiation which, emitted from luminous bodies such as the sun and stars, stimulates the nerve cells contained in the retinas of our eyes. When these nerve cells are stimulated by light, we *see*. Any non-luminous body, such as the paper before us, is made visible as the result of light from a luminous body (the sun, an electric lamp, a candle) striking it and being reflected into our eyes.

Although our sense of sight is activated by the presence of light, no information as to the nature of light itself follows from the act of seeing. If, for example, the light from a candle flame reaches our eyes, we are made aware of the form, colour, and extent of the flame, but not of the nature of the light which it emits. It is thus desirable to try to establish a model or picture of the nature of light, both by a careful study of the properties of light, and from the knowledge which we have accumulated from previous chapters.

Accepting light as some ultimately 'unseen' radiation, then, as was the case with 'cathode rays' in Chapter 12, we have to decide whether to regard light as *corpuscular* and obeying Newton's laws of motion, or as *wave-like* and exhibiting the properties of waves which we discussed in the last chapter. Isaac Newton first suggested that light is composed of tiny material particles (or corpuscles) emitted from any luminous body. These particles, according to Newton, were emitted at high speed, and travelled in straight lines in accordance with the first law of motion. The size of the particles emitted was responsible for the colour of the light, and their assumed perfectly elastic nature would explain the reflection of light from a polished mirror surface. This theory, backed by Newton's standing as a scientist of outstanding eminence, survived throughout the whole of the

eighteenth century, despite the fact that Huygens' more flexible wave theory of light had been proposed earlier in 1690. Huygens had been impressed by the facts that (i) light is transmitted in all directions with an extremely high speed (this speed having been measured as approximately 3×10^8 m s^{-1} by Romer in 1676), and (ii) two beams of light may cross each other without either hindering the other (as we observed to be the case with two pulses meeting and crossing each other in a coil spring in the last chapter). In proposing a wave model for light however, Huygens also proposed the existence of a stationary undetected aether which filled all space, including vacuum and the gaps between all particles of matter. If such a medium were absent Huygens argued, then light would have nothing to 'wave' in, and so its passage through a vacuum (such as that between Sun and Earth) would be impossible. This argument is to a large extent parallel with that which states (correctly) that water waves cannot be transmitted in the absence of water. All experiments designed to reveal the presence of an aether have so far proved inconclusive. In 1905, Albert Einstein, in formulating his theory of relativity, ignored the concept of an aether. Let us follow his example and examine the theory that light is wave-like in nature. We shall attempt to interpret the behaviour of light in terms of wave characteristics and, at the same time, note weaknesses in the corpuscular theory as Newton understood it.

15.1 The Reflection of Light

The paper in front of us is made visible to us from all angles of elevation, and so we may conclude that light is reflected from it *diffusely*. That is, light is reflected from it in all directions. When light is incident on a highly polished surface such as a mirror, however, it is reflected *regularly* and in a particular direction. Regular reflection, being less complicated than diffuse reflection, is more easily investigated, and in its investigation, we may proceed as follows using the apparatus illustrated in Fig. 15.1(a).

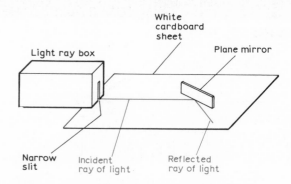

Fig.15.1(a)   The regular reflection of a ray of light.

Using this apparatus in a darkened room, direct a ray of light (made visible as it brushes the surface of the white cardboard sheet) on to the surface of a plane mirror. You should find (as in Fig. 15.1(b)) that the reflected ray (again, made visible as it brushes the surface of the cardboard sheet) is sharply defined as is the incident ray. Mark on the cardboard sheet the position of the mirror surface and the directions of the incident and reflected rays. Draw the normal to the reflecting surface through the point of incidence, and measure the angles of incidence and reflection as defined in the diagram of Fig. 15.2. These two angles will be found to be equal, within the limits of experimental error, for all directions of the incident ray.

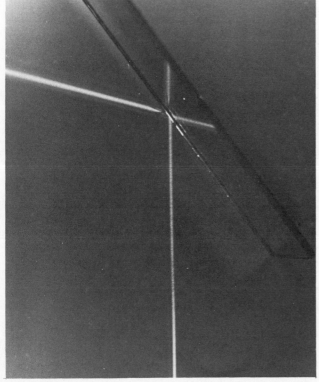

Fig.15.1(b)

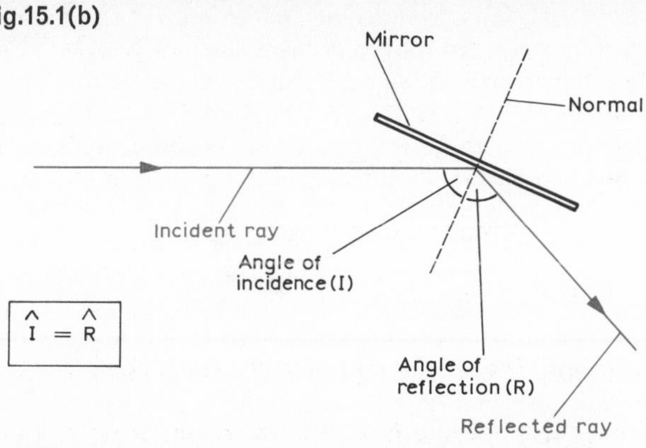

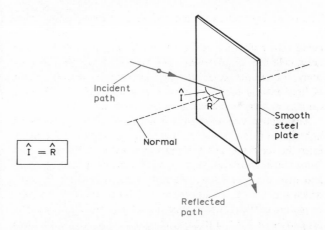

Fig.15.3 The reflection of a steel ball from a smooth steel plate.

This simple result is found to hold true regardless of the angle of incidence, and it is known as the second law of regular reflection of light.

In finding that the angle of incidence is equal to the angle of reflection for a ray of light undergoing regular reflection, and recalling the similar law of reflection which we established in our study of water waves in the last chapter, we might be tempted to conclude that light too is a wave motion. This conclusion can be valid only if a corresponding law of reflection does not hold true for material particles undergoing reflection from a surface.

It is found that when a steel ball bearing is fired at a smooth steel plate, it bounces off in regular reflection such that its angle of incidence is equal to its angle of reflection, as is indicated in Fig. 15.3. Further, the incident and reflected paths are both in the same plane perpendicular to the plane of the plate. If the ball bearing is fired at a plane surface such as wood however (so that the high degree of elasticity is removed from the system) then it is found that the reflected motion which results does not exhibit equal angles of incidence and reflection.

From these discussions therefore, we cannot say with certainty whether light is wave-like or corpuscular in nature. Although we hope to show the presence of wave properties in light, we cannot rule out the possibility (from the evidence here) that light might be composed of tiny material corpuscles which are perfectly elastic in their interaction with the reflecting surface. Of course it might be argued at this stage that light cannot possibly be corpuscular in nature, since it is possible for two light beams to pass through each other without either hindering the other. Surely, one might argue, material particles would give rise to considerable hindrance—observed as scattering—by their mutual collisions. If however we consider the particles to be sufficiently minute, and travel-

Fig.15.2 The second law of regular reflection of light.

ling with sufficiently high speeds, then the probability of any one particle in one beam colliding with any one particle in a second beam becomes negligibly small—even for two very intense beams. The lack of interaction between two beams, if they happened to be corpuscular, might therefore be explained in this way.

Clearly we must investigate further properties of light before coming to a conclusion.

15.2 The Refraction of Light

The bent appearance of an oar partly immersed in water was recognised correctly by the ancient Greeks as being due to the fact that rays of light reflected from the oar were being bent or refracted on passing from water to air. The fact that a ray of light is bent or refracted when it passes from any one medium to another of different optical density* may be demonstrated easily using the apparatus illustrated in Fig. 15.4.

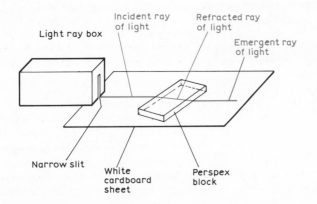

Fig.15.4   The refraction of a ray of light.

Using this apparatus in a darkened room, a ray of light is directed to the edge of a rectangular perspex block positioned so that this edge makes some angle (other than 90°) with the direction of the incident ray. It is found that on passing into the perspex block, the ray is no longer directed along its original path. It has been bent or refracted as a result of passing from air to perspex. Further, by marking on the cardboard sheet the position of the perspex block along with the directions of the incident and emergent rays, the path of the refracted ray may be deduced by joining the points of incidence and emergence of the incident and emergent rays respectively.

On drawing the normal to the first refracting surface (the leading edge of the block) through the point of incidence, it is found by measurement that the angles of incidence and

* Two materials are said to have different optical densities if light does not travel at the same speed in each.

refraction—defined in relation to the system as in Fig. 15.5—are quite different. It is found however that no matter what the angle of incidence, the ratio of the sine of this angle to the sine of the angle of refraction is constant for the perspex block employed. In our experiment, it is found that

$$\frac{\sin i}{\sin r} = 1\cdot5$$

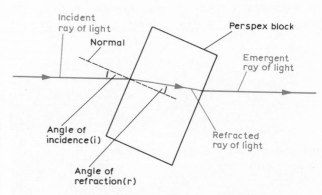

Fig.15.5   The second law of refraction of light.

This result is a specific instance of the more general second law of refraction of light which states that 'when a ray of light passes from one medium to another of different optical density, the sine of the angle of incidence bears a constant ratio to the sine of the angle of refraction'. The first law of refraction of light states that 'the incident and refracted rays are on opposite sides of, and in the same plane as the normal to the refracting surface through the point of incidence'.

In finding a constant ratio for the sines of the angles of incidence and refraction for two given media (in our case air and perspex), and recalling a somewhat similar relationship we established in the last chapter in our study of water waves, we might again be tempted to conclude that light must therefore be a wave motion. Again, such a conclusion is valid only if a similar relationship does not hold true for material particles undergoing refraction on crossing a surface between two regions or materials.

It is found that when a steel ball bearing is rolled along a smooth horizontal surface towards a steep slope leading down to a lower smooth horizontal surface, its direction of travel on the lower surface is quite different from that on the upper surface, provided that initially the ball is travelling in a direction other than at 90° to the edge of the steep slope. That is, a certain refraction is observed in its motion as it passes from one region to another. Further, the speed of the ball on the lower surface is observed to be greater than that on the upper surface, so that a change in the ball's direction has been accompanied by a change in its speed as it passes from one region to another. This situation is represented as in Fig. 15.6.

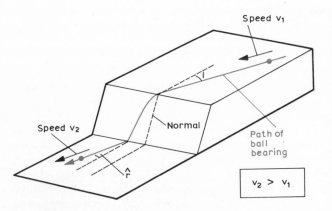

Fig.15.6   A particle model of refraction.

When the ball bearing reaches the slope, a component of its weight acts down the slope, and increases its velocity in the direction of the normal to the edge of the slope. There is no corresponding force parallel to the edge of the slope, and so the path of the ball is bent towards the normal. That is, the angle r on the lower surface is less than the angle i on the upper surface. With reference to Fig. 15.6,

$$v_1 \sin i = v_2 \sin r$$

Hence
$$\frac{\sin i}{\sin r} = \frac{v_2}{v_1} \quad \dotfill \quad (15.1)$$

(where v_1 and v_2 refer to the speeds of the ball in the first and second regions respectively.)

Newton in his corpuscular theory of light explained the sudden change in direction at the surface of a glass block by saying that light corpuscles were attracted into the block (that is, in a direction normal to the surface) by the particles present in the block. This of course implied that the ray of light, after being bent towards the normal during refraction, would be travelling at greater speed in the glass block. This is quite consistent with the last equation.

Equation 15.1 is thus a law describing the refraction of corpuscles. When we compare it with the law describing the refraction of waves as expressed in equation (14.3), we note an important difference. In the case of the refraction of waves

$$\frac{\sin i}{\sin r} = \frac{v_1}{v_2}$$

whereas in the case of the refraction of corpuscles;

$$\frac{\sin i}{\sin r} = \frac{v_2}{v_1}$$

(where, in the now usual notation, v_1 and v_2 refer to the speeds

of the particular motion—waves or corpuscles—before incidence and after refraction respectively).

In 1862, Foucault succeeded in measuring the speed of light in air and in water, and found that its speed in the optically denser material was less than in the optically less dense material. Further experiments have shown that the ratio of the speed of light in air to the speed in perspex is almost exactly 1·5. Since in our experiment the light was incident in air and refracted in perspex it would seem that the refraction taking place is described correctly by the equation

$$\frac{\sin i}{\sin r} = \frac{v_1}{v_2} \quad \text{(in the usual notation)}$$

so that the refraction of light resembles the refraction of waves rather than that of particles.

This result has strengthened our wave model of light at the expense of the corpuscular model: but some of the evidence still points in the reverse direction. For instance, the fact that light appears to travel in straight lines follows naturally from the corpuscular model, but, as we have seen, a wave model suggests that light should bend round corners. We must not, therefore, come to too hasty a conclusion, but rather look more deeply into the problem for further evidence on one side or the other.

15.3 The Interference of Light

It was in our investigation of water waves in the last chapter that we first met the phenomenon of the interference of travelling waves. We noted that the interference pattern produced by two point sources of waves—these sources producing waves of the same wavelength and phase—was symmetric, having a regular succession of nodal and anti-nodal lines. Clearly it is difficult to imagine how such a pattern could be produced by anything other than waves, so that on achieving such a pattern with two point sources of any radiation (such as light), we could be certain that the radiation in question is wave-like in its nature. Let us then attempt to produce an interference effect with light and thereby establish its wave-like nature beyond any doubt.

When we set up two small identical lighted torch bulbs side by side, each having a screen with a pinhole placed before it, and observe these point sources of light in a darkened room, we are unable to detect any signs of interference however. If interference was occurring, then we might expect that where light waves were reinforcing, we should observe bright regions, and where light waves were cancelling, we should observe dark regions. That is, the resulting interference pattern should be characterised by a succession of light and dark areas.

The fact is that interference *is* occurring, but the interference regions or bands can never be observed satisfactorily using two independent sources of light as we have here. The light from any one source is composed of millions of short wave trains—each train radiated from a different atom in the source and at a different time. It has been calculated that the emission period of a wave train from any atom is about 10^{-8} s, so that if we consider two independent light sources such as the torch bulbs, then during any particular 10^{-8} s, one atom in each source might be radiating light, but there is no guarantee that the wave trains from the two atoms are in phase—in fact they are most likely to be out of phase by a certain amount. During the following 10^{-8} s, a different atom in each source will be radiating light, but again, the probability that the two wave trains are in phase (or even out of phase by the same amount as in the previous 10^{-8} s) is extremely low. In practice, many more than one atom per source will be radiating light in any given 10^{-8} s, but the emissions are so spontaneous and random, that no synchronised phase changes or *coherence* can be hoped for between the two sets of wave trains being emitted from the sources. The use of two incoherent sources in this way gives rise to interference between the two sets of wave trains, but the symmetry of the interference pattern being produced is changing at the rate of 10^8 times per second, as a result of the interference bands continually changing their positions and overlapping. This means that there can be no sustained bright bands and dark bands, and so the eye registers no interference pattern at all.

To produce a regular and sustained interference pattern with light and thereby establish the wave nature of light, we must therefore synchronise the phase of the two light sources and thereby produce two coherent radiations.

This was first done by Thomas Young in 1801 when he used a single light source and split the light from it into two parts which could then, he hoped, interfere with each other. Young succeeded in producing an interference pattern by illuminating two fine pinholes in a barrier with sunlight passing through a distant single pinhole. The interference pattern, he observed on a screen placed behind the twin sources as illustrated in Fig. 15.7. In this arrangement,

light from the single pinhole passes through the twin pinholes 'simultaneously' so that these pinholes serve as coherent sources of light.

We can repeat Young's experiment in a darkened room by setting up the apparatus illustrated in Fig. 15.8, in which light is emitted from an incandescent bulb with a long straight filament. A red filter has been placed over this normally white line source for a reason which we shall discuss later. The reason for using a line source, which is in effect an extended point source, is simply that it emits much more light than the point source. The light from the line source is allowed to fall on an opaque barrier which has two narrow parallel slits scratched on it—the separation of these slits being of the order of $\frac{1}{4}$ mm. When we look at the transluscent screen held behind the double slit barrier, we observe an interference pattern consisting of red and black bands alternately. Such a pattern is illustrated in Fig. 15.9.

The fact that an interference pattern has been produced establishes the wave nature of light beyond any further doubt, and the fact that it has been produced in this way means that we have made use of the diffraction property of waves in the process. It is the diffraction of wavefronts from the line source by each of the parallel slits, which is responsible for the generation of semicylindrical wavetrains at each of these slits, and hence for the establishment of the symmetric and regular interference pattern on the transluscent screen.

By making measurements on the interference fringes produced on the screen, and performing a little mathematical analysis on the arrangement of the experimental apparatus, we find it possible to calculate the wavelength of the light which is incident on the double slit arrangement. This approach of making measurements on interference fringes is in fact one of the simplest approaches towards the determination of the wavelength of light. Let us now re-examine our experiment mathematically, and with reference to Fig. 15.10.

We recall from our earlier analysis of the interference pattern produced with water waves in the ripple tank, that we

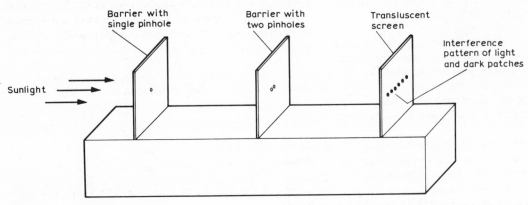

Fig.15.7   Young's Experiment.

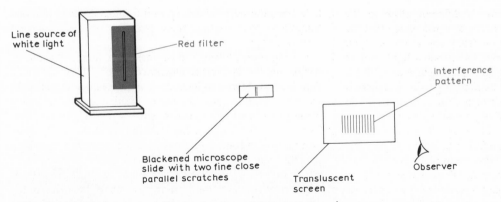

Red filter

Interference pattern

Blackened microscope slide with two fine close parallel scratches

Transluscent screen

Observer

Fig.15.8 Producing an interference pattern with light in the laboratory.

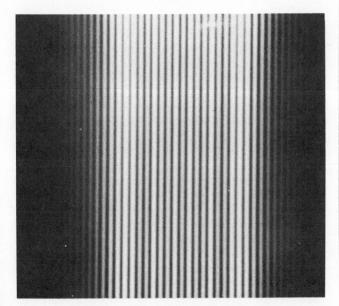

Fig.15.9 An interference pattern for light. (By kind permission of Mr. G. Y. Haig, Dept. of Physics, Paisley College of Technology.)

could predict whether a point in the vicinity of the wave sources would find itself on a nodal or on an antinodal line, depending on whether the path lengths—as measured between each source and the point in turn—differed by a half integral number of wavelengths or an integral number of wavelengths respectively. Let us translate the results of that analysis into the situation which we have represented in Fig. 15.10.

Since there is no difference in the path lengths S_1P and S_2P, the point P on the screen will lie on a bright fringe—the central bright fringe of the pattern. Let us suppose that Q is that point on the screen at which the next bright fringe is observed on the same side of P as S_1. Since Q lies on a bright

fringe, the difference in the path lengths S_2Q and S_1Q must be an integral number of wavelengths—in particular *one* wavelength, since Q lies on the *first* bright fringe after the central antinode. If the wavelength of the light incident on the slits is λ, then

$$S_2Q - S_1Q = \lambda$$

With reference to the geometry of Fig. 15.10, we may write

$$S_1Q^2 = \left(y - \frac{d}{2}\right)^2 + x^2$$

and

$$S_2Q^2 = \left(y + \frac{d}{2}\right)^2 + x^2$$

Hence $(S_2Q^2 - S_1Q^2) = \left[\left(y + \frac{d}{2}\right)^2 + x^2\right]$

$$- \left[\left(y - \frac{d}{2}\right)^2 + x^2\right]$$

$$= 2yd$$

That is, $(S_2Q + S_1Q)(S_2Q - S_1Q) = 2yd$

and so $S_2Q - S_1Q = \dfrac{2yd}{S_2Q + S_1Q}$

Now since the screen is usually some 40 to 50 cm from O whereas the slit separation is but a fraction of a millimetre, S_1Q and S_2Q are each almost exactly equal to OP. That is,

$$S_1Q \fallingdotseq S_2Q \fallingdotseq x$$

Hence $$S_2Q - S_1Q = \frac{2yd}{2x}$$

$$= \frac{yd}{x}$$

Hence $$\lambda = \frac{yd}{x}$$

where y is the distance between the central and first bright fringes.

It follows that the next bright fringe—at the point R say (on the S_1 side of P)—will be formed in accordance with the relationship

$$S_2R - S_1R = 2\lambda$$

If R is found to be at a distance y' from P, then

$$2\lambda = \frac{y'd}{x}$$

so that

$$y' = \frac{2x\lambda}{d}$$

But

$$y = \frac{x\lambda}{d}$$

and so

$$y' = 2y$$

This means that the centres of the bright fringes must be separated by the same distance, and this distance—known as the *fringe width*—is calculated as w, where

$$w = \frac{x\lambda}{d}$$

Hence

$$\boxed{\lambda = \frac{wd}{x}} \quad \dots\dots\dots\dots (15.2)$$

The fringe width in an interference pattern is a much more useful quantity to measure than the separation between the first bright fringe of the pattern and the central bright fringe. For one thing, it might be extremely difficult to locate the central fringe in the pattern since all of the fringes exhibit the same width and the same light intensity. Can you suggest another reason?

It is left as an exercise for the reader to show to his own satisfaction that the first dark fringe on the S_1 side of P in Fig. 15.10 is found at a distance y'' from P where

$$y'' = \frac{x\lambda}{2d}$$

and that the second dark fringe is found at a distance y''' from P where

$$y''' = \frac{3x\lambda}{2d}$$

What is the fringe width as measured between the centres of successive dark fringes?

Problem 1   When a red filter is placed over the line source in Fig. 15.8, the fringe width of the interference pattern on the screen is measured as 1·05 mm. When this filter is removed and a blue filter inserted in its place, the fringe width is measured as 0·75 mm. If the screen is located 50 cm behind the double slits and these slits are separated by 0·30 mm, calculate the wavelengths of the red and blue light transmitted by the red and blue filters in turn.

From equation (15.2),

$$\lambda = \frac{wd}{x}$$

In the case of the red filter, and hence the red light,

$$w = 1·05 \times 10^{-3}\,\text{m}, \quad d = 0·3 \times 10^{-3}\,\text{m}, \quad x = 0·5\,\text{m}$$

Hence
$$\lambda = \frac{(1·05 \times 10^{-3}) \times (0·3 \times 10^{-3})}{0·5}$$

$$= 6·3 \times 10^{-7}\,\text{m}$$

The wavelength of the red light is thus $6·3 \times 10^{-7}$ m. In the case of the blue filter, and hence the blue light,

$$w = 0·75 \times 10^{-3}\,\text{m}, \quad d = 0·3 \times 10^{-3}\,\text{m}, \quad x = 0·5\,\text{m}$$

Hence
$$\lambda = \frac{(0·75 \times 10^{-3}) \times (0·3 \times 10^{-3})}{0·5}$$

$$= 4·5 \times 10^{-7}\,\text{m}$$

The wavelength of the blue light is thus $4·5 \times 10^{-7}$ m.

This problem introduces us to the facts that different colours of light may be attributed to different wavelengths, and that the fringe width in an interference pattern is dependent on the spectral colour of the light being used to form the pattern. It is found that red fringes are about twice as broad as violet fringes.

When a white light source (rather than a monochromatic source) is used in establishing an interference pattern, it is found that the resulting pattern is composed of fringes which are apparently overlapping, of different colours, and of different widths. Only the central fringe of the pattern is white, and even it is tinged with red at its edges. This rather unfortunate pattern is easily explained when we realise that white light is the sum of all the spectral colours—a fact which we shall establish in Chapter 18—so that the pattern of interference fringes obtained with a white light source is formed as the resultant of the regular patterns of each of the constituent spectral colours, each pattern having a different fringe width. A white light interference pattern is thus characterised by a central white fringe and an array of multi-coloured fringes, only a few of which are quite distinct. For this reason a white light source is not particularly useful in the preliminary demonstrations of the interference of light. Hence the use of the coloured filter in the experimental arrangement of Fig. 15.8.

Finally in this section let us re-examine the statement which we made following the derivation of equation (15.2), namely that all the bright fringes in a monochromatic interference pattern exhibit the same light intensity.

With reference to Fig. 15.10, it is fairly obvious that the resultant wave amplitude at any point on the screen is determined by the difference in the path lengths as measured between each source and the point in question. That is, the

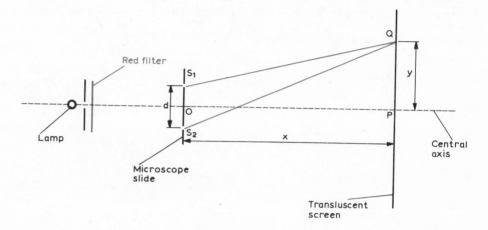

Fig.15.10 An analysis of the interference of light.

resultant amplitude is determined purely by the phase relationship between the two wave trains arriving at the point —assuming the amplitudes of the two trains to be equal. When we wish to add two waves of the same frequency, it is convenient to use a vector method in which the waves are represented in amplitude and phase relationship by appropriate vectors. The length of a vector in this situation is taken as representing the wave amplitude, while its direction and sense relative to that of another vector is taken as representing the phase relationship existing between the wave and another wave (represented by the second vector).

If we consider any two random wavetrains of the same frequency and amplitude, then they are likely to have a phase difference of some fraction of a wavelength. To relate this fraction to the relative orientation of two vectors, it is necessary to re-express the fraction of a wavelength as a fraction of one revolution of angular measure—that is, as a fraction of 2π radians.

In our derivation of equation (15.2), we established a general expression for the path or phase difference between two wave trains as equal to $\dfrac{Yd}{x}$, where Y refers to the distance between the central bright fringe and some arbitrary point on the screen. This difference may be re-expressed as $\dfrac{Yd}{x\lambda}$ wavelengths of light, when λ is the wavelength of each of the wavetrains.

Now a path difference of one wavelength would correspond to an angular difference of 2π radians, so that a path difference of $\dfrac{Yd}{x\lambda}$ wavelengths would correspond to an angular difference of $\dfrac{2\pi Yd}{x\lambda}$ radians.

Let us denote this arbitrary phase difference by the phase angle ϕ (radians).

The resultant wave amplitude at the arbitrary point on the screen (at a distance Y from the central bright fringe) may now be found as follows. A vector of length a units is drawn in the sense of the positive X-axis to represent one of the wave trains (of amplitude a). A second vector, also of length a units, is then added to this first vector inclined at an angle ϕ to the sense and direction of the positive X-axis. The resultant amplitude is then found as the vector sum of the two vectors.

This addition is performed in the diagram of Fig. 15.11.

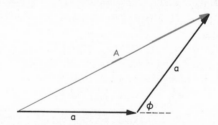

Fig.15.11 Combining light wave amplitudes.

Before considering the mathematics of this vector addition, it is fairly obvious that as the point Q (in Fig. 15.10) moves up the screen, the second vector (in Fig. 15.11) rotates anti-clockwise, clearly causing the resultant amplitude to swing between zero and $2a$.

Denoting the size of the resultant amplitude by A, then from the vector diagram it follows that

$$A^2 = a^2 + a^2 - 2a^2\cos(\pi - \phi)$$
$$= 2a^2(1 + \cos\phi)$$
$$= 4a^2\cos^2\frac{\phi}{2}$$

It may be shown that the intensity of light at any point on the screen is proportional to the square of the resultant wave amplitude at that point. Denoting the intensity of light at our arbitrary point by I, then we may write

$$I = 4ka^2 \cos^2 \frac{\phi}{2}$$

where k is a constant of proportionality.

Hence

$$I = 4ka^2 \cos^2 \left(\frac{\pi Y d}{x\lambda} \right)$$

Now this function exhibits maxima when $\cos^2 \left(\dfrac{\pi Y d}{x\lambda} \right) = 1$

That is, when $\dfrac{\pi Y d}{x\lambda} = n\pi$, where n may assume the values $0, \pm 1, \pm 2$ etc. That is, when $Y = \dfrac{nx\lambda}{d}$, or when $Y = 0$, $\pm \dfrac{x\lambda}{d}, \pm \dfrac{2x\lambda}{d}$, etc., as is consistent with our earlier findings.

The function exhibits minima when $\cos^2 \left(\dfrac{\pi Y d}{x\lambda} \right) = 0$. That is, when $\dfrac{\pi Y d}{x\lambda} = (m + \frac{1}{2})\pi$, where m may assume the values $0, \pm 1, \pm 2$ etc. That is, when $Y = \dfrac{(m + \frac{1}{2})x\lambda}{d}$, or when $Y = \pm \dfrac{x\lambda}{2d}, \pm \dfrac{3x\lambda}{2d}$ etc., as the reader should note to be consistent with his earlier findings.

A graph of the intensity of the fringe pattern against the distance Y as measured from (and on both sides of) the central antinode P (as it was denoted earlier) is thus as shown in Fig. 15.12.

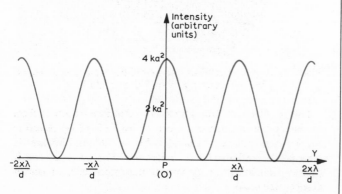

Fig.15.12 The intensity of light in an interference pattern.

Although the light intensity is zero at the positions of the interference minima, the energy originally carried in the light waves has not been destroyed as one might be tempted to think. The energy has been re-distributed so that the points at which interference maxima occur are brighter than they would have been had interference not taken place. The total energy of the system remains unchanged therefore, in accordance with the principle of conservation of energy.

15.4 Interference Effects in the Diffraction of Light

In Chapter 14, we noted that when plane wavefronts were incident on a narrow opening or slit—narrow in the sense that its width was comparable with the wavelength of the incident waves—then these wavefronts exhibited a semi-circular spreading beyond the region of the slit. We called this phenomenon *diffraction*. Having now investigated the interference of light, we can proceed with the investigation of the *interference effects* observed in the diffraction of light and so consider diffraction as the rather unique case of a single slit interference effect.

Diffraction effects with light may be classified according to whether the light waves incident on the aperture are spherical or plane. When spherical waves are incident on the aperture—these waves having been produced by placing the light source at a finite distance from the aperture—the diffraction pattern, which is observed on a screen also at a finite distance from the aperture, is known as a *Fresnel diffraction pattern*. This type of diffraction pattern was first studied and accounted for by Augustin Fresnel (1788–1827) (Fig. 15.13), a pioneer of the wave theory of light.

Fig.15.13 (By kind permission of the International Telecommunications Union, Geneva, Switzerland.)

When plane waves are incident on the aperture however— these waves having been produced by placing the light source effectively at infinity relative to the aperture—the diffraction pattern, which is observed on a screen also effectively at infinity relative to the aperture, is known as a *Fraunhofer diffraction pattern*. This type of pattern was first studied and accounted for by Josef Fraunhofer (1787–1826), the inventor of the diffraction grating. In the Fraunhofer diffraction system, the light source and the observation screen are effectively removed to infinity by the use of convex lenses.

The experimental arrangement required to demonstrate Fraunhofer diffraction at a slit is shown in Fig. 15.14 in which the slit source of monochromatic light is placed at the focal point of the convex lens L_1, so that a parallel beam of light (and hence plane wave fronts) fall on the single slit S at which diffraction is to take place. This single slit might perhaps be a very fine scratch on a blackened microscope slide. The observation screen is placed at the focal point of the convex lens L_2, so that the light transmitted by the slit S is brought to a focus on this screen. The performance of the pair of lenses in the absence of the single slit is illustrated in Fig. 15.15: it is hoped that this will be adequate for the reader's understanding at present, until we consider the properties of such lenses in the next chapter.

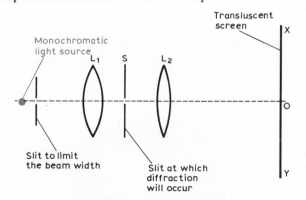

Fig.15.14 Demonstrating Fraunhofer Diffraction.

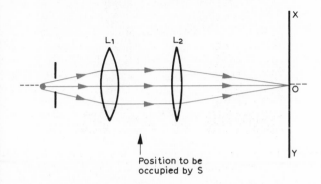

Fig.15.15 The action of the pair of lenses.

A Fraunhofer diffraction pattern is illustrated in Fig. 15.16.

(In setting up this pattern, a laser of the type shown in Fig. 15.17 was used as the source of light). This pattern is characterised by a central bright fringe of high intensity and of twice the width of all other bright fringes, which, arranged symmetrically around this central fringe, are such that their intensities fall off according to their distances from it. A graph of the fringe intensity against separation from the central fringe would therefore appear similar to that shown in Fig. 15.18.

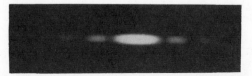

Fig.15.16 The diffraction pattern obtained with a narrow slit.

Fig.15.17 A group of low power school laboratory lasers. (By kind permission of Ferranti Ltd.)

Let us then attempt to explain the interference effects obviously present in the pattern of Fig. 15.16, by referring to the fundamental principles by which interference is understood, and also to the diagram of Fig. 15.19, in which part of the diffraction apparatus has been redrawn on an exaggerated scale.

We recall from Huygens' Principle that all points on a wavefront are responsible for the generation of forward-moving secondary spherical wavefronts. This means that all points on a wavefront passing through a slit will generate secondary wavelets expanding in all forward directions. Since a convex lens (L_2) is located behind the single slit in the

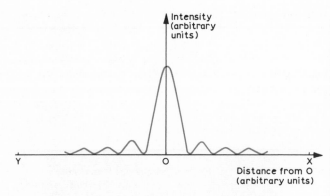

Fig.15.18 The intensity of light in the diffraction pattern.

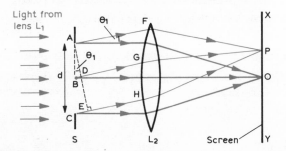

Fig.15.19 An analysis of the diffraction of light.

experimental apparatus—this lens having the property that it focusses parallel incident light at a point—then it follows (with reference to Fig. 15.20) that those portions of the secondary wavefronts leaving the slit in the direction ϕ_1 will be focussed at one point on the screen, while those portions leaving the slit in the direction ϕ_2 will be focussed at some other point on the screen. That is, each point in the diffraction pattern on the screen will have been formed by light rays leaving the aperture in one direction only.

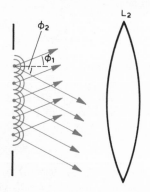

Fig.15.20 Rays leaving the diffraction aperture in one particular direction are focussed at a specific point on the screen.

Now with reference to Fig. 15.19, let us consider three points in particular (A, B, and C) on a wavefront passing through the slit. These points have been chosen such that A and C are located at the edges of the slit, and B is midway between them. In the direction perpendicular to the plane of the slit, portions of the secondary wavelets generated at A, B, and C all travel the distance between the slit and the lens L_2 in step, so that these portions or rays are focussed *in phase* at the point O on the screen. In fact rays from all point sources of secondary wavelets on the wavefront at the slit, and travelling in this direction, are focussed in phase at O, so that the point O is a point of brightness on the transluscent screen.

Let us now consider those rays or portions of the secondary wavelets generated at A, B, and C, which are travelling in that direction making an angle θ_1 with the direction of the rays considered in the last paragraph. Let this angle θ_1 be such that the distance BD (in Fig. 15.19) is $\frac{\lambda}{2}$ where λ is the wavelength of the incident monochromatic light. The rays AF and BG are therefore out of step by an amount $\frac{\lambda}{2}$ so that on being focussed by the lens at P, these rays will interfere destructively. Further, a ray parallel to AF from a point immediately below A will interfere destructively with a parallel ray from a corresponding point immediately below B, when these two rays are focussed and meet at the point P. The reason is that again the rays are out of step by an amount $\frac{\lambda}{2}$ on leaving the slit.

Similarly for the parallel rays originating from the next point below A, and the next corresponding point below B. When successive pairs of corresponding points in the upper and lower halves of the wavefront are considered in this way, it becomes clear that the upper half AB will interfere destructively with the lower half BC. It is therefore clear that the point P will have minimum light intensity—the minimum being zero if the destructive interference is complete.

It is fairly obvious that there will be a corresponding point of minimum intensity—at P′ say—at the same distance from O, and on the other side of the central maximum.

Now since $BD = \frac{\lambda}{2}$, and $\sin\theta_1 = \frac{BD}{AB}$ then $\sin\theta_1 = \dfrac{\frac{\lambda}{2}}{\frac{d}{2}}$

and so $$\sin\theta_1 = \frac{\lambda}{d}$$

This relationship defines the position of the first minimum in the pattern.

The second minimum in the diffraction pattern may be accounted for by considering that angle θ_2 at which rays or portions of the secondary wavelets leave the wavefront at the slit, such that the distance BD (in Fig. 15.19) is equal to λ. When rays are considered as leaving the wavefront at this angle, then the whole of the preceding argument may be applied to the whole of the first half of the wavefront (AB) by dividing it into two and then to the second half (BC). A second minimum is thus found in the pattern according to the relationship

$$\sin \theta_2\left(= \frac{\text{BD}}{\text{AB}}\right) = \frac{2\lambda}{d}$$

It seems therefore that all minima in the diffraction pattern may be calculated in their angular positions in terms of $\sin \theta$, where $\sin \theta$ assumes the values $\pm \dfrac{\lambda}{d}, \pm \dfrac{2\lambda}{d}, \pm \dfrac{3\lambda}{d}$ etc., where λ is the wavelength of the incident monochromatic light, and d is the width of the diffracting aperture.

The maxima in the diffraction pattern, other than the central maximum, may be accounted for by considering the diagram of Fig. 15.21, in which we have chosen four points in particular (A$'$, B$'$, C$'$, and D$'$) on a wavefront passing through the slit. These points have been chosen so as to divide the slit into three equal portions.

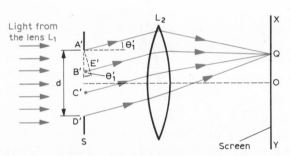

Fig.15.21 Explanation of the maxima in the diffraction pattern.

Let us consider those rays or portions of the secondary wavelets from A$'$, B$'$, C$'$, and D$'$ which are travelling in that direction which makes an angle θ_1' with the perpendicular to the plane of the slit. Let this angle be such that the distance B$'$E$'$ (in Fig. 15.21) is $\dfrac{\lambda}{2}$ where λ is still the wavelength of the incident light. It follows then that each ray originating from that portion of the slit A$'$B$'$ and travelling in the direction θ_1' will interfere destructively with a corresponding ray from the portion B$'$C$'$ (also travelling in the direction θ_1'), when the two meet at the focal point Q. Rays from that portion of the slit C$'$D$'$ do not experience destructive interference at the focal point Q as a result of meeting rays from other portions of the slit, and so contribute to some resultant intensity at Q. Can you suggest why this resultant intensity is not particularly large?

The position of this first maximum on the screen is defined

therefore according to the equation

$$\sin \theta_1'\left(= \frac{\text{B}'\text{E}'}{\text{A}'\text{B}'}\right) = \frac{\frac{\lambda}{2}}{\frac{d}{3}}$$

and so

$$\sin \theta_1' = \frac{3\lambda}{2d}$$

Again it is fairly obvious that there will be a corresponding point of maximum intensity—Q$'$ say—at the same distance from, and on the other side of, the central maximum.

If we were now to choose six particular points of secondary wavelets on the wavefront passing through the slit, evenly spaced so as to divide the slit into five equal portions, then the second maximum of the diffraction pattern could be accounted for by considering that angle θ_2' such that a path difference of $\dfrac{\lambda}{2}$ existed between the path lengths of rays from pairs of corresponding points in consecutive portions of the wavefront travelling in the direction θ_2'. This second maximum would then be defined by the equation

$$\sin \theta_2' = \frac{5\lambda}{2d}$$

It seems therefore that all maxima, other than the central maximum, may be calculated in their angular positions in terms of $\sin \theta'$, where $\sin \theta'$ assumes the values

$$\pm \frac{3\lambda}{2d}, \pm \frac{5\lambda}{2d}, \pm \frac{7\lambda}{2d}$$

etc., where λ is the wavelength of the incident monochromatic light, and d is the width of the diffracting aperture.

Having considered the values of $\sin \theta'$ and $\sin \theta$ for the angular positions of the maxima and minima in the diffraction pattern, we can now redraw the graph of the light intensity pattern of Fig. 15.18, as in Fig. 15.22.

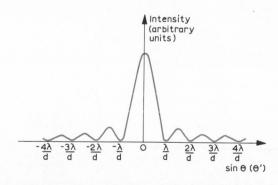

Fig.15.22 The intensity of light in the diffraction pattern as a function of angular position.

The linear width of the fringes observed on the transluscent screen is dependent on the focal length of the lens L_2, such that if this focal length is f, then the width of the central fringe is $\frac{2f\lambda}{d}$, while the width of every other fringe is $\frac{f\lambda}{d}$. The overall extent of the diffraction pattern is of course determined by both the width of the slit S and the wavelength of the incident light.

It is reported that when Fraunhofer moved the slit S parallel to itself at the same distance from and still in front of the lens L_2, he observed the diffraction pattern to remain in the same position, unchanged in its intensity. The reason for this is that all regions of a high quality convex lens bring parallel rays of light to the same focus. In an attempt to reinforce the diffraction pattern, Fraunhofer then employed two slits rather than one, in an arrangement like that illustrated in Fig. 15.23. Instead of reinforcing the diffraction pattern however, he succeeded in producing a mixture of an interference pattern and a diffraction pattern. The graph of light intensity against spatial distribution for this pattern is as illustrated in Fig. 15.24, in which the dotted line drawn as an envelope represents the diffraction pattern that would be observed with either of the two slits alone.

It was then an obvious follow-up to investigate the effect of introducing a parallel beam of light to a large number of narrow and closely spaced slits.

A large number of narrow closely spaced slits is the basis of an optical device known as the *diffraction grating*—a device which is extremely useful in the accurate determination of the wavelengths of light. A typical grating might contain as many as 5500 slits per cm! Let us now consider briefly the pattern produced by a diffraction grating in the Fraunhofer arrangement.

The diagram of Fig. 15.25 shows a diffraction grating having only eight slits, where the distance between the centres of consecutive slits—called the *grating element*—is d. As before, each slit acts as a source of secondary wavelets spreading out in all forward directions, and any point in the pattern on the screen is formed by those rays (or portions of the secondary wavelets) leaving the slits in some particular direction. In the direction perpendicular to the plane of the grating, all the rays leaving the grating arrive at the lens in step and are therefore focussed in phase so as to yield a bright central image which is known as the zero order maximum.

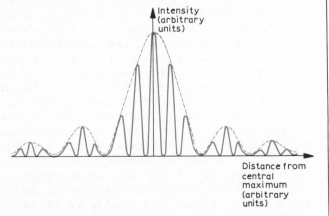

Fig.15.23 A Fraunhofer double slit arrangement.

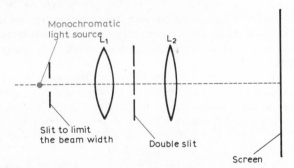

Fig.15.24 The diffraction pattern obtained with the Fraunhofer double slit arrangement.

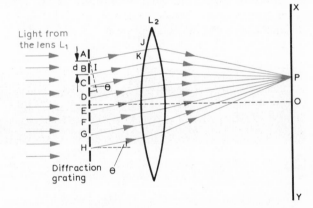

Fig.15.25 The analysis of a simple diffraction grating.

Let us now consider those rays diffracted by each slit at an angle θ to the perpendicular to the plane of the grating and brought to a focus at some point P on the screen. The rays AJ and BK are out of step by an amount equal to BI (with reference to Fig. 15.25) and $BI = d \sin \theta$. Although we have shown only one ray emerging at an angle θ from each slit, there would in fact be many such rays, each being derived from a point source of secondary wavelets in each slit. Further, for every different point considered in slit A, there will be a corresponding point in slit B and as far as any two corresponding points are concerned, parallel rays leaving them will be out of step by an amount $d \sin \theta$. Similarly for all adjacent pairs of slits in the grating (C and D, E and F, etc.).

Now if θ is such that $d \sin \theta$ is equal to one wavelength of light (λ), then all rays arriving at the lens from all slits and in the direction θ will be focussed in phase at the point P. That is, a maximum will be observed at P (and similarly at P' on the opposite side of O). Further, if θ' is such that $d \sin \theta'$ is equal to two wavelengths of light, then all rays arriving at the lens from all slits and in the direction θ' will be focussed in phase at some point Q on the screen. That is, a second maximum will be observed at the point Q on one side of O and similarly at Q' on the opposite side of O.

In general if $d \sin \theta = n\lambda$ where $n = 0, 1, 2, 3,$ etc., then maxima will be observed in the pattern on the screen. These maxima appear bright and widely spaced on the screen (Fig. 15.26), and are separated by a very large number of secondary maxima—almost equal in number to the number of slits in the grating, and of negligible intensity. The central maximum is referred to as the zero order maximum ($n = 0$), and on either side of this is found the first order maximum ($n = 1$), then the second order maximum ($n = 2$), and so on. A typical graph of intensity against angular separation, for a diffraction grating in the Fraunhofer arrangement, might appear as in Fig. 15.27, in which the dotted line represents the diffraction pattern that would be observed for any one slit in the grating alone. The diffraction pattern for each of the slits in the grating is of course identical.

Fig.15.26 The pattern produced with a diffraction grating using a low power laser as the light source.

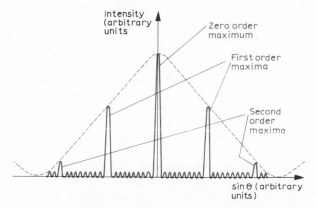

Fig.15.27 The distribution of light intensity produced with a diffraction grating in the Fraunhofer arrangement.

In the actual determination of the wavelength of mono-chromatic light using the diffraction grating, it is necessary to mount the grating on the turntable of a spectrometer which is provided with an accurate scale calibrated in degrees and fractions of a degree. The grating is then adjusted so that its plane is at right angles to the axis of the collimator, and its slits are parallel to the collimator slit. In the spectrometer (which we shall meet in Chapter 18) the collimator provides a parallel beam of light. The telescope of the spectrometer, which has previously been adjusted to focus the parallel light from the collimator, is then rotated until the images of the different orders of maxima are observed in turn at the intersection of the crosswires. The angular positions of these maxima are read from the scale of the spectrometer. The wavelength of the incident light may then be calculated from the formula

$$\lambda = \frac{d \sin \theta}{n} \quad \dots \dots \dots \dots (15.3)$$

where d is the grating element and θ is the angle through which the axis of the telescope must be rotated—starting from the zero order position—in order that the nth order maxima be observed. In practice, partly because of the excessive brightness of the zero order, one always focusses the telescope on the two nth order maxima and measures the angular displacement between them which will clearly be equal to 2θ.

With the diffraction gratings normally used in school laboratories, only the zeroth, first, and second order spectra are visible. Unless a very bright light source is used, the second order spectrum will have a very low intensity. The limit on the number of visible orders arises from the fact that $\sin \theta$ cannot be increased indefinitely.

In view of our discussions leading up to the development of the diffraction grating, we might begin to wonder why the Young's slits interference pattern, which we discussed earlier, was found to exhibit maxima of equal intensity and not of diminishing intensity. However, the Young's slits experiment for producing the interference fringes involved a Fresnel diffraction arrangement rather than the Fraunhofer arrangement with which we have been concerned until now. In the Fresnel double slit arrangement of Fig. 15.28, the diffraction patterns from each of the slits are in fact superimposed on the interference pattern and they may in certain circumstances result in a variation in the brightness of the interference fringes. Far enough away from the slits however, the central maxima of the two patterns tend to overlap, and it is in this region of overlap that the double slit interference pattern is observed. The other maxima of each diffraction pattern are usually too weak and too far removed to the sides of the central maxima to have any detectable effect on the interference pattern.

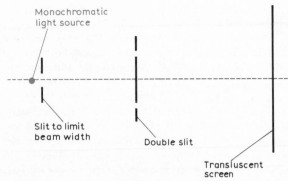

Monochromatic light source

Slit to limit beam width

Double slit

Transluscent screen

Fig.15.28 The Fresnel double slit arrangement.

Problems

1 The diagram of Fig. 15.29(a) shows light being reflected regularly from a polished surface. Can you indicate how diffuse reflection might be explained, with reference to the unpolished irregular surface of Fig. 15.29(b)?

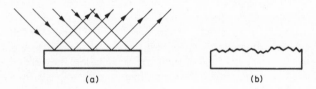

(a)   (b)

Fig.15.29 See Problem 1.

2 A laser is a device which produces coherent light. In an experiment with a laser, two narrow slits were placed in front of the aperture from which the laser beam emerges, and an interference pattern was observed on a white screen at a distance of 90 cm from the laser. If the slits were separated by 0·2 mm, and the wavelength of the laser light was $6·95 \times 10^{-7}$ m, calculate the separation of the bright fringes of the interference pattern.

3 In view of the results of the worked example in the text of this chapter, why is it essential that the slits employed in an interference experiment should be as narrow as possible?

4 Can you devise an experiment which might enable you to determine the average wavelength of white light?

5 In problem 2, how far from the double slits would the screen have to be placed in order to increase the fringe width to 1 cm?

6 It has been stated that the essential difference between Fresnel and Fraunhofer diffraction is that in one, each point in the diffraction pattern is formed by rays leaving the slit in many directions, whereas in the other, each point in the diffraction pattern is formed by rays leaving the slit in one direction. Which description refers to which type of diffraction?

7 Describe the diffraction pattern produced by a single slit if a white light, rather than a monochromatic light, was used as the source. Can you explain the result which you have described?

8 A beam of light of wavelength $6·4 \times 10^{-7}$ m is incident on a slit of width 0·4 mm behind which is located a lens of focal length 40 cm. This lens focusses the light on a transluscent screen. What would be the distance (measured on the screen) between the centre of the diffraction pattern and the centre of the first maximum on either side?

9 The manager of the precision instrument company with which you are employed has been asked in conversation if his company manufactures diffraction gratings. Not knowing what a diffraction grating is, the manager sends for you the following day, and asks you what a diffraction grating is and what it does. What would you tell him?

The manager later decides that manufacturing diffraction gratings and selling them might be economically viable, and puts you in charge of a development programme. How might you consider constructing a trial grating, and which of its features might you investigate as affecting its performance so that a more elaborate grating might be conceived?

10 A diffraction grating with 10 000 lines per cm is placed on the turntable of a spectrometer. A mercury lamp with a filter is placed in front of the collimator of the spectrometer. The two first order maxima are observed to be separated by an angle of 70° 30′. What is the wavelength of the light transmitted by the filter? Suggest two separate means by which you might check on your result.

Chapter 16

An Introduction to Mirrors and Lenses

Fig.16.0 In the study of mirrors and lenses, we may consider light as a radiation which travels in straight lines—as appears to be the case with the sunlight shining through the trees. (Photograph (taken with a Leica M3 camera) by kind permission of E. Leitz Ltd.)

In the last chapter, we saw that light exhibits wave properties. In Chapter 20 we shall discuss the fact that light may exhibit particle properties too! For most practical purposes however, it is sufficient to consider light as a radiation which travels in straight lines—as appears to be the case with the beam from a cinema projector. The design and construction of most optical instruments assume the facts that light rays travel in straight line paths and that these paths may be changed in direction by the introduction of mirrors, lenses, and prisms. Such changes in direction conform to simple geometrical principles and the study of *geometrical optics* is essential to an understanding of the operational principles of many optical instruments. We shall consider the construction of several instruments in the next chapter, concerning ourselves in the present chapter only with the basic principles of geometrical optics, by way of preparation.

Most optical instruments are concerned with the formation of an image of a given object, and although the instruments which we shall be considering form images by the process of refraction, we shall consider the formation of images by reflection, as well as by refraction, for completeness in this chapter.

What exactly is the image of an object? Each of us has seen an image of himself (the object) in a plane mirror, and the image appears to be located behind the glass although of course there is nothing really there. Any object is visible to us if it sends out light towards us, or if light is being reflected from it and towards us. For example, the paper before us is visible as a result of light being reflected from it towards our eyes. If the rays of light which we receive from an object are somehow bent or deflected between leaving the object and reaching our eyes, then we still see the object, but not in its true position. Since the eyes and the brain are unable to take account of the deflection process, we are in fact seeing an *image* of the object at the point from which the deflected rays seem to come.

In the case of an image formed in a plane mirror, that image is said to be imaginary or *virtual* for the simple reason that rays of light from the object do not pass through the position of the image. Such an image is formed only in the mind, and could not be focused on a screen placed behind the mirror at the apparent position of the image. This fact may be appreciated from the diagram of Fig. 16.1. Not all images are virtual however, and *real* images may be formed by concave mirrors and convex lenses. A real image is one through which rays of light from an object actually pass, and which can therefore be gathered on a screen.

Real and virtual images will assume greater significance when we consider their actual formation by various processes of reflection and refraction. The processes which we shall consider are:

1 the formation of images by a plane reflecting surface

2 the formation of images by curved reflecting surfaces (curved mirrors)
3 the formation of images by a plane refracting surface
4 the formation of images by curved refracting surfaces (thin lenses).

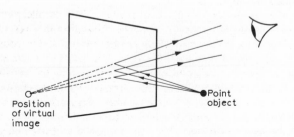

Fig.16.1 The image formed by a plane mirror is virtual rather than real.

16.1 The Formation of Images by a Plane Reflecting Surface

The simplest image which can be formed in a plane mirror is that of a point object which we might consider to be a tiny light bulb sending out light rays in all directions. Let us suppose that such an object is placed in the plane of the page, and in front of a plane mirror perpendicular to the plane of the page. Further, let an eye be present in the plane of the page looking towards the mirror, so that the complete system appears as in Fig. 16.2.

In particular, let us consider two rays OA and OC, lying in the plane of the page. The normals to the mirror at A and C will lie in the plane of the page since the plane of the mirror is at right angles to the page. Further, since the incident rays and the normals are in the plane of the page, the reflected rays AB and CD must also lie in the page and therefore be able to enter the eye. Note that $O\hat{A}A' = A'\hat{A}B$ ($= \theta_1$) and $O\hat{C}C' = C'\hat{C}D$ ($= \theta_2$). Since the eye cannot follow the directional changes at A and C however, it appears to the observer that the rays AB and CD have diverged from the point I behind the mirror, and so this point takes on the appearance of the object. The point I thus marks the position of the virtual image of the point object O.

It is left as a simple exercise for the reader to prove (geometrically) that *the virtual image is located as far behind the mirror as the object is in front.*

In practice, only a very few objects might possibly be considered as point objects, and it is more likely that any given object would be of an extended form. When an extended object is placed in front of a plane mirror, each point on the object will give rise to a corresponding image point so that an image of the whole object will be produced. Representing an extended object by a small arrow lying in the plane of the paper and in front of a plane mirror as in Fig. 16.3, we have drawn two rays from each extremity, for simplicity, to establish the position of the image of the object. If the reader cares to draw a pair of rays from any other point on the extended object, he will find that its virtual image lies on this same straight image line.

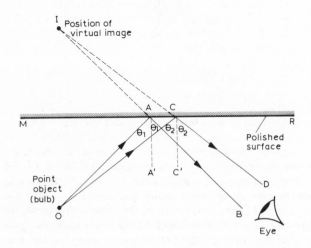

Fig.16.2 Finding the position of the virtual image.

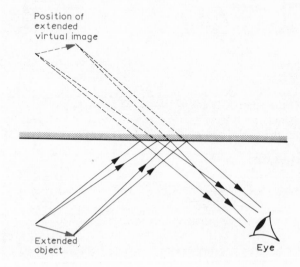

Fig.16.3 The virtual image of an extended object in a plane mirror.

An interesting problem concerning an extended object and plane mirror is to determine how long a plane mirror attached to a vertical wall, do we need in order to be able to see ourselves from top to toe. Let us solve this problem before considering the images which may be formed in two plane mirrors.

The diagram of Fig. 16.4 shows a man of height H standing in front of a large vertical plane mirror. We wish to determine just how much of this mirror is required in order for him to see his entire length. If the man's eyes are located at a distance h from the top of his head then we can say that if the point Y is chosen to be the lower extremity of the required mirror length, then this point must be such that rays from the tips of the toes will enter the eyes after reflection. It follows then that OY $= \dfrac{H-h}{2}$. (If Y were chosen lower than this, then the man would see the floor in front of his feet as well as his feet.)

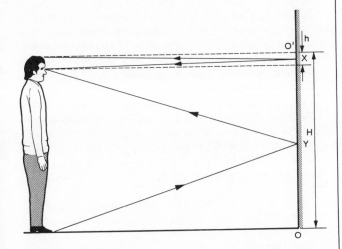

Fig.16.4

If the point X is chosen to be the upper extremity of the required mirror length, then this point must be such that rays from the top of the head enter the eyes after reflection. It follows then that O'X $= \dfrac{h}{2}$

Now OO' $= H$, O'X $= \dfrac{h}{2}$, and OY $= \dfrac{H-h}{2}$

Hence XY, the required mirror length, is given as

$$XY \, (= OO' - [O'X + OY]) = H - \left[\frac{h}{2} + \frac{H-h}{2}\right]$$
$$= H - \frac{H}{2}$$
$$= \frac{H}{2}$$

That is, the required mirror must be half the height of the person.

The reader should prove to himself that this height of mirror is independent of the distance between the person and the mirror, but that the height at which the mirror is positioned on the wall is critical.

When we look into a plane mirror faced by a parallel plane mirror (as might be the nature of the decoration in a restaurant) we see a very large number of images of the room stretching away, apparently towards infinity. Of course we should only see one image of ourselves (assuming the mirrors to be exactly parallel) since this image covers all others, but we are able to see a very large number of images of another person as a succession of alternate back and front views, in either mirror. We can explain the formation of these images as follows, referring to Fig. 16.5.

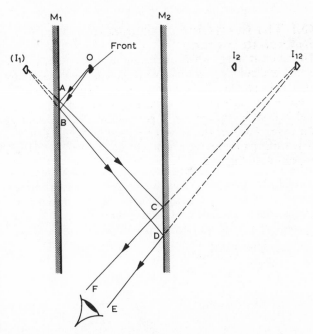

Fig.16.5   The images formed by parallel mirrors.

This diagram shows two parallel mirrors M_1 and M_2 and a small object O, placed between them—the front of the object towards M_2. Let us consider rays OA and OB, leaving the back of the object as shown and eventually giving rise to a virtual image of the back of the object at I_{12} in M_2, as detected by the observer. Had the observer looked along the paths of the rays AC and BD, instead of along CF and DE, then he would have seen an image of the back of the object in M_1. (Marked in brackets in the diagram as I_1.) Further, the image I_1 is as far in front of the mirror M_2 as I_{12} is behind it. That is, I_{12} is the virtual image of the virtual image I_1, so that it is possible for one virtual image in one mirror to give rise to an image of itself in a second mirror—provided the first image is in front of that second mirror.

It follows then that an image of the first frontal image in M_2 (that is I_2) will be formed in M_1 and that an image of I_{12} will be formed in M_1, and that these images will give rise to further images in each mirror. The result is that an alternate succession of back and front views of the object will be observed in either mirror.

When an object is placed between two mirrors which are hinged and inclined to each other—each perpendicular to the plane of the paper—then an increasing number of images of the object are seen as the angle between the mirrors is reduced. This effect may be explained in terms of the results of our last discussion—rays from the virtual image formed in one mirror being reflected by, and giving rise to an image of itself in, the other mirror.

Let us consider the case of two mirrors inclined to each other at an angle of 60° and a point object O placed in front of each of them. With reference to Fig. 16.6 it follows that O will give rise to an image I_1 in M_1 and an image I_2 in M_2—these images being located as far behind the mirrors as the object is in front. Further, the image I_1 will give rise to an image I_{12}, in M_2 and I_2 will give rise to an image I_{21} in M_1. The reason for this is that although I_2 is beyond the end of M_1 it is still in front of it, so that some of the rays leaving M_2 and appearing to come from I_2 will strike M_1 and thereby give rise to an image of I_2 in M_1. Again the images I_{12} and I_{21} are still in front of (although beyond the ends of) the mirrors M_1 and M_2 respectively, and so each gives rise to a further image. If the mirrors are inclined at exactly 60°, then further images should coincide at I. Since the point I is located behind each mirror, no further images are formed.

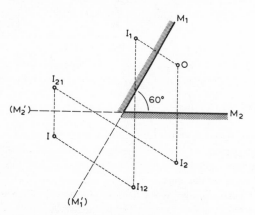

Fig.16.6   The images formed by inclined mirrors.

It follows then that an observer looking between these inclined mirrors could detect five images of a point object.

The reader may care to verify for himself that when the

mirrors are inclined at an angle θ (where θ is a submultiple of 360°), then the number of possible images of a point object placed between the mirrors is given as n where

$$n = \frac{360}{\theta} - 1$$

16.2 The Formation of Images by Curved Reflecting Surfaces (Curved Mirrors)

Anyone who has looked into the convex wing mirror of a car or into a concave shaving mirror must have realised that the images formed by these mirrors are quite different from the images formed by plane mirrors. Let us now consider the formation of images by curved reflecting surfaces, treating any given curved surface as a continuum of tiny plane mirror surfaces to each of which may be applied the laws of reflection of light.

The two types of curved mirror surface employed in optics are the sphere and the paraboloid, and these differ in as much as a spherical concave mirror reflects a parallel beam of light into a cusp whereas a paraboloidal concave mirror reflects such a beam into a sharp point focus. If the aperture of a spherical concave mirror is small compared to its radius of curvature, so that rays of light incident on it must lie close to its axis, then, to a close approximation, the mirror focusses these rays at a point, and it therefore gives rise to the same effect as its paraboloidal counterpart. In the discussion which follows, we shall consider only spherical mirrors which satisfy this condition so that the effects of *spherical aberration* may be ignored.

The illustrations of Fig. 16.7 show the reflection of light rays parallel and close to the axis, by a spherical concave mirror. Such a mirror obviously has the capacity to render a parallel beam of light convergent. In the diagram, the point C is the *centre of curvature* of the sphere of which the mirror forms a part—CP and CN being known as the radii of curvature. The point F is the *principal focus* of the mirror, and it is to this point incident rays parallel to the principal axis of the mirror converge after reflection. The point P is the *pole* or centre of the mirror itself, and the distance FP is the *focal length* of the mirror.

Now since C is the centre of curvature of the mirror, the dotted line is normal to the surface at the point N, and so the angles marked θ_1 and θ_2 must be equal. However, the angles θ_1 and θ_3 are also equal since the upper ray and principal axis are parallel, and so the triangle NCF is isosceles. Hence NF = FC. Now since the mirror is assumed to have a very small aperture, all angles considered are very small and so NF $\fallingdotseq$ FP. That is, FP $\fallingdotseq$ CF, and so the focal length of the mirror is almost exactly equal to half the radius of curvature.

The illustrations of Fig. 16.8 show the reflection of light rays parallel and close to the axis, by a spherical convex mirror. While the spherical concave mirror imposes convergence on such rays, the convex mirror imposes divergence, and to an observer the reflected rays appear to diverge from a virtual focal point F′ located behind the mirror. The geometry of this system is similar to that of the last, and the reader may care to show to his own satisfaction that the (virtual) focal length of the mirror is almost exactly equal to half its radius of curvature.

reflected through the principal focus of the mirror (F).

b) A ray through the principal focus of the mirror which is reflected parallel to the principal axis.

c) A ray incident on the pole of the mirror which is reflected in such a way that the angles of incidence and reflection, measured relative to the principal axis as normal, are equal.

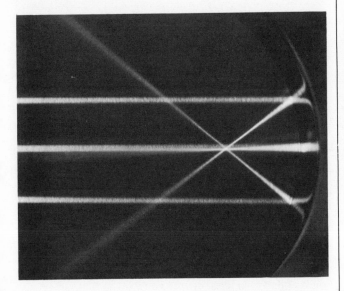

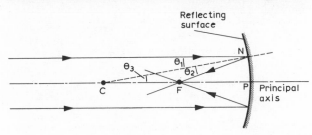

Fig.16.7 The focussing effect of a concave spherical mirror.

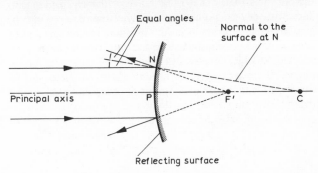

Fig.16.8 The de-focussing effect of a convex spherical mirror.

Let us now consider the formation of the image of an extended object in a spherical mirror—this object being placed at a finite distance from the mirror. The position, nature, and size of the image of such an object may be deduced by a simple graphical approach which involves the drawing of a scaled ray diagram. Such a diagram involves the tracing of a few specific rays from one extremity of the object before and after their reflection in the mirror.

With reference to Fig. 16.9 in which the object is a small lighted candle placed in front of a spherical concave mirror, it is convenient to choose the following three rays, the paths of which may be traced readily.

a) A ray parallel to the principal axis of the mirror which is

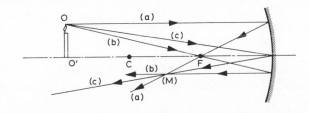

Fig.16.9 Any two of the rays (a), (b), and (c) may be used to locate the tip of the image of the object.

Since all three of these rays converge on the same point (M), it is obvious that this point marks the position of the image of the tip of the candle flame in the concave mirror. Further, all other points along OO′ will give rise to image points along the perpendicular through M towards the principal axis, and so the image of the candle in the mirror is located along this perpendicular. In practice it is sufficient to consider any two of the rays (a), (b), or (c) in determining the position of the image, since all three are concurrent at M following reflection.

Using this graphical approach, we can now consider the six groups of images which may be formed in a concave mirror, the constructions of these images being shown in Fig. 16.10.

With reference to Fig. 16.10, when an extended object of normal size is placed at an effectively infinite distance from the mirror, the rays which originate on all points of it are almost exactly parallel. Consequently the image of this object, when the mirror is adjusted so that its axis is parallel to the rays, is formed as a point on the principal axis. This point is of course the principal focus (Diagram A).

When the extended object is placed at a finite distance from the mirror, behind its centre of curvature, an image is formed between the centre of curvature of the mirror and its principal focus (Diagram B). This image is diminished and inverted. Further, it is real. That is, it may be formed on a screen placed between the points F and C since the reflected rays of light actually converge on its position. Such an image therefore is not one which is formed in the mind alone.

When the object is placed at the centre of curvature, of the mirror, the image is formed also at the centre of curvature. This image is inverted, real, and of the same size as the finite object (Diagram C).

When the object is placed between the centre of curvature of the mirror and its principal focus, the image formed is real, inverted, enlarged, and positioned beyond the centre of curvature (Diagram D).

When the object is placed at the principal focus, an infinitely large image is formed at infinity by the parallel reflected rays. If this image at infinity is then used as an object at infinity for a second concave mirror, the latter will form a finite image at its focus—as in Diagram A. This second image will be finite because the 'object' from which it is formed is infinitely large. The image is also real and so may be thrown on a screen placed in the focal plane of the second mirror and examined by an observer.

When the object is placed between the principal focus of the mirror and the mirror itself, all of the rays reflected from the mirror are divergent and so a real image can never be formed on a screen (Diagram F). To an observer, the ray appears to have come from a point behind the mirror, so that he locates an image of the object in his mind alone. This virtual image is upright, enlarged, and located behind the

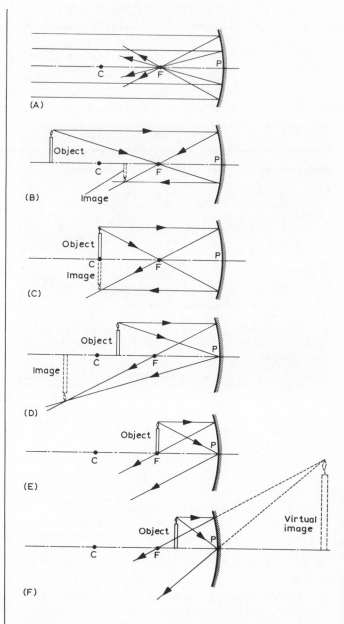

Fig.16.10 The six groups of images which may be formed by a spherical concave mirror.

mirror.

When a concave mirror is used as a shaving mirror, the face to be shaved appears enlarged, upright and in great detail only when it is positioned close to the mirror so as to lie between the mirror and its principal focus.

With reference to Fig. 16.11, in which the extended object (the lighted candle) is placed in front of a spherical convex mirror, we see that since the rays chosen from the upper extremity of the object diverge after reflection a real image can never be formed by such a mirror. To an observer the diverging rays would appear to come from a point behind the mirror so that a virtual image of the object would be observed. This image is always upright, diminished, and located between the mirror and its virtual focus, regardless of the position of the object. As the object is moved closer to the mirror, the image increases in size but it never becomes as large as the object itself. To anyone who has experienced using a car wing mirror, these statements will be immediately obvious. In what way is the location of the image important to the driver of a car?

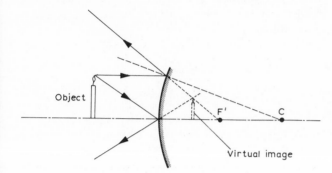

Fig.16.11 Locating the image formed by a spherical convex mirror.

The diagram of Fig. 16.10(C) suggests to us a simple experimental approach towards the determination of the radius of curvature and focal length of a spherical concave mirror. The theory of this approach is simply that if a finite object is placed at the centre of curvature of a spherical concave mirror then a real image of that object will be cast on a screen in the same vertical plane as the object.

In Fig. 16.12 a spherical concave mirror has been mounted on a carrier placed on an optical bench—a bench equipped with a scale on which optical components may be mounted so as to be in accurate alignment (Fig. 16.13). At one end of this bench is placed a box containing an electric lamp and on the front surface of the box a triangular aperture has been cut— its base at the same height as the principal axis of the mirror— and a piece of wire gauze placed over the aperture. The front surface of the box has been painted white to act as a screen.

By moving the mirror carrier along the optical bench, a position is found where a sharp image of the wire gauze aperture is cast on the front of the box beside and below the actual aperture. When this image is as sharp as is possible, then it is found to be as nearly as one can measure, the same size as the actual aperture. With the carrier in this position, the distance between the front surface of the box (or the gauze object) and the concave mirror is equal to the radius of curvature of the mirror. This may be read directly from the

scale on the bench, provided the lamp box has been positioned at the zero of this scale.

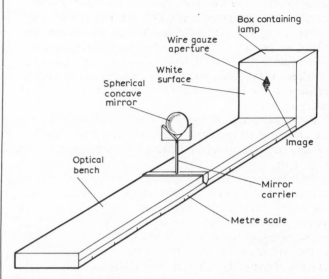

Fig.16.12 Determination of the focal length of a spherical concave mirror.

Fig.16.13 A simple optical bench. (By kind permission of Philip Harris Ltd.)

The focal length of the concave mirror may then be taken as equal to half the radius of curvature.

Although the position, nature, and size of the image of a given object in a spherical mirror may be obtained graphically as we have shown, they may also be obtained more accurately by a less time consuming numerical method. Let us search for a general formula which will enable us to do this.

Figure 16.14 shows a spherical concave mirror in front of which and on the principal axis of which has been placed an object OO'. By drawing two constructional rays as before, the position of the image of this object is found to be at II'.

In Fig. 16.14, the triangles OPO' and IPI' are similar. It follows therefore that

$$\frac{II'}{OO'} = \frac{PI'}{PO'}$$

Now let us suppose that the ratio of mirror aperture to focal length is small, so that that portion of the mirror, NP,

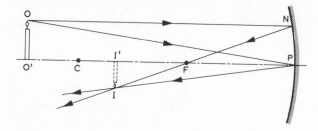

Fig. 16.14

is almost perpendicular to the principal axis, and $OO' \doteqdot NP$. Since triangles NPF and II'F are similar, we may write

$$\frac{II'}{PN} = \frac{I'F}{PF}$$

$$\Leftrightarrow \frac{II'}{OO'} = \frac{I'F}{PF}$$

$$= \frac{PI' - PF}{PF}$$

$$= \frac{PI'}{PF} - 1$$

$$\Leftrightarrow \frac{PI'}{PO'} = \frac{PI'}{PF} - 1$$

$$\Leftrightarrow \frac{1}{PO'} = \frac{1}{PF} - \frac{1}{PI'}$$

$$\Leftrightarrow \frac{1}{PO'} + \frac{1}{PI'} = \frac{1}{PF} \quad \cdots\cdots\cdots\cdots \quad (A)$$

Had we repeated this exercise for the case where the object was located between the pole and principal focus of the concave mirror, so that a virtual image was formed behind the mirror, we should have derived the equation

$$\frac{1}{PO'} - \frac{1}{PI'} = \frac{1}{PF} \quad \cdots\cdots\cdots\cdots \quad (B)$$

In the case of a convex mirror, the corresponding equation is found to be

$$\frac{1}{PO'} - \frac{1}{PI'} = - \frac{1}{PF} \quad \cdots\cdots\cdots\cdots \quad (C)$$

The reader should check these two equations for his own satisfaction.

If we now write PO' as u, PI' as v, PF as f in equation (A); PO' as u, $-PI'$ as v, PF as f in equation (B); and PO' as u, $-PI'$ as v, $-PF$ as f in equation (C), then each equation becomes

$$\frac{1}{u} + \frac{1}{v} = \frac{1}{f}$$

We have thus established a general mirror equation.

The quantities u, v, and f are now of course *algebraic quantities* in as much as each refers to a positive or a negative term. When we are substituting for u, v, or f in this general equation therefore, we must adhere to the following sign convention so that the substitution of values for u, v, and f will lead to the required form of mirror equation (A, B, or C):

1 Distances between the pole of the mirror and real objects, images, and foci are written as positive numbers.
2 Distances between the pole of the mirror and virtual objects, images, and foci are written as negative numbers.
3 The radius of curvature of the mirror is written as a positive number if the mirror converges incident parallel light, and as a negative number if the mirror diverges parallel light.

The general mirror equation is therefore

$$\boxed{\frac{1}{u} + \frac{1}{v} = \frac{1}{f}} \quad \cdots\cdots\cdots\cdots \quad (16.1)$$

where the boldface type reminds us that we are dealing with algebraic quantities rather than numbers. In using the equation we must always remember to substitute a sign as well as a number for each quantity. Let us suppose that in a problem a virtual image is formed by a concave mirror. We should therefore substitute a positive number for u, a negative number for v, and a positive number for f (according to the rules of the sign convention) so that equation (16.1) reduces to the correct form (i.e. to equation (B)). The sign convention thus allows us to remember one general mirror equation rather than three separate mirror equations and the situations to which they apply.

The *transverse magnification* of a mirror is defined as the ratio of image size to object size. It is a simple exercise to show that for any given mirror, the magnification may also be found as the ratio of image distance to object distance. (The reader should verify this for the case illustrated in Fig. 16.14.)

That is, the transverse magnification of a mirror (m) may be written as

$$m = \frac{PI'}{PO'}$$

If we wish to re-write this definition in terms of the algebraic quantities u and v, then it is useful to introduce a negative sign into the definition and re-write it as

$$\boxed{m = - \frac{v}{u}} \quad \cdots\cdots\cdots\cdots \quad (16.2)$$

If, using a real object, we are dealing with a virtual image, then v is negative, and m is positive. *In all cases where m is positive, the image is upright.*

If we are dealing with a real image, then v is positive, and m is negative. *In all cases where m is negative, the image is inverted.*

The sign convention used in this way thus enables us to deduce whether the mirror image is upright or inverted.

The application of the sign convention is illustrated in the following problem.

Problem 1 A small object 10 cm from the pole of a spherical mirror gives rise to a virtual image 12 cm from the pole. Find the focal length of the mirror, and whether the mirror is concave or convex.

Here $u = +10$ cm and $v = -12$ cm.

Now
$$\frac{1}{u} + \frac{1}{v} = \frac{1}{f}$$

hence
$$\frac{1}{f} = \frac{1}{10} + \frac{1}{-12}$$
$$= \frac{12 - 10}{120}$$
$$= \frac{2}{120}$$
$$= \frac{1}{60}$$

Hence
$$f = 60 \text{ cm}$$

The focal length of the mirror is therefore 60 cm and since it is described by a positive number, the focus is real. The mirror is therefore concave.

16.3 The Formation of Images by a Plane Refracting Surface

We are all familiar with several examples of the refraction of light in everyday life. For example, the bent appearance of a stick in water; the basin which appears shallower when full of water than when empty; the coin and the cup trick; all of these effects may be explained in terms of the bending of light rays which occurs when the rays cross the boundary between water and air. We recall that such bending may be attributed to the change in speed as light passes from one material to another of different optical density—the greater the difference in optical densities, the greater the amount of bending which results. A point which we did not stress in our previous discussions however (although the reader may satisfy himself on it by referring back to Fig. 15.5) is that when light passes from an optically dense material to a less dense material—perspex to air say—then the light rays are bent *away* from the normal to the boundary between the media on leaving that boundary. On passing from one medium to another of higher optical density—air to perspex say—then the light rays are bent *towards* the normal to the boundary.

In the last chapter we found that the amount of refraction occurring between two media A and B could be written in terms of the equation

$$\frac{\sin i}{\sin r} = {}_A\mu_B$$

where i and r are the angles of incidence (in medium A) and refraction (in medium B) respectively, and ${}_A\mu_B$ is a constant called the index of refraction. Its value is always the same provided the light always travels in the sense medium A → medium B.

Now in optics there exists a *principle of reversibility* which holds that if any ray is reversed in its direction of travel, it will retrace its path—regardless of the nature of the optical system through which the ray is passing. Let us suppose then that a ray travelling from medium A to medium B (with angles of incidence and refraction i and r in these respective media) is reversed, so as to travel now from B to A. This ray would now have an angle of incidence (in medium B) of r and an angle of refraction (in medium A) of i so that the index of refraction of light travelling from medium B to medium A could be written as ${}_B\mu_A$ where

$$ {}_B\mu_A = \frac{\sin r}{\sin i}$$

that is
$$ {}_B\mu_A = \frac{1}{{}_A\mu_B} \qquad \dots \dots (16.3)$$

Having revised our discussions of refraction this far, let us now consider the explanation of the three effects which we mentioned at the outset of this section.

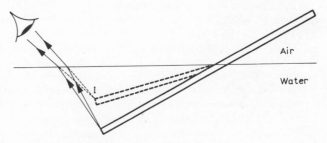

Fig.16.15 That portion of the stick below the water surface appears bent.

The bent appearance of a stick in water may easily be explained with reference to the diagram of Fig. 16.15. The diagram shows a straight stick partly immersed in water and inclined to the water surface. Two rays of light are drawn leaving the immersed end of the stick, and, after refraction at the water surface, they appear to the eye of an observer to be coming from a point I. If similar rays were drawn from every point on the stick then the images of these points would be contained within the dotted line in the diagram. That is, the dotted line represents the image which the observer perceives of that portion of the stick which is immersed. We note that this image is virtual.

The shallow appearance of a container full of water may be explained with reference to the diagram of Fig. 16.16 in which two rays of light are drawn leaving a point O on the base of the container. After refraction at the water surface, these rays appear to the eye of an observer to be coming from a point I above the point O. That is, the point O on the base appears to an observer to be shallower than it really is. Similarly for all other points on the base of the container so that in effect the actual depth of water is not appreciated by the observer. The image of the base of the container which he perceives is of course virtual.

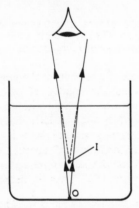

Fig.16.16 The container of water appears shallower than it really is.

The reader may care to show for himself that the image of an object at the foot of a pool of water changes in position when the eye is moved sideways away from the vertical, so that such a pool of water appears shallower when viewed obliquely than when viewed from vertically above; the image also moves towards the observer.

The relationship existing between the apparent depth of a container of water (when viewed from vertically above) and the true depth of water provides us with a means of determining the index of refraction of light travelling from air to water. Set up the apparatus shown in Fig. 16.17 in which a long focus microscope is mounted on a vertical scale so that its vertical travel may be recorded. The microscope is focussed first on a small paint mark on the bottom inside surface of an empty glass beaker, and its vertical position noted on the scale (i). The beaker is then filled with water and the microscope raised until the mark again comes into focus at I. The new vertical position of the microscope is then noted (ii). Finally some powder is sprinkled on the surface of the water and the microscope raised again until it is focussed on the powder. Its new vertical position is then noted (iii). The

difference in the positions (i) and (iii) is equal to the real depth of the water in the beaker, while the difference between (ii) and (iii) is equal to the apparent depth.

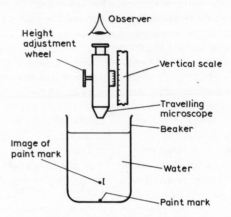

Fig.16.17 Determination of the index of refraction for light travelling from air to water.

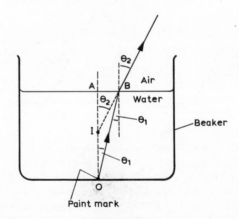

Fig.16.18

Let us suppose that the index of refraction for light travelling from air to water is μ, then with reference to Fig. 16.18, it follows that

$$\frac{1}{\mu} = \frac{\sin \theta_1}{\sin \theta_2} \quad \text{(applying the principle of reversibility)}$$

hence

$$\mu = \frac{\sin \theta_2}{\sin \theta_1}$$

$$= \frac{\dfrac{AB}{BI}}{\dfrac{AB}{BO}} = \frac{BO}{BI}$$

$$= \frac{AO}{AI}$$

assuming that θ_1 (and hence θ_2) is sufficiently small—as would be the case for observations from vertically above since the microscope will accept only a very narrow cone of light. That is, the index of refraction for light travelling from air to glass may be calculated as the ratio of the real depth to the apparent depth of water in the beaker of Fig. 16.17.

The coin and the cup trick may be described and explained with reference to the diagrams of Fig. 16.19. In diagram (a) a coin is placed in an empty cup so that it is just out of sight of the eye of the observer—as is indicated by the fact that a ray of light cannot pass from the coin to the eye. When water is added to the cup as in diagram (b) however, the observer is able to see the coin although it is still in its original position. The two rays of light drawn in diagram (b) are refracted at the surface of the water and hence appear to the observer to have come from a point on the image of the coin—located as indicated by the dotted lines. The observer thus perceives a virtual image of the coin after water has been added to the cup.

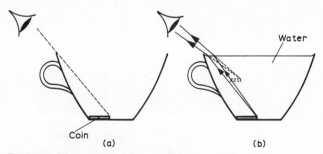

Fig.16.19 The coin and the cup trick.

As we have seen, a ray of light travelling from water to air is bent away from the normal and further, as the angle of incidence of the ray at the water surface is increased, the refracted ray is bent farther from the normal. But surely there must be some limit to how far this refracted ray can be bent?

Let us consider the diagram of Fig. 16.20 in which rays of light are shown leaving an object O under the surface of water.

The first ray OA is travelling at right angles to the refracting surface and consequently suffers no change in direction in passing into air as the ray AB. The ray OC however is travelling at an angle to the surface and hence is refracted as it passes into the air in the direction CD. The third ray OE makes a greater angle of incidence with the refracting surface than did OC and is therefore subjected to more bending on passing into air. As the rays leaving the object are chosen to make larger and larger angles of incidence with the refracting surface, there is reached a *critical angle of incidence* (marked c in Fig. 16.20) at which the angle of refraction is 90° so that the ray GH is directed along the refracting surface.

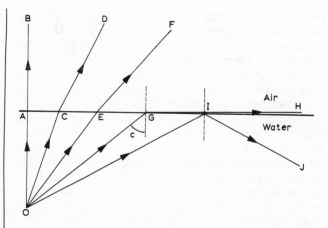

Fig.16.20 The phenomena of refraction and total internal reflection. The ray OG strikes the water surface at the critical angle of incidence.

The *critical angle* of a medium is the angle of incidence in the medium for which the angle of refraction in air is 90°.

When a ray is considered whose angle of incidence exceeds the critical angle, (e.g. the ray OI), that ray is unable to penetrate the refracting surface, and is *totally internally reflected* according to the laws of reflection of light.

Let us suppose that the index of refraction for light travelling from air to water is μ. Then the index of refraction for light travelling from water to air is $\dfrac{1}{\mu}$. Thus when a ray of light is incident on the water surface at the critical angle of incidence, we may write

$$\frac{\sin c}{\sin 90} = \frac{1}{\mu}$$

But
$$\sin 90 = 1$$

hence
$$\sin c = \frac{1}{\mu}$$

Thus knowing the index of refraction for light travelling from one medium to another of higher optical density the critical angle of incidence for light travelling from the denser to the less dense medium may be calculated.

For example, the index of refraction for light travelling from air to water is 1·33. Denoting the critical angle of incidence for light travelling from water to air by C, then

$$\sin C = \frac{1}{1\cdot33} = 0\cdot75$$

Hence
$$C = 48°\,35'$$

The critical angle for perspex may be determined experimentally with the apparatus shown in Fig. 16.21. A semicircular perspex block is mounted on the light-tracking board with its straight edge along the 90°–90° line of the 360° protractor, with its centre coincident with the centre of the protractor. A ray of light from the ray-box directed towards the centre of the protractor strikes the curved surface of the block normally and is therefore undeviated as it passes into the perspex, but on re-entering the air, the ray is bent away from the normal to the air-perspex boundary. The block and protractor are rotated simultaneously until that angle of incidence within the perspex is reached where the refracted ray is observed to graze the straight edge of the block. This angle of incidence is the critical angle for perspex and should be approximately 42°.

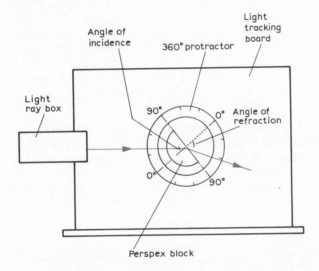

Fig.16.21 Determination of the critical angle for perspex.

The phenomenon of total internal reflection is put to practical use in the construction of light guides made in the form of a bundle of glass fibres. Figure 16.22 shows a ray being transmitted down one such fibre. Remember that the reflections are total: no light escapes from the fibre, so the only transmission losses are due to absorption in the glass. In a practical light guide many such fibres are grouped and bound together to give a flexible glass rod which may be used to direct light round corners and into inaccessible regions. Such a tube is now used by chest physicians in performing exploratory examinations into the lobes of patients' lungs.

The mirage is about the most fascinating and tormenting example of *atmospheric refraction*. The dehydrated desert traveller sees a shimmering pool of water in the distance in which the surrounding sand dunes are reflected. On reaching the apparent position of this pool however, the pool has disappeared, and the traveller begins to doubt his sanity. The pool he has observed is in fact an image of the sky due to

Fig.16.22 The transmission of light along a glass fibre is a series of total internal reflections.

atmospheric refraction. So too is the reflection of a sand dune.

The mirage effect may also be observed on a hot day as a pool of water on the road seen by car drivers generally just beyond the crest of a very slight rise. The mirage effect has been responsible for aircraft crashing when taking off from desert airstrips—the pilots having been mislead by the effect.

The effect may be explained with reference to Fig. 16.23 in which the air heated by the hot sand is shown in layers although of course in practice the change in air temperature and density would be gradual and continuous.

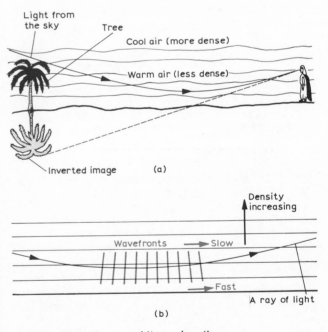

Fig.16.23 The mirage and its explanation.

Light coming from the top of a tree (or from the sky) in the direction shown, will be continually bent 'away from the normal' as it passes from regions of cooler to warmer air. Since the upper regions of the light wavefronts in a ray are travelling through denser air than the lower regions, these upper regions will travel more slowly than the lower regions, and so the ray will be continually bent upwards (Fig. 16.23(b)). When the ray reaches the observer, the observer traces it back along its final direction and thereby locates the top of the tree and the sky behind it below ground level. The tree thus appears upside down and the sky as a pool of water. Since it is only rays from the sky at near grazing incidence which will behave in this complicated way, the pool is of a limited size. The observer is of course able to see the actual tree and sky by direct rays of light travelling towards him.

The diagram of Fig. 16.24 shows a ray of light travelling from a distant star and towards Earth. The Earth's atmosphere is shown as a series of layer which decrease in density with height. The ray of light is thus bent successively 'towards the normal' as it passes through the atmosphere and so to an observer on Earth the star appears higher in the sky than it really is. Astronomers must make a correction for this effect in interpreting their measurements.

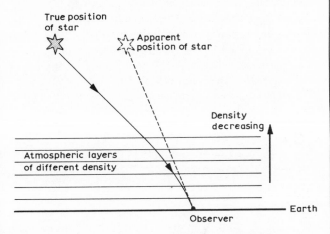

Fig.16.24 As a result of atmospheric refraction, a star appears 'higher' in the sky than it really is.

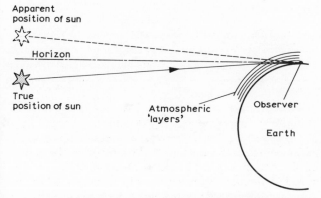

Fig.16.25 Atmospheric refraction is responsible for the lengthening of a day by approximately eight minutes.

The diagram of Fig. 16.25 shows a ray of light travelling from the sun which has (by definition) set. Because of the phenomena of atmospheric refraction however, this ray is bent in such a way that the sun may still be visible above the horizon even although it has set. By the same phenomenon the sun is also visible in the morning before it has (by definition) risen. These effects of atmospheric refraction are responsible for the lengthening of a day by approximately eight minutes.

(Does the phenomenon of atmospheric refraction give rise to real images or virtual images?)

16.4 The Formation of Images by Curved Refracting Surfaces (Thin Lenses)

The lens is that component common to each of the eye, the camera, the projector, the microscope, and the telescope. Its function is either to converge light, or to diverge light, depending on its design. It is defined correctly as a piece of transparent material (usually glass) bounded by two surfaces, at least one of which is curved. These boundary surfaces may be spherical, cylindrical, or parabolic, although spherical surfaces are by far the most common. A variety of common spherical lens sections is shown in Fig. 16.26.

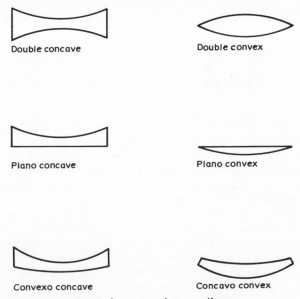

Fig.16.26 A variety of common lens sections.

A study of Fig. 16.26 reveals that thin lenses fall into two main categories—the convex lens and the concave lens. These categories are more often referred to as the converging lens and the diverging lens respectively for reasons which we shall now consider.

The illustrations of Fig. 16.27 show the refraction and transmission of light rays parallel and close to the axis of a thin spherical double convex lens. Each of the rays is bent 'towards the normal' on striking the first glass surface and 'away from the normal' on leaving the second glass surface, so

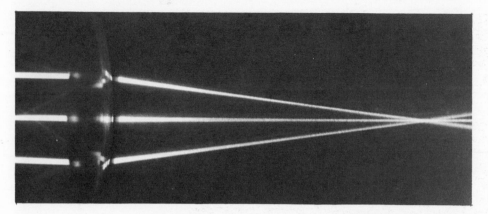

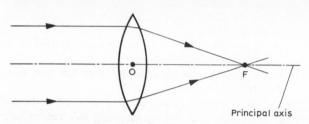

Principal axis

Fig.16.27 The focussing action of a thin spherical double convex lens.

that each is bent towards the principal axis of the lens. The point F at which the two rays converge on the principal axis, is called the *principal focus* of the lens. The point O within the lens is called the *optical centre* of the lens and this point is such that, provided the lens is sufficiently thin, any ray of light passing through it (whether along or at an angle to the principal axis) will do so without significant deviation. This follows by considering the middle of the lens as a small parallel sided block. A ray incident along the principal axis would strike this block normally and therefore by transmitted without deviation. A ray incident at an angle to the principal axis would emerge parallel to its original direction (see Fig. 15.5) and with insignificant lateral displacement, provided the lens block is sufficiently thin. The distance OF in Fig. 16.27 is the *focal length* of the lens and is usually denoted by f. The plane through the point F and at right angles to the principal axis of the lens is called the *focal plane* of the lens and it is to a point on this plane that any parallel beam of light inclined to the axis of the lens will be focused (Fig. 16.28).

From the diagrams we see that a convex lens has a certain converging power for an incident beam of light: this converging power of the lens is measured as the reciprocal of the focal length, so that the closer the point F to the lens in Fig. 16.27, the greater is the converging power of that lens.

The illustrations of Fig. 16.29 show the corresponding effects using a thin spherical double concave lens. In this case rays are again bent 'towards the normal' on striking the

first glass surface and 'away from the normal' on leaving the second glass surface. Each ray is therefore bent away from the principal axis of the lens at both faces so an observer on the far side of the lens sees the rays diverging from the point F′ on the principal axis. That is, the point F′ is the *virtual principal focus* of the concave lens. The distance OF′ is the focal length of the concave lens where O is again its optical centre.

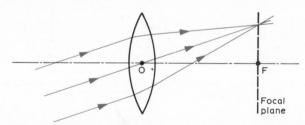

Focal plane

Fig.16.28 Incident parallel rays, regardless of direction, are brought to a focus at a point on the focal plane of the lens.

A focal plane may again be drawn through F′ at right angles to the principal axis of the lens so that for a parallel beam of light incident on the lens and inclined to its axis, the diverging rays would appear to an observer to have come from some point on this focal plane. (Fig. 16.30).

While the convex lens has a certain converging power for an incident parallel beam, the concave lens has a certain diverging power. The diverging power of a concave lens is measured, as for a convex lens, by the reciprocal of its focal length, so that a *short focal length* concave lens has a *large diverging power*.

Let us now consider the formation of the image of an extended object by a thin spherical lens—the object being placed usually at a finite distance from the lens. As was the case with spherical mirrors, the position, size and nature of the image of such an object may be deduced by a simple graphical approach which involves the drawing of a ray diagram to scale. Such a diagram involves the tracing of a

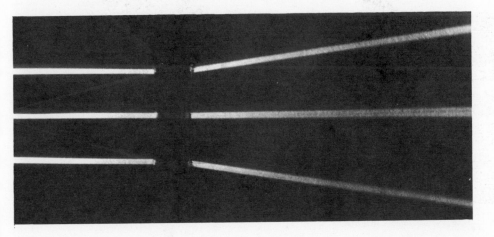

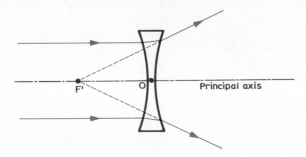

Fig.16.29 The de-focussing action of a thin spherical double concave lens.

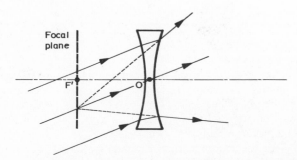

Fig.16.30 The focal plane of a spherical double concave lens.

few specific rays from one extremity of the object—rays which are refracted and transmitted in a known way.

With reference to Fig. 16.31 in which the object is again a small lighted candle placed in front of a double convex lens, it is convenient to choose the following three rays the paths of which may be traced readily.

a) A ray parallel to the principal axis of the lens is refracted and transmitted through the principal focus of the lens (F).

b) A ray through the principal focus of the lens on the object side of the lens (F_1) is refracted parallel to the principal axis of the lens.

c) A ray through the optical centre of the lens is un-deviated.

These rays have been drawn as being refracted at the mid-plane of the lens since we are assuming the lens to be of negligible thickness. All three rays are found to converge on the same point (M), and so M marks the position of the image of the tip of the candle flame as formed by the convex lens. Further, all points along OO' will give rise to image points along the perpendicular through M towards the principal axis so forming the complete image of the candle. (This discussion assumes that the ratio aperture/focal length of the lens is small: otherwise spherical aberration will be present.)

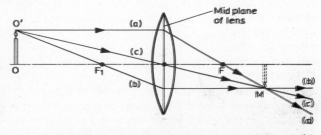

Fig.16.31 Any two of the rays (a), (b), and (c) may be used to locate the tip of the image of the object.

As in the case of mirror problems, it is sufficient to choose any two of the above rays to locate the image, the two chosen being those which can be drawn most easily. Let us now consider the six groups of images which may be formed with a convex lens. The construction of these images is illustrated in Fig. 16.32.

When an extended object is placed at an effectively infinite distance from the lens, the rays which it sends towards the

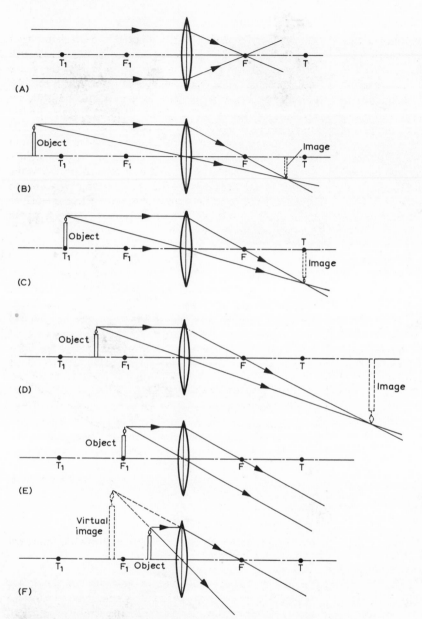

Fig.16.32 The six groups of images which may be formed by a spherical double convex lens. The points T and T_1 are each a distance of twice the focal length from the optical centre of the lens.

lens are almost exactly parallel. Consequently the image of this object is formed as a point on the principal axis of the lens and this point is, of course, the principal focus (diagram A).

When the object is placed at a finite distance from the lens exceeding twice its focal length, as would be the case with objects to be viewed with the eye or to be photographed with a camera, the image is formed on the opposite side of the lens at a distance between one and two focal lengths from the lens (diagram B). This image is inverted, diminished, and real—that is, it may be projected on a screen placed in the vertical plane where it is formed, since the refracted rays of light actually converge at points in this plane.

When the object is placed at a distance equal to twice the focal length of the lens, the image is inverted, of the same size as the object, and real. Further, it is located on the other side of the lens at distance equal to twice the focal length of the lens (diagram C).

When the object is placed at a distance between one and two focal lengths away from the lens, we are actually considering the converse of diagram **B**. That is, the image formed is real, inverted, enlarged, on the opposite side of the lens to the object, and at a distance from the lens greater than twice its focal length (Diagram D). This type of image formation finds application in the slide projector and compound microscope.

When the object is placed at the principal focus of the lens, an infinitely large image is formed at infinity—and as such may subtend a finite angle at the lens (Diagram E).

When the object is placed at a distance less than one focal length from the lens, the rays are diverging after refraction so that a real image cannot be formed. To an observer on the far side of the lens, the rays appear to come from a point behind the lens giving the impression of a virtual image. Further, this image is upright and enlarged: it is the type of image which is formed by the eyepiece lenses of telescopes, microscopes and binoculars. (Diagram F).

With reference to Fig. 16.33 in which the extended object is placed in front of a double concave lens we see that since the rays chosen from the flame diverge after refraction, the image formed by the lens must be virtual. To an observer, such an image would appear upright, diminished, and located on the same side of the lens as the object.

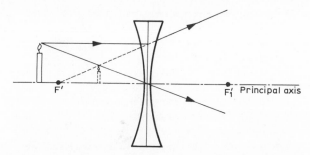

Fig.16.33 Locating the image formed by a thin spherical double concave lens.

The Sun is so far away from the Earth that its rays can be assumed to be parallel and so a convenient method of determining the focal length of a double convex lens is to use it to focus the sun's rays on a white sheet of paper. The distance between the optical centre of the lens and the sheet of paper is then the focal length of the lens.

The focal length of the double convex lens may also be determined using a plane mirror placed at one end of an optical bench as illustrated in Fig. 16.34. At the other end of the bench, is placed the light box with the gauze aperture, and in front of this is mounted the convex lens whose focal length is to be determined. The heights of the lens and the mirror are adjusted so that the centre of the mirror and the gauze aperture both lie on the principal axis of the lens.

The plane of the mirror is then adjusted to be at right angles to the principal axis. If the lens is moved along the bench until the distance between its optical centre and the gauze object is equal to the focal length, then rays of light from the object transmitted by the lens are parallel to the principal axis and are therefore reflected back along their own paths by the plane mirror at the end of the bench. On reaching the lens again these rays of light are therefore focussed at the position of the object or at the side of the object if the mirror is slightly tilted. Thus when a sharp image is formed on the white surface of the light box beside the aperture, the distance between the box and the optical centre of the lens is equal to the required focal length. This may be read directly from the centimetre scale on the bench.

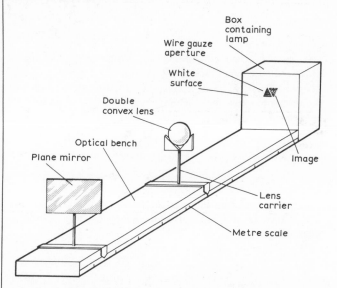

Fig.16.34 Determination of the focal length of a thin spherical double convex lens.

Although the position, nature, and size of the image formed by a thin lens may be found graphically, they may also be found numerically. There exists a general lens equation which may be written in exactly the same form as equation (16.1). The general lens equation is also an algebraic equation in as much as the object distance, the image distance, and the focal length are all regarded as algebraic quantities whose signs are defined thus:

1 Distances between the optical centre of the lens and real objects, images, and foci are written as positive numbers.
2 Distances between the optical centre of the lens and virtual objects, images, and foci are written as negative numbers.

Denoting the object distance by u, the image distance by v, and the focal length by f, then the general lens equation may be written

$$\frac{1}{u} + \frac{1}{v} = \frac{1}{f} \quad \cdots\cdots\cdots \quad (16.4)$$

(The reader may care to verify this equation for the particular case illustrated in Fig. 16.35).

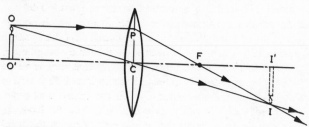

Fig.16.35

As was the case with spherical mirrors, the *magnification* produced by a lens is defined as the ratio of the height of the image to the height of the object. It is left as an exercise for the reader to show that the magnification might equally well be defined as the ratio of image distance to object distance. That is, in Fig. 16.35, the magnification of a lens (*m*) may be written as

$$m = \frac{CI'}{CO'}$$

Re-writing this definition in terms of the algebraic quantities *u* and *v*, it is useful to introduce a negative sign into the definition, and write it as

$$m = -\frac{u}{v} \quad \cdots\cdots\cdots \quad (16.5)$$

By the correct use of sign when substituting for *u* and *v*, we find that when *m* is positive, the image formed by the lens is *upright*. When *m* is negative, the image formed is *inverted*.

The sign convention thus enables us again to deduce whether the lens image is upright or inverted.

The simplicity of the sign convention is illustrated again in a straightforward problem.

Problem 2 A pin at a distance of 12 cm from a lens produces a virtual image 3 cm nearer the lens. What is the nature and focal length of this lens?

Here $u = 12$ and $v = -9$

Since $$\frac{1}{u} + \frac{1}{v} = \frac{1}{f}$$

then $$\frac{1}{f} = \frac{1}{12} + \frac{1}{-9}$$

$$= \frac{9 - 12}{108}$$

$$= -\frac{3}{108}$$

Hence $$f = -36 \text{ cm}$$

The focal length of the lens is therefore 36 cm, and since it is described by a negative number, the lens is concave in nature.

Problems

1. What is the shortest length of vertical mirror which will allow a man 2 m tall to see his full image? Would this length of mirror inclined to the wall at 30° still allow him to see his full image?

2. Two plane mirrors stand vertically on the bench and inclined to each other at 90° with their reflecting surfaces facing inwards. A small object is placed 2 cm from one mirror and 3 cm from the other. By drawing a scaled diagram, show the positions of the images seen by an observer looking into the mirrors.

3. Discuss the nature of the mirrors which would produce a tall thin image and a small fat image of a 'normal' person in a 'hall or mirrors'.

4. A pin 2 cm high is placed at a distance of 8 cm from the pole of a concave mirror whose radius of curvature is 7 cm. By means of a scaled diagram find the position, nature, and size of the image formed.

5. An object 3 cm high is placed 20 cm from a convex mirror whose radius of curvature is 10 cm. By means of a scaled diagram, find the position and size of the image. Check your answer by calculation.

6. A spherical concave shaving mirror has a radius of curvature of 25 cm. What magnification is achieved when the face to be shaved is placed 8 cm from the pole of the mirror?

7. A concave mirror is used to form an image of the filament of a car headlamp on a screen 5 m from the mirror. The filament is 5 mm high, and the image formed is 50 cm high. Find the radius of curvature of the mirror, and the distance between the filament and the pole of the mirror.

8. A man whose eyes are 1·8 m above ground stands 0·8 m from the vertical edge of a swimming pool 3 m deep. He can just see a coin lying at the foot of the pool. If the index of refraction for light travelling from air to water is 1·33, find the distance between the coin and the side of the pool.

9. In Fig. 16.36 a ray of light is incident on a cylindrical piece of transparent material in a plane at right angles to the axis of the cylinder. The point A is such that $\hat{AOC} = 60°$. The refracted ray leaves the cylinder at B, COB

being a diameter. Calculate the angle of incidence at A and also the angle of deviation between the incident and final emergent rays. Do not look up tables for the values of sines, but express them as fractions of the sides of a well known triangle—e.g. $\sin 60°$ (which you will not require) $= \dfrac{\sqrt{3}}{2}$. (The index of refraction for light travelling from air to the transparent material is $\sqrt{2}$.)

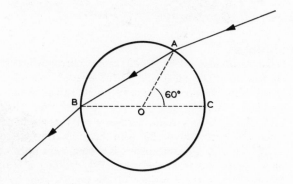

Fig.16.36 See Problem 9.

10 A ray of light in air strikes the horizontal surface of a frozen pond at 45° and is refracted at an angle of 30°. What is the apparent depth of a small leaf embedded in the ice at a depth of 2 cm?

11 A triangular glass prism has two angles of 70°. Will a ray of light be reflected or refracted at one of the larger sides if it enters the prism normally to the other larger side? (The index of refraction for air to glass is 1·5.)

12 An object 2 cm high is placed 20 cm from a double convex lens of focal length 10 cm. By drawing, find the position and size of the image. Check your answer by calculation.

13 A colour slide has dimensions 35 × 24 mm and is to be projected so as to fill a screen of dimensions 1·12 × 1·12 m to the best possible advantage. If the screen is at a distance of 3·2 m from the projector lens, how far from the lens must the slide carrier be placed? What is the focal length of the lens? Is the lens convex or concave? Is the image real of virtual?

Chapter 17

Optical Instruments

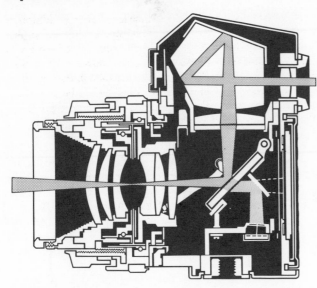

Fig.17.0   The construction of the Leicaflex SL Camera. (By kind permission of E. Leitz Ltd.)

In the final sections of the last chapter, we discussed the formation of images by thin lenses. In this chapter we shall extend this discussion to consider the uses to which lenses may be put in the construction of a number of optical instruments. From our personal point of view, the most vital optical instrument of all is the human eye. In the design of those optical instruments which are intended to improve and extend vision it is essential that the structure and optical properties of the eye itself be taken into account. Bearing this point in mind, we begin the chapter with a study of the human eye. We shall then study the slide projector and the camera as instruments which form real images, and the microscope and telescope as instruments which form virtual images. It is this latter class of instruments which is employed to extend the vision of the eye towards the realms of the microscopic and macroscopic worlds. These instruments are generally used for direct viewing of a virtual image by the eye, though they are often modified for recording a real image photographically or, today, by a television camera in say an earth satellite which transmits the picture which it 'sees' back to earth.

17.1 The Human Eye

The diagram of Fig. 17.1 shows a horizontal section through a human (right) eye as seen from above. This diagram shows the eye to be a complicated optical system, but, as we shall see, this system is equivalent to a converging lens of variable focal length.

The outermost layer of the eye (called the *sclerotic coat*) is white, tough, and opaque, except at the extreme frontal part where it meets the slightly bulging and transparent

cornea. The cornea is the window of the eye.

Inside, the eye is divided into two compartments by its crystalline lens—a complicated structure which is composed of layers of transparent tissue in such a way that each layer has a slightly different index of refraction from the next. The lens is supported by *ciliary muscles* and ligaments, and the combined actions of these serve to alter the curvature and hence the focal length of the lens.

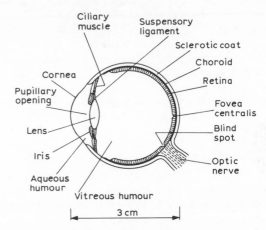

Fig.17.1   A section through a human right eye.

The forward compartment of the eye—called the anterior chamber—is filled with a transparent salty liquid called *aqueous humour*; it is in this chamber that we find the *iris*. The iris is the coloured portion of the eye (usually blue or brown) which is seen through the cornea, and which is in fact an extension of the pigmented *choroid* coat of tissue. The opening formed by the iris is the *pupil* of the eye, and is seen as the black spot in the centre of the eye. The size of the pupil is controlled by a reflex action stimulated by the amount of light falling on the eye. In bright sunlight the diameter of the pupil is about 2 mm, whereas in blackout conditions this may increase to 7 or 8 mm.

The rear compartment (or posterior chamber) of the eye is filled with an irreplaceable transparent jelly-like substance called the *vitreous humour*. At the rear of this chamber we find the *retina*—a light sensitive tissue which is backed by the light absorbing choroid, the two being joined to the sclerotic coat. The retina is composed of many millions of light sensitive nerve cells of which there are two types—*rods* and *cones*. When light falls on these sensory receptors, electrical impulses are generated by photochemical action and conducted to the brain along the *optic nerve*. According to the von Kries Theory, the rods function in night vision at low illuminations, while the cones function as daylight receptors, operating when there is high illumination. It is the cones which see colour, while the rods distinguish only shades of black and white. The cones are most numerous at the centre of the retina or *fovea centralis*, and are involved in space perception and visual acuity. The rods are most numerous at the periphery of the retina and are required for intensity vision, rather than for spatial vision. The image of any object we perceive is normally brought to a focus at the fovea on the retina, for it is this region which gives the most detailed picture of all. In fact we move our eyes automatically so that the image formed by the eye will be formed at the fovea. For example when we are reading a book, we see only a small group of words clearly at any instant although we are totally conscious of all words on the page before us. Since only a few words may be focussed at the fovea at any time, (the fovea being extremely small) the reading of a line of print necessitates a series of small movements of the eyes across the page being read.

At that part of the retina where the optic nerve enters the eye, there are neither rods nor cones present, and so any object whose image is formed on this *blind spot* is invisible. The existence of the blind spot may be verified simply by holding the book at arms length in front of you, closing the left eye, and looking at the cross in Fig. 17.2 with the right eye alone. Bring the book slowly towards you (still concentrating on the cross) and you will be aware that at some point, the black square suddenly disappears. This is because the image of the black square is now being formed on the blind spot. The square re-appears as the book is then brought closer (still looking at the cross) but at another point, the black circle suddenly disappears—re-appearing as the book is brought closer still.

Fig.17.2

When the image of an object is formed on the retina, it is formed by the refraction of light at curved surfaces. Most refraction occurs at the cornea of the eye and not at the crystalline lens as is often wrongly assumed. Since the cornea is bulging outwards slightly, light entering the eye is converged. This light is converged further by the action of the crystalline lens and so, as the diagram of Fig. 17.3 indicates, the image formed on the retina is real. This image is also diminished and inverted, although the idea of an inverted image may seem quite unacceptable. After all, we observe our surroundings the right way up and most certainly not upside down. Although the image formed on the retina is inverted however, the brain interprets the information which it receives in terms of an upright image—this power of interpretation developing in the first 3 weeks of life.

When the eye is forming the image of a very distant object, it is in its most relaxed state. Its ciliary muscles are in their least state of stress and the crystalline lens is in its condition of least converging power. With the normal healthy eye in this state the very distant object is clearly seen. When the eye is forming the image of a very close object however, it is in its most tense state. Its ciliary muscles are then in their greatest state of stress for the purpose of compressing the crystalline lens towards its condition of greatest converging power so that diverging rays of light from the nearby object may be converged on the retina.

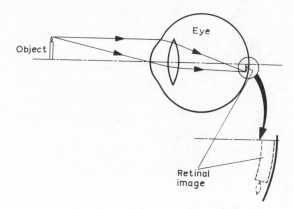

Fig.17.3   The formation of the retinal image is due to the refraction of light at curved surfaces.

There is of course a limit to the amount of compression of the crystalline lens, so objects closer to the eye than a certain minimum distance will give rise to images which are not focussed clearly on the retina. For the normal healthy eye, the *least distance of distinct vision* is about 25 cm, although for young children, it may be as little as 10 cm.

17.2 Optical Instruments which Record Real Images

A real image is one through which rays of light from the object actually pass, and which may therefore be gathered on a screen. Thereafter, the image may be observed by many people simultaneously. To achieve this result with a lens system, then the lens system must effectively be convergent, as is the case with those systems in each of the slide projector and the photographic camera. Let us now consider these instruments in turn.

1. The Slide Projector
The purpose of the slide projector is to form a much magnified image of a small transparent object—usually a colour slide—on a screen, and in such a way that the image is illuminated strongly, uniformly and efficiently.

Efficient illumination of the image requires that all of the light passing through the transparency is gathered on the screen. If the area of the screen is say 1 m² (10^4 cm²) and the area of the transparency is approximately 7 cm² (35 mm × 21 mm), then for an average required intensity of illumination I on the screen, the transparency must be illuminated with light whose intensity is at least 1430 I—assuming that the image is to fill the screen. That is, efficient and strong illumination of the image demands that the transparency be illuminated intensely.

For the image to appear uniformly illuminated, the light from the source in the projector must be concentrated on to the transparency with the same intensity at the edges as at the centre.

For a satisfactory reproduction of the transparency, it is also essential that no image of the projector's light source should appear on the screen: if it did, the illumination of the image would clearly not be uniform.

The construction of the slide projector which satisfies all of these requirements is illustrated in the diagram of Fig. 17.4(a). The diagram of Fig. 17.4(b) illustrates the formation of the image of the transparency on the screen.

The presence of the concave mirror behind the lamp ensures that light from the lamp travelling to the left is reflected back to be collected by the condenser lens. This lens then converges and hence concentrates the originally divergent light towards the slide. The coiled filament of the lamp is positioned on the central axis of the instrument at a distance of two focal lengths from the optical centre of the condenser lens, and an image of the filament is thus formed at a distance of two focal lengths from the condenser on its far side. The objective lens (which has been corrected for both spherical and chromatic aberration) is placed so that its optical centre coincides with the image of the coiled filament, and hence this lens cannot possibly form an image of the filament on the screen.

The slide is placed close to the condenser lens where the illumination is uniform, and just outside the principal focus (F_0) of the objective lens, so that a real enlarged image is formed by this lens. As the last chapter predicted and the last diagram shows, the image formed on the screen is inverted, and so the slide must be inserted upside down in the projector.

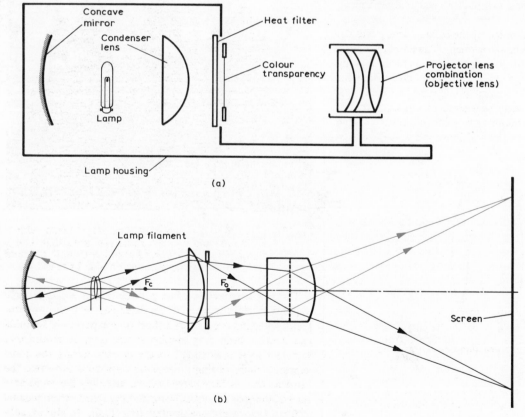

Fig.17.4 The construction and action of the slide projector. For simplicity, we have shown refraction as taking place in one plane (the dotted line), in the objective lens.

A projector without a condenser lens gives rise to a dim picture which is less brightly illuminated at its edges than at the centre. This picture is also likely to include an unwanted image of the bulb's filament slightly out of focus.

2. *The Photographic Camera*

In its simplest form, the camera is a light proof box with a shuttered convex lens at the front and a light sensitive film or plate at the back. Its function is to form a small real image of a distant object on the photographic film, but obviously not all distant objects can give rise to the formation of sharp images simultaneously, since the image distance varies with object distance for any given lens. In an expensive camera (Fig. 17.0), proper focussing of the image on the film is achieved by moving the lens towards or away from the film and in the modern camera this movement involves the rotation of one of the components of the compound lens such that the component is screwed towards or away from the film. In an inexpensive camera, no mechanical focussing arrangement is provided, and such a camera is equipped with a lens of short focal length which forms an image very nearly at its principal focus for all object distances except those which are extremely small.

The amount of light admitted by the camera determines the quality of contrast in the image formed. The amount of light admitted may be varied in the expensive camera by altering either or both of the size of the lens aperture and the time for which the lens shutter is opened (the exposure time). The size of the lens aperture may be altered by changing the diameter of the hole in the diaphragm which is located between different portions of the compound lens system as illustrated in Fig. 17.5.

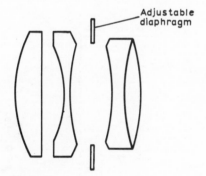

Fig.17.5 A compound camera lens showing the adjustable diaphragm.

In most cameras with a variable lens stop, the diameter of the diaphragm hole may be adjusted to the following fractions of the focal length of the lens system:

$$\frac{f}{2 \cdot 8}, \quad \frac{f}{4}, \quad \frac{f}{5 \cdot 6}, \quad \frac{f}{8}, \quad \frac{f}{11}, \quad \frac{f}{16}$$

where f denotes the focal length.

These diameters are known as the *stop numbers* and their squares are naturally proportional to the areas of each of the possible diaphragm holes and hence to the amount of light which may be admitted by each hole in a given time. The amounts of light are thus proportional to:

$$\frac{f^2}{7 \cdot 5}, \quad \frac{f^2}{16}, \quad \frac{f^2}{31 \cdot 4}, \quad \frac{f^2}{64}, \quad \frac{f^2}{121}, \quad \frac{f^2}{256}$$

that is, the amount of light admitted at the stop number $\frac{f}{2 \cdot 8}$ is almost double that at $\frac{f}{4}$ in the same time, so that on stopping down from $\frac{f}{2 \cdot 8}$ to $\frac{f}{4}$, the exposure time would have to be doubled if the same amount of light were to be admitted to the camera.

Fig.17.6 This action photograph has been taken with a Leica camera using a short exposure time and a large lens aperture. As a result, the depth of focus is limited. (By kind permission of E. Leitz Ltd.)

The correct selection of stop number and exposure time requires careful thought. If, for example, we wish to photograph an action event, then a short time exposure is desirable and hence a large stop number is necessary to ensure that sufficient light is admitted to the camera during the short exposure time. Using a large lens aperture however, the camera achieves little *depth of focus* and only the immediate surroundings of the object being photographed are sufficiently in focus to look reasonably clear (Fig. 17.6). In photographing a landscape, it is desirable to achieve a large depth of focus and this requires the selection of a small stop number together with a larger exposure time.

17.3 Optical Instruments which Extend the Range of Vision

Optical instruments which form virtual images aid and extend the vision of the eye so that a small object can be made to appear larger, or a distant object to appear closer. Before considering the construction and operating principles of these instruments however, let us first consider how we judge the size and location of a given object.

The apparent size of an object depends on the size of the image which is formed on the retina of the eye. The size of the retinal image depends on the size of the *visual angle*, which the object subtends at the eye—the larger the visual angle, the larger the object appears. The visual angle which an object subtends at the eye is defined in the diagrams of Fig. 17.7.

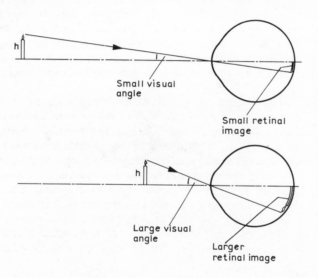

Fig.17.7 The definition of visual angle.

The size of an object is not judged only by the visual angle which it subtends at the eye however. In judging its size, we take into account its distance from us and our past experience, along with the size of the retinal image. For example, although our thumb held at arm's length may cover a distant tree, we do not conclude that the thumb and the tree are of the same order of size. From past experience we know the general size of a tree, and, by employing binocular vision, we realise that the tree is located at a far greater distance from the eyes than the thumb held at arm's length.

In general, we estimate the size of an object *together with* its distance from us, by comparing each with known sizes at known distances. This becomes obvious when we try to cross mountainous country at night—a small hillock at a short distance appears like a large mountain a great distance away. In conditions of good lighting, we may be able to judge the size of a given small object fairly accurately, but in order to make out fine detail in the object, it is desirable to increase the size of the retinal image. This is easily accomplished by bringing the object closer to the eyes so that it subtends a larger visual angle. On bringing the object closer than 25 cm however, the image becomes blurred, because the normal eye can no longer focus a clear image on the retina. When we are confronted with a large object at a great distance—such as a mountain several miles away—the retinal image can only be increased in size by moving closer to the mountain so that the visual angle subtended by the mountain is gradually increased.

Let us now consider those instruments which extend the vision of the eye by making small objects appear larger.

1. The Simple Magnifying Glass

The magnifying glass is a convex lens which is placed immediately in front of the eye and behind the object which is to be examined in greater detail.

Let us suppose that the unmagnified object subtends a visual angle α when placed at the least distance of distinct vision (D) as in Fig. 17.8(a). By introducing the magnifying glass as in Fig. 17.8(b) with the object just within one focal length of the optical centre of the glass, it is possible to form an upright virtual image of the object at the least distance of distinct vision. This image then assumes the role of an object, and the angle which it subtends at the glass is practically equal to that subtended at the eye—assuming the two are sufficiently close. Denoting this angle by β, then we see that $\beta > \alpha$.

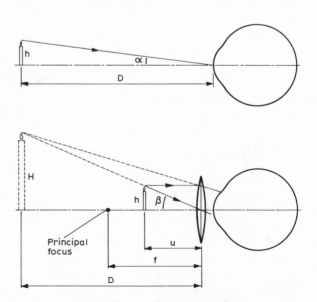

Fig.17.8 The effect of the simple magnifying glass (image formed at the least distance of distinct vision).

The *magnifying power* of an optical instrument is defined as the ratio

> angle subtended at the eye by final image seen through the instrument
> ──────────────────────────────
> angle subtended at the eye by object when viewed normally without the instrument

With reference to Fig. 17.8, the magnifying power of the glass is thus the ratio $\frac{\beta}{\alpha}$. Denoting this power by m, we may write

$$m = \frac{\beta}{\alpha} \doteqdot \frac{\tan \beta}{\tan \alpha} \quad \text{(since } \theta \text{ in radians equals } \tan \theta, \text{ for small angles)}$$

$$= \frac{h/u}{h/D}$$

$$= \frac{D}{u}$$

Now $\quad \dfrac{1}{u} - \dfrac{1}{D} = \dfrac{1}{f}$ (applying the general lens equation to Fig. 17.8)

$$\Leftrightarrow \frac{1}{u} = \frac{1}{D} + \frac{1}{f}$$

$$= \frac{D + f}{fD}$$

Hence $\quad m\left(= \dfrac{D}{u}\right) = D\left(\dfrac{D + f}{fD}\right)$

$$\Leftrightarrow m = \frac{D}{f} + 1$$

Hence a magnifying glass of focal length 5 cm would have a magnifying power of 6.

2. The Compound Microscope

The maximum magnification to be gained with a simple magnifying glass is of the order of 20 times, and this is quite insufficient for the detailed examination of extremely small objects such as living cells. The compound microscope improves on the performance of the simple convex lens by arranging for the magnification process to occur in two stages by means of two lens systems.

The diagram of Fig. 17.9 shows a very simple form of compound microscope in which the two lens systems are simply convex lenses. The objective lens has a short focal length, and is used to form a real and enlarged image of the object. The eyepiece lens assumes the role of a simple magnifying glass, and gives rise to an enlarged virtual image of this real image.

Since the objective lens forms a real and enlarged image of the object, the object distance to this lens must be slightly greater than the focal length of the lens. In order that the eyepiece lens may act as a magnifying glass, the real image formed by the objective lens must be arranged to lie at a point slightly closer to the eyepiece than its principal focus (marked F_e).

In the diagram of Fig. 17.9, the final image is formed at the least distance of distinct vision from the eyepiece, and hence the eye—assuming the two to be extremely close. If observations are to last for some time however, then the accommodation required to form a retinal image of an object at the least distance of distinct vision may result in eyestrain. To avoid eyestrain, many microscopists adjust their instruments so that the final image is formed at infinity and can be viewed by a fully relaxed eye. Note this means that the intermediate real image in Fig. 17.9 must be formed at the principal focus of the eyepiece lens as in Fig. 17.10. Used in this way, the

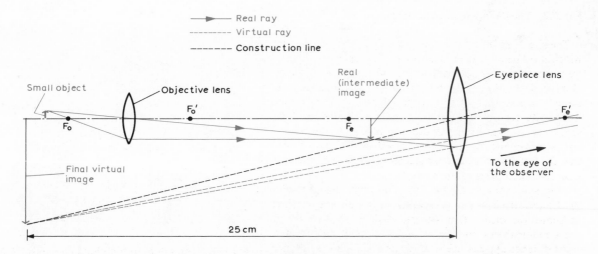

Fig.17.9 Image formation by a compound microscope.

205

microscope is said to be in *normal adjustment*.

With reference to Fig. 17.10, the angle subtended at the eye by the final image is β, where

$$\beta = \frac{h'}{f_e}$$

Now since triangles $OO'C$ and $II'C$ are similar,

$$\frac{h}{f_0 + O'F_0} = \frac{h'}{g + f_0}$$

Since triangles $OO'F_0$ and PCF_0 are similar,

$$\frac{h}{O'F_0} = \frac{h'}{f_0}$$

Hence

$$O'F_0 = \frac{f_0 h}{h'}$$

Hence

$$\frac{h}{f_0 + \frac{f_0 h}{h'}} = \frac{h'}{g + f_0}$$

$$\Leftrightarrow \frac{h}{\frac{f_0 h' + f_0 h}{h'}} = \frac{h'}{g + f_0}$$

$$\Leftrightarrow \frac{h}{f_0 h' + f_0 h} = \frac{1}{g + f_0}$$

$$\Leftrightarrow gh + f_0 h = f_0 h' + f_0 h$$

$$\Leftrightarrow gh = f_0 h'$$

$$\Leftrightarrow \frac{h'}{g} = \frac{h}{f_0}$$

Hence

$$\beta = \frac{hg}{f_0 f_e}$$

If the object were viewed at the least distance of distinct vision (D), and in the absence of the microscope, then the angle subtended at the eye would be written as α, where

$$\alpha = \frac{h}{D}$$

By definition, the magnifying power of the microscope may be calculated as

$$\text{magnifying power} = \frac{\dfrac{hg}{f_0 f_e}}{\dfrac{h}{D}}$$

$$= \frac{Dg}{f_0 f_e}$$

The magnifying power of the microscope may therefore be regarded as the product of terms $\left(\dfrac{D}{f_e}\right)$ and $\left(\dfrac{g}{f_0}\right)$. The first of these terms is in fact the magnifying power of the eyepiece lens (see problem 6 at the end of the chapter). The second term can be shown to be equal to $\dfrac{h'}{h}$. That is, the second term is the linear magnification of the objective lens.

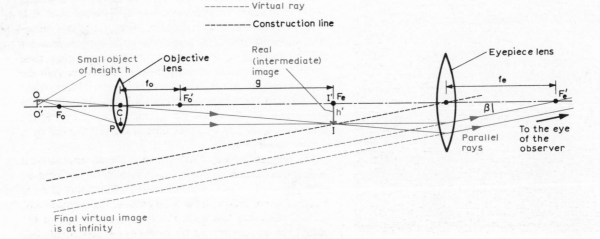

Fig.17.10 The compound microscope in normal adjustment.

The magnifying power of the microscope is thus the product of a magnifying power, and a linear magnification factor.

For high magnifying power, the focal length of each lens should therefore be as small as possible, and the separation of the foci F_0' and F_e as large as possible. High magnifying power in a microscope is not the ultimate requirement however. A large image is of little use if it is indistinct. The detail of the image is finally determined by the *resolving power* of the instrument—a topic which we leave for study at a more advanced level.

In a typical microscope for use in a school biology laboratory, the microscope tube is of the order of 16 cm long. The high power objective lens has a focal length of approximately 4·5 mm, and magnifies 40 times. The eyepiece lens magnifies 7·5 times, and so the magnifying power of the instrument is 40 × 7·5 or 300.

In some advanced instruments, as many as ten separate lenses may form the objective system, while two or three lenses might form the eyepiece system—the two systems having the combined power to magnify over 2000 times. The constructions of the objectives shown in Fig. 17.11 are shown in Fig. 17.12. With such high magnification however, it is not easy to illuminate the object with sufficient intensity. To achieve this, and at the same time maintain uniformity of illumination, a powerful condensing lens is mounted beneath the object (the sub-stage condenser) which concentrates a wide angled beam of light into a small uniformly bright spot.

Fig.17.12 This photograph shows the construction of each objective lens system shown in Fig. 17.11. (By kind permission of E. Leitz Ltd.)

Let us now consider those instruments which aid vision by making distant objects appear closer, and hence examinable in more detail.

3. The Telescope

The compound microscope principle—by which the real image of an object is magnified—is used to advantage in the telescope. This principle affords the only feasible approach towards increasing the visual angle subtended by a distant object, and hence towards increasing its apparent size. It is futile to try and increase the apparent size of a distant mountain by viewing it through a magnifying glass, but if we examine the real image of the mountain with a magnifying glass, then we find an increase in its apparent size, and hence gain the impression that it has been brought closer. Since, using refraction, a real image can be formed only by means of a convex lens, it follows that the optical system of a refracting telescope consists of a convex objective lens followed by a convex magnifying lens.

The diagram of Fig. 17.13 shows a simple astronomical telescope in which rays of light from a distant star are focussed in the focal plane of the objective lens. This focal plane is arranged to coincide with the focal plane of the eyepiece lens, so that this latter lens gives rise to a virtual image of the distant star at infinity. As far as the eye is concerned, this virtual image assumes the role of an object and so a real retinal image is formed with the eye completely relaxed.

Fig.17.11 This photograph shows five microscope objective lens systems. (By kind permission of E. Leitz Ltd.)

By definition, the magnifying power of the telescope may be written as m where (with reference to Fig. 17.13)

$$m = \frac{\beta}{\alpha}$$

$$= \frac{\dfrac{h}{f_e}}{\dfrac{h}{f_0}} \quad \text{(for small angles measured in radians)}$$

$$= \frac{f_0}{f_e}$$

Hence in order that the magnifying power be as large as possible, the objective lens should be of a large focal length and the eyepiece lens of a short focal length.

Can you suggest why the aperture of the objective lens should be as wide as possible?

The final image formed by the telescope is inverted, but as far as astronomical observations are concerned, this is of little importance. For terrestrial observations however, the inversion is undesirable, and so a means whereby the final image may appear erect must be found. In the terrestrial telescope, the final image is made to appear erect by the presence of an erecting lens placed between the objective and eyepiece lenses as in Fig. 17.14. The objective lens forms a real inverted image of the object; the erecting lens then forms a re-inverted image of this image; and finally, the eyepiece lens magnifies the second image—giving a final image which is upright, as required. If the terrestrial telescope were in normal adjustment the final image would be formed at infinity. For the sake of showing the final image however, the diagram of Fig. 17.14 shows the telescope adjusted to form the final image at the least distance of distinct vision.

In Fig. 17.14, the erecting lens has been placed such that the first real image formed in the telescope is at a distance of twice the focal length from the erecting lens. This means that the second real image (formed by the erecting lens) is exactly the same size as the first real image, and so the magnifying power of the instrument is unaffected by the introduction of the erecting lens in this way. The length of the instrument is increased by four times the focal length of the erecting lens however.

4. Prism Binoculars

In prism binoculars, one telescopic tube is available for each eye, so that the instrument lends depth and perspective to the the object being viewed.

In each telescopic tube, two prisms take the place of the erecting lens found in the terrestrial telescope. By the process of total internal reflection, these prisms provide for both

i) the erection of the real image formed by the objective lens system

and

ii) a reduction in the overall length of each telescopic tube.

Although the tube is effectively folded by the action of the prisms, the optical path lengths are still the same so that the required relationship between the focal lengths of the objective and eyepiece lenses is maintained.

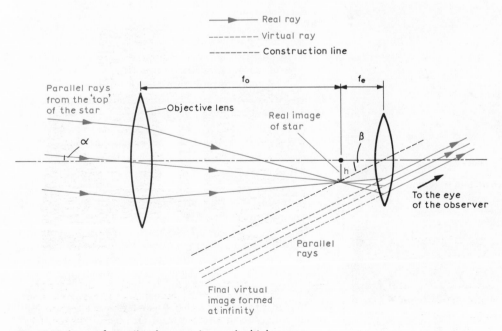

Fig.17.13 Image formation by an astronomical telescope.

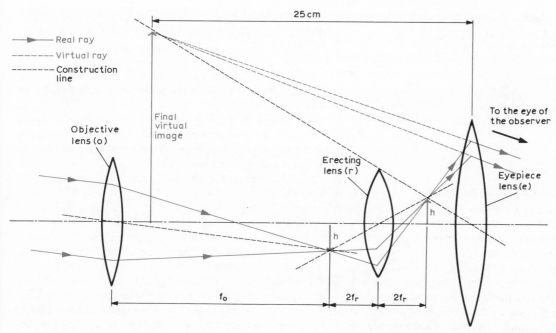

Objective
lens (o)

Final
virtual
image

Erecting
lens (r)

To the eye of
the observer

Eyepiece
lens (e)

25 cm

f_o $2f_r$ $2f_r$

h   h

Fig. 17.14 The formation of an image at the least distance of distinct vision by a terrestrial telescope.

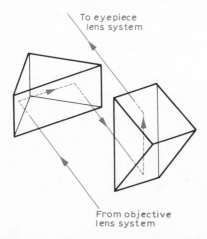

To eyepiece
lens system

From objective
lens system

Fig. 17.15 The action of the prisms means that light traverses the tube three times, so that the optical path is effectively folded.

As Fig. 17.15 shows, the light traverses the tube three times, and so the binoculars need only be one-third as long as a telescope of the same magnifying power.

New light-weight binoculars ('Trinovid') are now being manufactured by the Leitz Company in Germany. These new binoculars are much more compact than more conventional binoculars, and they owe their stylish shape to the nature

of the prisms which they contain. Instead of using two large conventional 'Porro' prisms in each binocular tube, the 'Trinovid' employs three smaller prisms, one of which is referred to as a 'penta prism'. The photograph of Fig. 17.16 shows the construction of the 'Trinovid' binoculars in relation to that of the conventional prism binoculars.

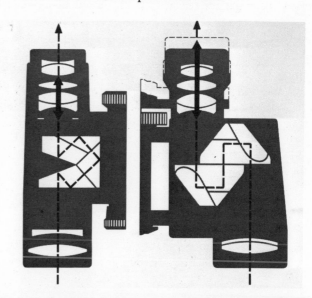

Fig. 17.16 On the left, 'Trinovid' binoculars; on the right, conventional prism binoculars. The comparison of optical paths clearly illustrates the reason for the stylish shape of the 'Trinovid' glasses. (By kind permission of E. Leitz Ltd.)

Problems

1 In what respects are the optical systems of the eye and the the camera alike, and in what respects are they different?

2 A man's least distance of distinct vision is 1 m. Find the focal length of the spectacle lenses he must wear in order to read a newspaper held 25 cm from his eyes.

3 Why must a slide be placed upside down in a slide projector?

What is the focal length of the objective lens of a slide projector which projects a $2 \cdot 5 \times 2 \cdot 5$ cm slide so as to fill the whole of a 2×2 m screen 4 m away?

4 Why is it that when a photograph is taken of a person lying on the ground with his feet towards the camera, his feet appear disproportionately large in the picture? Why do the feet not appear disproportionately large when we put our eyes in place of the camera?

5 The lens of a camera has a focal length of $5 \cdot 5$ cm. If the aperture is set with a diameter of $0 \cdot 5$ cm, calculate the stop number setting. A photograph is taken at this setting with a shutter speed of $\frac{1}{15}$ s. Under the same conditions, what stop number would be required for an action photograph taken at a shutter speed of $\frac{1}{120}$ s? In what respect would the two photographs differ?

6 Show that when a small object is placed at the principal focus of a simple magnifying glass, the magnifying power of the glass may be written as m, where

$$m = \frac{D}{f}$$

(D is the least distance of distinct vision, and f is the focal length of the glass).

7 In using a magnifying glass, is it more or less tiresome to place the object at the principal focus of the glass, or just inside the principal focus? Which arrangement gives the greater magnifying power?

8 In a compound microscope the focal lengths of the objective and eyepiece lenses are 1 cm and 4 cm respectively, and the two lenses are 20 cm apart. If the final image is formed at the least distance of distinct vision, find the distance between the object and the objective lens.

9 In what respects are the structure and operation of the compound microscope and astronomical telescope alike, and in what respects are they different?

10 A telescope magnifies an object 8 times and has an objective lens of focal length 24 cm. What is the focal length of its eyepiece? What is the distance between the two lens systems when the telescope is (i) in normal adjustment (ii) adjusted so as to form the final image at the least distance of distinct vision?

Chapter 18

Spectroscopy

Fig.18.0   A modern laboratory spectrometer. (By kind permission of Griffin & George Ltd.)

I know not what I may appear to the world, but to myself I seem to have been only like a boy playing on the seashore, and diverting myself now and then finding a smoother pebble or a prettier shell than ordinary while the great ocean of truth lies all undiscovered before me.

Isaac Newton

Of all Newton's contributions to physics, perhaps his researches into the spectrum and the origin of colours fascinated him most, and the above quotation reflects his thoughts on this work in 1666. Enthralled as he was at that time, Newton had no idea of the large contribution which his work on colour was to make—possibly because so many of his contemporaries were severely critical of it.

The study of colour is indeed a fascinating one, although for most of us with normal vision, the colourful world in which we live is all too often taken for granted. In this chapter, we shall analyse light in terms of its colours, first, by reviewing Newton's experiments on the spectrum. We shall then consider how each chemical element may be identified by its own characteristic spectrum—concerning ourselves here with the analytical technique employed and not with what the characteristic spectrum can tell about the atomic structure of the particular element. (This latter aspect of spectroscopy will be dealt with in Chapter 20.)

18.1 Newton's Experiments on Dispersion

Dispersion is the name given to the splitting of white light into many colours as a result of the light passing through a transparent medium of a particular shape. This phenomenon occurs when colourless glass is used, and so the production of the colours cannot be attributed to colour present in the glass.

Newton began his extensive study of dispersion and colour when attempting to construct an astronomical telescope. The need to understand colour arose from his frustration in finding that the image formed by the objective lens of the telescope was always surrounded by a coloured border. One of his first investigations was conducted with a small triangular glass prism which he placed in the path of a beam of sunlight shining through a small circular hole in the shutters of his room in Trinity College, Cambridge. Instead of finding a small white circular patch on the wall opposite the shutters, Newton was surprised to find an elongated coloured patch of light, which he measured to be five times as long as it was broad. The colours present in the patch were those of the rainbow, and the ends of the patch were semicircular as is indicated in Fig. 18.1. Newton named this coloured band the *spectrum*.

Newton distinguished the seven colours labelled in Fig. 18.1. Today, since we associate colour with wavelength, we think rather of an infinity of colours, each merging imperceptibly into the next. Newton's seven colours are still useful in naming the main bands of colour which we can identify— though most people find it difficult to distinguish a definite indigo colour between blue and violet.

In an attempt to explain the origin of the colours and the formation of the elongated patch, he then investigated the passage of white light through different thicknesses of glass,

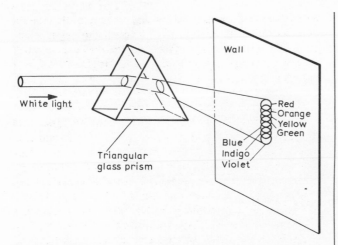

Fig.18.1   A reconstruction of Newton's first experiment on dispersion.

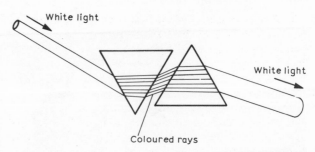

Fig.18.2   Newton's second experiment on dispersion.

and changed the size of the hole in the shutter, but with no further success—the same spectrum of colour was always produced.

He then argued that the phenomenon might be due to irregularities or flaws within the glass of which the prism was made. If the phenomenon were due to regularities in the prism, then a second reversed prism should serve to cancel the spectrum, whereas if it were due to irregularities, then a second reversed prism should serve to enhance the effect. Newton thus set up the apparatus of Fig. 18.2, and he found that on passing the spectrum through the second reversed prism, the colours were recombined to form white light again. Dispersion was thus a regular process, and not a result of flaws in the prism.

The result of this investigation gave additional support to Newton's original belief, which was that white light is composed of many colours, and the colours of the spectrum are in no way manufactured in the prism. Instead, each of the component colours in white light is refracted by a slightly different amount on passing through the prism, so the two successive refractions serve to disperse or spread the beam out into the elongated spectrum.

The fact that each component colour is refracted by a slightly different amount was demonstrated by Newton when he set up his apparatus as in Fig. 18.3, in which one colour from the spectrum produced by a triangular prism is selected and directed towards a second triangular prism. The point at which the final ray touched the screen was noted. The first prism was then rotated slightly so that a second colour was selected and directed towards the second prism at the same angle of incidence as the first colour. The point at which the final ray touched the screen was again noted, and found to be different from the first point. Newton found that for the same angle of incidence on the second prism, red light was refracted least and violet light was refracted most. The elongated spectrum produced in his original experiment could therefore be thought of as a large number of overlapping coloured circular spots, ranging in order from red through orange, green, and blue towards violet.

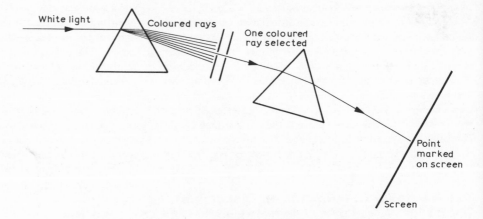

Fig.18.3   Showing that different colours are refracted by different amounts.

This last investigation showed also that monochromatic light is merely deviated by a second prism—the amount of deviation depending on the particular colour—and no fresh colour is formed.

18.2 Producing a Pure Spectrum—the Spectroscope and Spectrometer

The optical instruments which we considered in the last chapter are usually referred to as image-forming instruments. Other optical instruments are referred to as analysing instruments, which are employed when we wish to investigate the intensity, the composition, or the state of polarisation of a given light beam. We now wish to consider the spectroscope as an instrument by means of which we may determine the composition of a given light beam in terms of the different colours (and hence wavelengths) present.

The triangular glass prism employed by Newton in his early experiments is in fact a simple spectroscope since it splits white light into its component colours. Its value is limited however because, after splitting, the coloured images of the light source merge with one another as a series of overlapping circular patches. The constituent colours are therefore not all in perfect focus, and we say that the spectrum produced is impure.

A purer spectrum may be produced using the apparatus of Fig. 18.4 in which a convex lens L_1 focusses light from a 6 V or 12 V electric lamp on to a narrow slit in a metal plate. A second convex lens L_2 then forms an image of the illuminated slit at I in the absence of a prism. When a triangular glass prism in then introduced in the path of the light leaving L_2, as shown, a spectrum is formed on the screen S. This spectrum is found to consist of a series of coloured images of the slit, each touching the other. The distinction between the different colours becomes more and more apparent as the slit width is reduced. This spectrum is purer than that originally achieved by Newton since its colours are all *approximately* in focus.

A purer spectrum still may be achieved by setting up the apparatus illustrated in Fig. 18.5, in which a narrow illuminated slit is again the object under observation. The lens system L_1 (corrected for the usual defects) is placed so that the slit coincides with its principal focus. This collimating system thus ensures that all rays of light in the beam leaving L_1 are parallel. These parallel rays then strike the triangular glass prism, and dispersion occurs—the different colours being refracted each by a different amount as they pass through the prism. Each colour thus emerges as a separate parallel beam travelling in its own direction. To an observer, these beams are apparently travelling from infinity, and so, by means of a second lens system L_2, the beams may be focussed on a screen. This system ensures that a sharp image of the slit is formed by each colour on the screen, and that the overlapping of colours is practically nil, provided one uses a very fine slit. With a wide slit, each coloured image will be wide, and overlapping will occur. For a 'pure' spectrum therefore, it is necessary to use an optical system of the type shown in Fig. 18.5 and as fine a slit as possible.

If instead of viewing the spectrum on a screen we examine it through a magnifying glass L_3 then the lens system formed by L_2 and L_3 acts as a simple telescope, since it receives parallel light from the prism. With L_2 and L_3 acting as a telescope, the complete apparatus is known as a *spectroscope*. When the spectroscope is equipped with an angular scale so that the angle between the axes of the collimating system and the telescope can be measured, the instrument is called a *spectrometer*. Its appearance and construction are as illustrated in Fig. 18.0 and Fig. 18.6 respectively.

As Fig. 18.6 shows, the collimating system, or collimator, is a light-tight tube with the slit and lens system L_1 contained at opposite ends. The lens L_2 and the eyepiece form the telescope arm, also a light-tight tube, and the telescope is normally adjusted to form a virtual image of the spectrum at infinity so that the observer may examine the spectrum with a relaxed eye. The collimator tube is usually fixed, and the prism platform and telescope may be rotated together, or separately, relative to this tube.

In using the spectrometer, the observer sees a number of images of the slit arranged side by side—each image formed by light of a particular wavelength. In the case of a white light

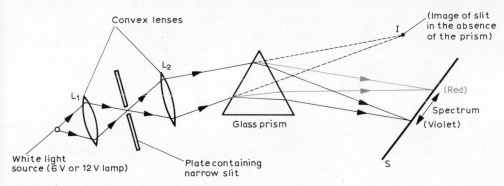

Fig.18.4   The production of a reasonably pure spectrum.

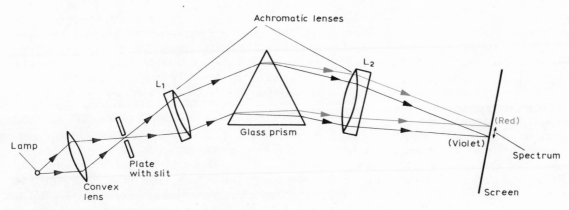

Fig.18.5   The production of a very pure spectrum.

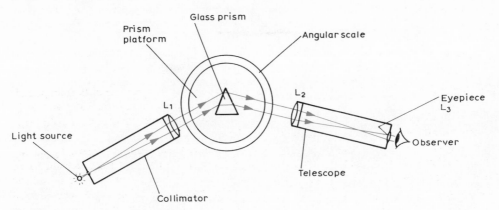

Fig.18.6   The construction of the spectrometer.

source, the spectrum produced is continuous and appears as a continuum of colour spreading from red, through yellow and green towards blue and violet. If however the light source emits only a few specific wavelengths, then the coloured images of the slit are quite distinct and separate so the observer sees a series of bright lines—one line for each wavelength emitted. Such a spectrum is referred to as a line spectrum.

The spectrometer arrangement of Fig. 18.6 is known correctly as a prism spectrometer. If we replace the prism by a diffraction grating, then the apparatus is known correctly as a grating spectrometer, its appearance being illustrated in Fig. 18.7. We recall from Chapter 15 that by means of a grating spectrometer it is possible to obtain a value for the wavelength corresponding to light of a particular colour by making simple angular measurements. In this respect the grating spectrometer offers an advantage over the prism spectrometer which can only be used for wavelength determinations after it has been calibrated—an exercise which requires prior knowledge of the wavelengths of particular colours of light. The spectrum produced by a prism is however brighter than that produced by a grating, although in the case of a line spectrum, the separation of lines achieved with the grating is greater than that achieved with the prism.

18.3 Types of Spectra
When an iron poker is gradually heated, it begins to emit light of a dull red colour at a temperature of about 550 °C. When the poker is heated further, light of shorter wavelengths is emitted too, and the colour of the poker changes gradually, until at about 1000 °C, it is white hot. At this temperature the poker is emitting light of all wavelengths and, placing it in front of the collimator slit of a spectrometer, we observe a *continuous spectrum* of colour (Fig. A)*, similar in nature to that which we have already discussed. A continuous spectrum may be produced by heating any suitable solid or liquid to a sufficiently high temperature so that it glows white. In an electric lamp which is emitting white light, the solid being heated is the tungsten of which the filament is made.

Light is emitted from a gas whenever it is excited, either by heating it to a high temperature (as would be the case in putting a volatile substance into a flame), or by an electric discharge (as in a yellow sodium street lamp, in which the gas is sodium vapour once the lamp has warmed up). The light emitted in such cases gives rise to a completely different type of spectrum.

* See the back cover.

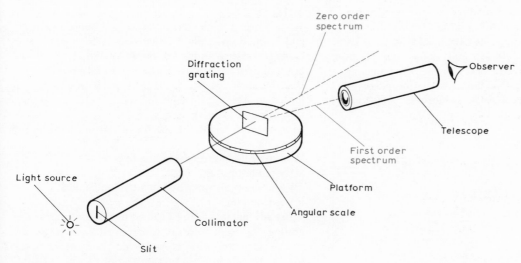

Fig.18.7 The grating spectrometer.

The light emitted by various excited gases was first investigated by the Scottish physicist Thomas Melvill, who examined the spectra of various gases (excited by heating) with the aid of a crude prism spectroscope. Melvill observed that these gaseous spectra were quite different from the continuous spectrum of a glowing solid in as much as they were composed of isolated coloured areas separated by dark gaps.

An accurate picture of a gaseous spectrum may be obtained by placing a gas discharge lamp in front of the collimator slit of a prism spectrometer as in Fig. 18.6. With the collimator slit sufficiently narrow, the spectrum of the excited gas is observed to be a set of narrow coloured lines. This spectrum is known as a *line emission spectrum* and the diagrams of Fig. B* show two of these. From these diagrams, it would seem that the light emitted by an excited gas is composed of only a few particular colours and hence a few wavelengths.

The diagrams of Fig. B* also show that the emission spectra of chemically different gases are quite different in appearance, and in fact each chemical element has its own set of coloured lines in its emission spectrum. For some gases the emission spectrum is very simple, helium, for instance, showing only six lines in the visible range. Other gases give rise to very complicated spectra, iron vapour, at the other extreme, producing about 6000 lines in the visible range.

In 1823 Herschel proposed that each chemically different gas could be identified from its characteristic line emission spectrum. This can be done with the same degree of certainty as that with which a person may be identified by his fingerprints. Herschel's proposal provided the basis of spectrum analysis—a powerful method of analysis in which the presence of particular elements in a compound may be revealed by a

* See the back cover.

careful study of the line emission spectrum of the compound. It was in the spectrum analysis of a mineral water vapour in 1860 that Bunsen and Kirchhoff discovered the elements rubidium and caesium.

When Newton examined the spectrum of the sun by passing sunlight through a prism, he reported the spectrum to be continuous in appearance. When Fraunhofer examined the sun's spectrum at a later date, using more sophisticated apparatus, he found that the sun's spectrum was crossed by a large number of dark lines. Fraunhofer counted over 500 of these lines which are now called the *Fraunhofer lines*.

Fraunhofer found that the positions of these dark lines in the sun's spectrum were the same as the positions of some of the bright lines in the spectra of certain excited gases. He found, for example, that the position of a dark line in the red portion of the sun's spectrum was exactly the same as that of the red line in the emission spectrum of excited hydrogen.

These dark lines in the sun's spectrum may be explained by assuming that the sun radiates energy in the same way as an electric lamp so that the light emitted should form a continuous spectrum. This light, once emitted, has to pass through the cooler outer layers of the solar atmosphere however, and in so doing some of it is absorbed by the gases present there. The sun's spectrum is thus not completely continuous, because gaps will occur for those wavelengths which have been absorbed by the different gases in the solar atmosphere. These gaps appear as dark lines crossing an otherwise continuous spectrum, and the resulting spectrum is known as a *line absorption spectrum*.

By studying the positions of the dark lines in the solar spectrum and comparing these positions with those of the bright lines emitted by known excited gases, we may deduce which gaseous elements are present in the solar atmosphere.

In such a study, Lockyer discovered a group of lines which formed a regular pattern but which belonged to no known line emission spectrum. He concluded that the solar atmosphere contained an element not known on earth, and called it Helium (Greek: *helios*, sun). Subsequently (in 1895) helium was found in the earth's atmosphere by Ramsey. Figure C* shows a helium absorption spectrum.

* See the back cover.

Problems

1 What is meant by the terms 'dispersion', 'pure spectrum', and 'impure spectrum'? Why does a triangular prism alone give rise to an impure continuous spectrum when a beam of light from a white light source falls on it?

2 Describe how you would set up spectrometer apparatus to demonstrate, (i) the emission spectrum (ii) the absorption spectrum, of sodium gas.

3 In what ways might the spectra of the sun and the full moon differ?

4 What type of spectrum is emitted by
 i) a red hot poker?
 ii) a sodium salt vaporised in a bunsen flame?
 iii) a neon lamp?

5 What advantages are to be gained by placing a diffraction grating on the platform of a spectrometer in place of a triangular prism. In what way is the quality of the resulting spectrum inferior to that formed by the prism?

Chapter 19

Radioactivity

Fig.19.0   The fast reactor at Dounreay, Caithness. (Copyright: United Kingdom Atomic Energy Authority.)

Prior to the eighteenth century, it was generally believed that all matter was composed of combinations of the four 'elements' *earth*, *water*, *air*, *and fire*. During the eighteenth century however, Lavoisier and others showed that certain substances such as iron and oxygen could not be broken down into simpler chemical components. Substances like these are true chemical elements. At the beginning of the nineteenth century, Dalton proposed that each chemical element was composed of individual atoms—all atoms of a particular element being of the same size and mass. According to Dalton, chemical compounds are formed by the atoms of different elements combining in certain proportions.

Each of these three contributions to science was concerned with providing an answer to the question, what is the basic material of which the universe is made? The search for this 'basic material' is still going on, and in the present day, it is hoped that the field of nuclear physics will provide the ultimate answer.

Nuclear physics is regarded as *modern* physics rather than *classical* physics in as much as it has developed (at an ever increasing rate) in the twentieth century. For physicists

however, the twentieth century began in the year 1895 when Rontgen discovered X-rays, followed by Becquerel's discovery of radioactivity in 1896. This latter discovery has proved to be of paramount importance, and the reader is advised to read an account of Becquerel's investigations (*The Foundations of Modern Physical Science*—G. Holton, D. Roller—Addison-Wesley Publishing Co.).

By studying some of the developments which followed Becquerel's investigations, we shall be able to appreciate the existence and significance of some of the tiny components of which atoms are themselves made. Such an appreciation naturally brings us closer to an understanding of the 'basic material' from which the universe is constructed.

It is now known that all naturally occurring elements with atomic numbers greater than 83 are radioactive (that is to say, these elements emit invisible penetrating radiations), although isotopes of certain elements whose atomic numbers are less than 83 have also been found to be radioactive. As well as the naturally occurring elements, certain artificial radioactive elements have now been produced. All of these radioactive elements, whether naturally occurring or artificially produced, are alike in as much as:

1 They decay in time and form the atoms of other elements—these elements being radioactive or non-radioactive depending on their atomic numbers.

2 The emissions from these elements can be physiologically harmful. The penetrating radiations can cause dissociation of organic molecules and thereby upset certain biological mechanisms.

3 Their radiations affect light sensitive photographic plates and this affords a means for the detection of these radiations. Although the plates are usually wrapped in thick black paper, the radiations usually have sufficient penetrating power to reach them.

4 Their radiations can also penetrate paper, glass, wood, and metal.

5 The radiations from these elements ionise the surrounding air. This ionisation is a dissociation of the surrounding air molecules, resulting in the generation of negative ions (electrons) and heavier positive ions. (This ionising effect may be easily demonstrated by holding a radioactive source (which emits 'alpha' radiation) within 2 cm of the cap of a charged electroscope. The electroscope is then observed to discharge at a much faster rate than it would in the absence of the source.)

It is this ionising property of radioactive elements which is used in the design of many important instruments for detecting and measuring the radiations.

19.1 Radioactivity Detectors

The radiations emitted by radioactive substances are far too small for direct observation, and so special instruments and techniques have had to be developed to 'observe' and measure these radiations. To 'observe' any quantity indirectly requires the observation of some reproducible and characteristic effect of that quantity. Towards the indirect observation and measurement of radioactive emissions, physicists have found it useful to consider the effects of

1 producing ionisation in certain substances

2 producing changes in photographic emulsions

3 producing scintillations or fluorescence in certain substances.

which are all due to these emissions. Here we discuss only the first of these effects as a basis for radioactivity detection.

In the next section we shall find that there are three completely different types of radioactive emission, and so it is often desirable that a detector should be available to detect one type of emission but not the other types. This aspect of detection we shall consider in the next section while concerning ourselves here with describing the principles of operation of several detectors.

1. The Expansion Cloud Chamber

The expansion cloud chamber is perhaps the most satisfying

radioactivity detector for the simple reason that it makes the paths of the ionising radiations directly visible.

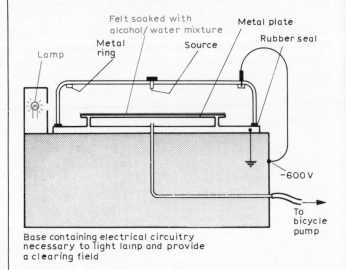

Fig.19.1   A school laboratory cloud chamber.

The original expansion cloud chamber was invented in 1911 by the British physicist C. T. R. Wilson, but a more up to date demonstration version is illustrated in Fig. 19.1. The chamber is essentially a perspex container filled with air saturated by the vapours of alcohol and water. When this vapour is expanded rapidly by means of the bicycle pump attachment, it is also cooled. In its cooled state, it will condense on any dust particles or gaseous ions present in the chamber. Assuming the space inside the perspex cover to be dust free, then when an ionising radiation passes through the vapour, it will leave behind it a trail of positive and negative vapour ions. Condensation takes place on these ions the liquid droplets forming a fine white trail easily visible as a result of light from the lamp being scattered from it. This trail does not of course show the actual ionising particle, but marks the path along which the particle has travelled. Similarly the vapour trail of a high flying aircraft doesn't show the aircraft itself but indicates the track taken by the aircraft.

In the cloud chamber shown, the source of radioactivity is placed at the centre of the perspex container and this source continually emits radiations. These radiations are only seen immediately after an expansion however, because condensation will not take place unless the vapour has been properly cooled. The vapour trail is swept away almost immediately after it is formed by the presence of an electrostatic 'clearing field'. Clearing is effected by maintaining a potential difference of several hundred volts between the metal ring at the top of the chamber and the metal base of the chamber. Depending on the nature of the ions formed in the chamber, they will then be attracted either to this ring or to the base. If a clearing field were not present 'fogging' would quickly occur within the chamber, making long rest periods essential to allow the liquid drops to settle under gravity.

2. The Bubble Chamber

The bubble chamber is another detector which forms a visible trail along the path of the radiation. While the cloud chamber operates by the presence of a supercooled vapour, the bubble chamber uses instead a superheated liquid. This device was invented in 1952 by the American physicist Donald Glaser, and is now in much wider use than the cloud chamber.

The principle of operation of the bubble chamber may be understood to some extent by considering the carbon dioxide contained in a bottle of lemonade. Before opening the bottle, the CO_2 above the lemonade is in equilibrium with that dissolved in the lemonade. When the cap is removed, unstable conditions result from the release of the CO_2 above the lemonade and so bubbling results within the lemonade. When the lemonade is poured into a glass, a stream of CO_2 bubbles may be seen to rise from any small irregularity inside the glass. Such an irregularity acts as a nucleus round which bubbles generate.

In a bubble chamber, a liquid such as liquid hydrogen is maintained at a temperature well above its normal boiling point, but the liquid is maintained under high pressure and is thereby prevented from boiling. If this pressure is reduced, the chamber is then in a state of unstable equilibrium and local boiling (or bubbling) will be produced around any small irregularity in the chamber. These chambers are usually constructed of smooth clean glass so that no boiling occurs around the walls. If an ionising radiation enters the chamber however, the ions produced act as bubble nuclei, and so a continuous trail of bubbles may be observed along the path of the radiation. Bubble tracks (Fig. 19.2) are visible for only a few milliseconds before general boiling is produced within the liquid.

Since liquid hydrogen has a greater density than alcohol/water vapour, the bubble chamber has a higher stopping power than the cloud chamber and so may be used in preference to the cloud chamber for the detection of more energetic radiations.

3. The Spark Discharge Detector

The spark discharge detector provides another visual indication that a radioactive emission is present—in this case by the passage of an electric spark. The development of a spark between two electrodes (between which a high potential difference is maintained) may be understood as a sort of 'chain reaction' which begins when an electron from an ionised atom is accelerated in the strong electric field between the electrodes. As it accelerates, it collides with other atoms and ionises them. Electrons produced from these atoms are

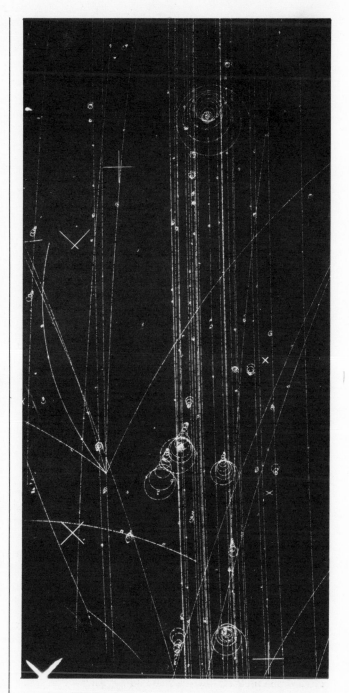

Fig.19.2 This photograph shows a liquid hydrogen bubble chamber immediately after high energy particles have passed through it. Near the bottom of the picture is an 'event' where an incident particle has struck and split a proton, resulting in the production of several particles with positive and negative charges. (By kind permission of Professor I. Hughes, University of Glasgow.)

accelerated in turn and themselves cause further ionisation. In a very short time an impressive spark is seen.

The photograph of Fig. 19.3 shows a simple demonstration spark discharge detector, and the diagram of Fig. 19.4 shows its experimental arrangement for the observation of sparks as in Fig. 19.5. One terminal (to which the wire gauze is connected) is connected to the negative terminal of a variable E.H.T. supply, and the other terminal (to which a fine wire—stretched below the gauze—is connected) is joined to the positive E.H.T. terminal. The output voltage of the E.H.T. unit is then adjusted to be *just below* the point where sparking occurs as a result of ionisation of the air by the strong electric field between the electrodes. When certain radioactive sources are then held close to and above the wire gauze, random sparking occurs, thereby detecting the presence of ionising radiations.

Fig.19.3   The demonstration spark discharge detector. (By kind permission of Philip Harris Ltd.)

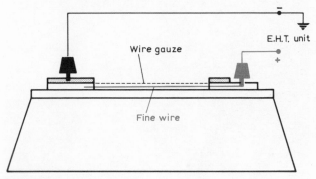

Fig.19.4

4. The Ionisation Chamber and d.c. Amplifier

The ionisation chamber differs from each of the last three detectors in as much as it provides an electrical technique (as opposed to a visual technique), for the detection of radioactive emissions. In its simplest form, the ionisation chamber is a metal can with a wire gauze lid. Immediately below and within a few millimetres of the wire gauze, there is fixed a small brass disc supported on a metal rod lying

Fig.19.5   Sparks may be produced when a radioactive source is brought up close to the detector.

along the central axis of the can. This rod (and hence the disc) is insulated from the can itself. The can is connected to the positive terminal of a small battery and the disc to the negative terminal, so that if the air inside the can is ionised—by say the passage of some ionising particles—electrons will flow towards the can and positive ions towards the disc. That is an ionisation current is generated.

In attempting to measure this current however, we find that an extremely sensitive current meter is required—the current is a tiny tiny fraction of a microamp when a strong radioactive source (strong by school laboratory standards) is responsible for the ionisation. Clearly, some means of current amplification is required if the ionisation chamber is to be of any great use in radioactivity detection.

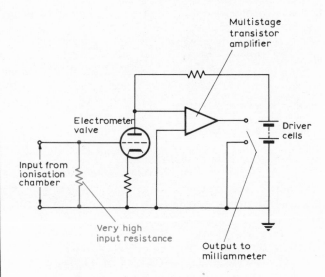

Fig.19.6   The d.c. amplifier used in conjunction with the ionisation chamber.

Towards this end, a d.c. amplifier is used in conjunction with the ionisation chamber, the gain of this amplifier being sufficiently high that the output may drive a milliammeter. The design of such an amplifier is illustrated in the diagram of Fig. 19.6.

The very small ionisation current flows through the very high input resistance of the amplifier (usually $10^{11}\Omega$) and the potential difference across this resistance thus appears between the grid and cathode of the electrometer valve. The valve amplifies this potential difference and passes it to the multistage transistor amplifier where further amplification takes place.

For an input current of 10^{-11} A (corresponding to an input potential difference of 1 V) the amplifier output will register as 1 mA—on a milliammeter. This is much more satisfactory.

The ionisation chamber and a d.c. amplifier assembly is shown in Fig. 19.7. The current registered on the milliammeter gives an indication of the average amount of ionisation taking place within the chamber per unit time.

5. The Geiger-Muller (G.M.) Tube and Scalar

The principle of the ionisation chamber is used again in the Geiger-Muller tube so that this latter instrument also provides an electrical technique for radioactivity detection.

In the G.M. tube, a hollow metalised glass cylinder acts as the negative electrode, and a very fine tungsten wire along the central axis of the cylinder acts as the positive electrode.

Between these two is contained an inert gas (usually neon) at a low pressure of the order of 13 500 N m^{-2}. (We recall from Chapter 7 that normal atmospheric pressure has the value 101 400 N m^{-2}.) One end of the tube is fitted with a thin sheet of mica, and this end acts as a window through which radiation enters the tube.

The central wire (or anode) is maintained as a potential of about 400 V positive with respect to the earthed metalised cylinder (or cathode), and a uniform axial electric field is thus set up within the tube. When an ionising radiation enters by the window, a neon atom is ionised and the electron produced is accelerated towards the anode. As this electron gains more and more energy, it causes further ionisation in colliding with other neon atoms. An electron avalanche is finally produced and when it reaches the anode, a current pulse is generated which flows through the circuit shown in Fig. 19.8, so that a potential difference is developed across the large resistor R. This potential difference may then be amplified so as to activate an electronic counting device called a scalar.

The magnitude of the electron avalanche increases drastically as the accelerating electrons move closer and closer to the fine wire. The heavy positive ions produced in ionisation move slowly outward from the region of the thin wire towards the cathode—reaching it a considerable time (100 ms) after the electron pulse has reached the anode. If these positive ions were allowed to reach the cathode, they would

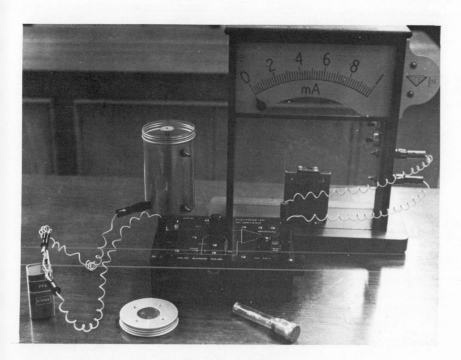

Fig.19.7　The ionisation chamber and d.c. amplifier.

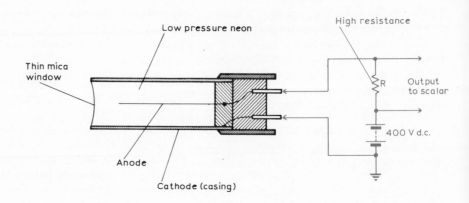

Thin mica window — Low pressure neon — High resistance — R — Output to scalar — Anode — Cathode (casing) — 400 V d.c.

Fig.19.8 The construction of the G.M. tube, and its associated circuitry.

eject secondary electrons from it, and the avalanching effect would begin all over again. To avoid this happening, a small amount of chlorine gas is introduced to the tube as a *quenching agent*. The accelerating positive ions tend to decompose the chlorine molecules and thereby give up their energy. The decomposed molecules then recombine and are thus available for further quenching in the next cycle of events. The sluggish action of the positive ions in reaching the cathode results in the G.M. tube having a certain *dead time* of about 200 μs, during which ionising particles entering the tube will not be registered individually. This implies that a G.M. tube will not provide sensible recognition of radioactive emissions which arrive with a frequency greater than 5000 per second. This shortcoming is of little significance in the school laboratory where most of the radioactive sources met are effectively 'weak'.

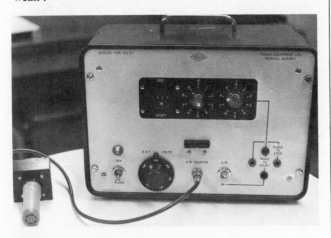

Fig.19.9 The G.M. tube and electronic scalar.

The voltage pulses developed across the resistor R in Fig. 19.8 are usually fed to the input circuit of the electronic counting unit called a scalar (of which R forms an integral part). The scalar provides us with an exact recording of the total number of pulses which have been received from the G.M. tube and counted. In most school laboratories the scalar contains two 'dekatron' tubes—one for counting 'units', the other for counting 'tens'—and a mechanical register which counts 'hundreds'. (The scalar may also be used as a very sensitive timing device.)

A G.M. tube and electronic scalar are shown together in Fig. 19.9. Figure 19.10 shows a more up to date form of scalar than that shown in Fig. 19.9.

Fig.19.10 A very recent electronic scalar. (By kind permission of Panax Ltd.)

19.2 The Three Radiations

The penetrating radiations from radioactive substances were originally thought to be similar in nature to X-rays. In 1897 however, Rutherford succeeded in showing that the radiations were of more than one kind, in as much as some were more penetrating than others. He called the more penetrating radiations *beta* (β) rays, and the less penetrating ones *alpha* (α) rays. Two years later, it was shown that β rays were deflected in a magnetic field in the same sense as cathode rays (or electrons). Further, the ratio of change to mass for β rays (or particles) was found to be exactly the same as that for cathode rays. Beta rays (or particles) *are in fact electrons*.

In 1900, Villard succeeded in showing that a third and much more penetrating radiation was emitted by certain radioactive substances. These radiations were named *gamma* (γ) rays.

We can verify the existence of the three different types of radiation in the following simple investigations.

1. An Americium (atomic mass 241) source is held close to the window of a Geiger-Muller tube (connected to a scalar), and the radiation count noted for one minute. When a thin sheet of paper is then introduced between source and G.M. tube, and the radiation count noted for another minute, this second count is found to be significantly different from the first (as the following table shows). It would seem that Americium (241) emits a weakly penetrating radiation (in fact *alpha*).

absorber between source and G.M. tube	radiation count per minute
none	1495
thin paper	74

2. A strontium (atomic mass 90) source is held close to the window of the G.M. tube (connected to a scalar) and the radiation count noted for one minute. When a thin sheet of paper is then introduced between source and G.M. tube, and the radiation count noted for another minute, this second count is not found to be significantly different from the first. When the thin sheet of paper is replaced by a thin sheet of aluminium and a further minute's count taken however, this third count is found to be significantly different from the first (as the following table shows). It would seem that Strontium (90) emits a more strongly penetrating radiation (in fact *beta*)

absorber between source and G.M. tube	radiation count per minute
none	6221
thin paper	5990
thin aluminium	309

3. A Cobalt (atomic mass 60) source is held close to the window of the G.M. tube (connected to a scalar) and the radiation count noted for one minute. When a thin sheet of paper is then introduced between source and G.M. tube, and the radiation count noted for another minute, this second count is not found to be significantly different from the first. Neither is a third count taken when the paper is replaced by a thin sheet of aluminium. When the aluminium is removed and a thin block of lead put in its place, the radiation count noted for one minute is found to be significantly different from the first (as the following table shows). It would seem that Cobalt (60) emits a very strongly penetrating radiation (in fact *gamma*).

absorber between source and G.M. tube	radiation count per minute
none	6247
thin paper	6201
thin aluminium	5997
thin lead	2214

The radioactive sources employed in these investigations are usually sealed or 'closed' sources. The radioactive material itself is wrapped in very thin metal foil and contained in a small metal holder equipped with a 4 mm stem. A small piece of wire gauze at the front of the holder protects the foil inside from damage. Figure 19.11 shows a laboratory source and its container.

Fig.19.11 (By kind permission of Griffin & George Ltd.)

Alpha rays (or particles) are in fact helium nuclei (composed of two protons and two neutrons) as Rutherford and Royds showed when they collected a large quantity of alphas in a tube and passed an electric discharge through the tube—the resulting spectrum was the same as that for helium. Alpha particles—which carry two positive charges—are 'slow' moving, (having speeds of the order of $\frac{1}{10}$th of the speed of light) fairly massive, and deflected only slightly in a magnetic field. Although their power of penetration is low, they cause heavy ionisation in gases, and are thus detectable by each of the five detectors we have discussed.

The range of alpha particles in air may be deduced to be of the order of 5 cm by lowering an Americium (241) source vertically downwards and towards the gauze in the lid of an ionisation chamber (connected to a d.c. amplifier and milli-ammeter). When the source is brought to within 5 cm of the gauze, the milliammeter suddenly registers, thereby detecting the presence of alphas.

Beta rays or particles are, as we have said, electrons or cathode rays. Each carries one negative charge and moves at high speed (of the order of $\frac{4}{5}$th of the speed of light). The mass of each beta is very much less than that of an alpha, and so the betas are much more easily deflected by a magnetic field. (Will the sense of deflection be the same for alphas and betas in a given magnetic field?) The high speed (along with having only one electric charge) accounts for the greater penetrating power which is observed with betas. The beta produces much less ionisation in gases than does the alpha, and although the beta may be detected by each of the gold leaf electroscope, the cloud chamber, the ionisation chamber (with d.c. amplifier), and the G.M. tube (with scalar), its detection by means of the spark discharge detector is impossible.

The behaviour of beta radiation in a magnetic field is found to conform to the 'right hand motor rule', (which we discussed in Chapter 10) thereby suggesting that betas carry negative charge. This behaviour is demonstrated in the following investigation.

The diagram of Fig. 19.12 shows a G.M. tube, brass collimating plate, and collimated beta source, all in alignment along a common central axis. This apparatus has been selected from the kit shown in Fig. 19.13. The slits in the brass plate and beta source are parallel. In this arrangement, the betas travel in straight line paths (determined by the collimated source), pass through the slit in the brass plate, and enter the G.M. tube for detection. A radiation count is noted on the scalar for say one minute.

When two magnets (separated by a spacer) are introduced to the apparatus, as indicated by the dotted lines in Fig. 19.12,

so that a vertical magnetic field is set up, then, depending on the proximity of the magnets to the central axis, subsequent scalar count rates may be significantly different from the first.

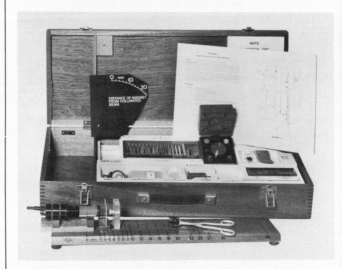

Fig.19.13 A radioactivity kit. (By kind permission of Panax Ltd.)

As the magnets are gradually brought closer to the central axis of the apparatus, (that is, towards us in Fig. 19.12) starting from a distance of say 3 cm from this axis, scalar count rates are gradually reduced, until, when the magnets are in the central position, the count rate is almost negligible. By keeping the magnets in this central position, and gradually moving the brass plate 'away' from us (in Fig. 19.12), the count rate is found to rise gradually, until after a displacement of several millimetres, it almost reaches its original value (as in the absence of the magnetic field).

This investigation shows that the deflection of beta radiation in a magnetic field is perpendicular to the magnetic field, and also perpendicular to the direction of the beta beam. These relationships are consistent with the 'right hand motor rule' (as the reader should have checked), and so we may conclude that the beta particles behave like an electric current (moving electrons).

Gamma rays are short bursts of electromagnetic radiation—the same kind of radiation as visible light—travelling at the same speed as light, but having much shorter wavelengths, and hence higher frequencies. While visible light is produced by transitions in atomic electron energy levels, gamma rays are produced by transitions in nuclear energy levels. These rays are uncharged and are thus undeflected on passing through a magnetic field. Because of their high speeds and lack of electric charge, they have little interaction with matter through which they might pass—hence their high penetrating

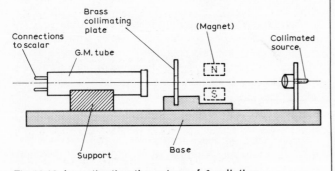

Fig.19.12 Investigating the nature of β radiation.

power. Because of their limited interaction with matter, the gammas are more difficult to detect than either alphas or betas. Gamma rays are most readily detected by a G.M. tube with scalar although under certain circumstances one can see that a gamma ray has passed through a cloud chamber by reason of the faint tracks of β particles which the γ ray has ejected from the atoms of the vapour in passing through the chamber. In a similar way, a γ ray may ionise silver particles in a photographic film which may subsequently be developed to show the path which the ray followed.

The absorption of gamma rays by matter is said to be *exponential*, and a graph of gamma count rate against the thickness of a lead absorber indicates what is meant by this statement. Such a graph has been plotted in Fig. 19.14. In the plotting of this graph, account has been taken of 'background' radiation—that radiation due to cosmic particles, and local sources other than that being used in the experiment, which gives rise to a count rate in the absence of the gamma source. Before plotting the gamma count rate, a background count rate was subtracted from the actual count rate on the scalar.

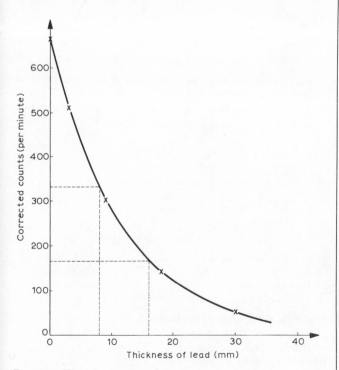

Fig.19.14 The absorption of γ radiation by lead.

A study of Fig. 19.14 reveals that with an absorber thickness of 8 mm, the original count rate is reduced by one half. Further, with an absorber thickness of 16 mm, the count rate is reduced by half again. That is, placing 8 mm of lead in front of a gamma source reduces the intensity of the gamma

beam by one half. For this reason, 8 mm of lead is referred to as the *half value thickness of lead* for gamma absorption. If it is decided that for a given gamma source more than $12\frac{1}{2}\%$ of its radiation would be biologically harmful, then it would be necessary to surround this source by lead 24 mm thick. This is because 8 mm of lead reduces the radiation intensity to 50%, a further 8 mm reduces the intensity to 25%, and a final 8 mm reduces the intensity to $12\frac{1}{2}\%$. That is, three 'half-thicknesses' of lead are required.

19.3 Radioactive Decay

When matter undergoes a *physical* change, no change occurs in the composition of the material substance, and the process is completely reversible. When a *chemical* change occurs in matter however, the atoms or molecules of the original material substance are re-arranged, and a new substance with different chemical properties is formed.

A third type of change may also occur in matter when the atoms themselves change their identity by their nuclei ejecting particles. This change is referred to as a *nuclear* change, and it occurs when a radioactive substance emits alpha or beta radiation. When a radioactive atom *decays* by emitting say an α, a new atom with different properties is formed. This new atom might itself be radioactive or completely stable. The original atom is referred to as the *parent*, and the final atom as the *daughter*.

Rutherford and Soddy first proposed that the atoms of radioactive elements are unstable, and that in the radioactive process, these atoms disintegrate or decay to form completely different atoms. Depending on the particular parent atom, many changes may occur (through a succession of daughter products), until a stable end-product is reached. This proposal was put forward in 1903 and received widespread criticism, because at that time the atom was regarded as permanent and indivisible. The proposal eventually gained acceptance however, in view of its power to explain experimental results which had been collected in the study of radioactivity.

Rutherford and Soddy proposed further that the nature of the daughter product could be deduced from a consideration of the nature of each of the parent atom and the particle emitted during disintegration. This deduction would involve obeying two *conservation rules* which, (anticipating the concept of the nuclear atom), could be stated in modern terms thus:

1 The mass number of the parent atom (that is, the number of nucleons—protons and neutrons—in its nucleus) must equal the sum of mass numbers of the daughter atom and the particle emitted.
2 The total electric charge of the parent nucleus must equal the algebraic sum of charges of the daughter nucleus and particle emitted.

Accepting these two rules we can describe nuclear changes conveniently in terms of nuclear equations—just as we describe chemical changes by chemical equations. In writing a nuclear equation, it is common practice to ascribe to each nucleus or particle (i) a symbol which is usually the same as the chemical symbol for the atom of which the nucleus forms a part (ii) a superscript to denote the atomic mass number represented, and (iii) a subscript to denote the atomic number (the number of protons and hence positive charges contained in the nucleus) represented. A nitrogen nucleus would thus be written as N_7^{14}. An alpha particle would be written He_2^4 (or sometimes α_2^4).

The nuclear change in which uranium (atomic mass 238) changes to thorium (atomic mass 234) by emitting an α is described by the equation

$$U_{92}^{238} \rightarrow Th_{90}^{234} + He_2^4$$

We note that this equation is unlike a chemical equation in as much as the same atoms do not appear on both sides of the equation. Instead, the total number of nucleons remains constant (in keeping with rule 1) and so too does the algebraic sum of electric charge (in keeping with rule 2).

Thorium (atomic mass 234) is itself unstable, and decays by beta emission. This nuclear change may be described by the following equation, in which the Rutherford and Soddy rules are again strictly obeyed.

$$Th_{90}^{234} \rightarrow Pa_{91}^{234} + e_{-1}^0$$

(The term e_{-1}^0 in this equation is used to denote a beta particle or electron. Why?)

The daughter product here (Protactinium) is also unstable and decays to form an isotope of uranium. (An *isotope* of an element is an atom which contains the same number of protons as the more abundant type of atom but a different number of neutrons. Isotopes have the same chemical properties as the more abundant type of atom, but they have different masses.) The uranium isotope is also unstable and decays to form an isotope of thorium. In fact a whole series of disintegrations occur following the decay of a uranium (238) nucleus, and this *disintegration series* is represented in Fig. 19.15.

As this disintegration series shows, fourteen separate transmutations occur before a stable atom is reached (lead 206). The disintegration of any given nucleus is a spontaneous event, and we cannot say with certainty that the given nucleus will decay at a particular time or even within a particular time limit. We can however calculate a statistical probability that a given nucleus X will decay in a particular time—this calculation being based on observation of the number of disintegrations which occur in a large population of nuclei of type X over a certain period of time. That is, because radioactive disintegrations are random in their occurrence, this occurrence can only be forecast statistically.

Experiments have shown that all radioactive substances

decay *exponentially* with time. (Recall that the penetration of γ-rays through lead was reduced exponentially with lead thickness.) If we are given a sample of pure radium (atomic mass 226) then after 1620 years, it will show only half of its original activity. This is not to say that half of the material has disappeared. Instead, half of the radioactive atoms have decayed into simpler atoms while the total mass of material remains almost constant. After a further 1620 years, the sample will show only a quarter of its original activity. After a further 1620 years, only an eighth of the original activity, and so on. The period 1620 years is known as the *half-life* of radium for the simple reason that the activity of any radium sample will be reduced by a factor of one half in that time.

The half-lives of different radioactive substances vary enormously: in the disintegration series shown, uranium (238) has a half-life of 4.5×10^9 years while polonium (214) has a half-life of 1.6×10^{-7} seconds. The half-life of a radioactive substance is inversely related to the energy released in each transmutation. That is, the shorter the half-life of an element, the greater is the kinetic energy with which the disintegration particle is emitted.

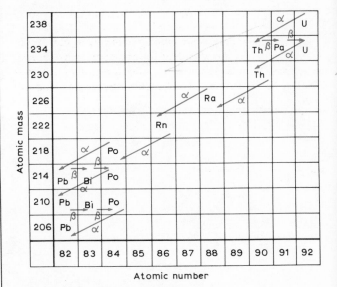

Fig.19.15 A disintegration series.

The fact that any radioactive substance decays exponentially with time may be deduced mathematically, on the assumption that the process is random, by making use of the theory of probability.

It is convenient to define the *decay constant* (λ) of a disintegration process as the probability that one specified nucleus will decay per unit time. Let us suppose that at time t, we have N radioactive nuclei remaining in a given sample. In the next dt seconds, the number of nuclei which will decay may be written as dN where

$$dN = -\lambda N \, dt$$

(the negative sign is necessary here since N decreases as t increases.) Hence

$$\frac{dN}{N} = -\lambda \, dt$$

Integrating both sides of this equation we may write:

$$\log_e N = -\lambda t + \text{constant}$$

If the number of radioactive atoms is N_0 at $t = 0$, then

$$\log_e N_0 = -\lambda \times 0 + \text{constant}$$

Hence the constant of integration equals $\log_e N_0$. Thus

$$\log_e N = -\lambda t + \log_e N_0$$

$$\Leftrightarrow \log_e \frac{N}{N_0} = -\lambda t$$

$$\Leftrightarrow \frac{N}{N_0} = e^{-\lambda t}$$

$$\Leftrightarrow \boxed{N = N_0 e^{-\lambda t}} \quad \ldots\ldots\ldots\ldots \quad (19.1)$$

This last equation is represented graphically in Fig. 19.16.

The relationship between half-life and decay constant may be deduced from Equation 19.1. After a period of one half-life (τ say), the number of radioactive nuclei remaining will be $\frac{N_0}{2}$. Substituting these values in equation (19.1):

$$\frac{N_0}{2} = N_0 e^{-\lambda \tau} \qquad (\text{at} \quad t = \tau)$$

Hence

$$e^{\lambda \tau} = 2$$

$$\Leftrightarrow \lambda \tau = \log_e 2$$

$$\Leftrightarrow \lambda = \frac{\log_e 2}{\tau}$$

$$\Leftrightarrow \boxed{\lambda = \frac{0 \cdot 693}{\tau}} \quad \ldots\ldots\ldots\ldots \quad (19.2)$$

The half-life of a radioactive substance may be found experimentally in the laboratory provided that the half-life is short—say of the order of minutes. Towards this end, it is convenient to measure the half-life of radon gas (atomic mass 220)—an alpha emitting gas which is produced by the decay of thorium.

The apparatus illustrated in Fig. 19.17 is set up as shown, with the gas cell as close to, and the radon generator as far from the G.M. tube as possible. With the clip closed on the rubber tube, a count of laboratory background radiation is taken over a period of one minute. This done, the clip is opened, the radon generator squeezed several times to fill the gas cell, and the clip is then closed.

Radiation counts from the cell are then recorded on the scalar in 10 second periods at half-minute intervals. These

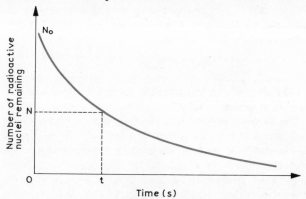

Fig.19.16 The nature of radioactive decay in relation to time.

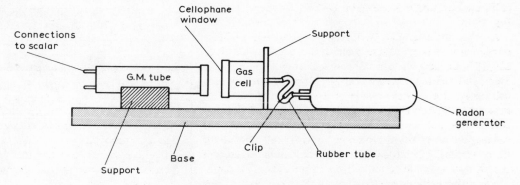

Fig.19.17 Determining the half-life of radon gas in the laboratory.

intervals allow for recording and resetting the scalar. The corrected count rate—that is, the actual count rate minus the background count estimated over a 10 second period—is plotted on a graph against time, and from the graph the half life of radon gas may be deduced.

The following table illustrates typical experimental results, which are plotted in Fig. 19.18.

Background
count = 24 per min.
(= 4 per 10 s)

Time (s)	G.M. counts	Corrected counts
0–10	188	184
30–40	128	124
60–70	95	91
90–100	57	53
120–130	48	44
150–160	33	29
180–190	23	19
210–220	17	13
240–250	22	18
270–280	19	15
300–310	19	15
330–340	14	10

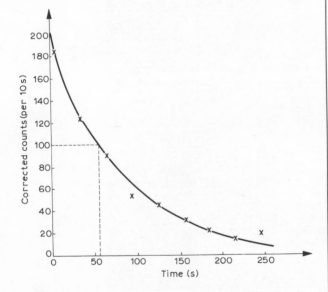

Fig.19.18 Experimental results for the half-life determination.

From the graph in Fig. 19.18, the half-life of radon gas would seem to be 55 s. (The half-life is actually 52 s.)

The reader will find an interesting half-life analogue experiment among the problems at the end of the chapter.

19.4 Artificial Transmutations

Having found that in radioactive decay, an atom of one element changes into an atom of another element, physicists were led to ask the obvious question—Is it possible to change one element into another artificially?—say by adding protons to the nucleus of an atom of that element. In 1919, Rutherford put this question to the experimental test by setting up apparatus similar to that shown in Fig. 19.19.

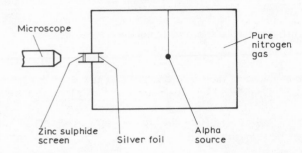

Fig.19.19 The apparatus used in the first artificial transmutation.

Rutherford had proposed that it might be possible to change nitrogen into another element by bombarding its nuclei with alpha particles—the hope being that these alphas would be captured by the nitrogen nuclei. In his apparatus, alpha particles not stopped by nitrogen atoms were stopped by a silver foil so that they would not produce scintillations in the zinc sulphide screen. Any scintillation observed on this screen would therefore be due to the production of high energy particles following the interaction of alphas and nitrogen nuclei. Rutherford observed scintillations on the screen and concluded that some interaction must have taken place. Indeed it had. Imagine his delight when he detected traces of oxygen in the container at the end of his observations!

The first observed artificial transmutations had taken place, and Rutherford described them by the equation

$$N_7^{14} + He_2^4 \rightarrow O_8^{17} + H_1^1$$

The alpha bombardment of nitrogen had resulted in the production of protons (H_1^1) which were responsible for the scintillations observed on the zinc sulphide screen.

In 1932, Cockroft and Walton (using the first particle accelerator) accelerated protons to a high speed and used them to bombard a lithium target. This experiment resulted in the production of alpha particles. At this time it was known that alpha bombardment often resulted in the production of protons, as in Rutherford's experiment above, but in the Cockcroft and Walton experiment the reverse effect was observed for the first time. Cockcroft and Walton concluded that the reaction which had taken place could be described by the equation

$$Li_3^7 + H_1^1 (\rightarrow Be_4^8) \rightarrow He_2^4 + He_2^4$$

Also in 1932, Chadwick bombarded a beryllium target with alpha particles and discovered the neutron. The neutron was detected as a particle with high penetrating power which had the ability to eject protons from a block of paraffin wax. In Chadwick's experiment, neutrons were produced according to the equation

$$Be_4^9 + He_2^4 \rightarrow C_6^{12} + n_0^1$$

where the term n_0^1 represents the neutron.

Being an electrically neutral particle, the neutron interacts with matter to a far less extent than the proton, and thus has a higher penetrating power. Further, a neutron may penetrate an atomic nucleus with far greater ease than any other charged sub-atomic missile. When charged particles are to be employed as missiles, physicists are faced with the problem of accelerating these missiles to sufficiently high speeds for penetration to occur (Fig. 19.20). When neutrons are to be employed however, the problem of making the neutron move sufficiently slowly (so that a transmutation might occur) arises.

When a slow moving neutron is captured by a uranium nucleus (atomic mass 238), an unstable isotope of uranium is produced. This transmutation is described by the equation

$$U_{92}^{238} + n_0^1 \rightarrow U_{92}^{239}$$

This isotope subsequently decays by beta emission, thus:

$$U_{92}^{239} \rightarrow Np_{93}^{239} + e_{-1}^0$$

The decay product (neptunium) is itself unstable and decays by beta emission to form plutonium:

$$Np_{93}^{239} \rightarrow Pu_{94}^{239} + e_{-1}^0$$

The bombardment of uranium (238) with slow neutrons results therefore in the creation of certain *transuranium* elements—elements with atomic numbers greater than 92. All of these elements are radioactive, and most have very short half-lives.

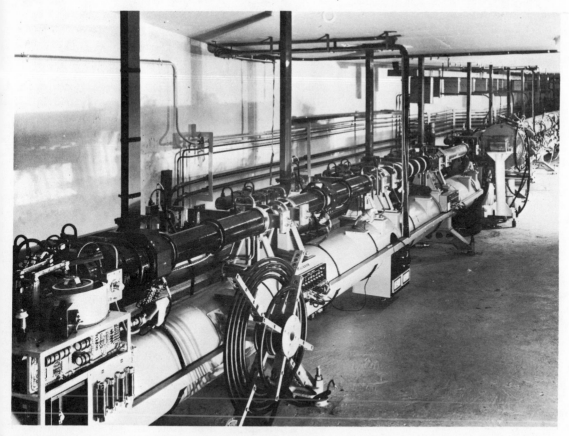

Fig.19.20 An electron accelerator. In this complicated piece of apparatus, electrons are accelerated from the gun (on the left) by a travelling wave, to an energy of 100 Mev. This accelerator ('linac') is about 50 m long, and situated in an underground tunnel with a few metres of concrete above. (Kelvin Laboratory, University of Glasgow.)

In any mass of pure uranium, the isotope of atomic mass 235 accounts for about 0·7% of the sample. When a nucleus of atomic mass 235 is bombarded with a slow neutron, a most fascinating transmutation takes place in which (i) three neutrons are produced (ii) two fairly massive nuclear segments appear in place of the original uranium nucleus, and (iii) a large amount of energy is released. This transmutation is described by the equation

$$U_{92}^{235} + n_0^1 \rightarrow Ba_{56}^{138} + Kr_{36}^{95} + 3n_0^1 + energy$$

This process whereby a heavy nucleus (uranium) splits into two nuclei of intermediate mass is known as *nuclear fission*—the name 'fission' having been adopted from biology, where it refers to cell division.

The total amount of energy released in the fission reaction discussed, can be realised when we consider that if a kilogram mole of uranium (235)—235 kg—were subjected to nuclear fission, then $1·9 \times 10^{16}$ joules would be released. To produce this amount of energy by the combustion of coal would require a mass of the order of four hundred million tons of coal!

If the three neutrons released in a fission process are allowed to produce further fissions, then nine neutrons will become available. If each of these produces fission, then twenty-seven neutrons will become available, and so on. If this process is allowed to continue unchecked, *an increasing chain reaction* results, and in a very short time billions of atoms will have undergone fission. An increasing chain reaction is only possible however if the sample of uranium (235) is sufficiently large. In a very small piece of uranium many neutrons escape. Clearly, the increasing chain reaction is only possible if the number of neutrons released by fission (per second) is greater than the number escaping through the surface of the uranium (per second). A certain *critical size* or *critical mass* of uranium is therefore required if only a small number of neutrons are to escape without striking a nucleus.

In the atomic bomb (which, when exploded in Hiroshima in 1945, brought the second world war to an abrupt end), an uncontrolled chain reaction was effected by exploding two blocks of uranium 235 (each smaller than the critical size) into each other, so that the composite block was larger than the critical size. The chain reaction might be triggered by any atmospheric neutron (of which there are a great number) entering the composite block, or by any free neutron within the uranium.

Not all chain reactions need be of an increasing or un-controlled nature however, and a *steady chain reaction* provides us with a means of generating useful power.

In a nuclear power station, a nuclear reactor provides the heat necessary to produce steam, whereas in a coal fired station, coal is required for this purpose. The nuclear reactor is a device which makes use of energy released in fission for the generation of power, but which also provides a means of producing new radioactive substances and a supply of neutrons for experimental investigations.

The first reactor (called the *atomic pile*) was constructed in 1942. It was built from bricks of uranium contained between bricks of graphite. At certain places in the pile, cadmium rods were inserted. A neutron from an external neutron source started the pile operating by causing fission in a uranium 235 nucleus. The three neutrons produced in fission were slowed down by the graphite *moderator* (after many collisions with carbon atoms) so that they could either cause further fission (if they collided with uranium 235 nuclei), or be absorbed by uranium 238 nuclei—thereby producing plutonium (neptunium has a very short half-life). Because of the large amounts of uranium 238 and the presence of the cadmium rods (which are excellent neutron absorbers) it was found that the atomic pile never ran out of control, and a steady release of energy resulted. The plutonium could be extracted from the system by withdrawing the uranium bricks and effecting a simple chemical separation.

A reactor of this type is known as a *thermal* reactor (since it operates by neutrons having thermal speeds). In the modern *fast breeder* reactor however, a core of uranium 235 is surrounded by a blanket of uranium 238. This blanket is steadily converted to plutonium by neutrons ejected from the core fission processes. Plutonium is itself fissionable so that while uranium 235 fuel is being consumed, new fissionable material is being created—usually at a higher rate than the uranium 235 is being consumed.

Fig.19.21 Neutron beam work at Harwell. (Copyright: United Kingdom Atomic Energy Authority.)

In July 1963, the Fast Reactor at Dounreay attained its full power of 60 MW, and since then, it has been used as an irradiation test facility for future fast reactors, although it is generating 15 MW of electricity, some of which is fed to the grid. The core can accommodate 324 fuel elements, and the blanket 1872 breeder elements of natural uranium. The driver charge of fuel consists of enriched uranium in the form of hollow rods, canned in niobium. Surplus neutrons from the fission chain reaction in the core are captured in the breeder blanket, and produce plutonium which will ultimately be used as fuel in this type of reactor.

The heat produced in the core is removed by liquid sodium-potassium alloy, and transferred to a secondary liquid metal circuit in the primary heat exchangers. These heat exchangers and the reactor are enclosed in a concrete vault within the 45 m diameter steel sphere shown in Fig. 19.0.

The Materials Physics Division at Harwell uses the reactor PLUTO for neutron diffraction and scattering applications in addition to its use for reactor materials testing. Figures 19.21 and 19.22 show the specialised apparatus which has been developed for this work. Such apparatus is referred to as diffractometer equipment.

Fig.19.22 Neutron beam work at Harwell. (Copyright: United Kingdom Atomic Energy Authority.)

19.5 Radioisotopes and Their Uses

A radioisotope is a radioactive isotope of an element. A great number of radioisotopes have been artificially prepared by inserting different elements into a nuclear reactor while it is operating (Fig. 19.23). A non-radioactive element may be changed into a new radioactive element (when inserted in a reactor) if its atoms absorb neutrons and immediately eject protons. The atomic number of the atoms is then lowered while the mass number is unaffected. By inserting pure sulphur into a reactor, radiophosphorus may be produced

by the following nuclear reaction.

$$S_{16}^{32} + n_0^1 \rightarrow P_{15}^{32} + H_1^1$$

The radiations from radioisotopes are used to practical advantage in (i) changing or destroying matter (ii) 'tracing' investigations (iii) industrial production monitors.

In the first category, radiation from radioisotopes is used to treat cancer by destroying cancerous tissue. Radiation is also used to kill bacteria and is thus a sterilising agent—finding its application in the sterilisation of food, drugs and surgical instruments. (Food treated in this way is quite safe to eat!) Also in this category, the irradiation of rubber causes hardening of the rubber, and thus eliminates the need for vulcanising.

When (in the second category) a radioisotope is used as a tracer, it becomes possible to follow the course of a somewhat complicated biological or chemical process. For example, in the modern research programmes on friction, it is common practice to introduce a small quantity of radioactive iron into bearings, and to measure wear and tear in the bearings in terms of the level of radioactivity measured in the lubricating oil.

Fig.19.23 Removing an isotope from the PLUTO reactor at Harwell. (Copyright: United Kingdom Atomic Energy Authority.)

When (in the third category) radiation is absorbed or scattered by matter, information can be gathered as to the characteristics of the material concerned. For example, the thickness of linoleum or paper can be checked by placing a beta source above the linoleum (or paper) and a G.M. tube below it. The thickness of linoleum can then be checked in terms of the G.M. count rate which may be calibrated to read thickness directly. The absorption of radiation is also frequently used as a 'level indicator' in the checking of levels in say tubes of toothpaste.

Problems

1   What do you understand by the terms 'electron avalanche', 'quenching agent'?

2   How would you demonstrate that a radium (226) source emits alpha, beta, and gamma radiation simultaneously?

3   How would you estimate the range of alpha particles in air, using a spark discharge detector?

4   If the half-value thickness of a metal for a given gamma beam is 18 mm, what thickness of the metal would be required to reduce the intensity of the gamma beam to 1% (or less) of its original value?

5   Why are the terms 'half-value thickness' and 'half-life' useful in the study of radioactivity?

6   In a radioactive decay analogue experiment, a collection of dice are thrown many times. Those dice which show '6' after a throw are removed from the collection, and the remainder are thrown again. Can you explain the analogy between this procedure and radioactive decay?

Suppose that 600 dice are available at the start of the experiment. Estimate the number remaining after each throw, and hence draw a graph of 'number of dice remaining' against 'number of throws'. Hence estimate the half-life of dice (in throws).

Can you verify your answer by calculation?

7   Write an equation for the alpha decay of Po_{84}^{210}.

8   What is meant by the statement 'Ca_{20}^{45} is a beta emitter with a half-life of 164 days'? Write an equation for the decay of Ca_{20}^{45}.

9   A sample of radioactive material has 10^{20} radioactive atoms initially. The half-life of the material is 1 hour. How many of these atoms will decay in the first second?

10   What is the probability that a bismuth (214) nucleus will decay in a second, given that the half-life of the transmutation

$$Bi_{83}^{214} \rightarrow Po_{84}^{214} + e_{-1}^{0}$$

is 19 minutes?

11   A radioactive atom of element X has atomic mass number A and atomic number Z. Write the symbol for its nucleus. How many neutrons does this nucleus contain? X decays to Y by alpha emission and Y decays to Y' by beta emission. How many protons are contained in a Y nucleus? How many neutrons are contained in a Y' nucleus?

Chapter 20

The Structure of the Atom

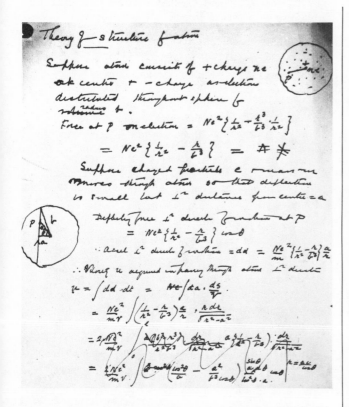

Fig.20.0 Rutherford's original notes on the theory of atomic structure. (Copyright: Cavendish Laboratory, University of Cambridge.)

Things on a very small scale behave like nothing that you have any direct experience about. They do not behave like waves, they do not behave like particles, they do not behave like clouds, or billiard balls, or weights on springs, or like anything that you have ever seen.

Richard Feynman

The physics with which we are concerned in this our final chapter is almost purely modern physics. Before beginning our discussions however, let us look back briefly, at the accomplishments of classical physics with which most of the book has been concerned.

With Newton's laws of motion, we explained accelerated motion, projectile motion, and circular motion. After introducing the nineteenth century idea of atoms and molecules, we applied the laws of motion to explain heat in terms of a kinetic theory model. The phenomena of electricity and magnetism we explained by discussing the concept of electric charge, and the interactions which occur when charges are in motion.

The crowning achievement of classical physics is regarded by many as the derivation of the electromagnetic wave theory of light from a consideration of Maxwell's equations of the electromagnetic field. Classically, any wave motion required

a medium in which to 'wave', but experiments to detect an aether (in which light 'waves') were quite unsuccessful. The need for an aether was discarded by Albert Einstein, when, in formulating his theory of relativity, he revised our fundamental concepts of space and time. This revision was a violation of 'common sense' to many people, but then, as Professor Feynman points out, common sense is again likely to be violated in the modern physics of small scale phenomena.

Let us then disregard common sense for the present, and trace some of the developments of modern physics, by examining the contributions which were made in the early years of this century towards providing an accurate picture of the structure of the atom. We begin by discussing two models of the atom which had been proposed before the turn of the century.

20.1 The Atomic Models of Dalton and Thomson

The *atomic theory of chemistry* proposed by John Dalton (Fig. 20.1), is in effect a series of postulates abstracted from his treatise of 1810, which he called *A New System of Chemical Philosophy*. Before Dalton's treatise, the words 'particle', 'atom', 'corpuscle', were used frequently, but with little attention being paid to their detailed description. Dalton established a basis for the accurate usage of the word 'atom', thereby providing chemical science with a firmer footing.

Fig.20.1 (By kind permission of the Science Museum, London. Neg. no. 491/58.)

We can list Dalton's postulates as follows:

1 *Matter consists of indivisible atoms.* Matter although divisible, is not infinitely divisible. Atoms are in fact the ultimate particles of which matter is composed, and as such, they cannot be divided themselves.

2 *Each element consists of a characteristic kind of identical atoms. Consequently, there are as many different kinds of atoms as there are elements.* Dalton was suggesting here that all atoms of a particular element are alike in mass and form—a view which had *not* been adopted by earlier theorists!

3 *Atoms are unchangeable.* There is no possibility of a transmutation of elements occurring—as the failures of alchemy had emphasised.

4 *When different elements react to form a compound, the smallest portion of the compound consists of a grouping of a definite number of atoms of each element.* Today, we call these smallest portions *molecules*.

5 *In chemical reactions, atoms are neither created nor destroyed.* Instead they are re-arranged or re-grouped.

It is left as an exercise for the reader to comment critically on the validity of these postulates, in the light of the findings of the last chapter, and also in the light of the chemical knowledge which he (the reader) may possess.

Perhaps the most serious shortcoming of Dalton's atomic theory arises from its failure to take account of the atomic nature of *electricity*. By the beginning of the 20th century, the whole concept of the atom had gained a greater significance than in Dalton's day, and the fact that electrons could be produced from many substances suggested that electrons themselves must be of atomic origin. If an atom was to be accepted as an electrically neutral entity however (since all substances are normally uncharged), then in possessing negatively charged electrons, the atom must also contain an equal amount of positive charge.

Such was the reasoning of the English physicist J. J. Thomson (Fig. 20.2) who pictured the atom as a globule of positively charged fluid in which electrons were embedded in a similar fashion to currants embedded in a Christmas pudding.

Thomson suggested that in the simplest atom (having one electron), the electron should be located at the centre of the globule, since it would be attracted equally in all directions by the presence of the surrounding positive charge. If the electron were momentarily displaced to one side (say by the attractive force due to a charged particle passing the atom) then following this displacement the electron would oscillate about its undisturbed position until it again came to rest at that position. During this oscillation, the electron would radiate electromagnetic energy, and this radiation would correspond to light of a particular wavelength and frequency (equal to the frequency of the electron oscillation).

This theory was very encouraging—particularly so when, on calculating the frequency of electron oscillation, Thomson

Fig.20.2   Sir J. J. Thomson and Lord Rutherford. (Copyright: Cavendish Laboratory, University of Cambridge.)

found that it fell in the visible region of the spectrum! The theory could not account for the emission of light of different frequencies in the hydrogen spectrum however, and so, encouraging as it was, the theory was not completely adequate and therefore not entirely correct.

20.2 Rutherford's Nuclear Model of the Atom

In 1907, while working in Manchester, Ernest Rutherford (Fig. 20.2)—a New Zealander, and brilliant experimentalist—observed that when a stream of α-particles passed through a very thin sheet or foil of metal, the stream was slightly broadened by the order of 1°. Rutherford attributed this broadening to the large number of small deflections which would result (on the basis of the Thomson model of the atom) from the α-particles interacting with the widely distributed positive and negative charge in the atoms of the foil. Rutherford thus pictured the process as in Fig. 20.3.

About this time, Dr. Geiger (one of Rutherford's col-

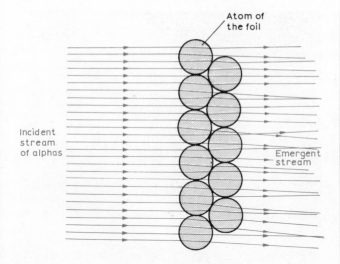

Fig.20.3   Rutherford's original picture of the alpha scattering process.

leagues) suggested that Marsden (one of his trainees) should be given a small research project in radioactivity. Rutherford suggested that Marsden might attempt to find whether or not any α-particles (incident on a thin gold foil) are in fact scattered through a large angle. (Rutherford expected this investigation to be fruitless.) Several days after Marsden's investigation began, Geiger excitedly reported to Rutherford:

We have been able to get some of the α-particles coming backward!

Rutherford was truly amazed. In his own words:

It was quite the most incredible event that has ever happened to me in my life. It was almost as incredible as if you fired a 15-inch shell at a piece of tissue paper and it came back and hit you! On consideration, I realised that this scattering backward must be the result of a single collision, and when I made calculations, I saw that it was impossible to get anything of that order of magnitude unless you took a system in which the greater part of the mass of the atom was concentrated in a minute nucleus. It was then that I had the idea of an atom with a minute massive centre carrying a charge.

Rutherford was thus led to conceive the *nuclear model of the atom.* According to this model, the atom is not composed of a positively charged fluid, but instead, it has its mass concentrated mainly at the centre in the form of a tiny positively charged nucleus. Around this tiny nucleus, electrons are in orbit in much the same way as the planets are in orbit around the sun, so that in effect, the atomic volume is mainly empty space (see section 8.2).

Rutherford had reasoned that the back-scattering of the α-particles could not possibly be due to interaction between α's and electrons. After making the necessary calculations, he likened the interaction of an α and an electron to the interaction of a fast rolling ball with a grain of sand.

Rutherford therefore pictured the thin metal foil as containing 'substantial objects' (positively charged atomic nuclei) and these were so massive that an alpha particle travelling directly towards one would be stopped and made to retrace its path—as a result of the force of electrostatic repulsion established between the two. Since most of the atomic volume was empty space, most α-particles would travel straight through the metal foil undeflected. Some would be deflected through small angles, but only a very few would be back-scattered—as Marsden had observed to be the case. Rutherford now pictured the scattering process as in Fig. 20.4.

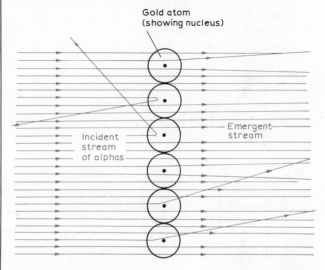

Fig.20.4   Rutherford's revised picture of the alpha scattering process.

After further deduction, Rutherford suggested that the observed amount of scattering would be related to the charge on the atomic nucleus (Q), and also to the thickness of the metal foil (t). The effects of each of these factors on the scattering process were subsequently investigated by Geiger and Marsden, using a piece of apparatus similar to that illustrated in Fig. 20.5. Alpha-particles were emitted from a radon source, and allowed to pass through a thin gold foil. The number of particles deflected through each angle ϕ was observed by counting the number of scintillations occurring on the zinc sulphide screen. Observations were made for different angles up to and including $\phi = 150°$, and from these, Geiger and Marsden concluded that the number of α-particles (q) scattered through an angle ϕ could be written as

$$q \propto Qt \operatorname{cosec}^4 \frac{\phi}{2}$$

This result confirmed the theoretical deductions which Rutherford had made beforehand on the assumption that the repulsive force between an α and a nucleus obeyed the inverse square law of charge separation.

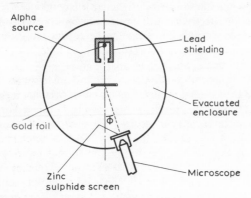

Fig.20.5   The apparatus of Geiger and Marsden.

This experiment is regarded as one of the most significant contributions to the whole of physics. Not only did it provide for the acceptance of a new picture of the atom, but it also established the technique of using atomic missiles (α-particles in this case) as atomic probes. As we pointed out in the last chapter, this technique has contributed greatly to developments in the whole field of nuclear physics.

The nature of the α-particle scattering process may be demonstrated in the school laboratory by using a mechanical model (Fig. 20.6) which reproduces the essential features of the process. In this model, the α-particle is represented by a steel ball, which, after being launched from a curved ramp, rolls with little friction on a smooth curved hill. The nucleus is pictured as being at the flat central region of the hill, and *the height of the hill at any point represents the electric potential energy of the α-particle* in the vicinity of the nucleus. The height of the hill has no spatial meaning.

Fig.20.6   The mechanical analogy to the alpha scattering process. (By kind permission of Griffin & George Ltd.)

If an α-particle is at a distance R from a nucleus, then the electric potential energy of the α is proportional to $1/R$. The hill is so constructed that the height of any point on the hill is also proportional to $1/R$. This is represented in the sectional drawing of Fig. 20.7, in which k is a constant.

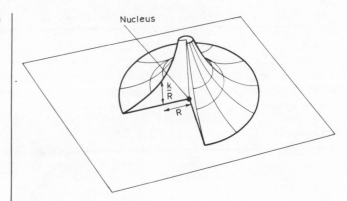

Fig.20.7   The construction of the scattering analogue apparatus.

If the steel ball is launched towards the centre of the hill, it will travel straight up until its potential energy is equal to its kinetic energy at the foot. Thereafter it will roll back down. (If this kinetic energy is sufficiently large of course, the ball may reach the top of the hill, and thereby 'penetrate' the nucleus.) This situation of the ball rolling back down the hill represents the backscattering of an α from the nucleus. If the steel ball is launched towards some point say to the right of centre of the hill, the ball will be deflected towards the right on passing over the hill—the scattering angle from the original path being inversely related to the distance between the central approach to the hill and the actual approach (Fig. 20.8). Similarly with the motion of α-particles suffering electrostatic repulsion in the field of the nucleus.

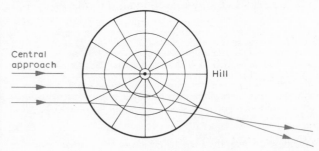

Fig.20.8   The scattering angle is inversely related to the distance between the central approach to the hill and the actual approach.

20.3 The Apparent Failures of the Rutherford Model

Although the Rutherford model of the atom provides us with an attractive and acceptable picture, it has certain flaws when examined from a classical physics viewpoint. Perhaps the most serious flaw is that relating to the behaviour of the atomic electrons, which, according to the nuclear model, are in orbit around the nucleus—just like the planets are in orbit around the sun. This motion (since it involves a continual change of direction) is by definition an accelerated motion, and according to the laws of classical physics, an accelerating charge emits electromagnetic radiation. If this is the case, energy must continually be radiated by electrons in orbits, so eventually they should spiral into the nucleus. The inconsistency between the model and the classical theory of electromagnetic radiation was obvious to Rutherford, who commented:

> I was perfectly aware that when I put forward the theory of the nuclear atom, that according to classical theory, the electron ought to fall into the nucleus.

The deeper we look into the Rutherford model in terms of classical theory, the deeper seems to be the split between them. Applying classical theory to the Rutherford model, we might expect that the frequency of the light emitted from a hydrogen atom should be related to the frequency with which the electron orbits the nucleus. As light is emitted and the diameter of the electron orbit subsequently decreases (according to classical theory), light of a higher frequency should then be emitted (since the electron's period of revolution will also have decreased). In a large population of hydrogen atoms, different atoms will be at different stages in the emission process, and so a continuous spectrum of light should be emitted at any time. This is clearly not the case when we examine a hydrogen emission spectrum. Instead of observing a continuum, we observe a finite number of sharp lines, and thereby infer the presence of a finite number of light frequencies.

An attempt to reconcile the Rutherford model with the classical theory of electromagnetic radiation clearly puts the stability of the atom in question. Accepting atoms as stable entities (in as much as their electrons do not spiral into their nuclei), it might seem that the Rutherford model is in some way deficient. A simple revision of the model does not resolve the obvious difficulties, but by adopting a revolutionary approach to the whole problem, the nuclear model of the atom may be retained with far greater confidence. We now consider this revolutionary approach.

20.4 The Bohr Theory

The results of α-scattering experiments had emphasised the need to accept a nuclear model of the atom, and yet the accepted classical theory of electromagnetic radiation suggested certain flaws in this model. Such was the problem which confronted the Danish physicist Niels Bohr. For his work on atomic structure, Bohr received the Nobel Prize in Physics in 1922. In 1913, Bohr developed a theory whose mathematical predictions agreed with the data observed in the emission spectrum of hydrogen.

In the solution of the problem, Bohr postulated that clas-

sical electromagnetic radiation theory was inapplicable to systems of atomic dimensions. In systems of these dimensions, it would be necessary to unite the nuclear model of the atom with the novel *quantum theory of radiation*—a theory which Planck and Einstein had shown to be relevant to systems of atomic dimensions. Two of Bohr's postulates are relevant to us at present, and these may be written thus:

1. Only certain allowed electron orbits exist in an atom. In these allowed orbits, electrons do not radiate energy, and in such orbits, the electrons could circulate for ever without ever radiating energy. The motion of the electrons in their orbits satisfies the laws of classical mechanics.

2. If an electron changes its motion by moving from one allowed orbit to another allowed orbit of smaller radius, then this change will be accompanied by the emission of a short burst of electromagnetic radiation. If its energy in the first orbit is E, and in the second orbit E', then the frequency of the radiation emitted (ν), is calculated as

$$\nu = \frac{E - E'}{h} \qquad \text{(where } h \text{ is Planck's constant)}$$

These postulates are accepted as a thorough mix-up of classical and modern physics, but this mix-up is valid if we are prepared to accept that the laws of classical physics (derived for macroscopic systems) might not be entirely correct in the realms of microscopic systems.

Let us suppose that the allowed orbits to which Bohr refers have radii r_1, r_2, r_3, etc., in ascending order. In a normal stable unexcited hydrogen atom, the orbiting electron will be in the first orbit (of radius r_1). If the atom absorbs energy, then it changes from its ground state to an excited state by the electron in the first allowed orbit jumping to an allowed orbit of greater radius—the particular orbit depending on how much energy the atom absorbs. The atom will then de-excite spontaneously by its electron returning to the first orbit in one jump (or by a series of jumps through allowed orbits). For each jump towards the first orbit, a quantum (or burst) of electromagnetic energy is radiated.

Let us suppose that the electron energy is E_1 in the orbit of radius r_1, E_2 in the orbit of radius r_2, E_3 in the orbit of radius r_3 etc. If in an excited atom, de-excitation begins by the electron jumping from the E_3 orbit to the E_2 orbit, then a short burst of light will be emitted. The frequency of this light (ν) is calculated as

$$\nu = \frac{E_3 - E_2}{h}$$

If the electron then jumps to the lowest orbit, the frequency of the light emitted in the transition (ν' say) is calculated as

$$\nu' = \frac{E_2 - E_1}{h}$$

Clearly, there are certain discrete frequencies at which light may be emitted from a hydrogen atom, according to the Bohr theory, and so here at last we have an answer to why the hydrogen emission spectrum exhibits certain discrete lines.

When the radii of the allowed orbits are calculated for the hydrogen atom, these are found to be as follows:

$$r_1 = 0\cdot53 \times 10^{-10}\,\text{m}$$
$$r_2 = 2\cdot12 \times 10^{-10}\,\text{m}$$
$$r_3 = 4\cdot77 \times 10^{-10}\,\text{m}$$

In general $\qquad r_i = i^2 \times 0\cdot53 \times 10^{-10}\,\text{m}$

$$(i = 1, 2, 3, \text{etc})$$

—as the reader may care to check.

That is, the radii of the allowed orbits (assumed circular) are arranged according to the squares of the natural numbers, so we might picture the orbits (along with a few of the possible transitions which can occur) as in the diagram of Fig. 20.9.

Although the Bohr model of the atom is extremely useful, it is now believed that there are no material particles travelling around the nucleus in the fixed orbits. Rather, we think that while the positive charge of the atom is concentrated in the nucleus, the negative charge is 'smeared' over certain concentric shells. The mean radii of these shells are equivalent to the radii of the Bohr orbits, and the imagined shells are 'pictured' as in Fig. 20.10. We shall return to this idea at the end of the chapter.

20.5 De Broglie's Postulate

When α-particles are emitted from uranium (238) each has kinetic energy of the order of $6\cdot7 \times 10^{-13}$ J. According to classical physics, we should expect that, since energy is conserved, the α-particles each possess energy of the order of $6\cdot7 \times 10^{-13}$ J inside the nucleus before escaping—this energy being in the form of potential energy within the nucleus. Alpha-particles emitted from polonium (212) each have kinetic energy of the order of $1\cdot4 \times 10^{-12}$ J. When these α-particles are fired at a uranium (238) nucleus however, they

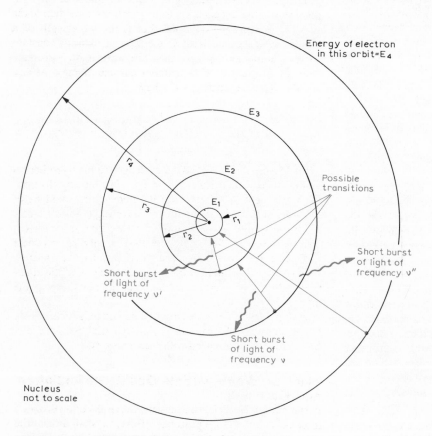

Fig.20.9   Illustrating the Bohr model of the atom.

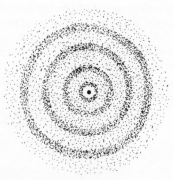

Fig.20.10

are turned back in their tracks, despite the fact that they have apparently more than sufficient energy to penetrate the 'energy barrier' of the uranium nucleus. That is, according to classical physics, we should argue that if an α with energy $6{\cdot}7 \times 10^{-13}$ J can penetrate the nuclear barrier in one sense, surely a more energetic α ($1{\cdot}4 \times 10^{-12}$ J) can penetrate the same barrier in the opposite sense.

Again it seems that classical physics is being violated in the realm of experiments at atomic level. But how do we explain the violation this time? Classical physics is being violated here because our familiar system of Newtonian mechanics is somewhat inadequate when applied to the tiny world of the atom. To explain the physical contradiction, we have to replace Newtonian mechanics by the more sophisticated system of *quantum mechanics*. This is not to say that Newtonian mechanics is being completely rejected, because its predictions agree with those of quantum mechanics in certain special situations. The development of the theory of quantum mechanics owes its initiation to the extremely important idea suggested by Prince Louis de Broglie in his doctoral dissertation of 1924.

De Broglie pointed out that although electromagnetic radiation exhibited pure wave properties classically, the work of Einstein (on photoelectricity) and Compton (on the scattering of X-rays) had demonstrated that in certain circumstances, it displays particle (or quantum) characteristics. He then went on to suggest that under certain circumstances, physical entities which we normally think of as particles (marbles, electrons, α-particles etc.) might exhibit *wave properties*. De Broglie argued further that if a quantum of radiation has a momentum associated with its wavelength (as the work of Einstein would seem to suggest) then to preserve a symmetry in nature, it was somewhat natural to expect that a particle should have a wavelength associated with its momentum.

If a photon (a quantum of light) has frequency f and wavelength λ, then

$$c = f\lambda \qquad \text{(where } c \text{ is the speed of light)}$$

The energy of the photon (E) may be written

$$E = hf \qquad \text{(according to Planck's quantum theory of radiation)}$$

Hence

$$E = \frac{hc}{\lambda}$$

According to Einstein's mass-energy relationship, a photon has an effective mass (m) when travelling at speed c. This mass is related to its energy (E) as follows:

$$E = mc^2$$

Hence

$$mc^2 = \frac{hc}{\lambda}$$

or

$$mc = \frac{h}{\lambda}$$

or

$$\boxed{\lambda = \frac{h}{mc}} \qquad \dots\dots\dots\dots\dots \text{(20.1)}$$

The product mc appearing in the denominator of the right hand side of the last equation is the effective momentum of the photon. De Broglie reasoned that if the wavelength of a photon could be calculated as the ratio of Planck's constant to the photon momentum, then the wavelength associated with the momentum of a material particle of mass M and speed v might be written as λ' where

$$\boxed{\lambda' = \frac{h}{Mv}} \qquad \dots\dots\dots\dots\dots \text{(20.2)}$$

De Broglie thus assigned a wavelength to his hypothetical matter waves, and calculated that for a fast moving electron, the wavelength associated with its momentum would be of the order of 10^{-10} m. Although this wavelength was extremely small, de Broglie was encouraged rather than discouraged, because it seemed likely that the wave properties of matter had never been observed since the associated wavelengths were so very small in relation to the dimensions of the apparatus which had previously been used in investigating the motions of particles.

Within a few years of de Broglie's postulate, a wide variety of experiments had confirmed that material particles had wave properties associated with their motions!

20.6 The Wave-particle Duality of Radiation and Matter

In this our final section, let us discuss the reality of de Broglie's most novel but strange postulate. First, we shall discuss the photoelectric effect as evidence supporting the idea that waves may exhibit particle properties. We shall then discuss certain situations where it is apparent that particles exhibit wave properties. In discussing the wave-particle duality of radiation or matter however, let us be clear on the point that the wave and particle properties of either are to be regarded as complementary rather than antagonistic.

1. The Photoelectric Effect

When two metal plates are sealed inside an evacuated glass tube and connected to a battery as in Fig. 20.11, a small current is registered on the ammeter whenever the negatively charged plate (the cathode) is illuminated with monochromatic light of a certain frequency. This photoelectric effect is more pronounced when the metal plates are particularly clean, and when the cathode is an alkali metal.

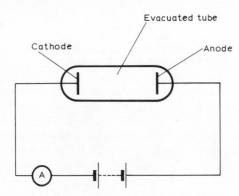

Fig.20.11 Demonstration of the photoelectric effect.

The photoelectric current would seem to consist of negative charges (electrons) emitted from the cathode whenever it is illuminated. It is observed that when the *intensity* of the monochromatic light is increased (say by bringing the lamp closer), then the size of the photoelectric current is increased proportionately—corresponding to a greater number of electrons being ejected from the cathode per unit time. The *speeds* of the ejected electrons are in no way affected by the intensity of the incident light however. That is, strong light ejects more electrons than weak light of the same frequency, but the speed of these electrons is the same.

According to the classical wave theory of light, the energy carried by light waves should decrease in density as the light spreads farther from the source, and yet according to the photoelectric experiments, it would seem that an exact quantity of energy is being absorbed by each of the photoelectrons whenever light strikes the alkali metal cathode—no matter how close the light source happens to be.

When different alkali metals are used for the cathode, it is found that a different basic light frequency is required before the photoelectric effect can be observed. That is, different metals have different *light threshold frequencies*, below which

photoelectrons will not be ejected—regardless of the intensity of illumination. If the light frequency exceeds the threshold frequency by even a tiny amount, then electrons are ejected from the metal immediately—regardless of the intensity of illumination. Perhaps the most mysterious aspect of the photoelectric effect is that as the *frequency* of the illumination is increased, the *speed* of the electrons ejected is increased.

The mysteries of the photoelectric effect were solved in 1905 when Albert Einstein published a paper entitled *On a Heuristic Point of View Concerning the Generation and Transformation of Light*. In this paper, Einstein pointed out that in classical physics, a great deal of attention had been paid to the propagation of light and very little attention had been paid to the interaction of light with matter. A violation of classical physics was therefore not too surprising. He then went on to propose a *photon theory of light* according to which the energy carried by light is localised in discrete small regions or corpuscles, instead of being distributed evenly over a whole wave front. In this photon theory, Einstein was actually applying the more general *quantum theory of radiation* (of 1901) to the photoelectric situation. (Planck's quantum theory had proposed that an oscillator could only radiate energy in quanta each of an amount $h\nu$, where ν is the frequency of the oscillator.)

With this new 'picture' of light, Einstein was able to provide a quantitative explanation of the photoelectric effect by formulating his photoelectric equation. Einstein reasoned that in order for an electron to escape from the metal, certain amount of work would have to be done (by some external agency), against the electrostatic binding forces in the metal. In terms of Planck's theory this amount of work could be equated to an amount of energy $h\nu_0$ where ν_0 is the threshold light frequency for the metal. This quantity $h\nu_0$ is called the *work function* of the metal. If an electron absorbs a photon of energy $h\nu$, then assuming $\nu > \nu_0$, the electron will be able to escape from the metal. The difference in energies $h\nu$ and $h\nu_0$ will appear as kinetic energy of the free electron. Einstein thus wrote his photoelectric equation in the form

$$h\nu = h\nu_0 + \tfrac{1}{2}mv^2 \qquad \ldots \ldots \ldots \ldots (20.3)$$

where m is the electronic mass, and v is the speed of the electron emitted. The equation mixes classical physics with modern physics by including the principle of conservation of energy along with the quantum nature of radiation.

The photoelectric effect may be demonstrated in the laboratory by attaching a small *clean* sheet of zinc to a 'Braun' electroscope as in Fig. 20.12, and giving the electroscope a negative charge by induction. When ultraviolet radiation from a mercury vapour lamp is allowed to fall on the zinc plate, the electroscope is observed to discharge fairly rapidly. When the electroscope is given a positive charge instead, no such effect is observed.

What do you conclude from this experiment?

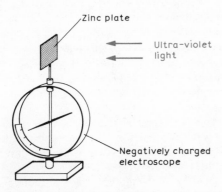

Fig.20.12 The laboratory demonstration of the photoelectric effect.

2. The Experiment of Davisson and Germer

In 1927, Davisson and Germer conducted an investigation which provided the first experimental confirmation of de Broglie's Postulate. Davisson and Germer calculated that the wavelength associated with a low energy electron (say the electron in the lowest allowed orbit in the hydrogen atom) was of the same order of size as the interatomic spacing in a nickel crystal. This suggested the possibility of looking for diffraction effects in the transmission or reflection of a beam of electrons by or from a nickel crystal, and so the two set up an experiment (illustrated simply in Fig. 20.13) to investigate the reflection of electrons from the surface of a single nickel crystal.

In this experiment, the electron detector detected only those electrons which had been back-scattered from the surface of the nickel crystal. The number of electrons $N(\theta)$ back-scattered at an angle θ (defined as in Fig. 20.13) was plotted against θ in a graph, with results as shown in Fig. 20.14.

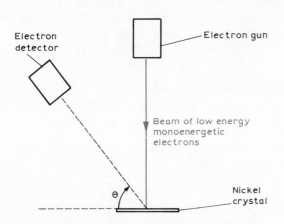

Fig.20.13 The experiment of Davisson and Germer.

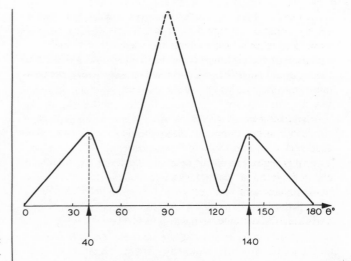

Fig.20.14 The distribution of scattered electrons in the Davisson and Germer experiment.

The distribution of scattered electrons clearly resembles the distribution of light intensity produced with an optical diffraction grating. The peaks at $\theta = 40°$ and $\theta = 140°$ can only be explained as the constructive interference of waves scattered or diffracted by the regularly spaced atoms of the crystal surface—just as the peaks in an optical diffraction pattern are explained by the constructive interference of light diffracted by the regular rulings on the diffraction grating. (To keep the analogy strictly correct, we should say that the crystal surface acts like an analogous optical device called the reflection grating—rather than like the actual diffraction grating.)

Electrons were thus shown to be capable of showing interference effects, and so de Broglie's Postulate had received its first experimental confirmation. By making measurements on the electron diffraction pattern, Davisson and Germer showed the postulate to be quantitatively correct too! The de Broglie wavelength of the incident electrons has been calculated (using equation (20.2)) to be $1\cdot67 \times 10^{-10}$ m. By applying the diffraction or reflection grating equation $n\lambda = d \sin \phi$ (where ϕ is measured from the centre of the pattern), and assuming that the small peaks correspond to the first order spectrum, then

$$n = 1, \quad \phi = 50°, \quad \text{and} \quad d \, (= \text{grating element})$$
$$= \text{interatomic spacing}$$
$$= 2\cdot15 \times 10^{-10} \text{ m}$$

Hence
$$\lambda = \frac{d \sin \phi}{n}$$

$$= 2\cdot15 \times 10^{-10} \times \sin 50$$

$$= 1\cdot65 \times 10^{-10} \text{ m}$$

The two values 1.67×10^{-10} m (calculated) and 1.65×10^{-10} m ('observed') agree to within 1.3% of each other—within the accuracy limits of the experiment.

The interference giving rise to the first order peaks must not be regarded as interference between waves associated with one electron, and waves associated with another electron. Instead, the peaks are produced by the interference of the waves *associated with a single electron*. These waves associated with the single electron have been diffracted by various parts of the crystal. This fact was demonstrated in the experiment by arranging for the electrons in the beam to go through the apparatus one at a time. The pattern of the scattered electrons remained the same!

Particles were thus shown to have associated wave properties. But what is the associated wave like? What is 'waving', and what is it 'waving' in? These are the obvious questions which spring to mind—perhaps because our train of thought is 'blinkered' and conditioned by thinking of wave motion in terms of the familiar nature of water waves.

The de Broglie particle waves are not changes of shape in the particle or changes in its motion or in any medium through which it is moving. *They are in fact patterns of probability, or probability amplitudes.*

To help clarify this intangible idea, let us consider the experiment of G. I. Taylor in which a two-slit apparatus was placed in front of a light source, so weak that only one photon was in the apparatus at any time. With reference to Fig. 20.15, Taylor found that a two-slit interference pattern was obtained on the screen, but that a detector placed at S_1 or S_2 detected only a whole photon or none—never a fraction of a photon. But surely to produce an interference pattern (we might argue) a photon passing through S_1 must somehow be influenced by S_2. Taylor found that if he covered either slit, the interference pattern was destroyed, and photons then began to arrive at points on the screen where dark fringes had previously occurred!

Taylor's experiment suggested that *probability* would have to be introduced into quantum mechanics, and that each photon would have to be ascribed some probability wave function or amplitude, if it (the photon) was to be described completely. The square of this probability amplitude (the probability 'intensity') would yield information as to the probability of finding the photon at a particular point in space. The probability amplitude associated with the photon would propagate as a typical wave—exhibiting known wave properties.

In the case of a particle which sometimes behaves like a wave, the wave properties can be interpreted in terms of a probability amplitude associated with the particle. The square of this amplitude at some point in space, is a measure of the probability of finding the particle at that point.

Although such probability waves are difficult to imagine, we can derive some comfort from the fact that they have similar properties to water waves in the ripple tank. The fact that the two wave types are unlike in nature is of less importance.

3. *The penetration of the Nuclear Barrier*

In section 20.5, we discussed the violation of classical physics which resulted from consideration of the escape of α-particles from a uranium (238) nucleus. The escape can be explained however, from consideration of the probability amplitude associated with the α-particle inside the nucleus. The diagram of Fig. 20.16 is a graph of the potential energy (U) of an α-particle in and around a nucleus of radius R, as a function of the distance (x) from the centre of the nucleus. The negative potential energy inside the nucleus represents the strong attractive forces which are thought to exist between nucleons inside the nucleus. Outside the nucleus, the increasing force of electrostatic repulsion on an approaching positively charged particle is represented by a potential energy hill (as before)—this force varying inversely with distance from the centre of the nucleus.

At $x = R$, an energy ε is required (classically speaking) before an α-particle could escape from, or penetrate, the nucleus. For uranium (238), this energy has the value 4.8×10^{-12} J but as we pointed out, most alphas emitted from uranium nuclei each have energy of an amount 6.7×10^{-13} J. In the diagram, we see that an α of this energy (E) is faced with the problem of penetrating a non-physical region of width b, before it can escape. Classically, such an α has insufficient energy to escape, but by considering the de Broglie probability wave associated with the α-particle of energy E, we can accept the possibility of escape.

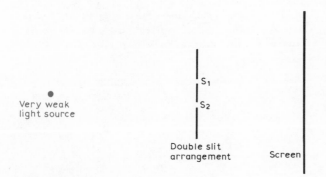

Very weak
light source

S_1

S_2

Double slit
arrangement

Screen

Fig.20.15 The experiment of G. I. Taylor.

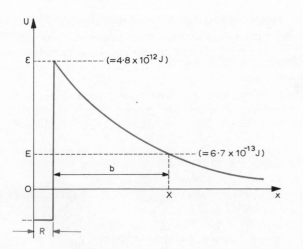

Fig.20.16 The potential energy of an alpha particle in and around the nucleus of radius *R*.

As the α-particle approaches and strikes the nuclear boundary ($x = R$), part of its probability amplitude (Ψ) is reflected (Ψ_r say). The remainder of the amplitude is transmitted through the nuclear boundary, but this transmitted component (like the transmitted component of a sound wave striking a wall) will be further and further attenuated with increasing x. Let us suppose that at $x = X$, the transmitted amplitude has the value Ψ_t. Then the probability of finding the α-particle of energy E at $x = X$—that is, outside the nucleus—is given as p where

$$p = \frac{(\Psi_t)^2}{(\Psi)^2}$$

Assuming that Ψ_t is non-zero, then p is finite, and so the escape of the α-particle is a distinct possibility.

To give an example of the probability of penetration, we can say that since the half-life of uranium (238) is $4\cdot5 \times 10^9$ years, then the probability of an α penetrating the 'barrier' of a uranium nucleus in $4\cdot5 \times 10^9$ years is $\frac{1}{2}$.

4. *Standing Waves in Bohr Orbits*

In the Bohr theory of the atom, only certain radii of electron orbits are permitted. When we consider the electron probability wave function rather than the electron itself, then

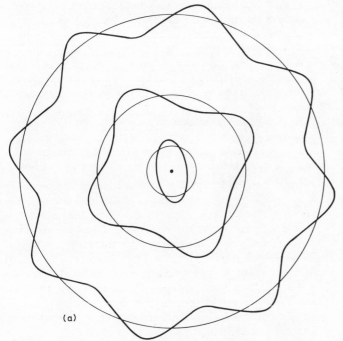

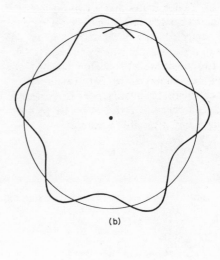

Fig.20.17 The idea of probability standing waves in the electron orbits is consistent with the requirement that only certain radii of electron orbits are permitted.

clearly for circles of certain radii, the probability wave will be able to reinforce itself, and hence maintain itself in the form of a standing wave—as in Fig. 20.17(a). For circles of other radii, the same probability wave functions would interfere with themselves (as in Fig. 20.17(b)), and so destroy themselves—corresponding to the disappearance of the electron in orbits of these radii. That is, the probability wave functions (and the associated electron orbits) will only be maintained when the circles considered have circumferences equal to a whole number of probability wavelengths. By calculation, it has been shown that the radii of these circles agree with the radii of the allowed Bohr orbits!

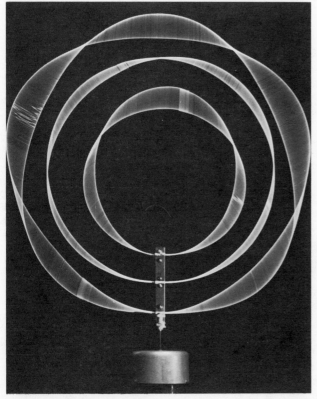

Fig.20.18 Standing wave patterns in a wire ring model of the Bohr atom. (I. D. Taylor.)

Figure 20.18 shows a mechanical model of standing waves in circular wire rings to simulate the electron orbits in a Bohr-type atom. The rings are attached to a metal strip linked to a vibrator. The radii of the rings are chosen such that a whole number of half wavelengths may be contained in the circumference of each ring when the vibrator is switched on. Rings of intermediate radii will not show stable patterns.

The idea of standing probability waves surrounding the nucleus is thus consistent with the Bohr hypothesis of allowed orbits. The idea of probability waves implies the uncertainty in position of each electron in its orbit however, and so our final picture of the atom is that of a minute, positively charged nucleus, surrounded by a 'smear' of, or probability distribution of, electrons.

Problems

(Take (i) Planck's constant as 6.6×10^{-34} J s; (ii) The speed of light as 3×10^8 m s^{-1}; (iii) The electronic charge as 1.6×10^{-19} C; (iv) The electronic mass as 9×10^{-31} kg;)

1 What is the effective mass of an X-ray photon of wavelength 8×10^{-11} m?

2 What is the de Broglie wavelength of
   a) an electron accelerated through a potential difference of 5 V
   b) a car of mass 800 kg travelling at 20 m s^{-1}?
   Why is the latter of little importance?

3 A monochromatic light source emits light of wavelength 5×10^{-7} m. The source is rated at 100 W, but only 1% of its power is developed as light. What energy is carried by each photon? How many photons are emitted each second?

4 When light from the source in the last problem is directed on to clean potassium (whose threshold light frequency is 4.6×10^{14} Hz), electrons are ejected from the metal. At what speed are they ejected?

5 In the laboratory demonstration of the photoelectric effect using a zinc plate and ultra violet light, is it necessary to conduct the experiment in an otherwise dark laboratory? Explain your answer.

6 Calculate the potential difference through which the electrons were accelerated in the electron gun in the Davisson and Germer experiment. (Take the associated wavelength as 1.65×10^{-10} m.)

7 In view of the discussion of the penetration of a nuclear barrier, do you think that a radioactive particle has high or low potential energy within the nucleus (before emission), when the decay process has a very short half-life? Explain your answer.

Numerical Answers To Problems

Chapter 1

1 (a) 2·1 cm, 3° W of N; (b) 9·1 km, 27° E of S
2 56 m, 0
4 804 km h^{-1}, 84° N of W
5 85° S of W, 2·68 hours
6 7·81 m at 50° to the direction of the positive X-axis
7 11·62 m, 50° N of E
8 5 ms^{-1} towards the centre of the circle.

Chapter 2

1 8 m s^{-1}, 1·33 m s^{-1} W
2 8 m s^{-1}
3 0·25 m s^{-2}, 0·5 s
4 10 s, 15 s
5 1250 m
6 1·3 m s^{-2}, 195 m
7 30 m s^{-1}, 45 m
8 5 s, 2 m s^{-2}, 654 m
9 9 m s^{-1}
10 35 m s^{-1}, 22 m, 18t.

Chapter 3

1 3 m s^{-2}
2 230 N
3 133$\frac{1}{3}$ N, 800 N
4 10 N, 5 m s^{-2}
5 5 N, 2·5 m s^{-2}, 4·4 s
6 3 s, 45 m
7 20 m
8 10 s, 500 m, 20 s, 3464 m
10 7·4 × 10^6 m s^{-1}, 1·05 × 10^7 m s^{-1} towards centre of orbit, 9·3 × 10^{23} m s^{-2}, 8·37 × 10^{-7} N.

Chapter 4

1 9/17 m s^{-2}, 265 N
2 6 N s
3 1·125 N s, 141 N
4 250 W
5 1·34 J, 1·64 m s^{-1}
6 1·6 m s^{-1}
7 0·67 m s^{-1} in the same sense as the original motion of the trolley
8 1·98 m s^{-1}, 0·196 m
9 7·5 m s^{-1}, 58° E of N
10 9·65 × 10^4 m s^{-1} in a direction making 338° 36′ with the original direction of motion of the proton
11 2·5 m s^{-1} in a direction making 91° with the original direction of motion of the 2 kg puck.

Chapter 5

1 200 J, 2 J, 0·99
2 1·92 °C
3 820 m s^{-1}

4 1·28 × 10^6 J, 1·22 × 10^6 calories
5 450 °C.

Chapter 6

1 1692 J
2 95·5 °C
3 154·2 J kg^{-1} °C^{-1}
4 −182 °C
5 672000 J
6 7·88 × 10^6 J
7 168 °C
8 60740 J
9 42 minutes, about $\frac{3}{4}$ minute longer
10 23 min 4 s.

Chapter 7

2 193 kN m^{-2}
3 12·84 cm^3
4 2 × 10^5 Nm^{-2}, 6 × 10^4 N
5 79 cm
6 1/24 kg mole
7 2·48 × 10^{26} molecules
8 2·73 m s^{-1}, 3·11 m s^{-1}, 3 m s^{-1}
9 428 m s^{-1}
10 939 °C
11 1310 m s^{-1}
12 3610 molecules.

Chapter 8

5 400 V
6 1 ev = 1·6 × 10^{-19} J, 5·9 × 10^5 m s^{-1}
7 50 μC
8 5 × 10^{-9} C, 3 × 10^{-9} C
9 1·28 × 10^{-15} kg.

Chapter 9

1 2·5 × 10^{-3} C, 1·25 A
2 1 mA
3 0·5 A, 0·4 A
4 5 Ω, 3$\frac{3}{4}$ Ω
5 12 Ω, 60 Ω
6 168 V
7 £36·44
9 1·5 V
10 179 °C
12 0·71 Ω.

Chapter 10

3 By placing a 39·9 Ω resistor in series with it
4 By placing a 0·003 Ω resistor in parallel with it, 1/333 Ω
5 By placing a 2390 Ω resistor in series with it
6 1200 Ω

Numerical Answers

11 40 V, 2/3 A

12 60 V, 360 J, 15·3 s, 1·5 A

13 320 kW lost, 200 W lost.

Chapter 11

1 622 V, 0·283 A

2 8 A, 16 V

5 3·15 mA, current lags applied e.m.f. by 0·24 cycle

6 32 mA, current leads applied e.m.f. by 0·143 cycle

7 628 Ω, 64 Ω, 15·8 Hz

9 17 V.

Chapter 12

3 7·07 V

4 $1·88 \times 10^7$ m s^{-1}

5 $2·66 \times 10^{-9}$ s, 3·0 mm, $1·9 \times 10^7$ m s^{-1} in a direction making 7·2° with the original direction of motion, 15·6 mm

8 16·7 Hz

10 Ripple will be reduced by a factor of approximately 20.

Chapter 13

4 By placing a 727 Ω resistor in series with the diode

5 0·33 A

8 7·7 mW, 2·7 kΩ (nearest value)

Chapter 14

4 50 s

7 At an angle of 6° 24′ to the normal to the surface

10 508 Hz.

Chapter 15

2 3·1 mm

5 2·88 m

8 0·96 mm

10 $5·77 \times 10^{-7}$ m.

Chapter 16

1 1 m

4 A real image 1·5 cm high is formed 6·22 cm from the pole of the mirror

5 An image 0·6 cm high is formed 4 cm behind the mirror

6 2·77

7 9·9 cm, 5 cm

8 0·96 m

9 45°, 30°

10 1·41 cm

12 Image is 2 cm high and located 20 cm from the lens on its far side

13 10 cm, 9·7 cm.

Chapter 17

2 33·3 cm

3 4·94 cm

5 f/11, f/4

8 1·065 cm

10 3 cm, 27 cm, 26·68 cm.

Chapter 19

4 126 mm

9 $1·93 \times 10^{16}$

10 $6·08 \times 10^{-4}$.

Chapter 20

1 $2·75 \times 10^{-32}$ kg

2 (a) $5·5 \times 10^{-10}$ m, (b) $4·1 \times 10^{-38}$ m

3 $3·96 \times 10^{-19}$ J, $2·52 \times 10^{18}$

4 $4·54 \times 10^5$ m s^{-1}

6 55 V.

Index

Index